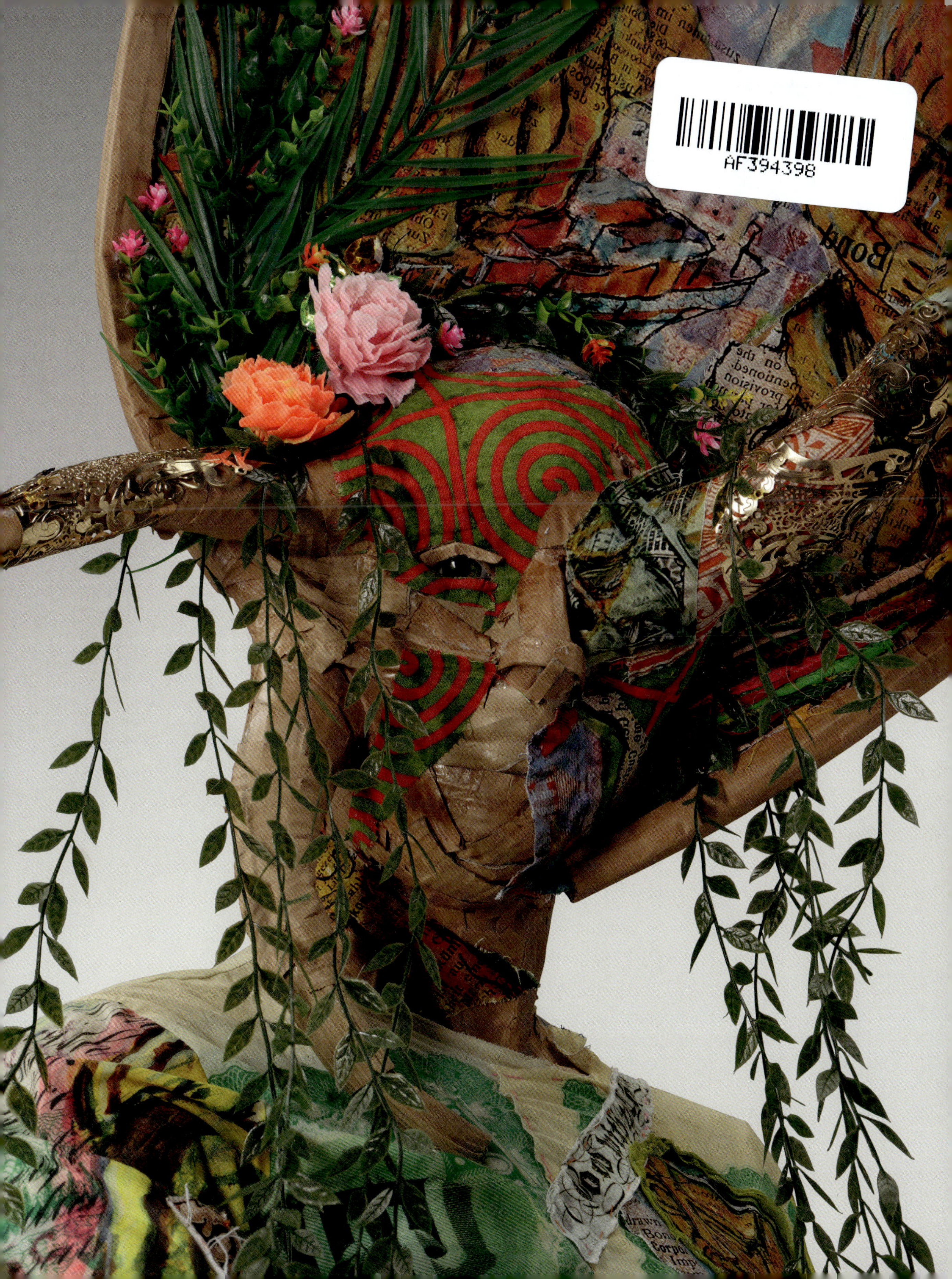
AF394398

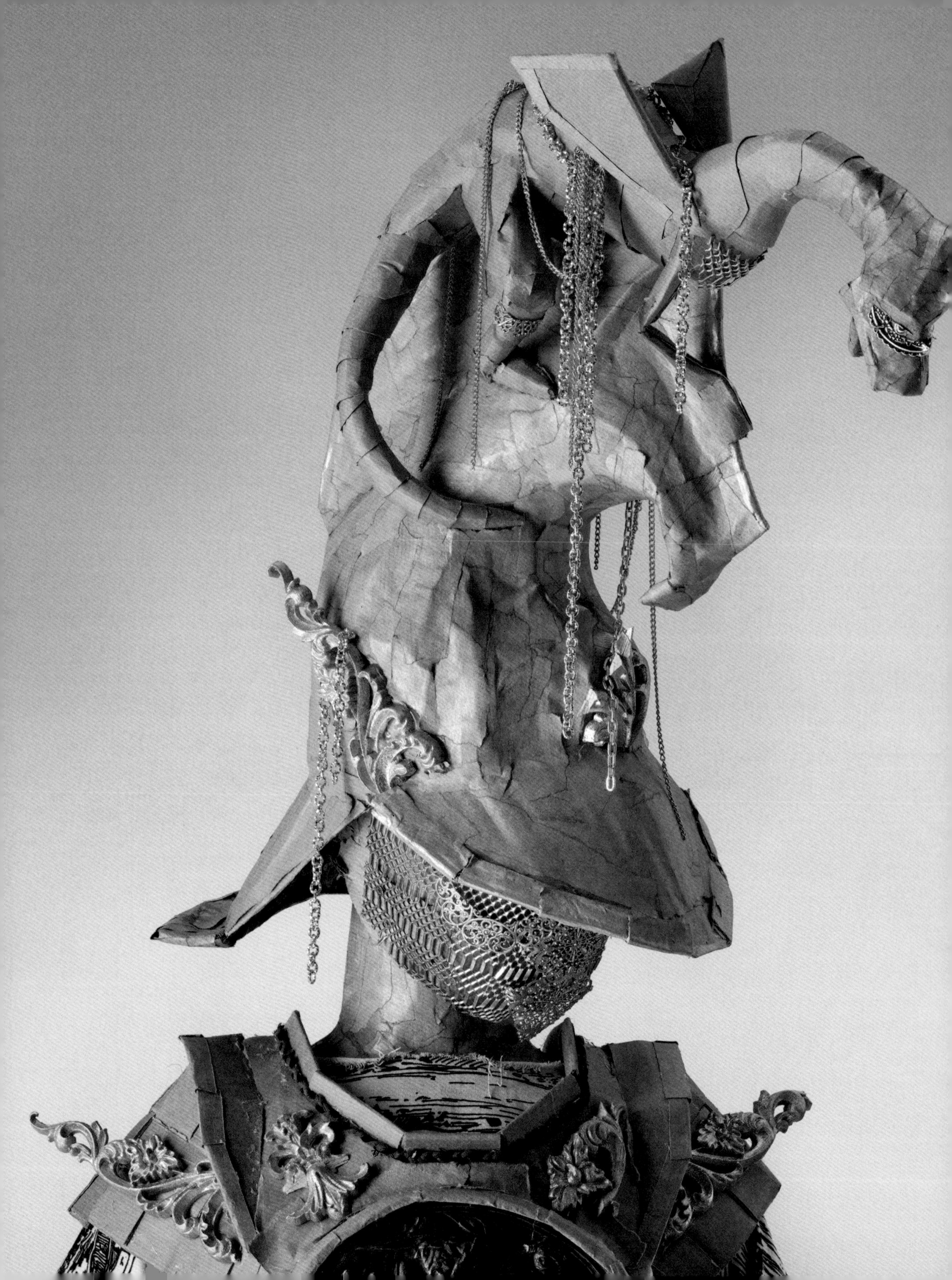

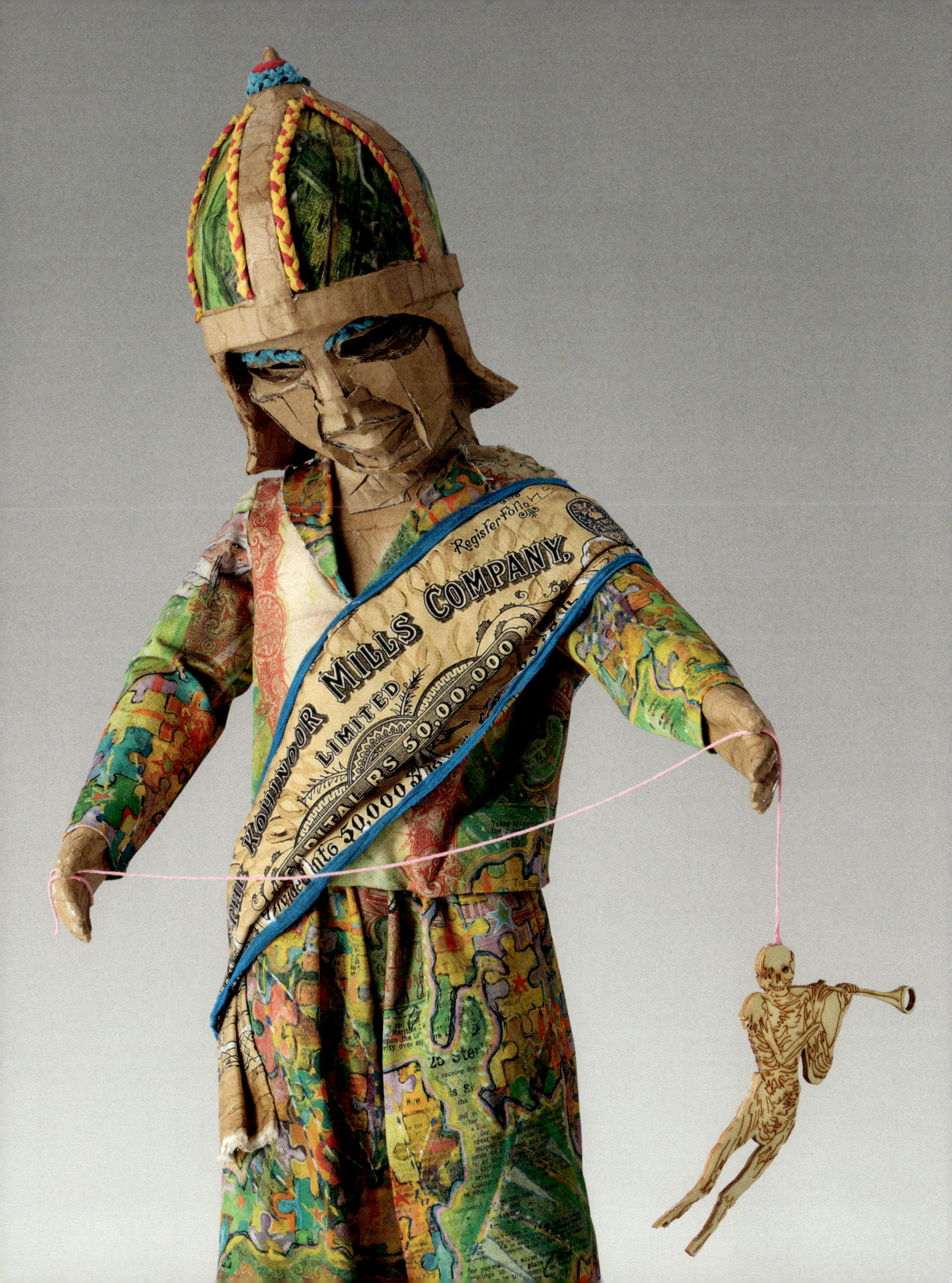

Register Folio
KOHINOOR MILLS COMPANY,
LIMITED
CAPITAL RS 50,00,000

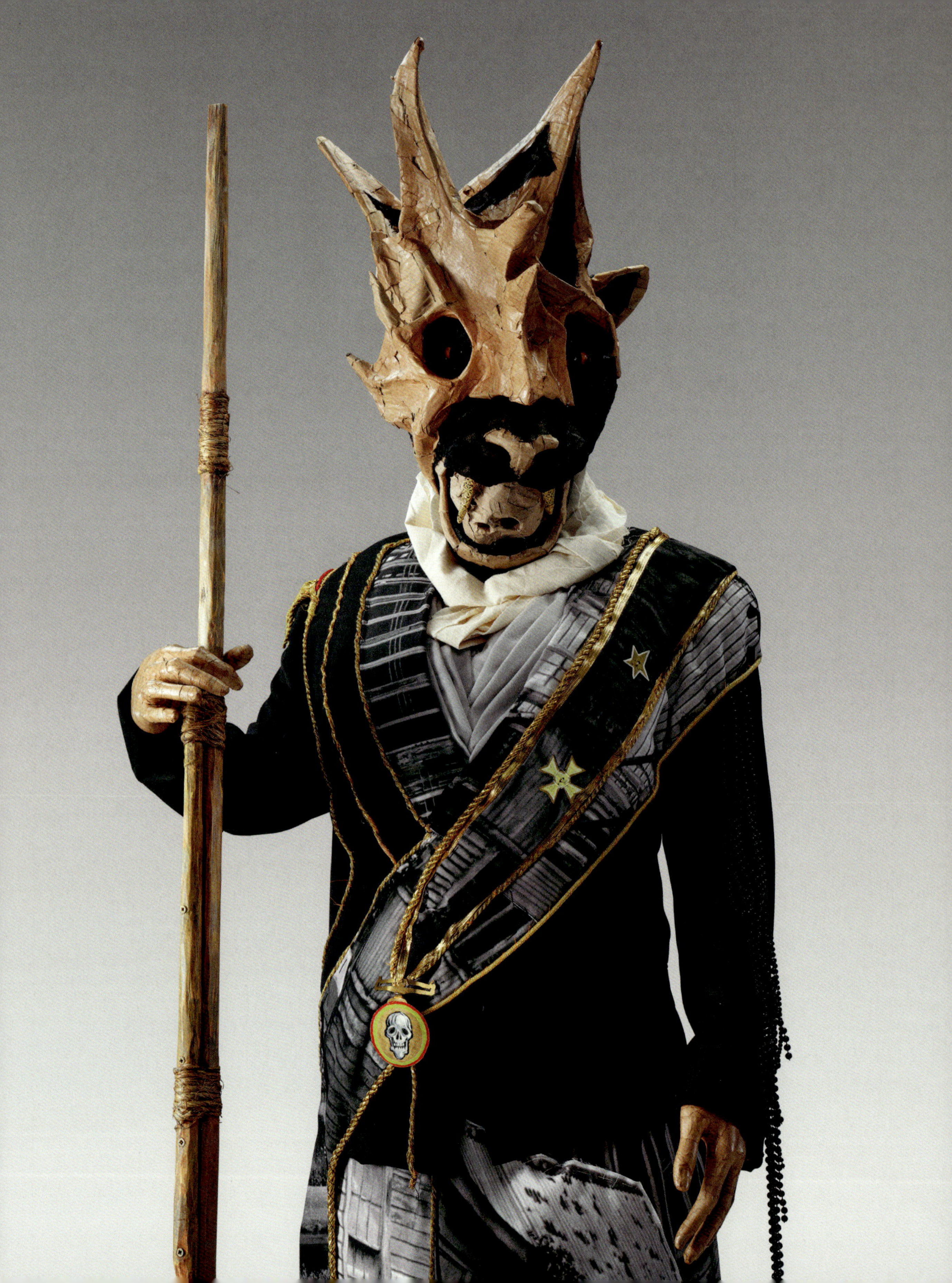

Hew Locke

what have we here?

Hew Locke, Isabel Seligman
and Indra Khanna

The British Museum

Published to accompany the exhibition
Hew Locke: what have we here? at the British Museum
from 17 October 2024 to 9 February 2025.

Supported by Cockayne – Grants for the Arts: a donor
advised fund held at The London Community Foundation.

COCKAYNE The London Community Foundation

With further support from the Stanley Thomas
Johnson Foundation.

This exhibition has been made possible as a result
of the Government Indemnity Scheme. The British
Museum would like to thank HM Government for providing
Government Indemnity, and the Department for Culture,
Media and Sport and Arts Council England for arranging
the indemnity.

Content notice: This publication contains
offensive historical wording and imagery.

For full details and provenance of objects, see pp. 181–7.

First published in the United Kingdom in 2024
by The British Museum Press

A division of The British Museum Company Ltd
The British Museum
Great Russell Street
London WC1B 3DG
britishmuseum.org/publishing
publicity@britishmuseum.org

A catalogue record for this book is available from the
British Library.

ISBN 9780714123509

Designed by Manon Veyssière at Fraser Muggeridge studio
Colour reproduction by Altaimage
Printed in Belgium by Graphius

Further information about the British Museum
and its collection can be found at britishmuseum.org.

Front cover and p. 38: Hew Locke, *Souvenir 20
(Queen Victoria)*, 2024.
Back cover and pp. 49, 174: William Jackson, *A Liverpool
Slave Ship, c.* 1780; Unrecorded Akan artist, Sankofa bird
gold-weight, 1700s–1900s.
pp. 1–7: Hew Locke, *The Watchers*, 2024.

The papers used in this book are natural, renewable and
recyclable and the manufacturing processes are expected
to conform to the regulations of the country of origin.

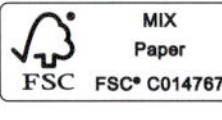

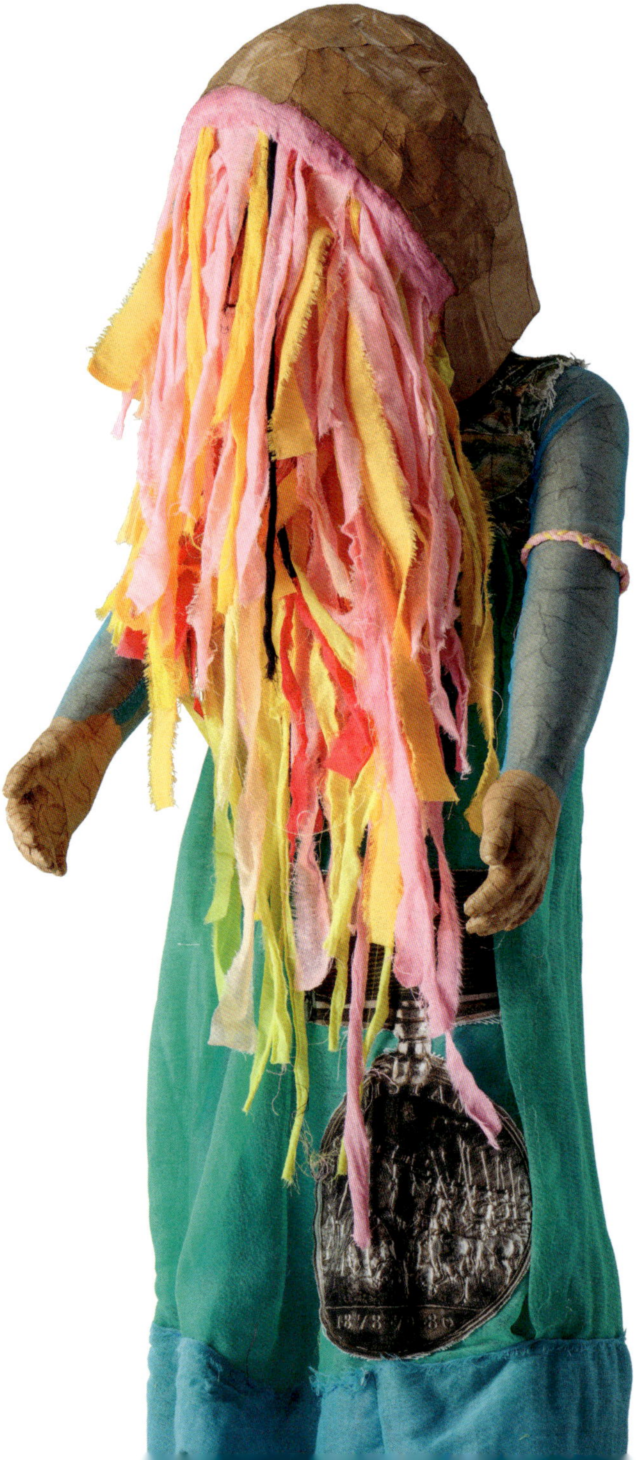

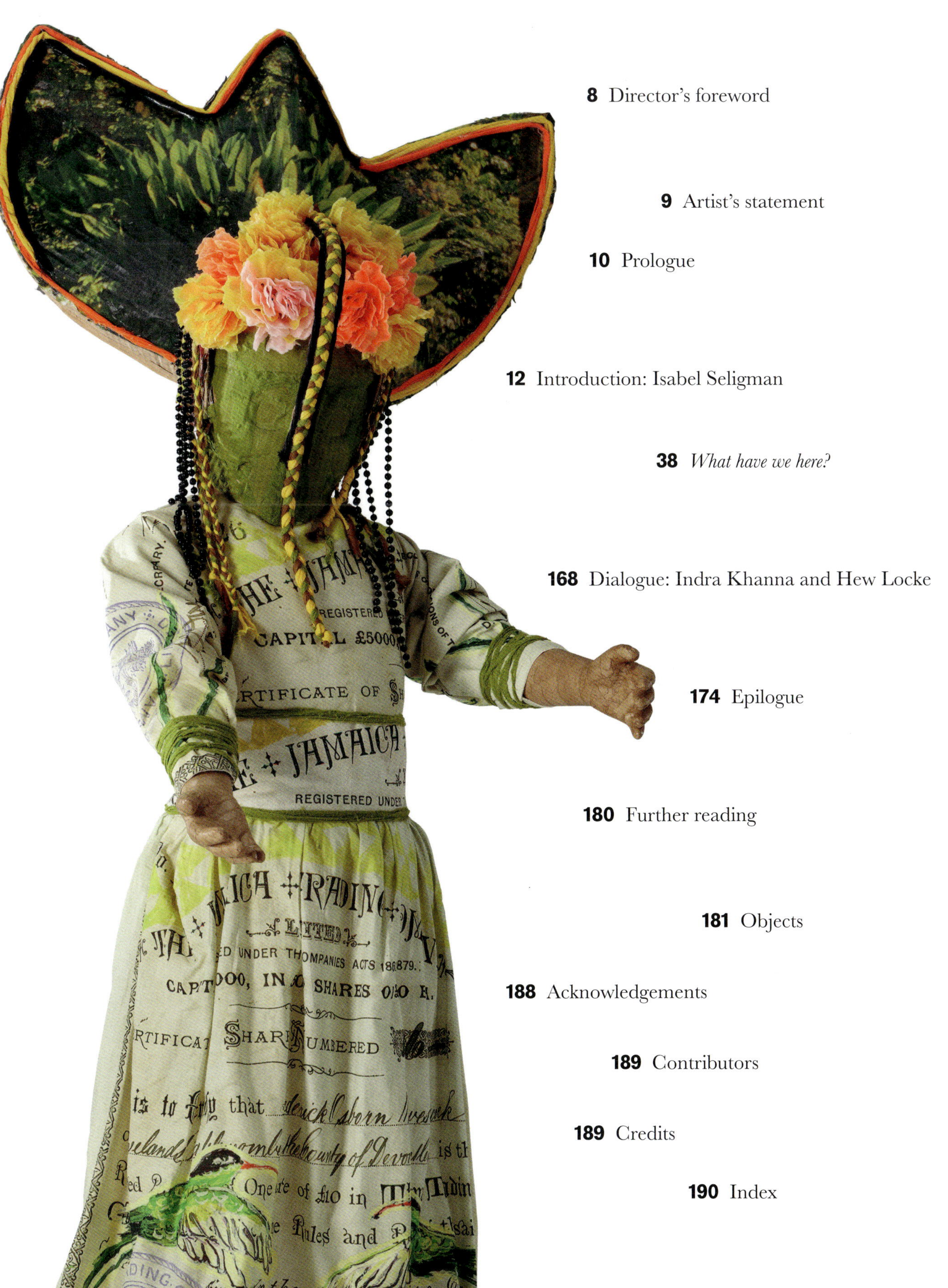

8 Director's foreword

9 Artist's statement

10 Prologue

12 Introduction: Isabel Seligman

38 *What have we here?*

168 Dialogue: Indra Khanna and Hew Locke

174 Epilogue

180 Further reading

181 Objects

188 Acknowledgements

189 Contributors

189 Credits

190 Index

There is a long and vital history of artists engaging with the British Museum collection – from Auguste Rodin in the 19th century, to Henry Moore in the 20th century, to, much more recently, Grayson Perry, Edmund de Waal and Maggi Hambling, among many others. The collection and galleries are a source of inspiration and fascination, generating new creativity and ideas as well as resulting in exhibitions and displays, publications, educational resources and much else besides.

The artist Hew Locke has been a regular visitor to the Museum for more than 40 years, and we were thrilled to have the opportunity to collaborate with him, and his partner, curator Indra Khanna, on a groundbreaking exhibition. Over the past year, Hew and Indra have explored the Museum in unprecedented depth, spending time in stores and study rooms, sharing ideas and thought-provoking conversations with curators.

The result is the exhibition *Hew Locke: what have we here?*, a constellation of objects and stories brought together by Hew and Indra, with colleagues at the British Museum. It is an assemblage interlinked by themes of colonialism, trade and propaganda, the structures of Empire that Locke has been critiquing for decades in his work, stretching as far back as *Restoration* in 2006 (fig. 1). Through this unique exhibition Hew is asking all of us to consider the complexity, and the questions, raised by a collection such as that of the British Museum.

I am pleased that the partnership has also inspired Hew to create new works, including a spectacular piece in his *Souvenir* series (see p. 38). *The Watchers*, figures in a brilliant new mixed-media intervention, feature in the exhibition as well as in the permanent galleries and survey visitors from all angles, acting, as the artist describes, in the manner of a Greek chorus, passing comment on the action.

It would not have been possible to stage this important exhibition without the generous support of Cockayne – Grants for the Arts: a donor advised fund held at The London Community Foundation. I would like to thank the lenders to the exhibition: Almine Rech Gallery; The British Library, London; Hales Gallery London and New York; Hew Locke; The Hitchin Family; HM King Charles III/ The Royal Collection Trust; Imperial War Museums; Jonathan Olsoff and Sophie de Bellissen; National Maritime Museum, Greenwich, London; National Museums Liverpool, Merseyside Maritime Museum; National Trust Collections, Powis Castle; and one Private Collection. Isabel Seligman, the Curator of Modern and Contemporary Drawings at the British Museum, has worked tirelessly to make the exhibition a reality, along with many other colleagues.

Above all, I am enormously grateful to Hew Locke and Indra Khanna for their powerful engagement with the collection. They have been wonderful partners on this journey. Locke's choice of subtitle, *what have we here?*, alludes to questions that should be explored more closely, and I hope that the exhibition inspires further debate and continuing conversations.

Dr Nicholas Cullinan OBE

I go to the British Museum to think.

I have been visiting the British Museum's collections for 40 years. When I go, I often visit the Egyptian boats, one of the influences on my own boat sculptures. In 1987, while a BA student at Falmouth Art School, I 'rescued' two fibreglass reproductions of Benin bronze plaques in the British Museum's collections that were being thrown out. The Falmouth staff offered them to me as they knew of my interest; I still have them on my wall today.

In 1988 I wrote my student thesis on 'Black Identity and the Ancient World', inspired by visits to the British Museum and my reading of alternative histories. Many people were talking about the idea that the culture of Greece had been foregrounded by most academics writing on the history of Europe, and that the links between the Minoan and Egyptian cultures had been downplayed – on top of which, Egypt was somehow not considered an African culture, despite obviously being in Africa. These ideas were exciting and changed my interaction with the Museum.

I moved to London in 1989 and started drawing in the Museum of Mankind, a totally different building over a kilometre away, where the British Museum's artefacts from sub-Saharan Africa were separated away from classical Greek and Egyptian art. I drew things such as Luba, Baule and Benin sculptures, which fed into my own work. I sometimes spent a whole day drawing one object. Since 2000 I have made extensive use of the image of the British Museum's Benin Queen Mother Idia's mask in my work. I am interested in the way this object has become an all-encompassing symbol of all of 'Sub-Saharan African culture'. It has become an icon and totem in modern times for many people in the African diaspora. For me, it is also a symbol of Africa's complex historical interactions with the West – the image is a shorthand for many things.

This project has enabled me to engage with the Museum's collections in a much deeper way than previously. With other work I have made inspired by museum collections, I have only been able to respond to items either on display or in their online collections catalogue. Here, I have engaged with a major museum collection in a way few artists have had the privilege. It has been so interesting visiting the stores, handling pieces and talking to the curators of many different departments.

I have always been fascinated by the way objects are interpreted through display in museums. What story has been distilled and is being told or implied about the past? How does it relate to the present? How can this telling be questioned, disrupted or complicated? These are the kind of questions I hope to raise with this project.

Hew Locke OBE RA

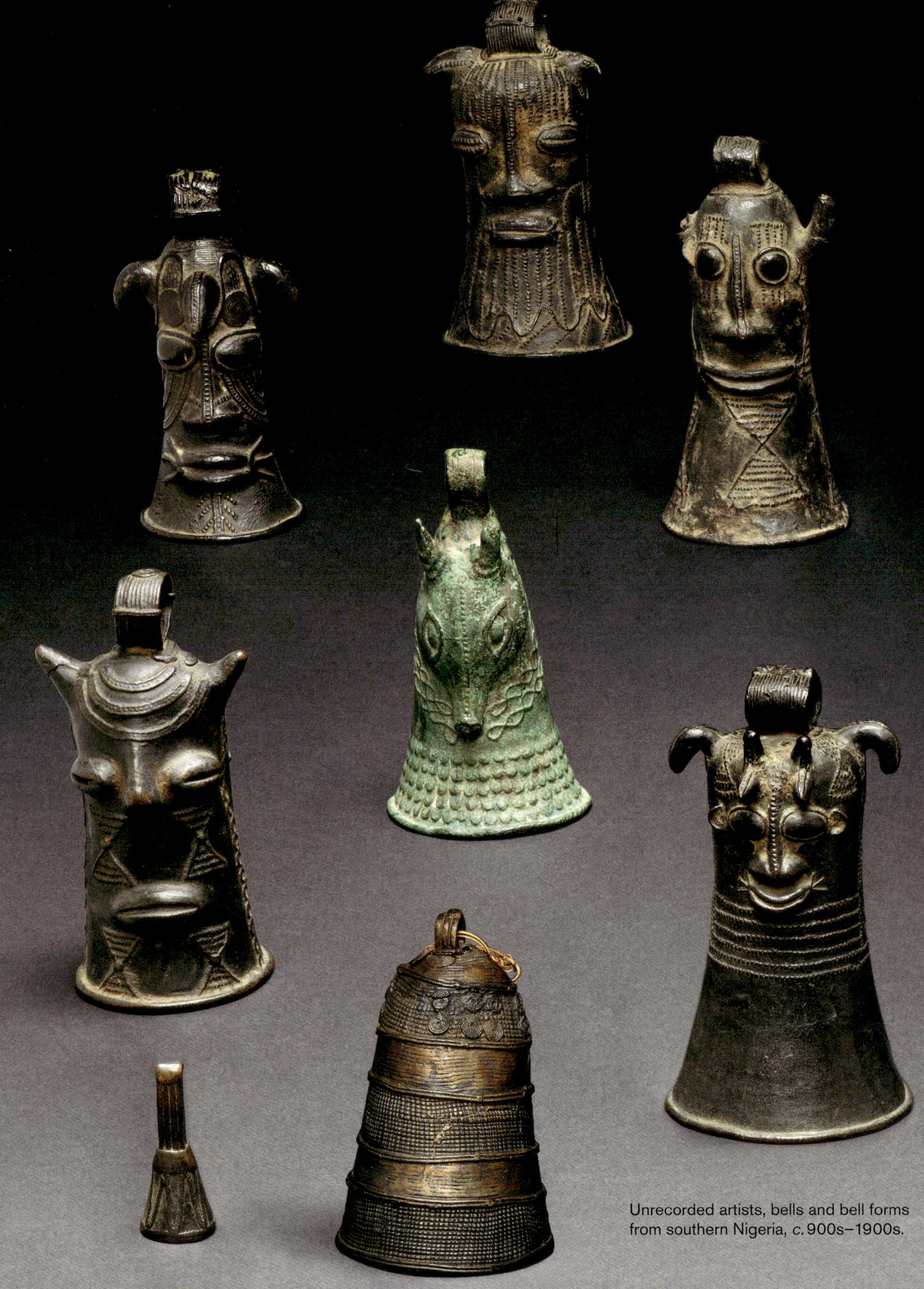

Unrecorded artists, bells and bell forms from southern Nigeria, *c.* 900s–1900s.

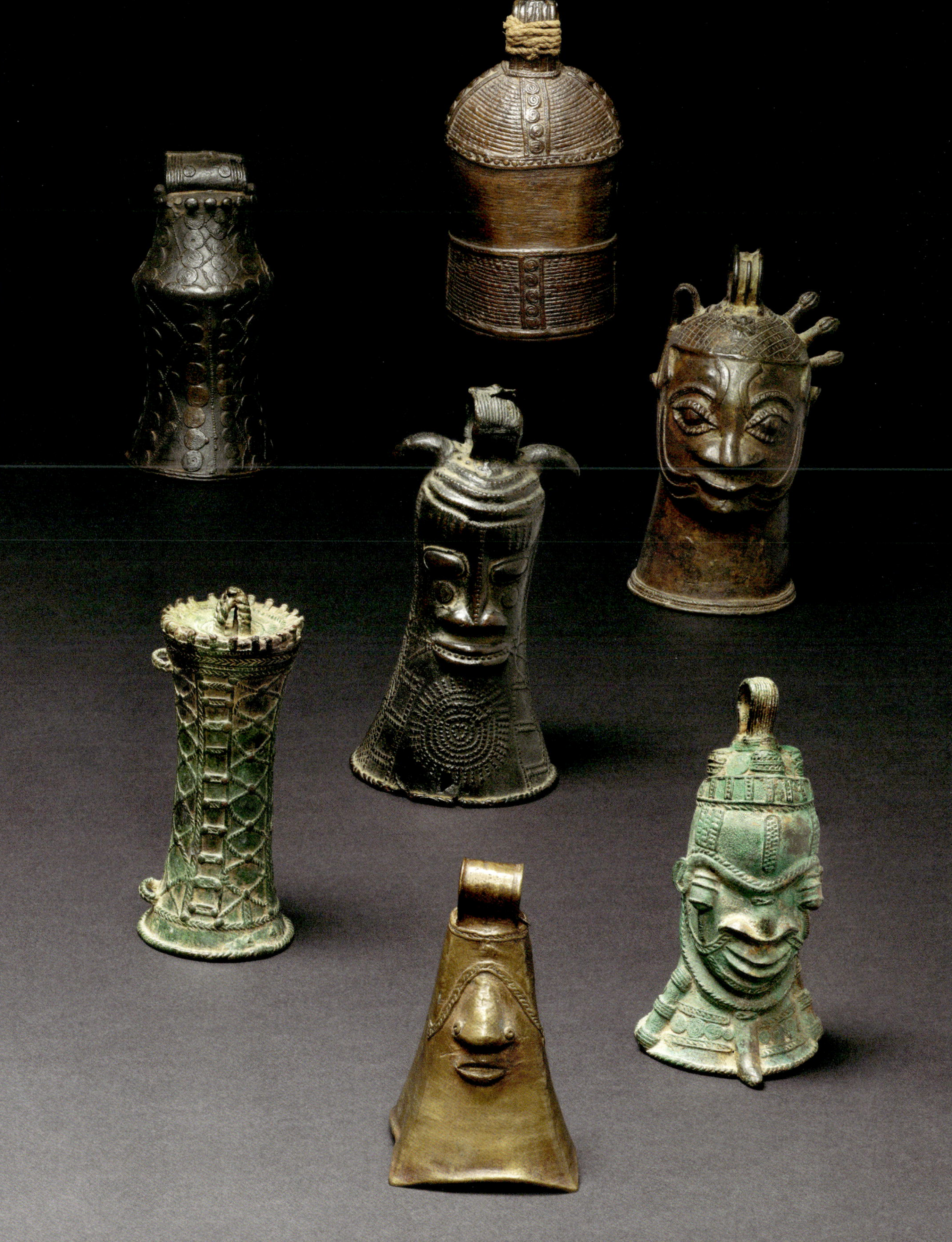

Introduction:
'The wrong side of history'

Isabel Seligman

In the summer of 2020, during global demonstrations protesting the murder of George Floyd by police officer Derek Chauvin in Minneapolis, a statue of Edward Colston was toppled into Bristol Harbour in the United Kingdom. The work by the Irish sculptor John Cassidy (1860–1939) had been the subject of local protest for decades. Edward Colston (1636–1721) was widely celebrated as a philanthropic founding father of Bristol, lending his name to Colston Tower, the music venue Colston Hall and even a Colston Bun.

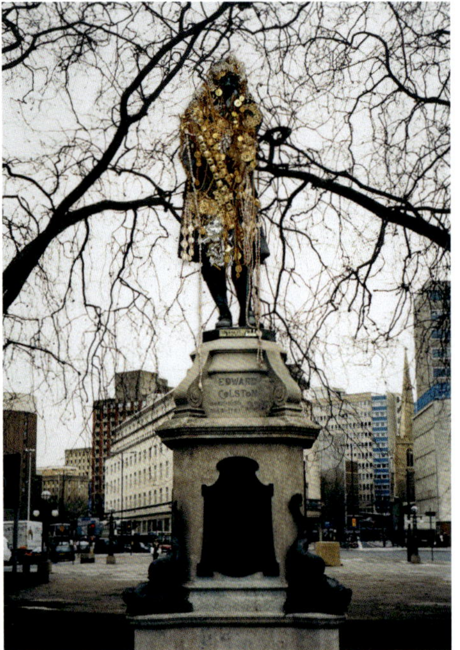

fig. 1. Hew Locke, *Colston*, 2006, from the series *Restoration*. C-type photograph mounted on aluminium, metal, plastic, fabric, mixed media. H. 182 cm, W. 121 cm, D. 15 cm.

Yet Colston was also a director of the Royal African Company (RAC), an entity that had been responsible for the enslavement of more African people than any other institution in the history of the transatlantic trade. As 2020's global demonstrations against the murder of Black citizens were the catalyst for wider conversations about systemic racial injustice, Colston's toppling by protesters into Bristol Harbour was the catalyst for a wider national conversation that focused on how to reckon with a colonial past.[1]

Nearly 15 years previously, the artist Hew Locke made a work detailing a radical intervention in the appearance of this same statue, an approach the artist described as a kind of 'mindful vandalism'.[2] In his series *Natives and Colonials* (2005–ongoing), *Restoration* (2006) and *Patriots* (2018), Locke encouraged viewers to examine monuments to British political, military and philanthropic heroes – including Queen Victoria, Winston Churchill and Oliver Cromwell – with a fresh and critical eye, asking them to see what had, in effect, been hiding in plain sight. In *Restoration* (2006), via mixed-media additions to a photograph, Colston was dressed in a dazzling assemblage of disparate items, including golden regalia fashioned from coins, chains, cowries, skulls and other grim reminders of Colston's involvement with the trade in enslaved people (fig. 1). Through this act of radically inventive commemoration, Locke reimagined and re-presented Colston's history.

The work neatly encapsulates Locke's ongoing concern with dominant narratives of British history and his interest in bringing hidden histories to the fore, as if turning over a rich tapestry to reveal a welter of colourful, tangled threads on the other side. The tapestry's image of power is calm, serene, beneficent; its reverse is messy and complex. Yet the web it reveals offers a different picture of British history, pulling at threads to show connections between seemingly disparate elements and asking how we arrived at where we are today. As Locke

1. These events led to the alteration of 70 tributes to enslavers and colonialists, 39 names for streets, buildings and schools, and 30 statues, plaques and other memorials. Aamna Mohdin, 'How the fall of Edward Colston's statue revolutionised the way British history is told', *The Guardian*, 5 May 2023.

2. 'Photography, painting and impossible sculpture: Hew Locke's *Natives and Colonials*. Jon Wood in conversation with Hew Locke', *Sculpture Journal*, 2006, vol. 15, no. 2, p. 282.

notes in an issue of the *Royal Academy of Arts Magazine,* 'today we're always sailing alongside the ghosts of the past.'[3]

The legalisation of racialised violence and chattel slavery began in the English colony of Barbados with the Slave Codes of 1661, which were adapted by other English colonies in the Caribbean and many of the 13 colonies of North America. Ongoing systemic racial injustice in America therefore has its roots in histories of English, and later British, imperial power. In the words of the Cameroonian historian and political philosopher Achille Mbembe, 'the history of Europe is not limited to the borders of Europe … The question of Europe is a world question.'[4]

COLLECTING HISTORIES

The British Museum's history and collection are intimately linked to the history of the British Empire. Objects within its collections, as well as arguably the Museum itself, are powerful and contested symbols of these imperial interactions. When the British Museum opened in 1753, it was the first truly public museum in the world. But the wealth that enabled its benefactor Sir Hans Sloane to amass a collection of more than 71,000 fabricated and natural objects, and the networks through which he acquired them, were dependent on the structures of British imperialism. Sloane's income as physician to Queen Anne and kings George I and II was supplemented by his wife Elizabeth's wealth, derived from the labour of enslaved Africans working on sugar plantations in Jamaica. Sloane himself had travelled to Jamaica as physician to the newly appointed governor, Christopher Monck, 2nd Duke of Albemarle, and visited plantations there. He collected many botanical specimens and other objects that formed the basis for his two-volume natural history of Jamaica (1707–25). Sloane's collecting and research were both enabled by chattel slavery and it is important to reckon with the brutal histories of human trafficking that underwrote the foundation of the Museum.

In the century following, as European Enlightenment thought developed, the Museum's collection evolved from a 'Wunderkammer' (room of wonder) of curious objects towards an encyclopaedic archive of knowledge as represented by human material culture. Often used as a means to assess the 'worth' and 'nobility' of its producers, this classificatory approach perpetuated a divide between European cultures (which produced both 'works of art' and material culture) and non-European cultures, whose objects did not fit into European categories and were considered through an ethnographic lens.[5]

As well as the numerous objects that were acquired by the Museum as the result of imperial activity – including the collections of officials and missionaries – objects also arrived as the result of colonial conflicts. Before the mid-20th century, there were no international laws proscribing the looting of cultural property following armed conflict; objects that were appropriated prior to these laws have been the subject of deeply felt debate between those who argue to keep them in the museums where they are held, and those who believe they should be returned to their country of origin. In the late 19th and early 20th centuries there were also specific instances in which the Museum would nominate a representative to collect objects on a military expedition (such as with Lawrence Augustine Waddell on the Younghusband

3. Dorothy Price and Hew Locke, 'Talking History', *Royal Academy of Arts Magazine,* no. 161, Winter 2023, special issue guest-edited by Hew Locke RA, p. 54.

4. Talk at the University of Cologne, 'Memory and Restitution / Achille Mbembe / AMP 2019', YouTube video, 18 July 2019, at 20:30 mins.

5. Scholars such as Annie E. Coombes have examined the ways in which discussions of 'aesthetic criteria and the artistic categories of art and design from the colonies contributed to both definitions of "race" and to the ideology of a national culture within Britain'. Annie E. Coombes, *Reinventing Africa: Museums, Material Culture and Popular Imagination in Late Victorian and Edwardian England,* New Haven, CT: Yale University Press, 1994, p. 5.

expedition to Tibet in 1903–4, see p. 154) or, on one occasion, send a member of staff.
This was the case with Richard Rivington Holmes (1835–1911), a member of the
manuscripts department at the British Museum who accompanied the British Expedition
to Abyssinia (as Ethiopia was then known in Britain) in 1867–8 as an archaeologist
(see p. 148). The 'punitive' expedition resulted in the death of hundreds of Ethiopians,
including Emperor Tewodros II (r. 1855–68); thousands more were wounded. During the
Younghusband expedition, around 2,000 to 3,000 Tibetans were estimated to have been
killed.[6] The presence of these objects in the British Museum's collection is indissoluble
from these violent events.

Although the collection represents Britain's desire to know other cultures, the
Museum might also be seen as a mirror for the British desire to collect and to categorise
as part of a colonial project; the collection of knowledge as a
means to power, domination and control. The Museum's collection
is particularly strong in areas that were previously colonised
by Britain. While studying the impact of displaying African
material culture in Britain at the end of the 19th century, Annie
E. Coombes – following in the footsteps of the scholar Edward
Said – has observed how 'representations of the African [during this period] necessarily
tell us more about the nexus of European interests in African affairs, and about the
coloniser, than they do about Africa and the African'.[7]

6. Alex McKay, 'The British Invasion
of Tibet, 1903–4', *Inner Asia*,
2012, vol. 14, no. 1, Special Issue:
The Younghusband 'Mission'
to Tibet (2012), pp. 5–25, p. 14.

7. Coombes, *Reinventing Africa*, p. 3.

HEW LOCKE

Born in Edinburgh in 1959, Locke spent his formative years in Georgetown, Guyana, the
son of Guyanese sculptor Donald Locke (1930–2010) and British painter Leila Locke (née
Chaplin, 1936–1992). He lived in Guyana from 1966 to 1980, during which time the country
experienced significant change, achieving independence from Britain in 1966 and becoming
the Co-operative Republic of Guyana in 1970. Locke's early experiences in this recently
postcolonial country – where Queen Victoria's statue was a landmark in the centre of the
capital, where he was taught about British heroes and his school exercise books still had
Queen Elizabeth II's face on them – deeply informed his thoughts about the way colonial
history impacts the experience of people across the globe.

Hew Locke has been visiting the British Museum's collections for over 40 years. As a
student, he used to visit the Museum of Mankind (a different site across town that housed
the Museum's ethnography collections from 1970 to 1997) to draw Luba, Baule and Benin
artefacts; objects such as the Kingdom of Benin Queen Mother Idia mask (p. 138) and
Portuguese mercenary figures (p. 67) have featured in his work for decades. He has a deep
fascination with objects and the stories they tell. In his words, he has 'always been interested
in the way objects are interpreted through display in museums. What story has been distilled
and is being told or implied about the past? How does it relate to the present?
How can this telling be questioned, disrupted or complicated?'[8] Locke's interest
in pulling at threads in the dominant narrative, and his focus on the 'wrong' side
of history, has meant embracing the messiness and complexity of these stories.

8. Artist's statement,
see p. 9.

In *what have we here?* Locke engages with the Museum's collection to an extent to which
few artists have had the opportunity. While the Museum has often collaborated with artists
to recontextualise and interpret its collections, this is the first artist co-curated exhibition
that has turned a critical eye on the Museum and its collections, questioning its role and the
way it came into being. Two comparable exhibitions were *Lost Magic Kingdoms and Six Paper*

Moons from Nahuatl by Eduardo Paolozzi (1924–2005) at the Museum of Mankind in 1985 and the *Tomb of the Unknown Craftsman* in collaboration with Grayson Perry (b. 1960) in 2011.

To put together the exhibition, Hew Locke and his partner, curator Indra Khanna, visited the Museum to view objects in the stores and study rooms and to discuss objects with specialist curators. Locke and Khanna also searched for objects using the Museum's database of objects, Collection Online. The themes of the exhibition were developed collaboratively, reflecting the concerns of Locke's work as manifested within the Museum's collection.

Newly commissioned sculptures by Locke form a central part of the exhibition. Locke's carnivalesque figures *The Watchers* (2024) are embedded into its build, viewing visitors from over the tops of exhibition cases and commenting on and judging the action in the manner of a Greek chorus (pp. 1–7). They spill out of the exhibition into the Museum's permanent collections in Room 1, also known as the Enlightenment Gallery. By interacting with objects from the Museum's collection, these figures prompt visitors to question their relationship with these artefacts and the cultures they represent. Drawing on often exploitative histories of ethnographic exposition, spectacles that saw objects and people displayed as trophies of empire, *The Watchers* seek to upset traditional dynamics of spectatorship and display.

Collage and assemblage are fundamental components of Locke's practice.[9] Rather than a traditional chronological approach, the objects in this book are presented in imaginative groupings, often with disparate juxtapositions to create an implied narrative – in Locke's words, each cluster of objects is 'like a little still life painting'.[10] The idea is that the groupings could be approached in any order and sometimes the same stories are refracted through different lenses like a poetic refrain. The 'what have we here?' section of this book does not intend to offer a single conclusion, but to provoke questions. Locke notes that 'museum exhibitions arrange things chronologically – there's a story, beginning, middle and end, whereas me, I randomly drift around a museum … this show is a bit like drifting around in my head. And that's what I want people to do – to make their own connections.'

9. For an analysis of the role of collage in Locke's work, see for example Kobena Mercer, 'Hew Locke's Postcolonial Baroque', *Small Axe*, Duke University Press, vol. 15, no. 1 (Mar 2011), pp. 10, 19.

10. Discussion during exhibition preparation between Hew Locke, Indra Khanna and Isabel Seligman, Dec 2022. All subsequent quotations by Locke are from exhibition workshop sessions at the British Museum, Dec 2022 to Apr 2024, unless otherwise stated.

SOVEREIGNS AND ICONS OF NATIONHOOD (pp. 38–63)

The way that a nation builds itself, both politically and symbolically, has been an ongoing concern of Locke's since he arrived in Guyana, aged six, at the moment of its independence from Britain. 'I saw a nation being born,' he recalls, 'I saw a flag being designed. I saw the money literally being designed.'[11] This instilled an enduring fascination with the way that a nation creates an idea of itself through visual symbols. The groupings of objects in this theme of the exhibition examine how the power of a nation or empire can become invested in a particular person, and the use of symbolic imagery to mediate and express this power.

11. 'Hew Locke – interview: "A lot of my work has to do with the burden of history and … how history affects us today"', *Studio International*, 15 Mar 2019, online.

12. Price and Locke, 'Talking History', p. 56.

Despite the nation's recent independence, Locke received a 'colonial education' in Guyana, taught by British nuns about King Alfred, General Wolfe and other heroes of the British Empire.[12] This fed into Locke's fascination with what stories a nation tells itself about its history. For his *Souvenir* series (2018–present), Locke has taken 19th-century busts of British royals, including Queen Victoria, her son Albert Edward and his future Queen Consort, Princess Alexandra, and covered them with an excess of military honours and mementos of imperial conflicts; these include the Asante War medal, Victoria crosses, medals from the Abyssinia Expedition, the Benin Expedition (1897), the Mahdist War (1881–99) and the Anglo-Egyptian War (1882), along with coins minted by the East India Company (EIC) and in British Guiana (a colony from 1831 until 1966, now Guyana).

Their intricate surface is seductive, illustrating Locke's technique of drawing in the viewer to confront them with a brutal history of violence – a process he has described as 'fly-fishing with a fancy lure'. Locke sees the sovereigns as 'weighed down by the literal burden of history' and touches on how this goes back to his 'idea of how a nation creates itself, what stories it sells to itself and how this relates to ideas of Britain and its history that are weighing down the minds of people today.'[13]

In *Souvenirs*, Locke uses principles of excess and exaggeration to reframe and recontextualise these royals: his approach draws on the fervour with which heroes of empire, such as Vice-Admiral Horatio Nelson (1758–1805), were venerated by contemporaries through mementos often revered in the manner of religious relics. For example, Nelson's victory at the Battle of Trafalgar secured British naval supremacy for the next century, yet his time serving in the Caribbean and a letter published after his death that appears to show support for anti-abolitionist causes has led to a reconsideration of his legacy.[14] The bullet that fatally wounded Nelson at Trafalgar was kept by the ship's surgeon, William Beatty (1773–1842), who had it mounted in a locket. On his death, it was presented to Queen Victoria and remains one of the most popular items in the Royal Collection (fig. 2).

Locke's work shows another side to British heroes, one that might have been hiding in plain sight, while asking what overly romanticised versions of these figures tell us about Britain's relationship to its imperial past.

Another facet of Locke's continued fascination with the British royal family is its historical links with the transatlantic trade in enslaved people. King Charles III (b. 1948) recently announced his support for research into these ties during the late 17th and 18th centuries, a time when the monarchy played a foundational role in formalising the English trade in enslaved African people.[15] Formed in 1663 by the House of Stuart and City of London merchants, the Company of Royal Adventurers of England Trading into Africa, which later became the Royal African Company, was granted a monopoly by Charles II (1630–1685) that was intended to last for a thousand years (see p. 48 for its charter). His brother James II (1633–1701) was its governor while also serving as the Duke of York. Between 1672 and the early 1720s, the RAC transported close to 150,000 enslaved African people across the Atlantic, mostly to the British Caribbean.[16] As Locke notes, 'A lot of these enslaved people had the initials "RACE" (Royal African Company of England) or "DoY" (Duke of York) branded on their backs, on their bodies. Once you hear that … it's very difficult for me personally to engage with those two beyond that.'

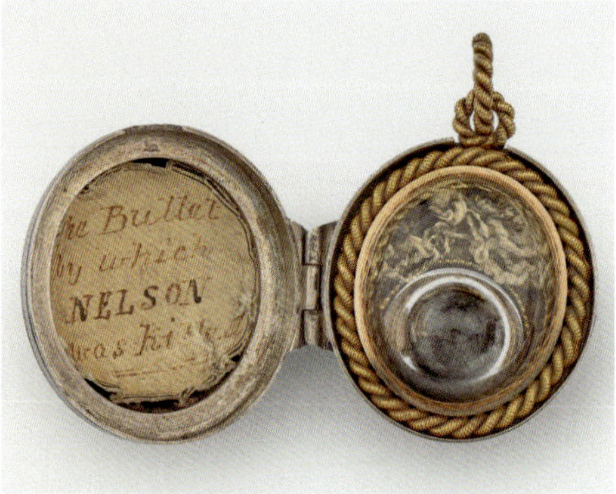

Boats have formed a part of Locke's artistic lexicon since 1987, when he created his first boat 'to take the souls of dead slaves back to Africa'.[17] Resonant and symbolic poetic works, they recall both the boats that brought him to Guyana and on which he sailed back

13. Louisa Buck, 'Hew Locke discusses monarchy and model boats in new survey show at Ikon Gallery', *Art Newspaper*, 11 Mar 2019.

14. See for example John McAleer and Christer Petley (eds), *The Royal Navy and the British Atlantic world, c. 1750–1820* (Basingstoke: Palgrave Macmillan, 2016), p. 98; Christer Petley, 'Lord Nelson and slavery: Nelson's dark side', *History Extra*, 8 June 2020, online.

15. David Conn, Aamna Mohdin and Maya Wolfe-Robinson, 'King Charles signals first explicit support for research into monarchy's slavery ties', *The Guardian*, 6 Apr 2023.

16. William A. Pettigrew, *Freedom's Debt: The Royal African Company and the Politics of the Atlantic Slave Trade, 1672–1752* (Chapel Hill, NC: University of North Carolina, 2013), p. 11.

fig. 2. The Nelson Bullet, 1805. Lead, silk, silver, glass, gilt metal. H. 7 cm, W. 5 cm, D. 2 cm. The Royal Collection, London / HM King Charles III, RCIN 61158.

to the UK. Since then, he has made a boat every few years (pp. 43–5), often amassing them into flotillas hung on trembling wires, as seen in *Wine Dark Sea* (2016), *On the Tethys Sea* at the Diaspora Pavilion of the Venice Biennale in 2017 and *Armada* (2017–19). Vessels from galleons to coastguard ships are bedecked with *memento mori* (reminders of death) and tattered sails, nets and cargo, bespeaking a ghostly fleet. They symbolise flows of goods as well as people, both historically, as part of the 'triangular trade' (the sailing route taken by British ships transporting goods to be traded for enslaved people from West Africa to the Caribbean, transporting products back from the Caribbean plantations to the UK) and also today. As Locke notes, 'They are not specifically talking about the current refugee crisis: it's about a longer, wider view of history where perhaps yesterday's refugee might be today's citizen.'[18]

17. Elizabeth Fullerton and Hew Locke, 'Mindful Vandalism: A Conversation with Hew Locke', *Sculpture Magazine*, 29 Sept 2020.

18. Buck 2019.

19. Adrian Ailes, 'Signs, Seals and Symbols of Imperial Power 1600–1960: A View from H. M. Government', *The Coat of Arms: The Journal of the Heraldry Society*, vol. 7, no. 221 2011, part 1, p. 14. For more on the imagery of the 'Indian' on colonial seals see Benjamin Justice, 'The Art of Coining Christians: Indians and Authority in the Iconography of British Atlantic Colonial Seals, 1606–1767', *Journal of British Studies*, vol. 61 (Jan 2022), pp. 105–37, p. 126.

20. See for example Hew Locke, unpublished statement sent by email to Alejandra Aguado by Ella Whitmarsh, Hales Gallery, 20 Nov 2007, Tate Acquisition file, 'all Caribbean countries have a European-originated coat of arms as their own national symbol, and also that they have all incorporated native symbols of native peoples' artefacts/plants/wildlife into this European format'.

Another subject that has continued to fascinate Locke is the iconography of sovereignty. Installation works such as *Evil to Him who Thinks Evil* (2004, fig. 3) and *Veni, vidi, vici* (2004) investigate how monarchs visually express their power through coats of arms. Locke is also particularly interested in seals as the legal expression of a sovereign's power. In his sculptural installation *The Procession* (2022), Locke included many Great Seals such as that of Edward the Confessor (*c.* 1003–1066), the first English king to use a Great Seal to symbolise his approval of state documents (fig. 4). During the period of the British Empire, the iconography of seals tells us much about Britain's self-fashioning as well as its perception of territories under its dominion. Common imagery included royal insignia, ships and local flora and fauna; images of supplicant Indigenous peoples, emphasising their submission to the crown, were also common. This imagery dates as far back as Charles II's Great Seal of Jamaica of 1662, which portrays a kneeling woman presenting Charles II with a dish of pineapples.[19] The way that Indigenous plants, animals and peoples have been incorporated into a European iconography of power is an enduring fascination for Locke.[20]

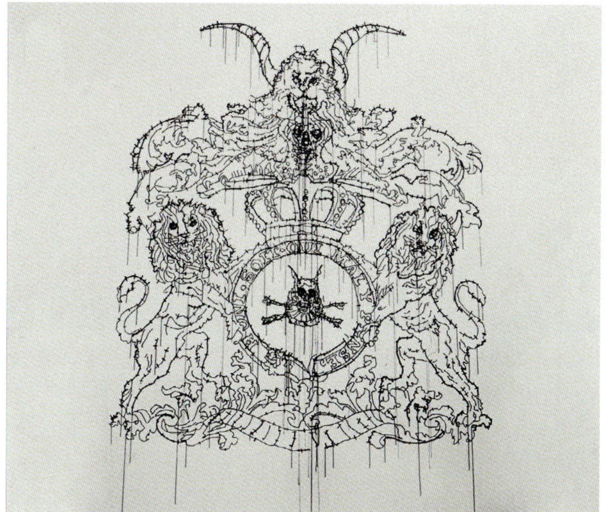

fig. 3. Hew Locke, *Evil to Him who Thinks Evil*, 2004. Mural with plastic beads and cord. Dimensions vary.

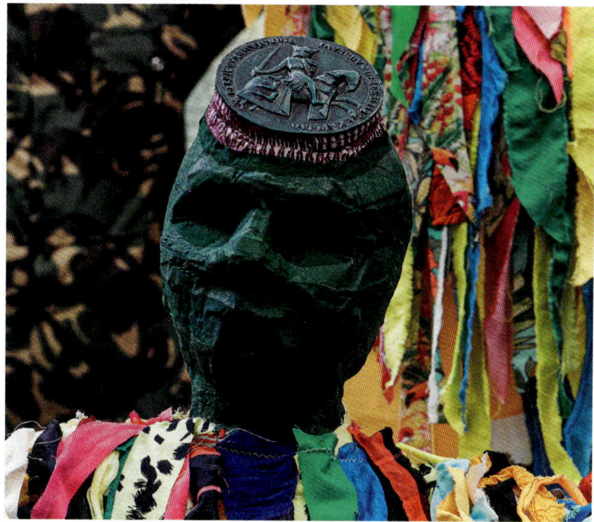

fig. 4. Hew Locke, *The Procession*, figure 63, 2022. Plastic, cardboard, fabric, wood, paper, metal, mixed media.

Locke has also paid keen attention to the ways in which potent symbols of British nationhood and power, such as a crown or a throne, can be made up of objects and symbols appropriated from other cultures. Coronations and royal pageantry are significant means of asserting a monarch's power, and the three Imperial Durbars of 1877, 1903 and 1911 proclaimed British royals (Victoria, Edward VII and Queen Alexandra, and George V and Queen Mary) as Emperor or Empress of India. An invented Victorian tradition drawing on Mughal precedents, the elaborate events produced by the Viceroys of India saw Indian rulers pay homage to their new monarch, although the Delhi Durbar of 1911 was the only one attended by the British royals. The Imperial Durbars served to emphasise the legitimacy of British rule over India and were also demonstrations of military force: in 1911, King George (1865–1936) reviewed a parade of 50,000 British and Indian troops. In the traditional durbar ceremony Indian monarchs heard petitions and exchanged gifts to mark reciprocal relationships between the ruler and his or her subjects. 'The British, however, appropriated the durbar as a ritual of subordination … Indian princes became subjects of Britain'.[21]

21. Julie Codell, 'On the Delhi Coronation Durbars, 1877, 1903, 1911', *BRANCH: Britain, Representation and Nineteenth-Century History*, June 2012, online.

The famous case of the Koh-i-Noor diamond is another example of the affirmation of British royal and imperial power through symbolic objects appropriated from other cultures (pp. 98–9). Locke explores the diamond's status as an icon, an object of myth repeatedly shaped by and imbued with specific ideas of power. He examines the long and fraught history of the diamond's ownership – passing, often as the result of violence, through many hands in places that are different nation states today – thereby complicating any calls for repatriation in the present day.

The final way in which Locke examines the intersection of British sovereignty and imperial power is through the lens of Queen Victoria's godchildren. Victoria became godmother to several children from across the British Empire for a number of different reasons, but often – as in the cases of Victoria Gouramma (1841–1864), Duleep Singh (1838–1893) and Prince Alemayehu of Ethiopia (1861–1879) – as the result of British military activity in their places of birth. Victoria Gouramma (baptised and named by the queen) was the daughter of Chikka Virarajendra (r. 1820–34), the last ruler of Coorg (modern-day Kodagu district, India), who was deposed by the British. Duleep Singh was the last maharaja (ruler) of the Sikh Empire until he was deposed at the age of 10 by the East India Company at the end of the Second Anglo-Sikh War. Prince Alemayehu was orphaned as a result of the British military invasion of Maqdala (now Amba Mariam, Ethiopia) in 1868, during which his father, Emperor Tewodros II, chose to die by suicide rather than be taken prisoner by the British, and his mother, Empress Tiruwork Wube, died on the journey to England accompanying her son.

Victoria's role as godmother to these children and benevolent 'Mother of Empire' was an expression of a wider attempt to shape the perception of the Empire's

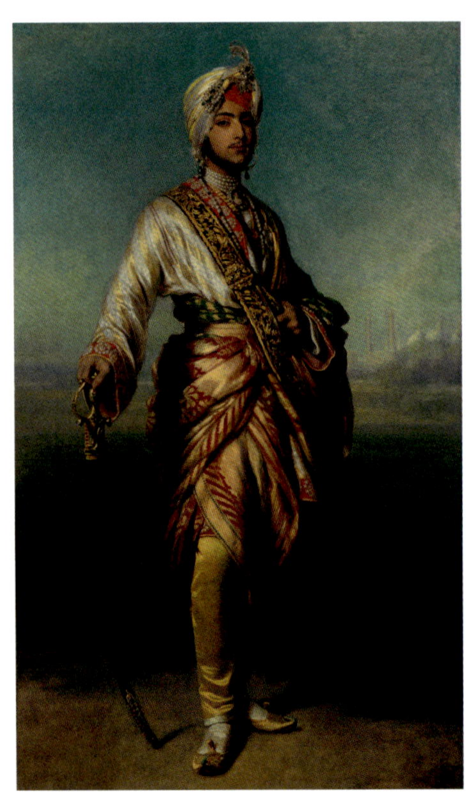

fig. 5. Franz Xaver Winterhalter, *The Maharaja Duleep Singh*, 1854. UK. Oil on canvas. H. 204 cm, W. 110 cm. The Royal Collection, London / HM King Charles III, RCIN 403843.

role as charitable, 'civilising' and humanitarian. While Victoria appeared to feel for these children – especially as fellow royals, and made much of Duleep Singh, who stayed with her at Osborne House and whose portrait was painted by the German artist Franz Xavier Winterhalter (1805–1873) (fig. 5) – their lives were often blighted by the attentions of the royal court. Locke cautions against any rose-tinted view: 'Victoria's legacy is interesting because she's highly romanticised in films such as *Mrs Brown* (1997) or *The Young Victoria* (2009) … We're cutting her too much slack here; she was the head of an Empire.'

TRADE (pp. 64–99)

During the early modern period (*c.* 1500–1700), much English imperial expansion was carried out through trading posts and corporations rather than military campaigns. Early modern connections between Europe and the continents of Asia and Africa opened routes for trade. The foundation in England of the East India Company in 1600 and the Company of Royal Adventurers into Africa in 1660 created trading monopolies that laid the foundations for the eventual military domination of India and much of Africa, as well as the trade in enslaved people who were transported from Africa and sold for labour in the Americas.

An interest in the intersection between histories of trade and Empire has long permeated Locke's work, stimulated by his awareness of Guyana's history as a Dutch and British colony. 'As a child, I would sit on the sea wall, watching boats coming in and out over the horizon and I was conscious that the winds cooling us were called "the trade winds". We had a deep psychological understanding that the country was created by trade – that was its purpose.'[22]

22. Price and Locke, 'Talking History', p. 56.

Two objects in this book point to early modern connections and trade on a more equal footing between the continents of Europe and Africa prior to the development of the transatlantic trade in enslaved people and subsequent imperial relationships. They illustrate the enmeshed histories of kingdoms in Europe and Africa – both in their significance to Edo and Akan peoples in the early modern period and in their later seizure during colonial wars. One is a jug (p. 66) that was made in the 1390s, possibly for King Richard II, and travelled all the way from England to the Asante royal court in modern-day Ghana. It is not known how the jug travelled to West Africa, but it might have arrived via trans-Saharan

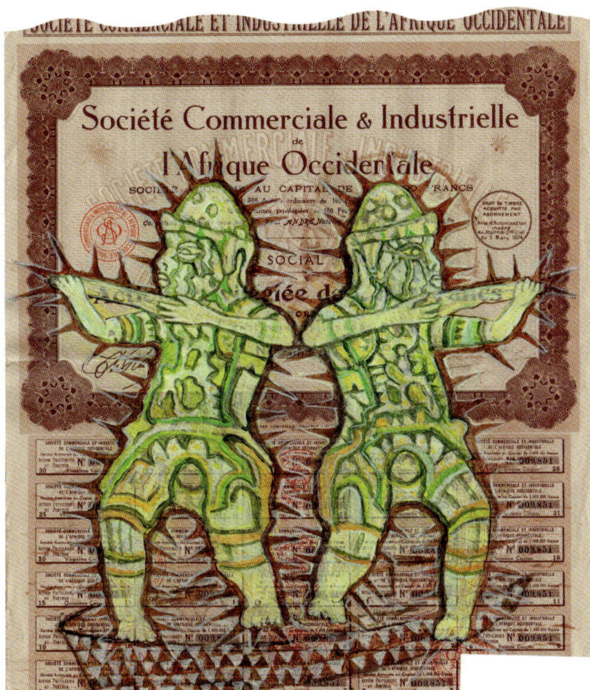

fig. 6. Hew Locke, *Société Commerciale & Industrielle de l'Afrique Occidentale 1*, 2014. Acrylic on antique share certificate. H. 38.5 cm, W. 31.5 cm.

trade, or via early European maritime journeys to the West African Coast. The jug was later taken as loot by the British during the Anglo-Asante War of 1895–6. Another is a sculpture of a soldier (p. 67, right), made for the Oba (king) in Benin from the late 1500s, depicting the

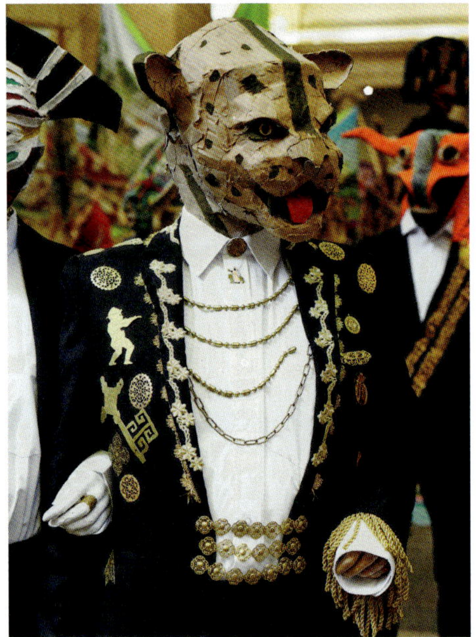

fig. 7. Hew Locke, *The Procession*, figure 16, 2022. Plastic, cardboard, fabric, wood, paper, metal, mixed media.

kind of Portuguese mercenary who often fought in his army. It was looted from the Oba's palace during the British invasion of Benin in 1897.

The Benin Portuguese mercenary has been a central motif of Locke's work since his days as a student in London when he would visit the Museum of Mankind to draw them. Since then, they have been painted onto share certificates (fig. 6), worn by figures in *The Procession* as brass badges (fig. 7), body adornments (fig. 8) or printed onto textiles (fig. 9), and mounted as brass plaques on boats in *Armada* and *Wine Dark Sea*. A symbol of cross-cultural exchange – 'I liked the fact that the people of Benin saw these strange-looking white newcomers and translated them into their own style of artwork'[23] – they also symbolise the power of the Oba of Benin and the European firepower that was at his disposal. In Locke's words, 'the firepower he's holding – today it would be a Kalashnikov.' The stance of the figure – musket or crossbow held aloft – is also transposed onto the figures that Locke describes as 'modern mercenaries', taking on different manifestations across his work from installation to embroidery (fig. 10, pp. 40, 43, 45).

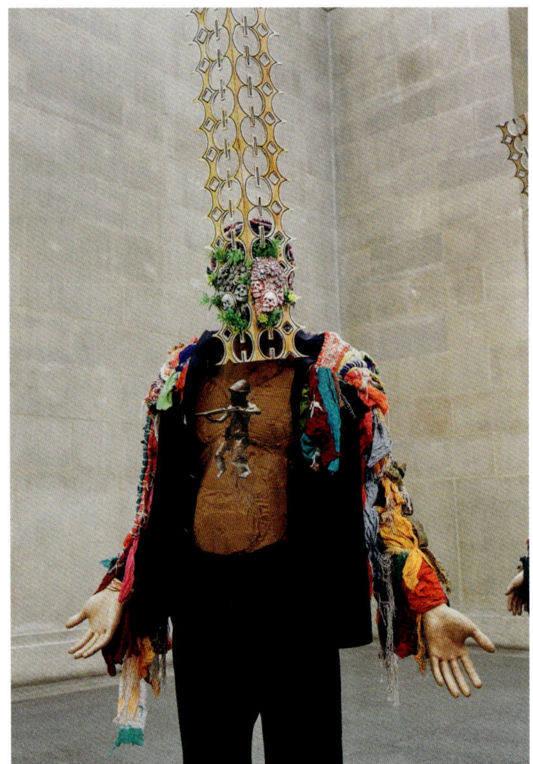

fig. 8. Hew Locke, *The Procession*, figure 33, 2022. Plastic, cardboard, fabric, wood, paper, metal, mixed media.

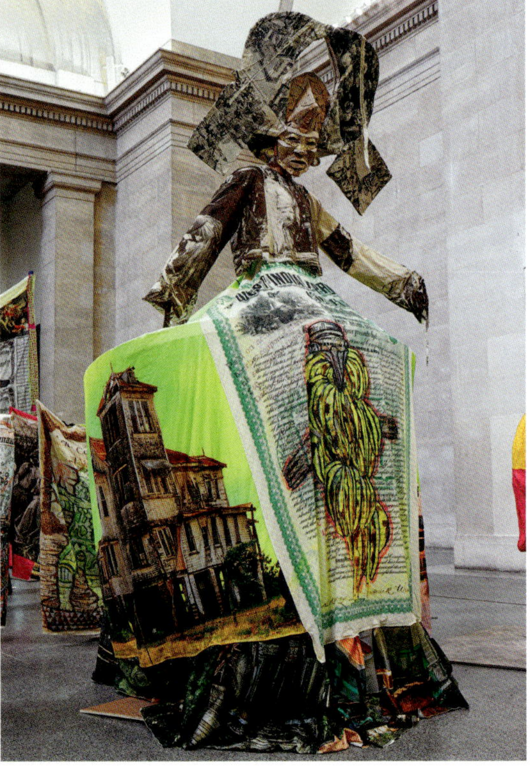

fig. 9. Hew Locke, *The Procession*, figure 86, 2022. Plastic, cardboard, fabric, wood, paper, metal, mixed media.

One of the principal companies trading between Europe and Africa in the early modern period was the Royal African Company, which dealt primarily in gold (pp. 72–3, 75) and enslaved people. The Company was responsible for the largest movement of enslaved people across the Atlantic in the history of the trade, transporting around 150,000 to 160,000 captives between 1672 and 1731 alone. Records show that in the early part of this period, as many as one in five would not survive the journey due to the horrifying conditions of the Middle Passage.[24]

One of the incredible material survivals of such a journey is the Akan drum (p. 69), the oldest African American object in the Museum. It was taken from West Africa to America – likely by an enslaver, as enslaved people were not allowed to carry objects with them – where it was collected by a Mr Clerk in Virginia (which was then a British colony). Mr Clerk gave it to Hans Sloane, who bequeathed it to the British Museum. In the Caribbean, drums were often confiscated due to their potential use for resistance; Locke notes that it makes sense to him 'that this thing [the drum] would have been given to Sloane because you're not giving this to a slave to remind them of when they were free'.

Locke is also particularly interested in the currencies that were exchanged for enslaved people in Africa, including glass beads, cowries and brass manillas (pp. 50–1, 74–5), all of which have featured in his work as symbolic dressing for figures involved in the trade, such as Colston (see fig. 1). Cowries were used as money in Africa from as early as the 14th century.[25] Small, portable and durable, they were also very hard to counterfeit. From the 16th century onwards there was an influx of cowries transported from the Indian Ocean by European traders, and they became a key currency in the trade. By the 1770s an enslaved person could be bought for between 160,000 and 176,000 cowries.[26]

Relating to currency forms that existed in West Africa prior to European trade, manillas (named after the Portuguese for 'bracelet') made from copper, bronze or brass were used as currency in West Africa from the 15th to the 20th centuries and were a frequent medium of exchange for enslaved people. From the 15th to the 18th centuries, most of the manillas in circulation in West Africa came from the copper mines of the Holy Roman Empire (800–1806), until Britain became Europe's leading brass manufacturer in the 18th century. These manillas were often smelted down by artists at the court of the Oba of Benin and were the source of much of the copper in the Benin Bronzes.[27] As Locke observes, 'It's not widely understood, the mass production [of brass] coming out of Birmingham, to be traded for human lives, and maybe melted down and made into Benin Bronzes … History is extremely perverse, I think.'

During the period of the 'triangular trade', roughly 12 million African people were forcibly transported from West Africa to the Americas. Around 40 per cent of them were taken to the Caribbean, where the rise of chattel slavery saw the forced cultivation of monocultural crops, mainly sugar, which was transported back to Europe to be sold at an enormous profit for the white plantation owners. In early 19th-century Trinidad the life expectancy for someone born into slavery was 17 years.[28] Strict racial hierarchies governed life in the Caribbean and racial categorisation became enshrined in English law for the first

23. Hew Locke and Charles Henry Rowell, 'An Interview with Hew Locke', *Callaloo*, vol. 37, no. 3 (Summer 2014), p. 535.

24. William Pettigrew, 'The Royal African Company', in Victoria Avery and Jake Subryan Richards (eds), *Black Atlantic: Power, People, Resistance*, exh. cat. (London: Philip Wilson Publishers, 2023), p. 70; Philip D. Curtin, *The Atlantic Slave Trade: A Census* (Madison, WI, and London: University of Wisconsin Press, 1969), p. 277.

25. Anne Haour and Annalisa Christie, 'Cowries in the archaeology of West Africa: the present picture', *Azania: Archaeological Research in Africa*, vol. 54, no. 3 (2019), pp. 287–321, p. 301.

26. Jan Hogendorn and Marion Johnson, *The Shell Money of the Slave Trade* (Cambridge: Cambridge University Press, 1986), p. 11, cited J. Guyer & K. Pallaver, 24 May 2018, 'Money and Currency in African History', *Oxford Research Encyclopedia of African History*, online.

27. Alissandra Cummins, 'Manillas', in *Black Atlantic*, ed. Avery and Richards, pp. 73–4.

28. A. Meredith John, 'Slave Mortality in Trinidad', *Population Studies*, vol. 42, no. 2 (July 1988), p. 172.

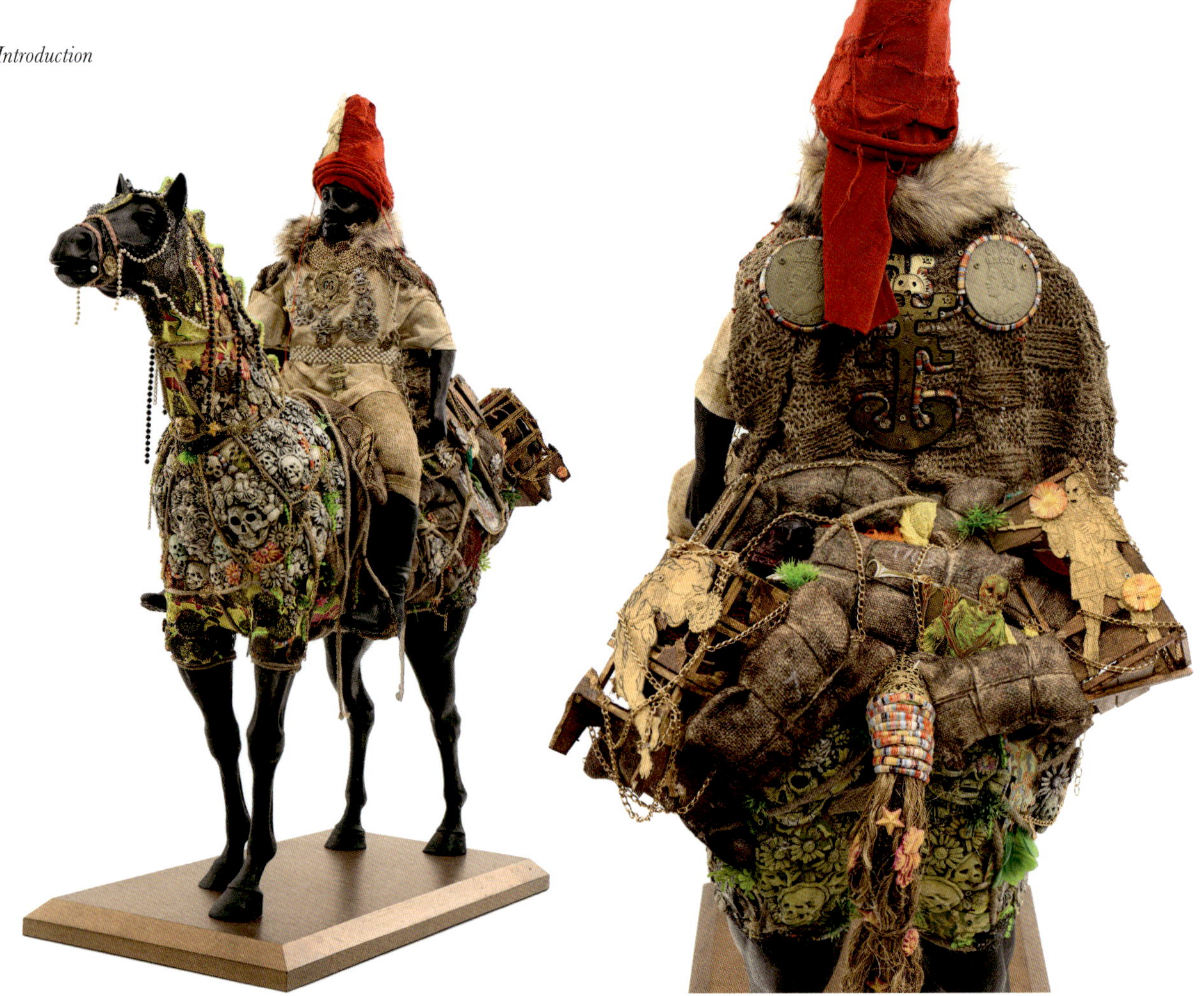

fig. 10. Hew Locke, *Ambassador 2*, 2021. Glass, plastic, metal, fabric, wood, leather, acrylic paint and mixed media. H. 146 cm, W. 128 cm, D. 53 cm.

time; the Barbados Slave and Servant Acts of 1661 stipulated that enslaved Africans were to be treated as 'other goods and Chattels'.[29] Both before and after abolition, life in the West Indies was structured according to an elaborate class system based on skin colour or 'pigmentocracy' ('the lighter your skin, the higher up the social ladder you go'[30]), as depicted in the highly romanticised scenes of Caribbean life of Agostino Brunias (1730–1796), which ignored the brutal conditions of enslavement (pp. 78–81).

29. Barbados Slave Act, 1661, cited in preamble, in *Slavery*, ed. Stanley Engerman, Seymour Drescher and Robert Paquette (Oxford: Oxford University Press, 2001), p. 105.

30. Andrew Gilbert, Hew Locke and Simon Grant, 'Legacies of Empire: Artist and Empire at Tate Britain', *Tate Etc*, no. 35 (Autumn 2015).

One souvenir of enslavement in the Caribbean has been a recurring motif in Locke's work: a coin showing the head of an African man. Often enlarged to show the detail of its modelling, it features, along with *memento mori* and Mesoamerican figures, on the back of *Ambassador 2* (2021, fig. 10), while its reverse (showing a pineapple, the 'king of fruits', associated with Barbados) hangs as a medal around the neck of a horned, beribboned figure in *The Procession*. Locke notes the head of the African man 'is not a caricature – that's what's interesting about it, it's really well modelled'; he also highlights how the head is positioned where the king or queen would usually feature, giving it equivalence with a head of state.

Britain did not supply currencies to any of its colonies until 1825. Parliament went as far as prohibiting the export of British silver coinage as it was felt that colonies should be providing the British with precious metals, rather than the other way around.[31] In 1788, to fill this gap, the planter and chair of the pro-slavery West India Planters' and Merchants' Association, Sir Philip Gibbes, privately commissioned the so-called 'Barbados penny' – a copper token intended to facilitate small transactions in the place of legal tender. The coins were struck from dies engraved by John Milton (1759–1805) of London, with a second issue struck by John Gregory Hancock (1775–1815) of Birmingham in 1792. On one side of the token is the head of an African man, crowned with a coronet and three ostrich feathers (the heraldic device of the Prince of Wales) along with his motto, 'I serve'. As Locke notes, 'it's a sick joke, basically', emphasising the Black Africans' subjection to white planters and the colony of Barbados's subjection to the crown.

Nearly two years after the Slavery Abolition Act was passed on 1 August 1834, outlawing the owning, buying and selling of enslaved people throughout British colonies, Philip Gibbes's grandson, Samuel Osborne Gibbes Jr, was compensated £6,536 for the loss of 292 enslaved people from his plantation, a sum that historian Alissandra Cummins estimates to be £6,076,000 in today's money.[32] Across British colonies, enslavers were given roughly £20 million for the loss of their 'property', while formerly enslaved people were given no compensation at all. Although legally declared free, many people spent further years in servitude as part of the apprenticeship system (a widely opposed stage between slavery and freedom, where enslaved people were required to work for their previous 'owner' without pay, in exchange for provisions); full freedom was not granted until 1 August 1838. A few different objects testify to this moment, including a carte de visite (calling card) featuring an emancipated child, Rebecca Huger, produced by a charity promoting education (p. 85), and an enslaver's claim for compensation in Essequibo, Guyana (p. 84).

After abolition, the British faced significant labour shortages on plantations in the Caribbean. They resorted to transporting indentured labourers from India to supply the shortfall. Locke notes, 'I grew up in a country where roughly 52 per cent of people are descended from indentured servants from India. I grew up celebrating Hindu festivals with friends at school. Some of them were Afro-Caribbean, some Indo-Caribbean. It's a mixed up and extremely complicated society and I'm constantly arguing for a complex view of the Caribbean rather than a one-dimensional view.'[33]

English imperial expansion in India began with the founding in 1600 of the East India Company, a joint-stock company (see p. 88) that the politician Edmund Burke (1729–1797) famously described as a 'state in the disguise of a merchant'.[34] The company was founded under a charter from Queen Elizabeth I to profit from the lucrative trade in spices in the Indian Ocean, which was already being pursued by the Dutch and Portuguese. By the mid-1700s the company had grown to dominate trade between Europe, South Asia and China, particularly in commodities including textiles, spices, tea and, later, opium.[35] A number of financial documents illustrate the extent of this economic extraction (pp. 90–1). In an attempt to strengthen the Company during a period of keen competition with the Dutch East India Company (leading to the Anglo-Dutch wars of the 17th and 18th centuries), King Charles II granted the East India Company rights to acquire territory, mint money (pp. 89, 91), command fortresses and troops, to make war and peace, and to exercise civil and criminal jurisdiction, essentially enabling the Company to act as a sovereign state. Described by one of its directors as an 'empire within an empire',[36] by 1803, when it defeated the Mughal Empire to become the dominant power in South Asia, the East India Company had a private military force twice the size of the British army.

31. Alissandra Cummins, 'Gibbes's plantation tokens: making, meaning and legacy', in *Black Atlantic*, ed. Avery and Richards, p. 78. Much of the information in this paragraph comes from Cummins's account.

32. Ibid., p. 83.

33. Emann Odufu, 'Interview with Hew Locke', *Brooklyn Rail*, Jul–Aug 2022.

34. Speeches in the Impeachment of Warren Hastings, First Day: Friday, Feb 15, 1788, in *The Works of the Right Honourable Edmund Burke* (12 vols), vol. 9, (London: John C. Nimmo, 1887), p. 350.

35. Anthony Farrington, *Trading Places: The East India Company and Asia, 1600–1834* (London: The British Library, 2002).

The Company was responsible for the bulk of British imperial expansion in the 18th century. In 1757 Robert Clive (1725–1774) defeated the Nawab of Bengal Siraj-ud-Daulah (1733–1757) and his French allies at the Battle of Plassey, a victory that allowed the East India Company to gain control of Bengal, one of the richest regions in the world; the Company proceeded to tax rapaciously, contributing to one of Bengal's worst famines (1769–70), which is estimated to have killed 1.2 million people.[37] Locke draws attention to the EIC's role in the destruction of Indian trade and manufacturing, particularly the textile industry, in his *Share* series (2009–ongoing, pp. 92–3, 95), elaborately decorated objects that highlight these histories of extraction.

36. William Dalrymple, *The Anarchy: The Relentless Rise of the East India Company* (London: Bloomsbury, 2019), p. xxxvi.

37. For figures on deaths caused by this famine see Rajat Datta, *Society, Economy and the Market: Commercialization in Rural Bengal, c. 1760–1800* (New Delhi: Manohar Publishers & Distributors, 2000), p. 264; for the East India Company's role see Tirthankar Roy, *An Economic History of India 1707–1857* (London: Routledge, 2021), p. 88.

CONFLICT (pp. 100–35)

While the trading relationships discussed above ranged from the mutually beneficial to the extractive, much was undergirded by violence, or the threat of it. An early series of charcoal drawings by Locke focuses on cross-cultural hybrid depictions of 'mercenaries' (fig. 11). 'Conflict' (pp. 100–35) examines encounters between cultures, including Columbus's journey to the Americas and the wider employment of mercenaries and violence, as well as examples of resistance, rebellion and revolution in the Americas, Africa and the Indian subcontinent.

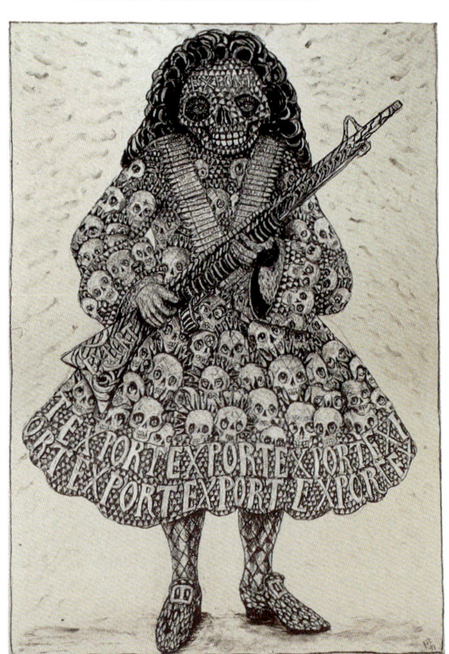

fig. 11. Hew Locke, *Mercenary 2*, 1998. Pastel and charcoal on mountboard. H. 154 cm, W. 128 cm.

The arrival of the European explorer Christopher Columbus (1451–1506) in the Caribbean was a seismic shift that exposed the American continents to European settlement and resource extraction, and alerted Europeans to the possibility of new markets. The common narrative of the 'discovery' of the 'New World' erases the complex histories and cultures of the diverse Indigenous peoples who had inhabited those lands, sometimes for thousands of years. While history has remembered Columbus's encounters on the mainland, he first arrived in the Caribbean. In opposition to a brick that was apparently used as ballast on Columbus's ship, Locke places two large wooden sculptures carved by unrecorded Taíno makers sometime between 800 and 1500 to symbolise this moment of encounter (pp. 103–5). Although once considered extinct, Taíno heritage is now reclaimed by many people across the Caribbean. As Locke notes, 'something of this age in the Caribbean is special – even the hardest woods don't survive the climate. They have become a symbol of collective memory, a myth, an idea of nationhood.' Elsewhere Locke has painted a Taíno figure onto a share of the West India Improvement Company, an American company formed to build a railway in Jamaica to ship bananas (see fig. 9, p. 122).

While it would be a mistake to project onto these (often peaceful) encounters the wholesale destruction of Indigenous peoples and ways of life that was to follow, Locke was also particularly drawn to a poster carrying a quote from Columbus's diary (p. 102), which illustrates his view of the people living there in a manner that foreshadows European interactions with Indigenous peoples in the Americas and later systems of enslavement.

> *They do not bear arms and do not know them, for I showed them a sword, they took it by the edge and cut themselves out of ignorance … They would make fine servants … With fifty men we could subjugate them all and make them do whatever we want.*[38]

Locke sought to challenge the insistence on Indigenous pacifism in this statement by juxtaposing Columbus's quotation with Guyanese Wai Wai clubs; one of these clubs was possibly brought over to England by a colonist who sold it to the collector and naturalist John Tradescant in the early 17th century. Locke also draws out the links between Columbus's statement and his Confederate share series *Song of the South* (2018–ongoing), painted on bonds drawn during the American Civil War (1861–5) to raise money for the Confederate cause. 'These shares are about the survival of Afro-Caribbean people in general … They're about survival against the odds.'

Similar themes recur in other accounts of the 'discovery' of the 'New World', including drawings by John White (fl. 1585–93), a governor of the Roanoke colony of Virginia (in modern-day North Carolina), the earliest surviving drawings of Indigenous Americans by a European artist (pp. 109–11). White's drawings were later published as engravings, in part to encourage potential colonists, emphasising the abundance of resources and alluding to the potential to convert Indigenous Americans to Christianity. The only account of the 1584 voyage, written by Arthur Barlowe (1550–1620), reads as a 'promotional tract for paradise':[39]

> *No people in the world carrie more respect to their King, Nobilitie, and Governors than these do … Wee found the people most gentle, loving and faithful, void of all guile, and treason, and such as lived after the manner of the golden age. The earth bringeth foorth all things in aboundance, as in the first creation, without toile or labour.*[40]

The prints were copied extensively, making them hugely influential on the European imagination and subsequent depictions of Indigenous Americans, particularly through White's borrowings from the poses of classical antiquity to give his subjects an air of power and authority; this contributed to the construction of the trope of the 'noble savage'.

Drawings by Maria Sibylla Merian (1647–1717) and her daughter Dorothea Graff (1678–1743) were also selected by Locke – partly for their beauty but also to illustrate the conflict and violence inherent within imperial structures (pp. 116–17). Made after Merian and Graff's self-funded voyage in 1699 to Suriname (at the time a Dutch colony), the drawings were groundbreaking for their careful observations, harmonious compositions and contributions to natural science. Merian and Graff drew heavily on the local knowledge and assistance of enslaved African and Indigenous people who laboured under horrifying conditions on Dutch sugar plantations.

Locke has juxtaposed these drawings with William Blake's engravings made nearly a century later, depicting the violence enacted upon a community of runaway and insurgent enslaved people known as the Maroons by the Dutch and their allies in Suriname; the book's illustrations of abject cruelty were later adopted by abolitionist campaigners

38. *Journal of Christopher Columbus*, Oct 1492, translation from the poster designed by Daniel Veneciano, p. 102.

39. Kim Sloan, 'An Elizabethan "Governour" in Virginia', in *A New World: England's First View of America* (London: The British Museum Press), 2007, p. 40.

40. Ibid.

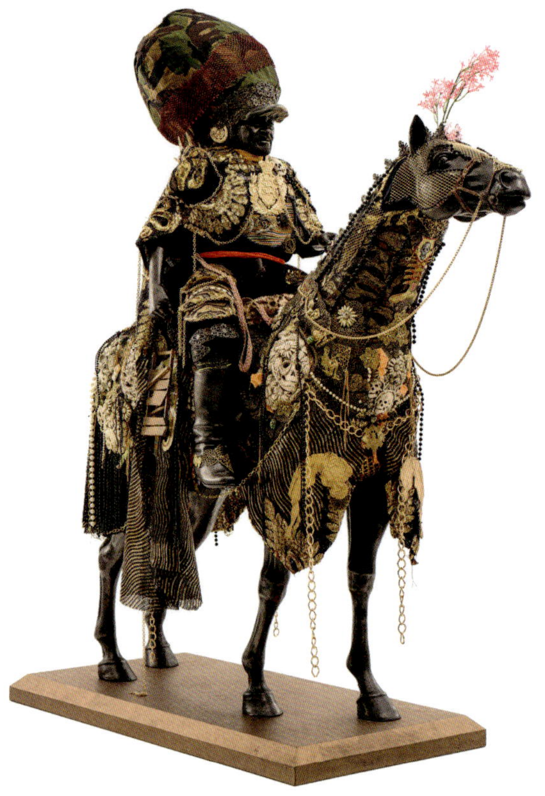

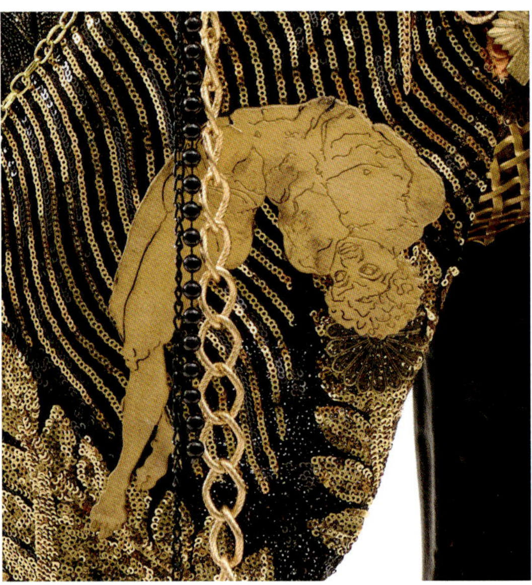

fig. 12. Hew Locke, *Ambassador 1*, 2021. Resin, metal, MDF, fabric, plastic and mixed media.
H. 155 cm, W. 137 cm, D. 50 cm.

in Britain. One horrifying image, showing an enslaved man hung from a gallows by a hook through his ribs, has been used repeatedly by Locke (fig. 12), although in such a way as to avoid simply replicating images of the brutalisation of Black bodies: 'if you paint them gold, then all of a sudden, they don't [seem] horrible anymore. They become very reminiscent of attractive baroque carvings that you see in historic stately homes. There is something perverse about that because, of course, that world was supported by the slave trade and by the plantation system.'[41]

Though Merian and Graff's drawings were made almost a century before Blake's engravings, Locke brings these disparate works together to highlight the struggle for life that is present in both. Merian was aware of the violence that circumscribed the lives of enslaved people in Suriname, noting in her description of the peacock flower, 'The Indians, who are not treated well in the service of the Dutch, abort their children with these [seeds], not wanting them to be slaves like themselves … [Enslaved women] sometimes even take their own lives, due to the typical harsh treatment they receive.'[42] Locke seeks to tease out this underlying tension in her drawings of botanical and animal life, a violence he sees reflected in her portrayal of struggle between different species and of predators devouring their prey.

As explored above, enslaved people in the Caribbean resisted their oppression in numerous ways. Objects in this section represent different forms of resistance, ranging from the personal, including suicide and abortion, to forms of cultural resistance, such as Carnival, to larger-scale military uprisings, as with Maroons in Jamaica and in the case of

41. Cosmo Whyte, 'Hew Locke: A World Before the World We Know', *Art Papers*, vol. 45, no. 2 (Winter 2021).

42. Maria Sibylla Merian, *Metamorphosis insectorum surinamensium* (Amsterdam: G. Valck, 1705), p. 45, translation by Charlotte Wytema, pers. comm., 2024.

Haiti, a revolution resulting in the world's first Black Republic. What began as an uprising of enslaved people, catalysed by the French Revolution in 1789, was transformed into a revolutionary movement thanks to the military and political acumen of the Haitian general Toussaint Louverture (*c.* 1743–1803) (see p. 118). Formerly enslaved, Toussaint fought with French Revolutionary forces under Napoleon but broke away from the French as the emperor moved to reinstate slavery in 1802.[43] The revolution was the largest ever on the North American continent, involving more than 100,000 enslaved Africans against the armies of France, Spain and Britain. In 1803 Jean-Jacques Dessalines (1758–1806), himself formerly enslaved, led the revolutionary forces to victory, announcing the creation of the new republic of Haiti (the Arawak name for the island) on 1 January 1804.

The new republic boldly attempted to implement universal human rights and was a turning point in the fight to abolish transatlantic slavery; three years after Haiti was declared an independent republic, on 25 March 1807, King George III (1738–1820) signed the Act for the Abolition of the Slave Trade, banning the trade of enslaved people within the British Empire (although this was not abolished in practice until 1838).[44] Henri Christophe (1767–1820), who had served as a general under Toussaint Louverture, went on to become the first King of Haiti (r. 1811–20). His self-presentation as a Roman emperor on the face of his 'one gourde' coin (p. 120) – which was commissioned from the British engraver Thomas Wyon Sr (1767–1830) in 1811, minted in London and shipped across the Atlantic to Haiti – illustrates the cosmopolitan and outward-looking nature of his government and constitutes a powerful declaration of Black sovereignty.[45]

Another powerful form of resistance in the Caribbean is the tradition of Carnival, which began as a hybridisation of African dances, celebrations and masquerades with European traditions of masked balls and parades, in a 'world turned upside down'. Mocking the behaviour and dress of white planters, or European and American sailors on shore leave, and drawing on spirits from African folklore and histories of African warriors, masquerade characters including John Canoe (or Koo Koo, p. 125), Moko Jumbie, Mother

43. The Colonial Williamsburg Foundation and UNESCO Slave Route Project, 'French Revolution', *Slavery and Remembrance* website, online.

44. Franklin W. Knight, 'The Haitian Revolution and the Notion of Human Rights', *Journal of the Historical Society*, vol. 5, no. 3, 2005, pp. 391–416; Hakim Adi, 'The Haitian Revolution: The Enslaved Africans who Rose Up Against France', *History Extra*, 10 June 2021, online.

45. Esther Chadwick, 'The Aesthetics of Postrevolutionary Haiti: Currency, Kingship, and Circum-Atlantic Numismatics', *Art History*, vol. 46, no. 5, Nov 2023, pp. 1014–45.

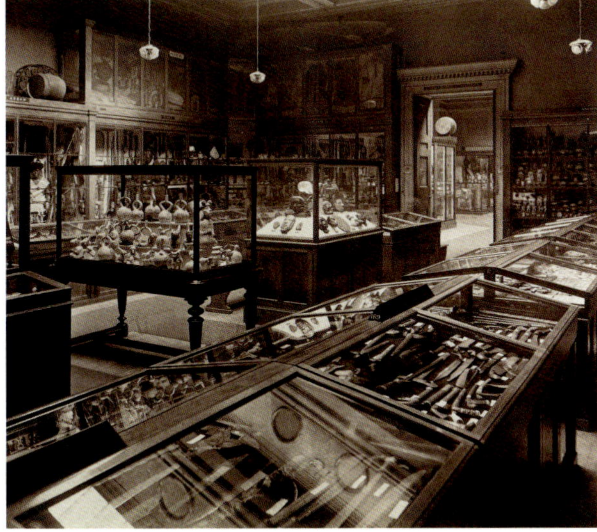

fig. 13. The British Museum ethnography galleries, view of the Asia section, 1908. London, UK.

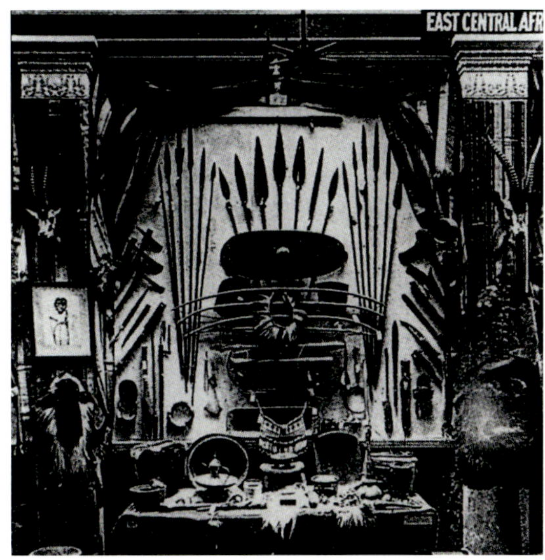

fig. 14. The Stanley and African Exhibition display from East Central Africa, 1890. London, UK.

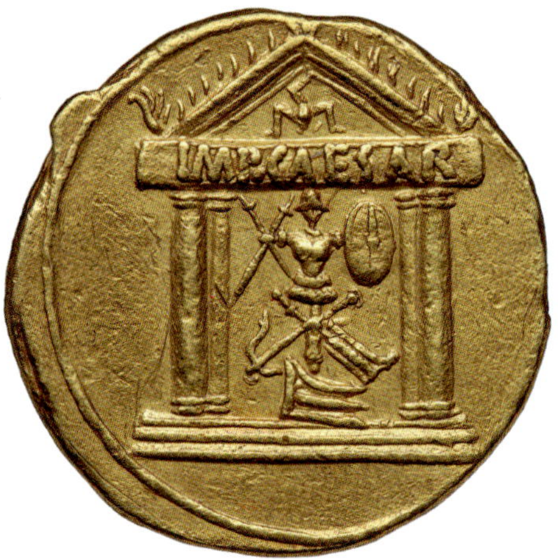

fig. 15. Gold aureus with military trophies inside a temple, 29–27 BCE. Minted in Italy. Gold. Diam. 1.9 cm, weight 8 g. British Museum, London, 1844,1008.63.

Sally, Midnight Robber, Pitchy Patchy and Sailor Mas were interpreted differently across the Caribbean.[46] Masquerade has formed an integral part of Locke's practice, not just in the sense that carnival masks and characters feature in works such as *The Procession* (see figs. 7–9) and his earlier installation *The Tourists* (2015), but in a structural manner that the art historian Kobena Mercer identifies as a kind of 'diaspora baroque'. This identification as 'diasporic' is not on account of Locke's biography but the '*double-sidedness of the mask* whereby the visuality of the exterior face serves to both solicit and deflect the gaze of others, while also containing and hence enabling the work of mourning that takes place on the other side of the black interior'.[47]

46. Emily Zobel Marshall, Max Farrar and Guy Farrar, 'Popular political cultures and the Caribbean carnival: Carnival is a rich resource for cultural resistance as well as pleasure', *Soundings*, no. 67 (Winter 2018), pp. 34–49; and Erol Hill, *The Trinidad Carnival* (London: New Beacon Books, 1997).

47. Mercer 2011, p. 6.

In the late 1800s Britain, along with other European powers, violently seized territory across the African continent in what became known as the 'Scramble for Africa', campaigns that were met with fierce resistance from Indigenous peoples. Locke juxtaposes British medals for African conflicts with various African weapons, noting that 'weaponry features strongly because violence underpins the enlargement of any state – even if you don't use it, the threat is there'. Their arrangement echoes a common format for ethnographic displays in museums, including, historically, the British Museum, which often grouped objects by type or function within a particular region (fig. 13), and exhibitions such as the Stanley and African Exhibition of 1890 (fig. 14), which arranged weapons in a 'trophy' format, similar to classical coins (fig. 15). This drew on Roman traditions that saw weapons seized from a defeated opponent as *spolia opima* (rich spoils), the highest military honour, and which, when arranged in this format, sought to impress upon the audience the fearsomeness of the defeated foe.

Theatrical arrangements of weapons occur often in Locke's work, most notably in his series of life-size photographs *How do you want me?* (2007, fig. 16) and his installations *Koh-i-Noor* (2005) and *El Dorado* (2005), while medals from African conflicts have also been woven throughout his works (pp. 33, 38, 41). Insignia such as the East and West Africa medal (p. 132) show British troops fighting African soldiers. 'Because there

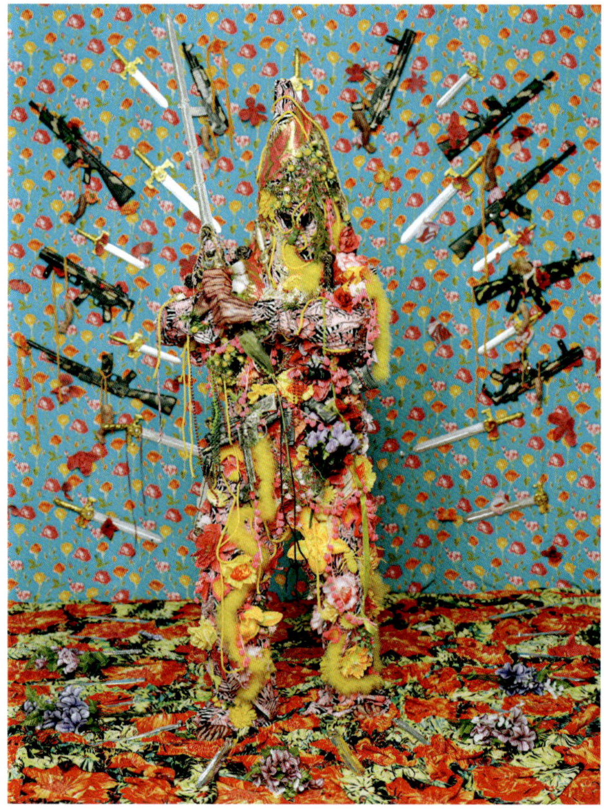

fig. 16. Hew Locke, *Chevalier*, 2007, from the series *How do you want me?*. C-type print. H. 227 cm, W. 177 cm.

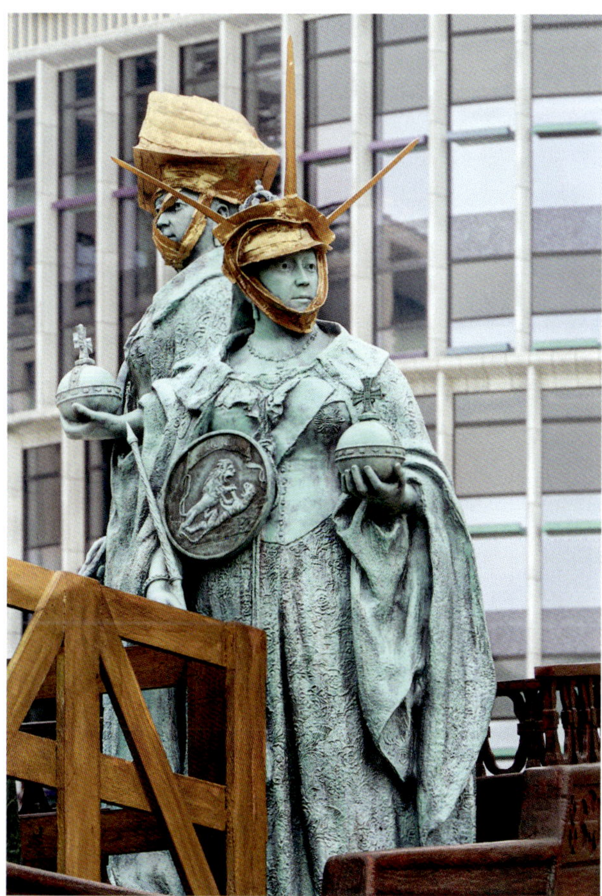

fig. 17. Hew Locke, *Foreign Exchange*, 2022. Steel, glass fibre, wood, resin and acrylic. H. 7.3 m, W. 4.4 m, D. 4.4 m.

were so many conflicts in Africa, they didn't design a new one for each conflict – they'd put a small bar on it … The idea of "Pax Britannica" (British Peace) was a lie. Someone would rebel and they would have to be suppressed.' Many of Britain's military victories during the 'Scramble for Africa' were enabled by the Maxim gun, the world's first fully automatic machine gun. In Locke's words, 'this is industrialised killing, basically. The gun that won an empire.' Yet the gun is conspicuously absent from contemporary depictions of warfare, particularly medals, which preferred to focus on the individual heroism of hand-to-hand combat.[48]

Locke has also selected a number of objects symbolising resistance to colonial rule on the Indian subcontinent. One medal commemorating the East India Company's defeat of Tipu Sultan (1751–1799) in 1799 has been reclaimed by Locke as a symbol of Indian resistance to British rule, forming the face of a hooded figure in *Procession* and draped over the arm of Queen Victoria in his public sculpture *Foreign Exchange* (2022) (fig. 17). Tipu Sultan, known as the 'Tiger of Mysore', was the ruler of the Kingdom of Mysore and a tireless opponent of Company rule. The Siege of Seringapatam (1799) culminated in Tipu's death and

objects associated with him had a lasting impact on the British imaginary. In Locke's words, 'Tipu became mythologised in history paintings, almost like the Death of Napoleon. These are important to Britain's idea of itself, the enemy has to be strong in order for the victory to mean something.'

Half a century later, the Indian Uprising of 1857–8, a major insurrection against Company rule, led to the dissolution of the East India Company and the establishment of the British Raj. Other objects illustrating resistance to British rule and how it was represented in the collective imagination include a 1952 film poster featuring the legendary Rani of Jhansi (p. 130) and a photograph of the proposal for the east terrace garden at Windsor Castle (p. 127). The composite photograph shows a kiosk from Lucknow in northern India placed into the landscaped gardens, another example of an attempt to incorporate symbols of Indian rule into the British monarchy's identity. On 1 November 1858 Queen Victoria issued a proclamation, promising Indians rights similar to other British subjects. The subsequent contravention of these promises was then used by Indians to call for a new nationalism and self-government, the legacy of which Locke examines in shares such as *Middleton & Tonge Cotton Mill* (2023, p. 95), which explores the development of India's independence movement.[49]

48. Ramey Mize, '"Whatever happens, we have got, the Maxim, and they have not": The Conspicuous Absence of Machine Guns in British Imperialist Imagery', *Rutgers Art Review: The Graduate Journal of Research in Art History*, vol. 33/4 (2018), pp. 43–65.

49. Ainslie Thomas Embree, Stephen N. Hay and William Theodore De Bary, 'Nationalism Takes Root: The Moderates', in *Sources of Indian Tradition: Modern India and Pakistan* (New York: Columbia University Press, 1988), p. 85.

TREASURE (pp. 136–67)

A final thread running through this book relates to the spoils of Empire, particularly those seized as a result of military conquest. A particular interest of Locke's is the way that objects change their meaning as they move from place to place, context to context, over time. During the British colonial period, there were dozens of 'punitive' expeditions intended to target and punish peoples or kingdoms seen as dissident or morally wrong, conditions that were sometimes used as a pretext for subjugating uprisings and acquiring objects of material or cultural value. Three major confrontations include the British Expedition to Abyssinia (1867–8, Ethiopia and Eritrea), the Benin Expedition (1897, modern-day Nigeria) and the Expedition to Tibet (1903–4, the 'Younghusband Expedition').

'Punitive' expeditions

Ethiopia (known in Britain at the time as Abyssinia) was ruled by Emperor Tewodros II. Tewodros sought to bring the whole of Ethiopia under his control through military conquest, and he was cosmopolitan in outlook, prizing foreign artistry, military strategy and technology. During his campaigns, he collected books, manuscripts and other objects from churches across Ethiopia with the intention of establishing the mountain fortress of Maqdala as a seat of learning. Ethiopia (and the preceding Kingdom of Aksum) had been Christian since the 4th century CE and Tewodros sought to ally himself with other Christian monarchs. For this reason, in 1857 and 1862 he wrote to Queen Victoria requesting assistance in military training.

While Britain had previously sought to influence political developments in Ethiopia, their commitments were limited, and these communications were ignored. When Tewodros realised this, he took hostage around 30 European diplomats and missionaries currently living in Ethiopia. In response, the British launched a punitive expedition and in 1867, 13,000 British and Indian soldiers were led by Sir Robert Napier from Bombay (Mumbai) to Ethiopia with the stated aim of freeing the hostages and punishing Tewodros. The massive military assault, carried out in 1868, resulted in the destruction of Maqdala's fortress, the deaths of hundreds of Tewodros's army and the wounding of thousands more, with only limited British casualties.[50]

During the invasion, Tewodros chose to die by suicide rather than be taken prisoner. The objects plundered from Maqdala by British and Indian troops were said to have required 15 elephants and almost 200 mules to transport them to the Delanta Plain, where items were auctioned off by an Army Prize Committee on 20–21 April 1868.[51]

Unusually, the Expedition was accompanied by a British Museum employee, Richard Rivington Holmes, assistant in the Department of Manuscripts, in the official capacity of 'archaeologist'. Holmes was one of the principal buyers at the auction, and returned to the UK with over 300 manuscripts (now at the British Library) and other important and sacred objects, many of which entered the British Museum collection via Holmes and the Secretary of State for India. Holmes also engaged in looting himself, having been given permission by Sir Robert Napier (Commander in Chief of the Abyssinian Expedition) to keep some objects, described as 'prizes'. While celebrated by many in Britain at the time, the destruction and

50. For more information see www.britishmuseum.org/about-us/british-museum-story/contested-objects-collection/maqdala-collection. For more information on Holmes's role in the expedition see Zoe Cormack, 'The British Museum and the Abyssinian Campaign, 1867–8' (forthcoming article).

51. Henry Morton Stanley, *Coomassie and Magdala: The Story of Two British Campaigns in Africa* (London: Sampson Low, Marston, Low, & Searle, 1874), p. 470, cited in Alexandra Watson Jones, 'Maqdala and the South Kensington Museum: 150 years later', *Intersectional Encounters in the Nineteenth-Century Archive: New Essays on Power and Discourse*, ed. Rachel Bryant Davies and Erin Johnson-Williams (London: Bloomsbury, 2022), p. 72.

pillaging of Maqdala also had fierce critics, most notably the British prime minister William Gladstone, who particularly regretted the seizure of church property.[52]

Hew Locke has been making work about Ethiopia since 2012. His *Company of the Imperial Railway of Ethiopia* (fig. 18) is painted on a sheet of shares for a company founded in France in 1894, under a royal charter from Emperor Menelik II (1844–1913), to build a railway across Ethiopia. The firm collapsed after the difficulty of building on mountainous and desert terrain, political instability and a lack of investment halted construction in 1904; Locke notes that in 2010 China started construction on Ethiopia's new rail system.[53] Locke's interest in Ethiopian history and the Ethiopian collections at the British Museum has also resulted in the creation of a new *Share* work (p. 149).

Another large-scale military expedition by the British was the invasion of Benin City, triggered by an allegedly peaceful but clearly provocative British trade mission, which had been attacked in January 1897 on its way to Benin City. This led to a large-scale retaliatory mission, and in February 1897 Benin City was captured by British forces. The Oba was deposed and sent into exile in Calabar in southern Nigeria (pp. 141–3). No exact figure can be given for the number of people killed during the occupation of Benin City, but there were many casualties as well as widespread destruction and pillaging by British forces.[54] Along with other monuments and palaces, the Benin Royal Palace was burned and partly destroyed (p. 145). Its shrines and associated compounds were looted by British forces and thousands of objects of ceremonial and ritual value were taken to the UK as official 'spoils of war' or distributed among members of the expedition according to their rank (p. 146).

52. See e.g. www.britishmuseum.org/collection/object/E_Af1868-1001-9. For Gladstone's comments see UK Parliament Hansard, Commons Chamber, 30 June 1871.

53. 'Compagnie Impériale Chemins de Fer Éthiopiens Bond, 1899', University of Illinois Springfield (Manuscripts and Special Collections), digitised on 15 Oct 2007; see www.hewlocke.net/goldstandard.html.

54. For more information see www.britishmuseum.org/about-us/british-museum-story/contested-objects-collection/benin-bronzes.

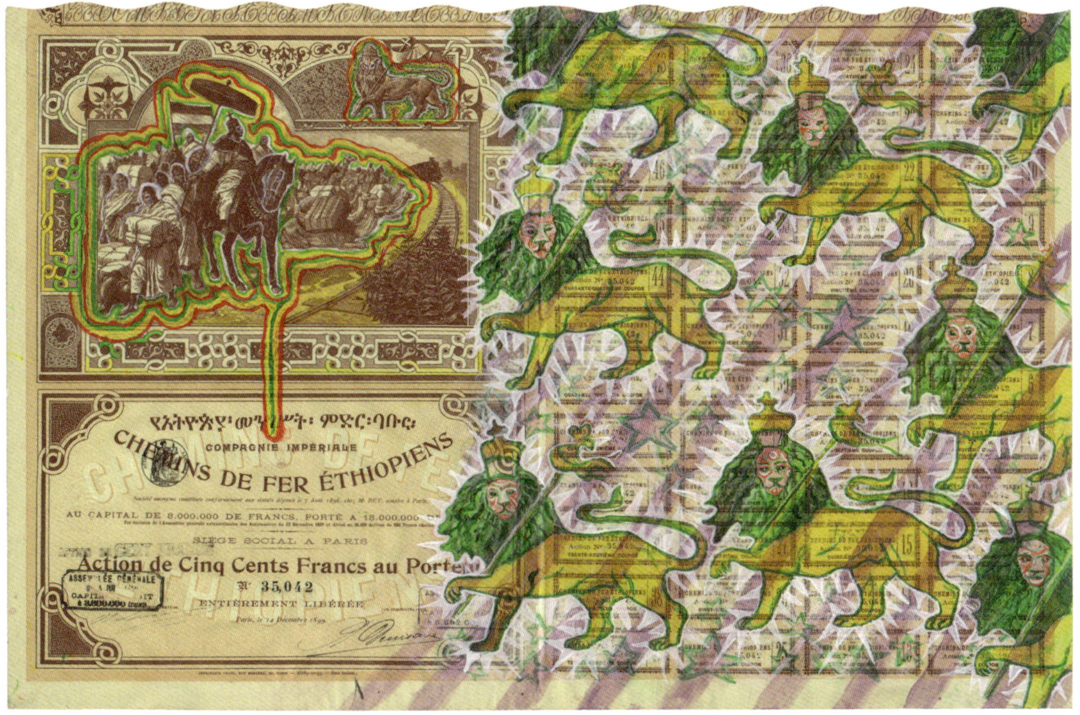

fig. 18. Hew Locke, *Company of the Imperial Railway of Ethiopia 1*, 2012. Acrylic ink on antique share certificates. H. 42 cm, W. 64.5 cm.

Locke's own interpretation is that 'a culture has been boxed up and shipped out'. He has been interested in Luba, Baule and Benin sculpture since his student days and has had two fibreglass reproductions of Benin Bronze plaques on his kitchen wall since his time at Falmouth Art School. There are over 900 objects from the historic Kingdom of Benin currently cared for by the British Museum, with the majority directly related to the looting that took place under the aggressive imperial expansion on the part of the British. More than 5,000 objects from Benin are catalogued by the Digital Benin initiative across 136 institutions in 20 countries worldwide, and some of these collections have also now been legally transferred or repatriated.

Another instance of widespread looting by British troops occurred during the British invasion of Tibet, led by Francis Younghusband, known as the 'Younghusband Expedition' (1903–4). Initiated as a result of tensions between the British and Russian empires over control of Central Asia during the period referred to as the 'Great Game' (a term popularised by Rudyard Kipling in his novel *Kim*, 1901), the invasion led to the deaths of 2,000–3,000 Tibetans.[55] At what became known as the Massacre of Chumik Shenko, more than 700 soldiers armed with swords and single-shot matchlock rifles were cut down by rapid-fire Maxim machine guns. Lieutenant Arthur Hadow, commander of the British detachment, later wrote: 'I got so sick of the slaughter that I ceased fire, though the general's order was to make as big a bag as possible. I hope I shall never again have to shoot down men walking away.'[56]

Many cultural objects were looted by soldiers from monasteries and elsewhere, especially around the town of Gyantse. The British Museum had nominated two representatives, Lawrence Augustine Waddell (1854–1938) and Perceval Landon (1869–1927), to collect books and manuscripts for the British Museum. Waddell was given 10,000 rupees by the British Government and amassed over 2,000 items, allowing an average of just 5 rupees per item.[57] While Waddell was only charged to collect books and manuscripts, in January 1905 his assistant, David Macdonald, sorted over 400 mule-loads of objects in the India Museum, Calcutta, containing 'many rare and valuable manuscripts, armour, weapons, paintings and porcelain'.[58] Items brought back from Tibet included objects of religious significance – gilt and brass Tibetan Buddhist statues filled with the remains of important lamas, bells, prayer wheels and lama robes – that were unlikely to have been willingly sold to the British.[59]

55. McKay, 'The British Invasion of Tibet' p. 14.

56. Simon de Bruxelles, 'The first pictures of Tibet by unwelcome British troops', *The Times*, 3 Aug 2013.

57. Michael Carrington, 'Officers, Gentlemen and Thieves: The Looting of Monasteries during the 1903/4 Younghusband Mission to Tibet', *Modern Asian Studies*, vol. 37, no. 1 (Feb 2003), pp. 81–109, p. 106, n. 116.

58. Ibid., p. 104, n. 107.

59. Ibid., p. 106.

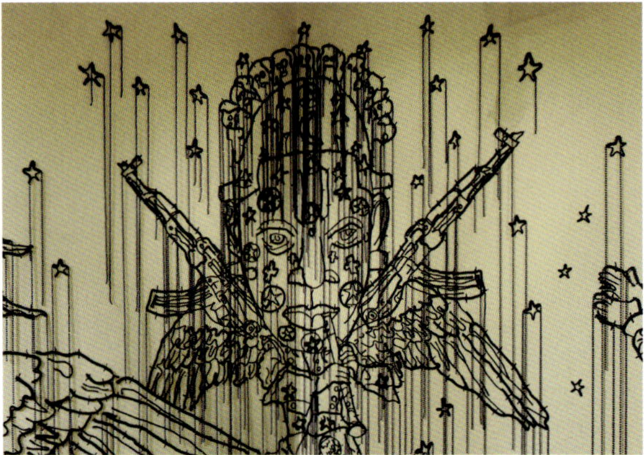

fig. 19. Hew Locke, *The Nameless*, 2010. Mixed-media installation. Dimensions vary.

Queen Mother Idia

One of the most significant and highly contested objects in the British Museum's collection is the Queen Mother Idia pendant mask from Benin, seized during the 1897 Expedition (Af1910,0513.1). The political title of Iyoba (Queen Mother) was created specifically for Idia by her son Oba Esigie (r. 1504–50), and the ivory pendant mask (Uhunmwu-Ẹkuẹ) is one of five known masks made in a similar style to commemorate her. It was worn on the hip by the Oba during important ceremonies.

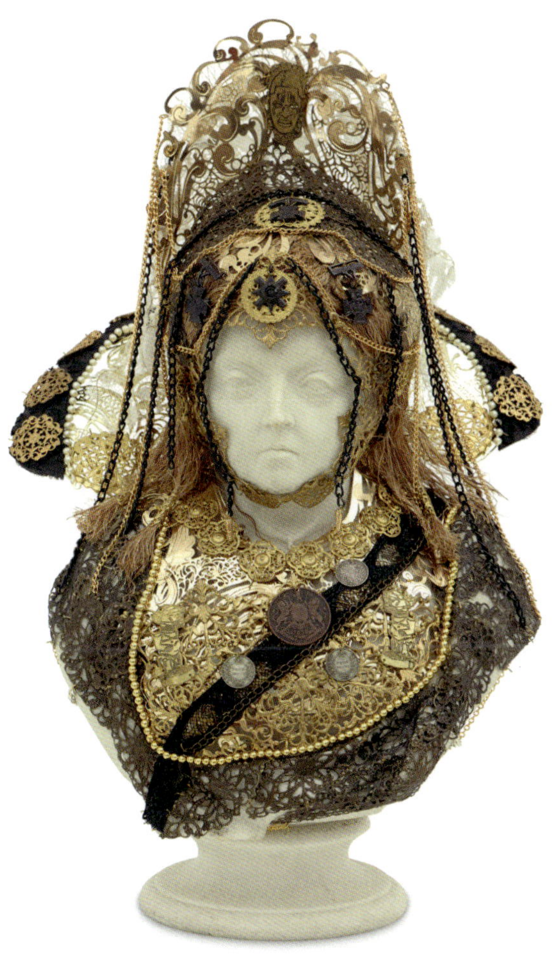

fig. 20. Hew Locke, *Souvenir 9*, 2019. Mixed media on antique Parian ware. H. 44.1 cm, W. 27 cm, D. 26 cm. Birmingham Museums and Art Gallery, 2021.7.

During the British Expedition of 1897, the pendant mask was looted from the Oba's bedroom by British soldiers, and in 1910 it was purchased by the British Museum. The Queen Mother Idia mask has been a recurring motif in Locke's work since around the year 2000, whether surrounded by Kalashnikovs and travelling on winged feet in his beaded installation *The Nameless* (2010) (fig. 19) or featuring as brass plaques on his *Souvenirs* (fig. 20) and boats such as *Armada 6* (p. 45). Locke has sometimes seen the Queen Mother Idia mask as a victim of its own ubiquity: 'It's a clichéd shorthand symbol for the heights of culture from sub-Saharan Africa. I've used it sometimes as a trope. But then I would underestimate how beautiful the thing is and I'd go and look and remind myself that though it's a cliché image, it is something very, very special.' It remains 'a symbol of Africa's complex historical interactions with the West – the image is a shorthand for many things'.

One of the reasons the Queen Mother Idia mask has become a 'shorthand' for many people stems from its role as the emblem of FESTAC '77, the Second World Black and African Festival of Arts and Culture held in Lagos in 1977. Around 500,000 people from more than 50 countries attended this celebration of pan-African culture, which was a seminal moment highlighting the contributions of Black and African peoples to the fields of science, technology and culture. It has been described as one of the most important Black cultural events of the 20th century.[60] Commissioned to design the visual concept of FESTAC, renowned artist Erhabor Emokpae (1934–1984) took part in selecting and requesting the loan of the Queen Mother Idia mask to the festival. As a pre-eminent example of African carving, and one of the many African objects held in Western museums, it was intended to be a symbol of unity and hope.[61] The British Museum issued a press release to the effect that the loan had been considered and refused on conservation grounds, offering to send a replica in its place (see p. 137). Instead, several established Nigerian artists descending from the original carvers' guilds, including Joseph Alufa Igbinovia (b. 1949) and Emoruyi Omoregie, were commissioned by the Nigerian government to create replicas of the mask for the festival. One was carved in ivory (based on a postcard of the original).[62] Emokpae centred the mask in the iconic logo and poster (p. 139) and many other reproductions that

60. Julian Lucas, 'The Photographer who Immortalized a Pan-African Pageant', *New Yorker*, 28 Oct 2022.

61. Nigerian President Olusegun Obasanjo, Guest of Honour at FESTAC's opening ceremony, said: 'We wanted a symbol which was taken away from here.' Cited Pelu Awofeso, 'Day I met artist who carved FESTAC '77 logo', *Medium*, 24 Nov 2020.

62. Dominique Malaquais and Cédric Vincent, 'Replicate This: Into the FESTAC Loop', in *Condition Report: On Art History in Africa*, ed. Eva Barois de Caevel et al. (Berlin: Motto, 2020), p. 45.

ensured Idia's image was seen all over Lagos in an act of virtual restitution that has been described as 'a potent decolonial move and a brilliant branding project all rolled into one'.[63]

Locke's work similarly employs ideas of replication and the use of facsimiles. While he remembers reading about FESTAC in magazines as a teenager in Guyana, he says that his real memories of it were formed vicariously through talking to the Guyanese artist Aubrey Williams (1926–1990), who had travelled to the festival. 'Living in England wouldn't have been the easiest place for a Black artist back then. I knew that from my dad as well. You were second-class artists basically, and second-class citizens as well. I think FESTAC gave him a real boost.' The story of the Queen Idia mask had a profound impact on Locke, the tale of the loan's refusal by the British Museum contributing to its status as a cultural icon: 'that's how you make something iconic, in the same way that you make the *Mona Lisa* iconic, by pointing at the empty space that was left behind after it was stolen'.

Gold

In the early 19th century the Asante Kingdom in modern-day southern Ghana reached the peak of its power, but by the end of the century faced five disastrous confrontations with British colonial powers known as the Anglo-Asante Wars. In 1874 the British Army invaded the capital Kumasi and destroyed part of the city. They deposed the Asantehene (king) Kofi Karikari (r. 1867–74) and obliged him to make an 'indemnity' payment to cover the cost of their military expedition.[64] One of the gold items 'paid' included the Asante awisiado (soul priest's ornament), most likely worn by one of the Asantehene's soul priests. The pendant was originally bi-facial, but when it was taken back to the UK, the centre of its reverse was removed in order to mount it onto a dish (p. 159).

As Locke notes, 'it looks like a European object, the aesthetic of the original Asante object has been trapped in the European design. Like the Koh-i-Noor being damaged to fit a European aesthetic … Its function is ignored, it's trapped and killed, it becomes just a trophy.' Locke has surrounded the dish with other items of Asante, Ethiopian, Edo and pre-Columbian gold, with the context of each different culture removed to indicate how they were perceived by those who took them, not for their enormous cultural, historical and spiritual significance, but for their weight in gold: 'I wanted to show the objects' position as loot. It's been taken as gold.'

*

Some of the final objects presented in this book are Locke's OBE and RA medals. Locke was awarded the Order of the British Empire in the King's Birthday Honours list in 2023 and has spoken about the absurdity of being awarded a medal "for God and the Empire" while his work interrogates the whole concept of Empire.[65] As well as drawing attention to the fact that this honour is problematic for so many on whom it is bestowed, Locke also emphasises his implication within the systems he is critiquing. 'We're not like gods looking down and judging, this is my stuff too.' Locke's medals are placed in dialogue with an Akan gold-weight in the form of a bird looking back over its tail, known as a Sankofa bird. The Sankofa bird embodies a Twi proverb emphasising the importance of looking to the past in order to learn and to make a better future.[66] This can be interpreted as both encouragement to preserve

63. Ibid., p. 47.

64. For more information see www.britishmuseum.org/about-us/british-museum-story/contested-objects-collection/asante-gold-regalia.

65. Hew Locke, Instagram post, 17 June 2023. Locke also noted that such an honour could easily be updated to an Order of British Excellence, as advocated by the 'Excellence not Empire' campaign, founded in 2021 by nearly 100 honours-holders, of which Locke is a member.

66. 'Pick it up if it falls behind you.' Fiona Sheales, *African Gold-weights in the British Museum*, London: The British Museum, 2014.

things that were valued in the past – forms of cultural memory and identity including forms of dress, language or worship, embodied in objects including many of those presented in this exhibition – and the idea that one should not be afraid to attempt to redeem the mistakes of the past, that, in fact, building a stronger future will depend on it.

Locke's work brings the past and present together to show the points at which they touch. In his hands, artefacts are not merely remnants of the past but part of living stories that continue to shape the structural inequalities of our present and future. In his words, 'I'm trying to bend the past and the present together. Back to the future or something like that.' Elsewhere he asks, 'What do you do with the truth of British history? You can't ignore what happened with empire. If you brush it under the carpet it's gonna come back to bite you.'[67] In the same way that Locke shows us the 'wrong' side of history, the shadow side to a history of power, in reading the British Museum's collections against the grain, he underscores the urgent need to confront our historical narratives in order to build a more truthful and expansive account of British narratives and their impact on global histories.

Through articulating the imperial shape and shaping of the British Museum's collections, as well as webs of connections, Locke also draws attention to its gaps and omissions, the millions of stories that are missing, the perspectives not represented, which are perhaps alluded to by the silent figures of Locke's *Watchers*. The figures' carnivalesque costumes and masks, as Kobena Mercer has highlighted elsewhere in Locke's work, 'both solicit and deflect the gaze of others', shielding the subjects' interiority. In this way perhaps the masked figures might gesture towards the millions of stories and subjectivities that are denied to us by the archive's silences and erasures.

Ultimately Locke's work demonstrates the importance of inviting artists and others to enter into dialogue with museum collections and the power of art to question, to provoke, to move. As Locke notes, 'So this of course is all speculation, and [this book] is all about the real facts of history, but also we weren't there, so this is us projecting multiple short stories onto these objects. That's what we do when we go to museums, try to bring the things to life in our minds with the history that we've been given. You yourself have to fill in the gaps.' The cultural historian Saidiya Hartman has used the term 'critical fabulation' to describe a method of working both with and against the archive in a manner that acknowledges its structural imbalances of power, 'both to tell an impossible story and to amplify the impossibility of its telling'.[68]

In Locke's case this is partly enacted through the open-ended grouping of objects that disrupts conventional narratives, encouraging the visitor to forge their own connections and actively participate in the creation of meaning. This diversification and multiplication of perspectives within an institutional space traditionally dominated by a singular narrative emphasises that this book does not aim to provide definitive answers, but rather open spaces for questioning our collective memory and shared histories. Locke's imaginative explorations challenge the museum's role not just as a custodian of history but as a space for critical engagement, dialogue, and ultimately, understanding. As such, *Hew Locke: what have we here?* issues a call to action for institutions and audiences alike to engage in a wider complex and more nuanced conversations about museum collections in Britain, their relationships to imperial power, and the space to imagine what a different present and future might look like.

67. Price and Locke, 'Talking History', p. 56.

68. Saidiya Hartman, 'Venus in Two Acts', *Small Axe*, vol. 12, no. 2 (June 2008), pp. 1–14, p. 12.

Overleaf: Hew Locke, *Société de Transit de Grand-Lahou 1*, 2014.

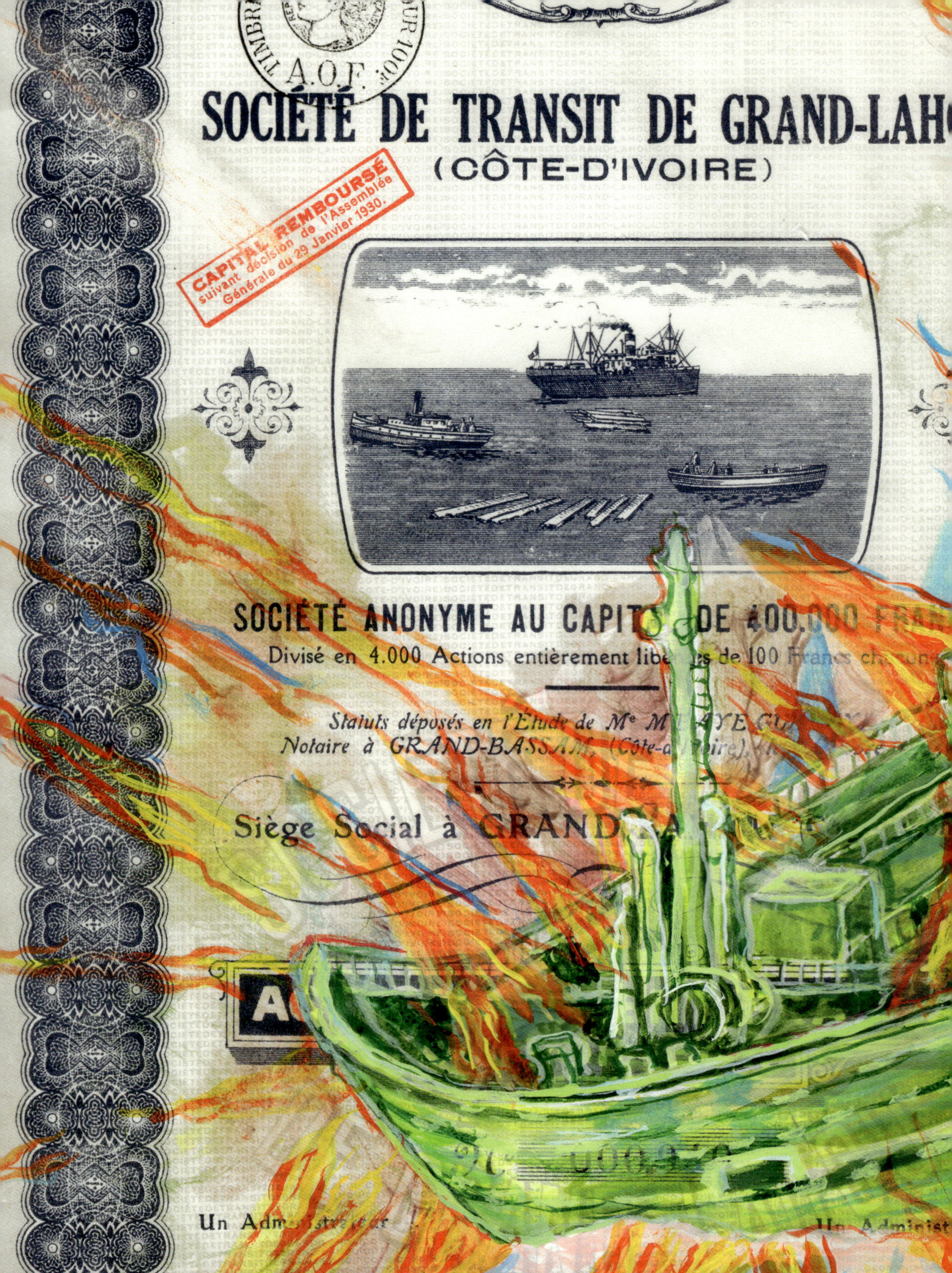

A.O.F.
CAPITAL REMBOURSÉ
suivant décision de l'Assemblée
Générale du 29 Janvier 1930.

SOCIÉTÉ DE TRANSIT DE GRAND-LAHO
(CÔTE-D'IVOIRE)

SOCIÉTÉ ANONYME AU CAPITAL DE 400.000 FRAN
Divisé en 4.000 Actions entièrement libérées de 100 francs ch

Statuts déposés en l'Étude de Me M... AYE G...
Notaire à GRAND-BASSAM (Côte-d'Ivoire)

Siège Social à GRAND-LAHOU

Un Administrateur   Un Administ

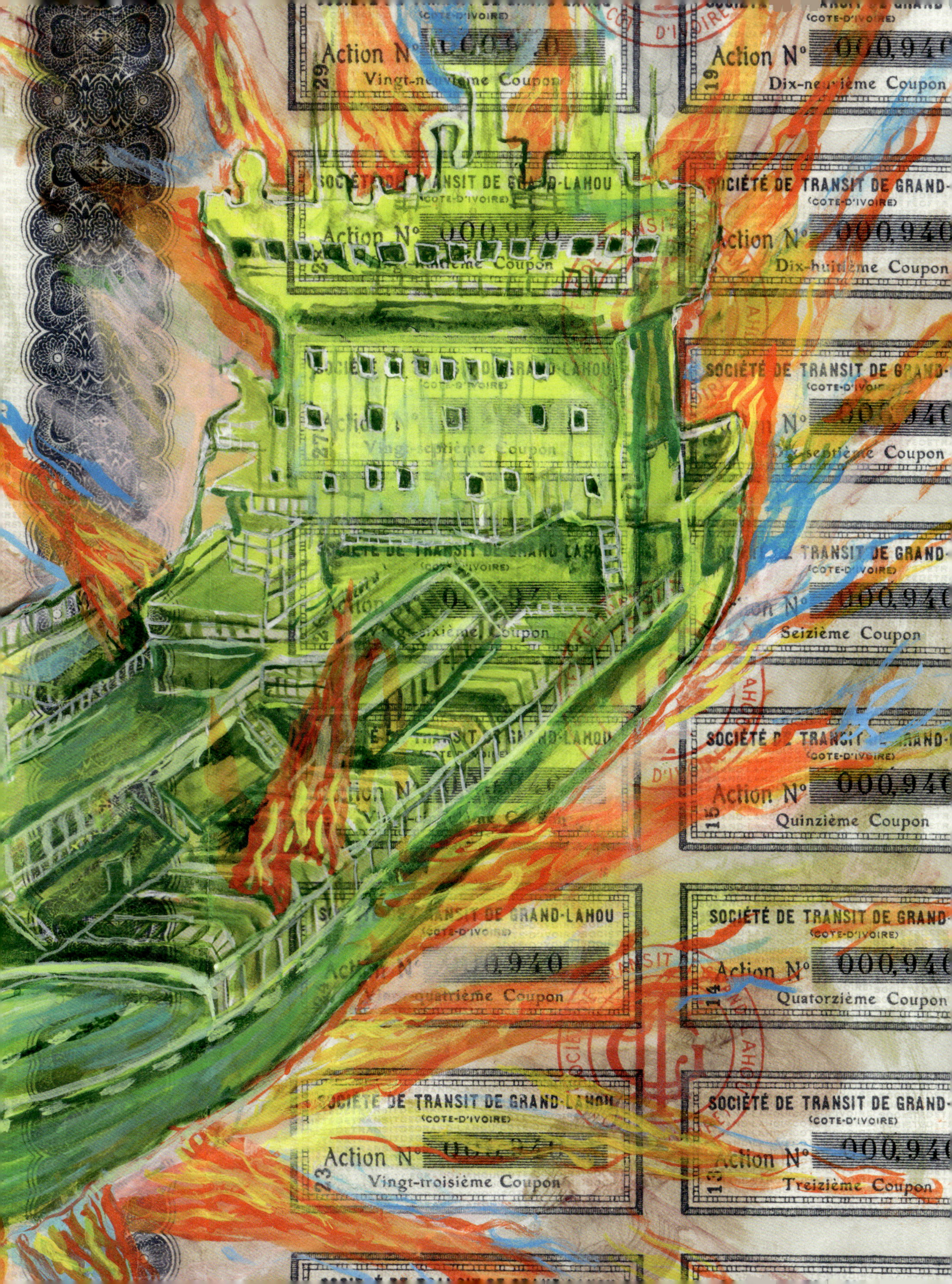

Action Nº AL 000 940
29
Vingt-neuvième Coupon
Action Nº 000 940
19
Dix-neuvième Coupon
SOCIÉTÉ DE TRANSIT DE GRAND-LAHOU
(COTE-D'IVOIRE)
Action Nº 000 940
28
Vingt-huitième Coupon
SOCIÉTÉ DE TRANSIT DE GRAND-
(COTE-D'IVOIRE)
Action Nº 000 940
18
Dix-huitième Coupon
SOCIÉTÉ DE TRANSIT DE GRAND-LAHOU
(COTE-D'IVOIRE)
27
Vingt-septième Coupon
SOCIÉTÉ DE TRANSIT DE GRAND-
(COTE-D'IVOIRE)
Nº 000 940
17
Dix-septième Coupon
SOCIÉTÉ DE TRANSIT DE GRAND-LAHOU
(COTE-D'IVOIRE)
26
Vingt-sixième Coupon
TRANSIT DE GRAND-
(COTE-D'IVOIRE)
Nº 000 940
16
Seizième Coupon
SOCIÉTÉ DE TRANSIT DE GRAND-
(COTE-D'IVOIRE)
Action Nº 000 940
15
Quinzième Coupon
SOCIÉTÉ DE TRANSIT DE GRAND-LAHOU
Action Nº 000 940
24
Vingt-quatrième Coupon
SOCIÉTÉ DE TRANSIT DE GRAND
(COTE-D'IVOIRE)
Action Nº 000 940
14
Quatorzième Coupon
SOCIÉTÉ DE TRANSIT DE GRAND-LAHOU
(COTE-D'IVOIRE)
Action Nº 000 940
23
Vingt-troisième Coupon
SOCIÉTÉ DE TRANSIT DE GRAND
(COTE-D'IVOIRE)
Action Nº 000 940
13
Treizième Coupon

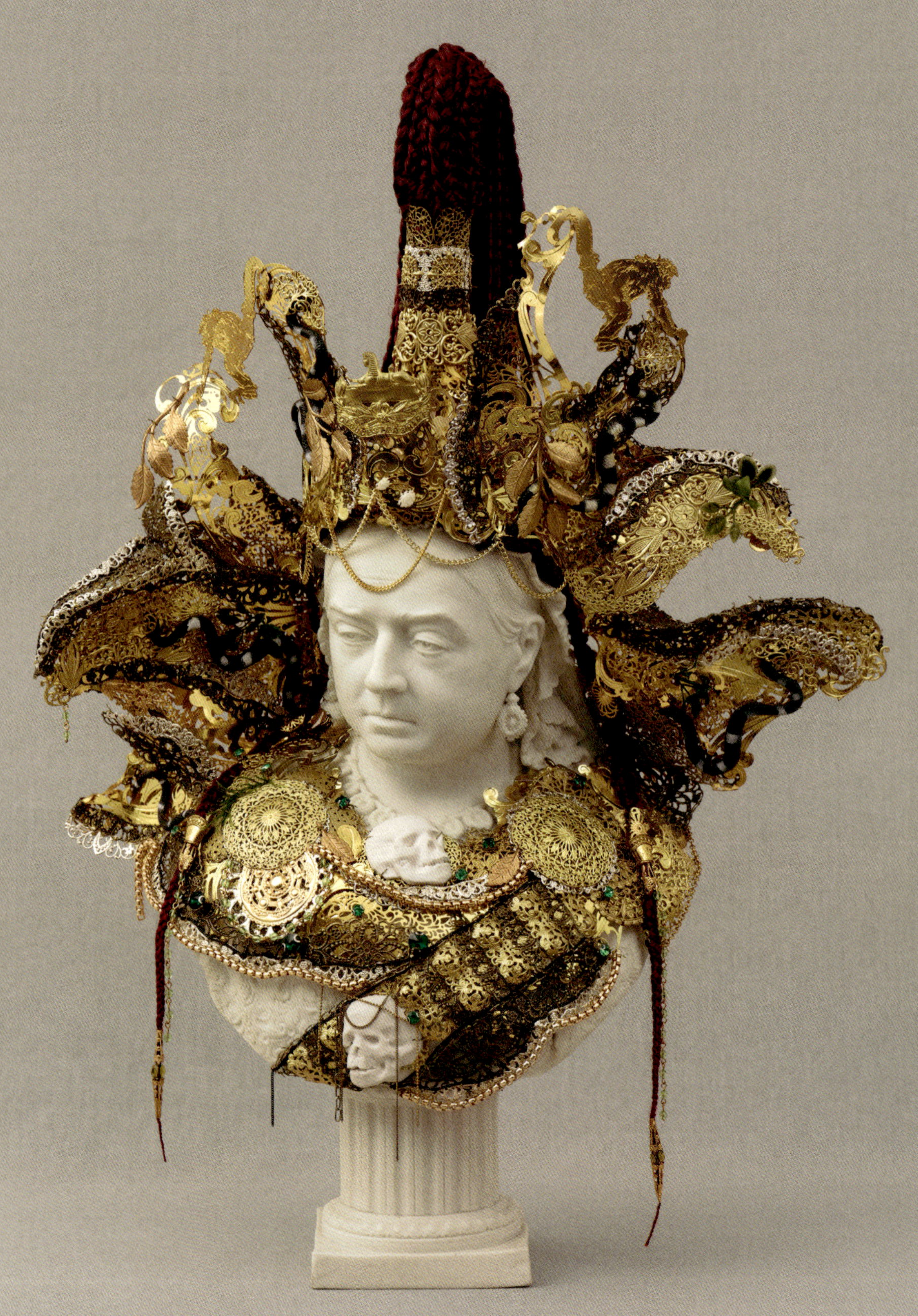

Hew Locke, *Souvenir 20*
(Queen Victoria), 2024.

Heroes are a key part of a nation's identity-building and myth-making. Hew Locke is interested in how these images are constructed, especially having grown up in newly independent Guyana, a nation engaged with the process of building its self-image. In Britain, national heroes are often linked with the figure of the monarch; Queen Victoria's portrait was successfully used across the British Empire as a propaganda tool to transmit its status as a benign and charitable enterprise. In his *Souvenir* series, Locke explores ideas of sovereignty and legacy. Antique Parian ware busts, souvenirs of the Great Exhibitions of 1851 and 1862 are decorated with regalia that include skulls, tropical foliage, brass plaques and replicas of military insignia such as medals from imperial conflicts. The figures of Queen Victoria, Prince Albert Edward (1841–1910) and Princess Alexandra (1844–1924) are almost engulfed by the objects that previously expressed the power of the British Empire.

"These are not just portraits of a person; they're symbols of an idea."

"*Souvenir 20 (Queen Victoria)* (opposite) has two *memento mori* images woven into the metal on her chest, two white skulls. She has hair extensions added, a ponytail, exploding out of the brass filigree. It's made from braids of synthetic hair sold in Brixton hair shops. From a distance it's one thing but when you get closer, you realise the black and white lines on her headdress are not lines, they're snakes. She's becoming a Medusa-like figure. It looks attractive and draws people in but the more time you spend with it the more you start to think.

I enjoy making beautiful work but I also like luring people in to think about what's beneath the skin. In and amongst the crown are two spider monkeys. I've been obsessed with these animals since I was a child. I'd go to the zoo and see them. They seem to symbolise something for me, they always look like 1920s gangsters with centre partings and Bryl-creamed hair. Their expression says 'I'm going to get you bastards', you know? They are a disruptive force." HL

"These national figureheads are weighed down by the burden of British history. I arrived in Guyana just before Independence and I saw the flag created, the coat of arms created, the banknotes created, the national anthem written. The same process happens in Britain. Each nation re-invents itself, over and over again." HL

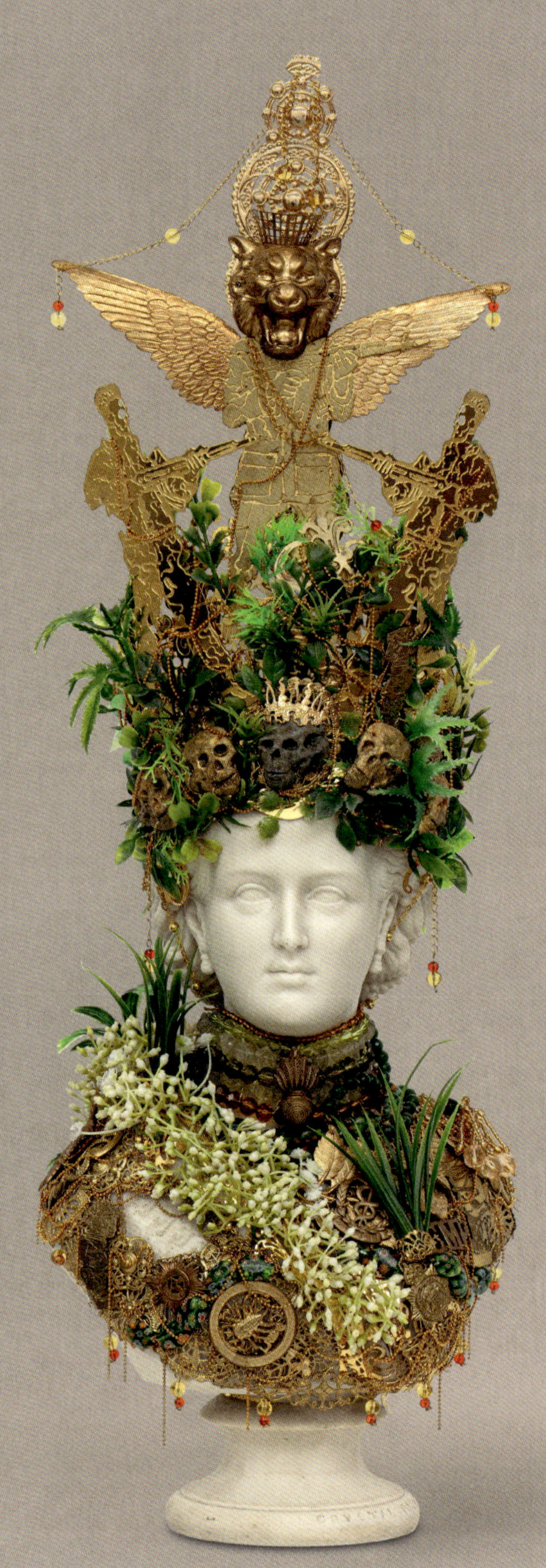

Hew Locke, *Souvenir 14
(Princess Alexandra)*, 2023.

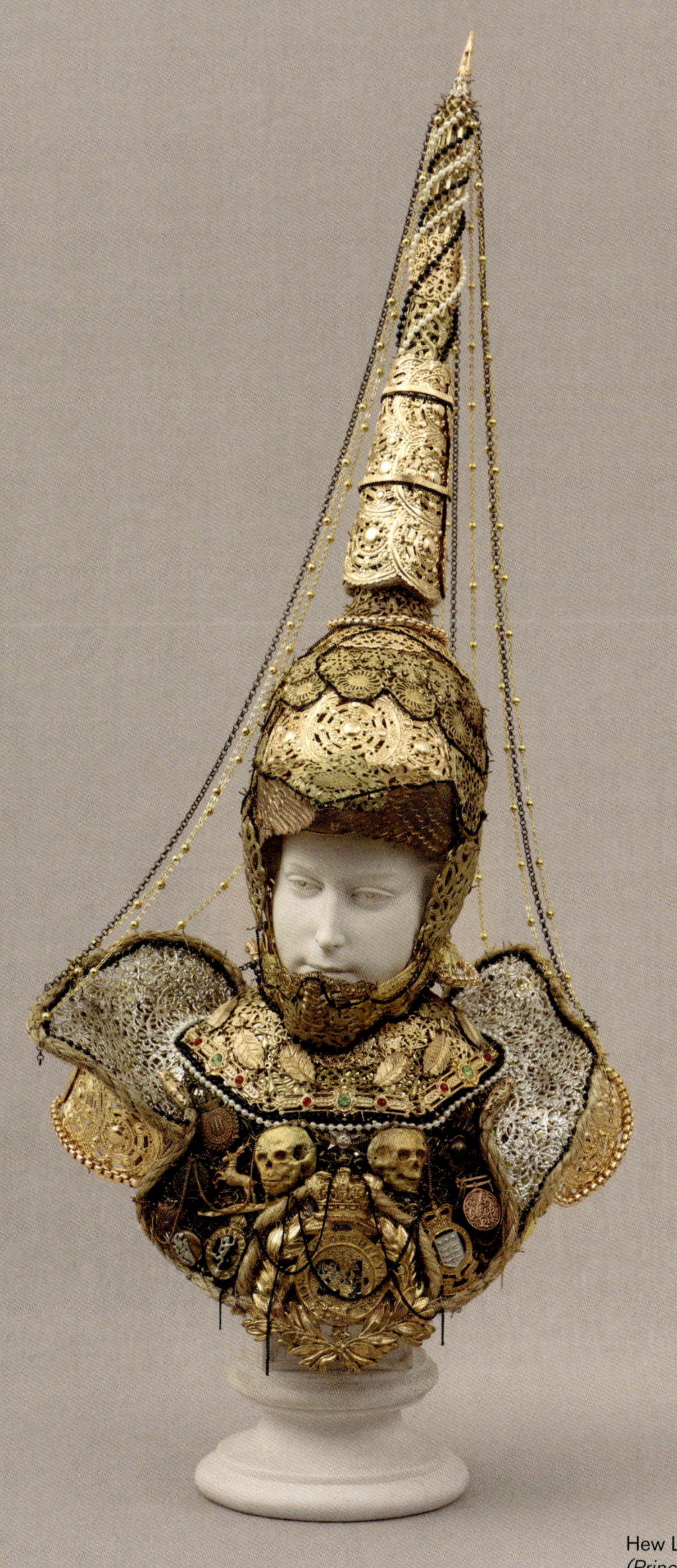

Hew Locke, *Souvenir 13*
(Prince Albert Edward), 2023.

"*Armada 6* (p. 45) is loosely based on the American boat the USS *Constitution*. It fought against the British in 1812 and defeated five ships. But it also protected American trade, so it was connected to the slave trade. It eventually ended up being involved in the Civil War. It is adorned with Queen Mother Idia masks (see p. 138) and brass gunmen as cut-outs. They're designed to imitate gold and make the ship into something it's not. The sails have been deliberately dirtied and wrecked a bit – the whole thing is designed to look like a religious icon, an object of veneration. I have used mercenaries a lot in my work (see p. 20), but they're not trying to present a cliché of African countries, they refer to many other places too. The mercenary represents what someone is fleeing from when they get in a precarious boat to cross the Mediterranean – a generic man with a gun, a figure to escape from." HL

"Why would somebody take such a perilous journey in a boat like this? You're hoping for a better life."

Boats stand in for many things – power, adventure, trade, war – and are an important motif in Hew Locke's work. Vessels symbolise flows of goods and ideas, as well as people, both historically and in the context of today's global migration crisis. Locke's *Armada* series takes the form of a flotilla of model boats or rafts that create an immersive large-scale fleet suspended from the ceiling. The models incorporate quasi-religious iconography, facsimiles and images of masks, pendants, skeletal figures and mythical symbols, recalling votive boats hanging in churches around Europe and offered as thanks for surviving a life at sea. *Armada 6* is decorated with the mask of Queen Mother Idia from the Museum's collection, a recurring image in Locke's practice. Covered in sheer mesh, *Wine Dark Sea Boat BB* (opposite) becomes a ghostly vision, its title recalling an epithet used by Homer in the *Iliad* and the *Odyssey*, and by the Saint Lucian poet Derek Walcott (1920–2017) in his epic poem *Omeros* (1990). 'Windward', meaning facing towards the wind, was used as a means of orientation in the Caribbean, for example the Windward Islands of the lesser Antilles. It may also allude to the Windward Passage, a strait between the islands of Cuba and Hispaniola, the latter of which Christopher Columbus established a colony on in 1492.

"*Wine Dark Sea Boat BB* came about in an interesting way. The boat was sitting in the studio for ages and I didn't know what to do with it; it was really beautiful but I wanted to try something new. I held up a piece of embroidered fabric over the boat and thought yes, this can work, creating some mesh to drape over it. I was very lucky to have someone who could help with the embroidering – Indra Khanna. This piece is covered in mercenaries, gunmen, lots of iconic figures but also a sunburst image of a Roman god. The imagery is almost like a stream of consciousness, becoming more poetic and less literal. In many cultures, boats symbolise the journey from life to death, or are the containers of the soul." HL

"*Windward* is an old 18th-century galleon. This model has been dirtied and aged with paint (p. 44). I wanted it to have a history. What's on the sails is crucial. A skeleton has been broken up over three sails and behind that are images of pre-Columbian objects. I grew up in Guyana and I like to nod towards Amerindian history and Indigenous imagery." HL

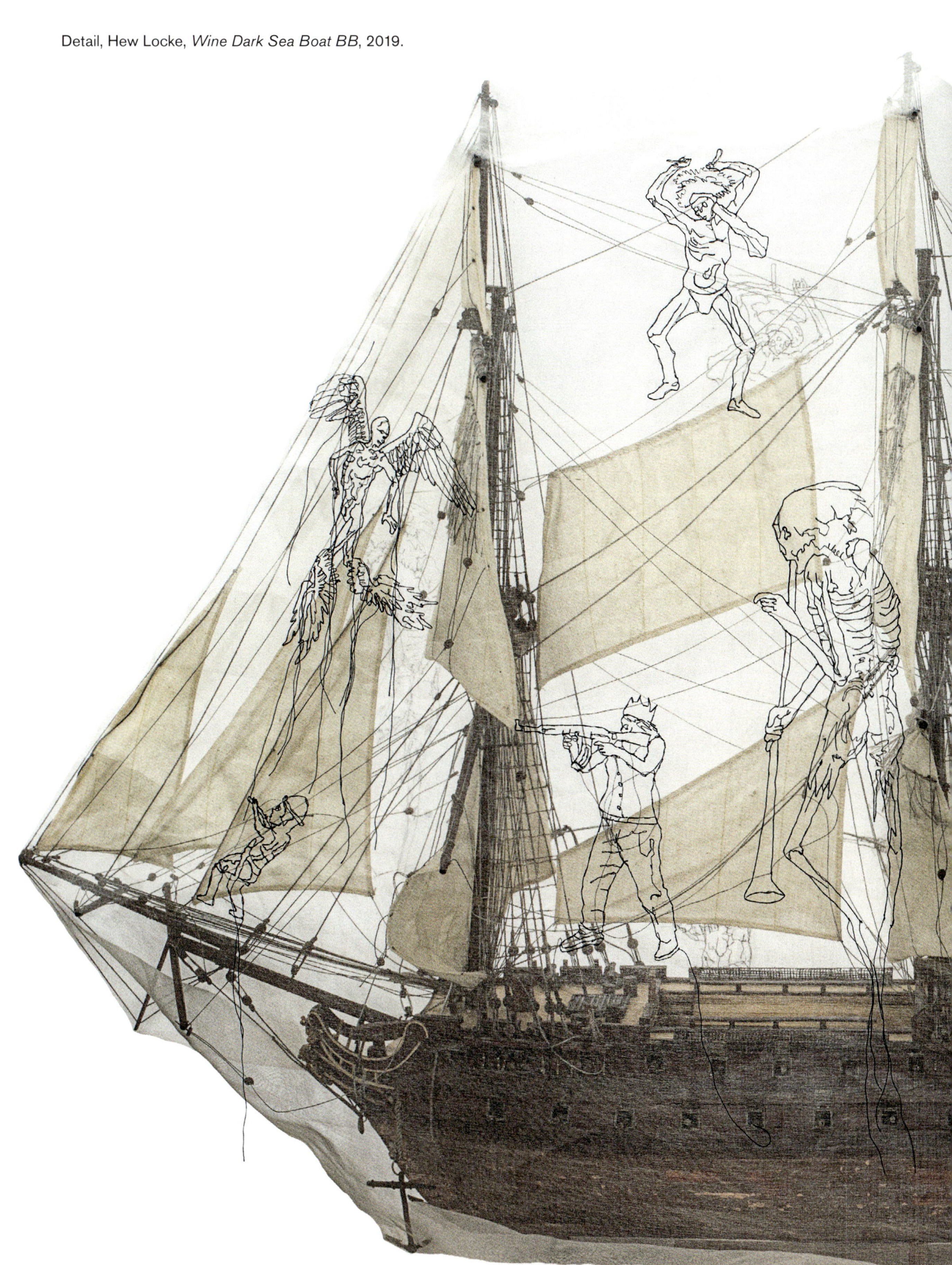

Detail, Hew Locke, *Wine Dark Sea Boat BB*, 2019.

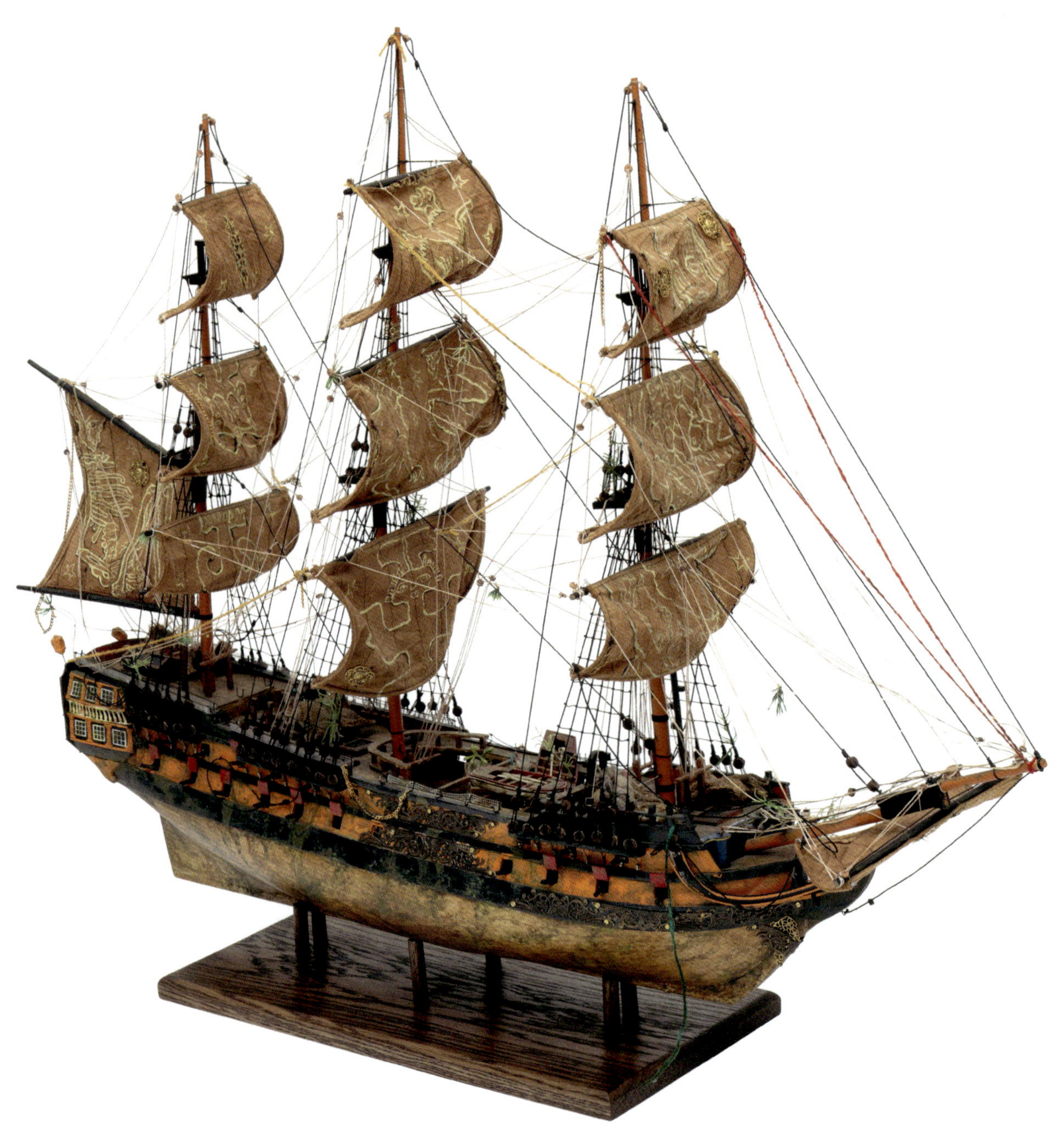

Hew Locke, *Windward*, 2019.

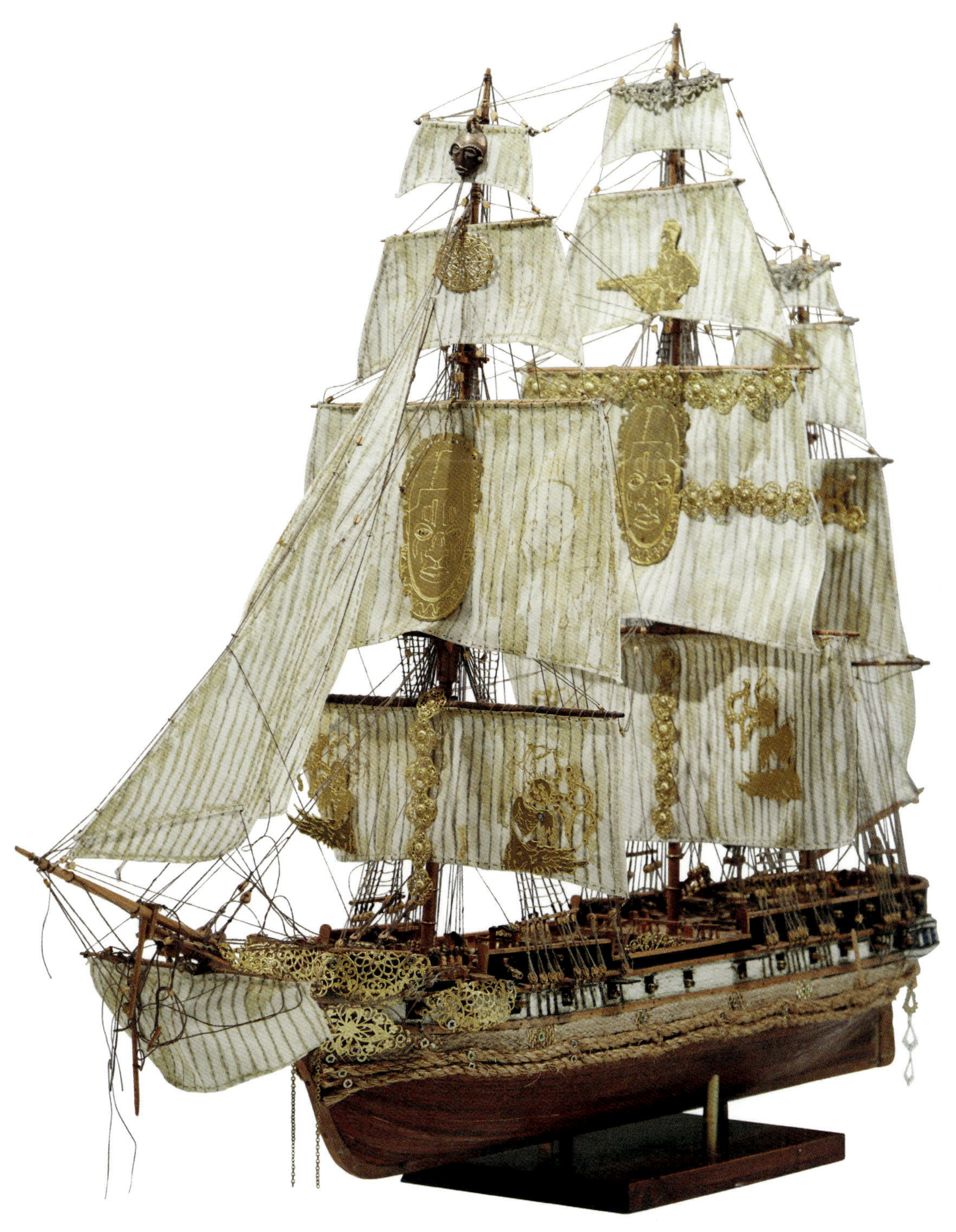

Hew Locke, *Armada 6*, 2019.

The Company of Royal Adventurers of England Trading into Africa was formed in 1663 by the House of Stuart and City of London merchants to trade in West Africa, and King Charles II granted it a monopoly. In 1672 it became the Royal African Company (RAC). Charles's brother, later King James II, was the RAC's governor while he was Duke of York. The motto on this seal-die (opposite) reads 'REGIO FLORET PATROCINIO COMMERCIUM COMMERCIOQUE REGNUM' ('By royal patronage trade flourishes, and by trade the realm'). From the 1500s, it is estimated that between 10 and 13 million enslaved people were transported across the Atlantic. Glass beads were made in Africa as early as 1000 CE and used in sophisticated trade currency systems. From the 1600s, European-made beads became part of this currency to take advantage of high demand. The beads on pp. 50–1 were stored in the Museum with handwritten cards that noted the types of trade they might have been used for: ivory, palm oil, gold and enslaved people. By the late 1700s, the trade in enslaved people was regarded as an abject horror by many across the British Empire. It was seen as a violation of the human rights that stood at the centre of Enlightenment ideals. Abolitionist activists demanded the end of the trade, including William Wilberforce (1759–1833), who stood in Parliament with a model of the notorious Brooks ship. This ship became an emblem of the horrific conditions imposed on enslaved people transported to the Americas. On top of Wilberforce's model was a diagram of the ship, highlighting the cramped conditions people were forced to endure. The jug on p. 49 is an example of pro-slavery propaganda, probably commissioned by someone in the trade as public opinion began to change. Its inscription reads 'SUCCESS TO THE BROOKS CAPT. NOBEL'. The unidentified ship in the painting by William Jackson (p. 49) was likely used to transport enslaved people; the coastline resembles West Africa, Black figures are seen on the shore and the vessel has four ventilation ports in the lower hull.

"Charles II is often portrayed as the 'merry monarch', but he sealed the document which started this Company that transported enslaved people (p. 48). His brother James was the Duke of York at the time – he was Edward Colston's boss. A lot of these enslaved people had the initials 'RACE' (Royal African Company of England) or 'DoY' (Duke of York) branded on their backs, on their bodies. Once you hear that … it's very difficult for me to engage with those two beyond that. The design for Elizabeth I's Great Seal of Ireland (p. 49) is here because Ireland was England's first plantation, a system that was then rolled out across the world.'

One of the themes in this book is currency in different forms, it echoes throughout, but this is the first example. The glass beads hide in plain sight; they're attractive and pretty. I've seen countless pictures of people in Africa wearing beads and I've read countless times that these were traded, but at first I didn't really make the connection. Similarly, paintings of ships like William Jackson's are very charming and quite common (p. 49). But then someone pointed out that some of them are slaving ships. You can tell by the hull – they've got a different configuration and ventilation ports. It's this bizarre thing of something hiding in plain sight, which is symbolic of a lot of history that's coming to light now in Britain." HL

"Which history is more important? Is it that this monarch was a Catholic or a Protestant? Or that this monarch kick-started something truly horrendous?"

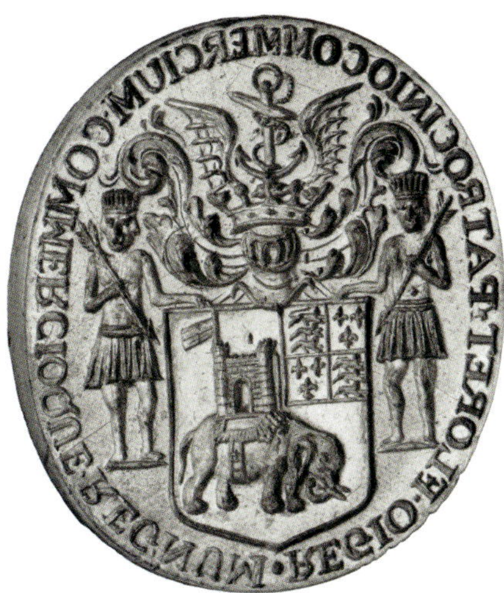

Unrecorded artist, seal-die with arms and motto
of the Royal African Company, after 1663.

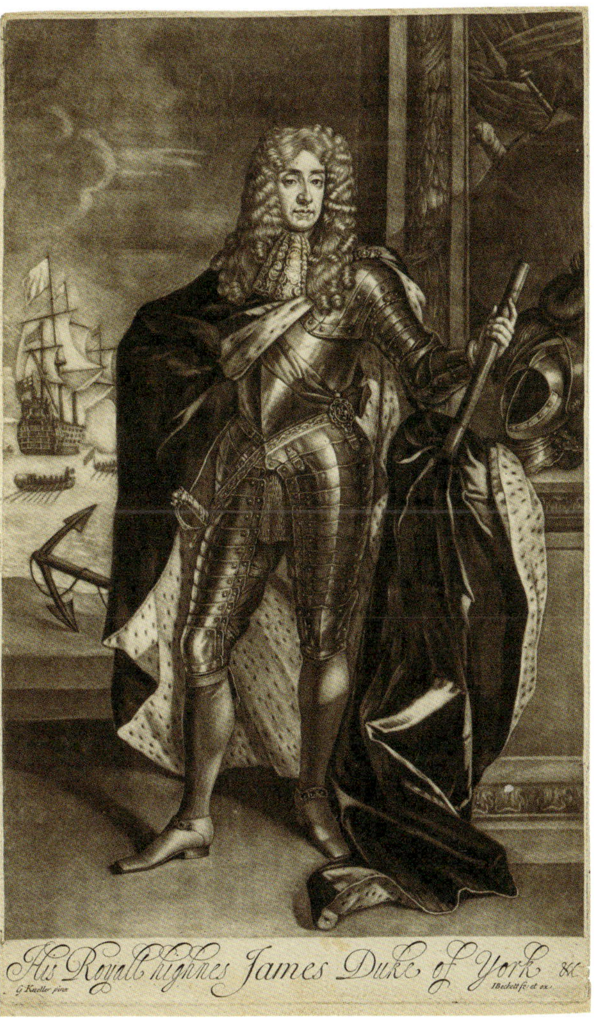

Isaac Beckett, after Sir Godfrey Kneller, *James, Duke of York*,
c. 1681–5.

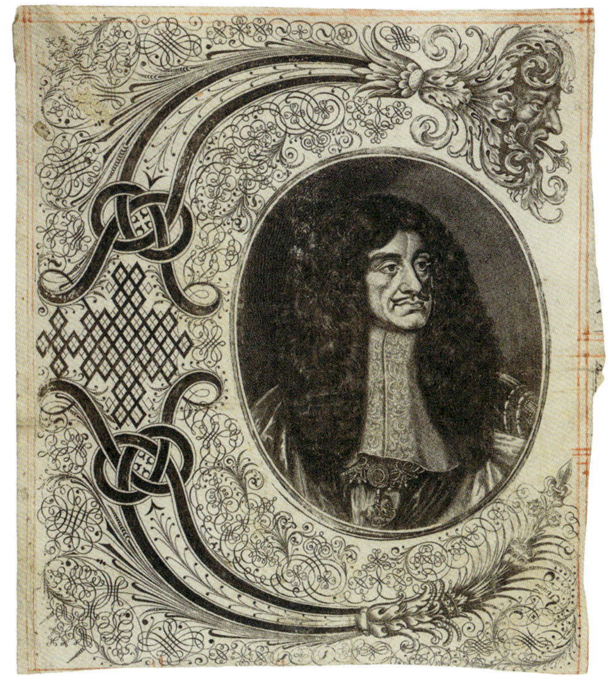

Unrecorded English artist, *King Charles II*, *c.* 1660–80.

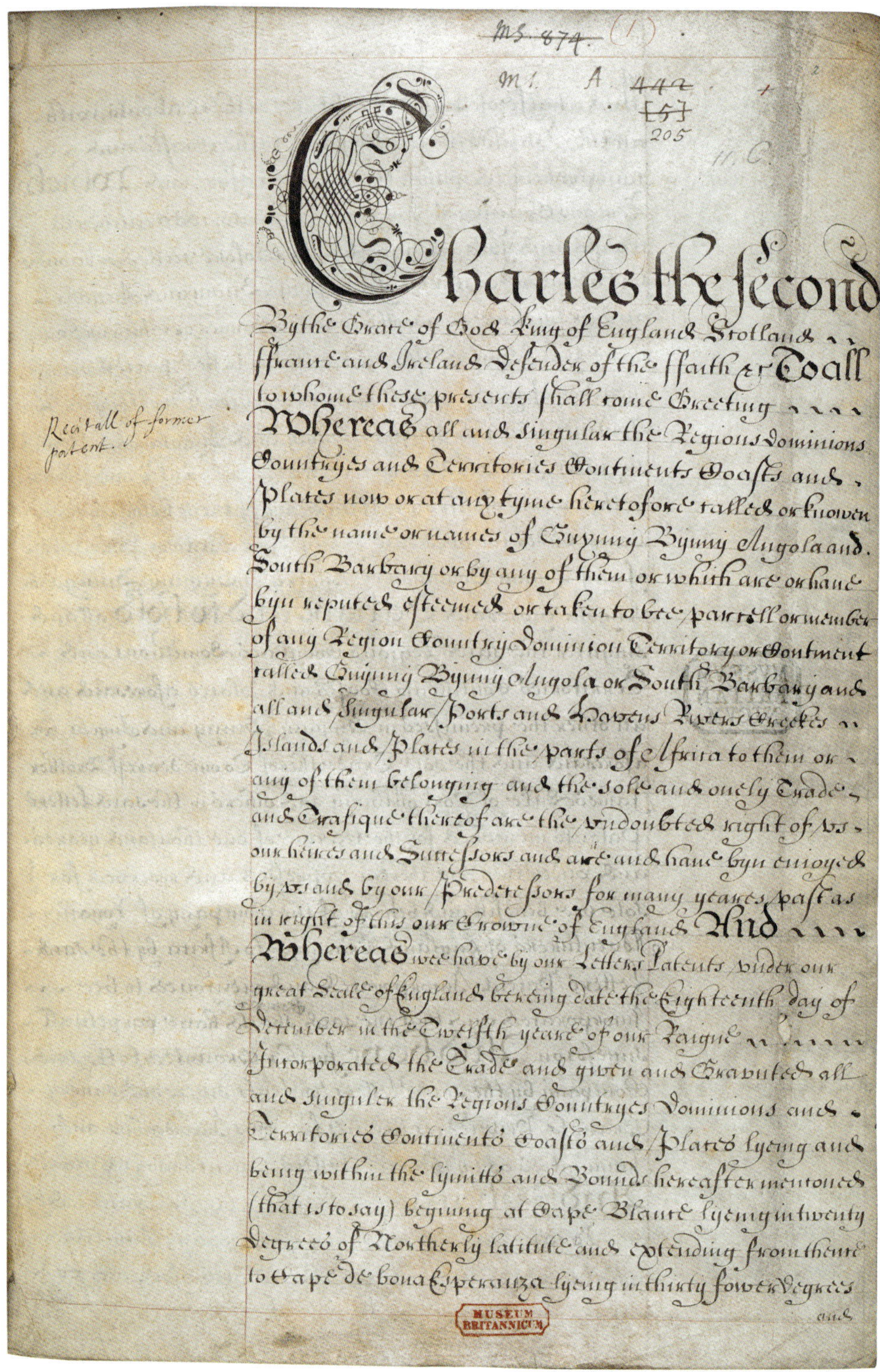

Charter for the Company of Royal Adventurers of England
Trading into Africa, 1663.

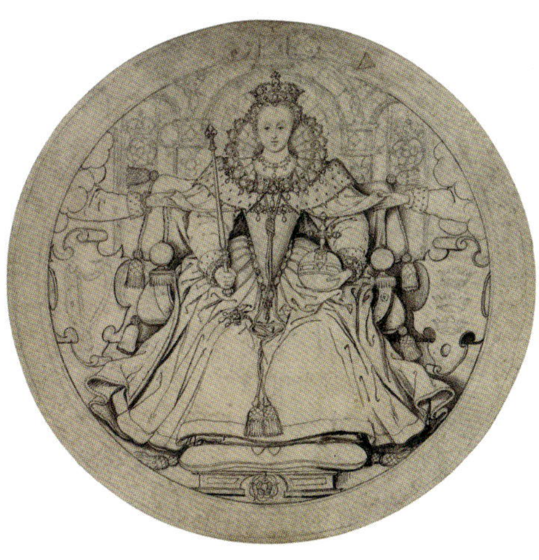

Nicholas Hilliard, design for Queen Elizabeth's Great Seal of Ireland, *c.* 1584–90.

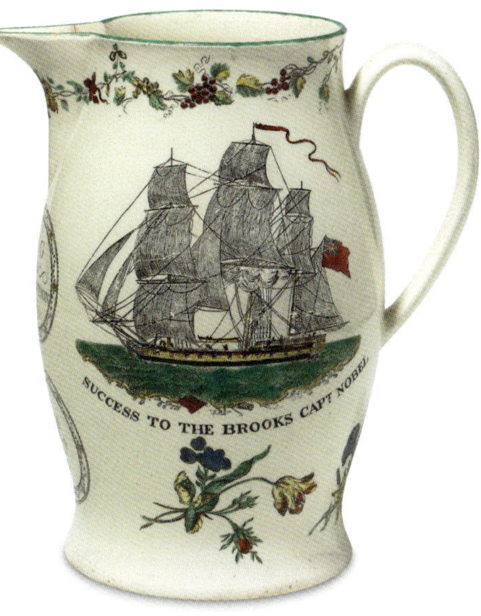

Brooks jug, 1793 or later.

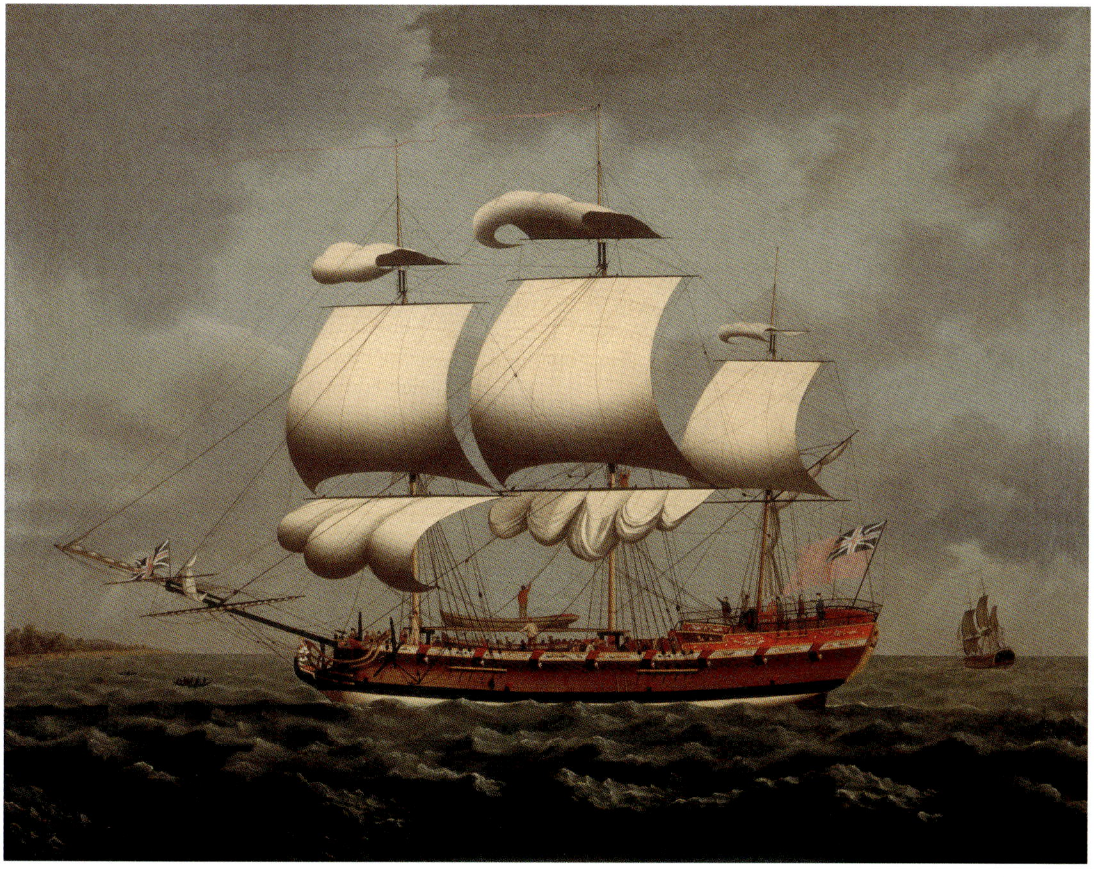

William Jackson, *A Liverpool Slave Ship*, *c.* 1780.

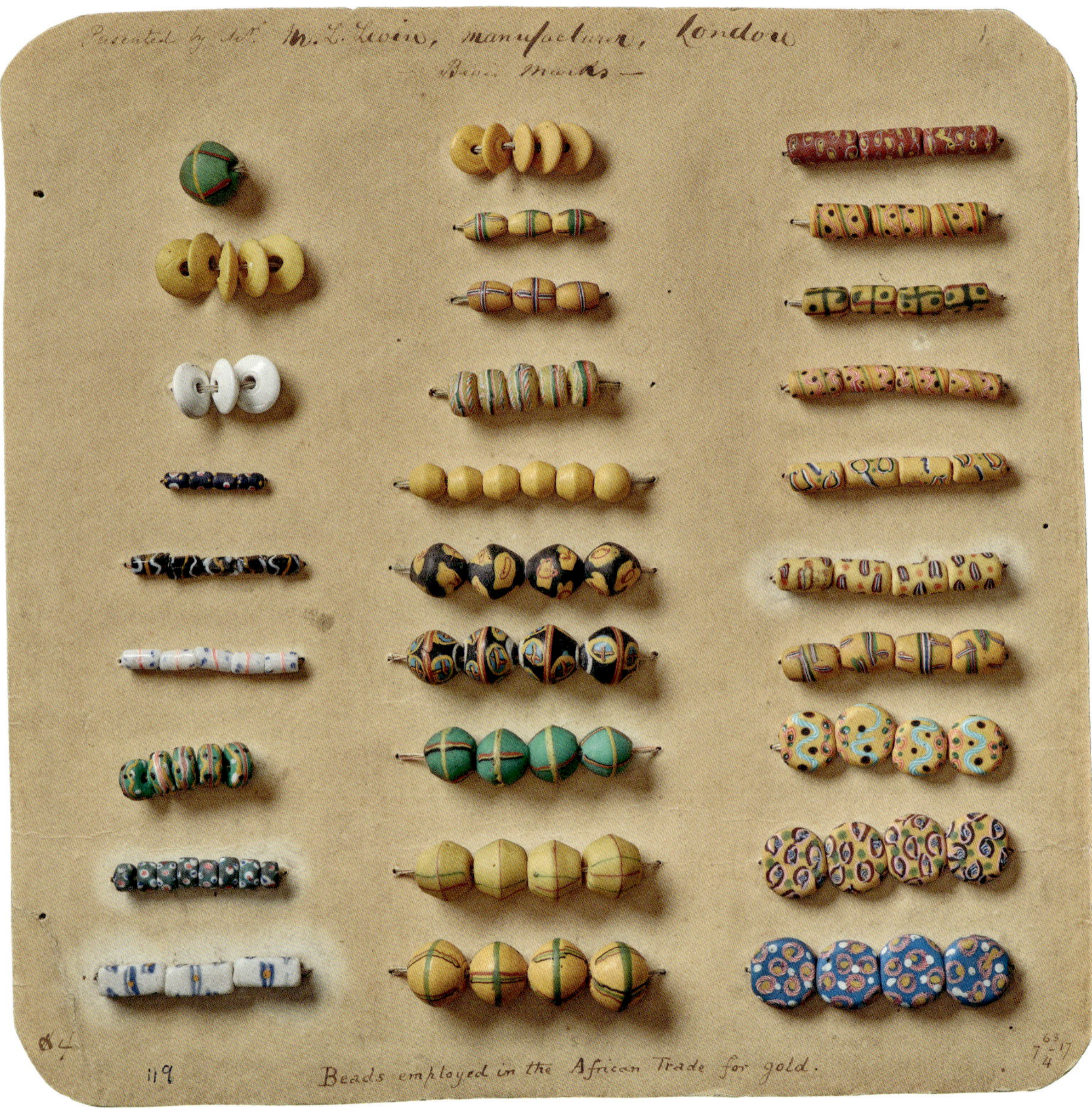

Trade beads from Venice and Bohemia, c. 1863.

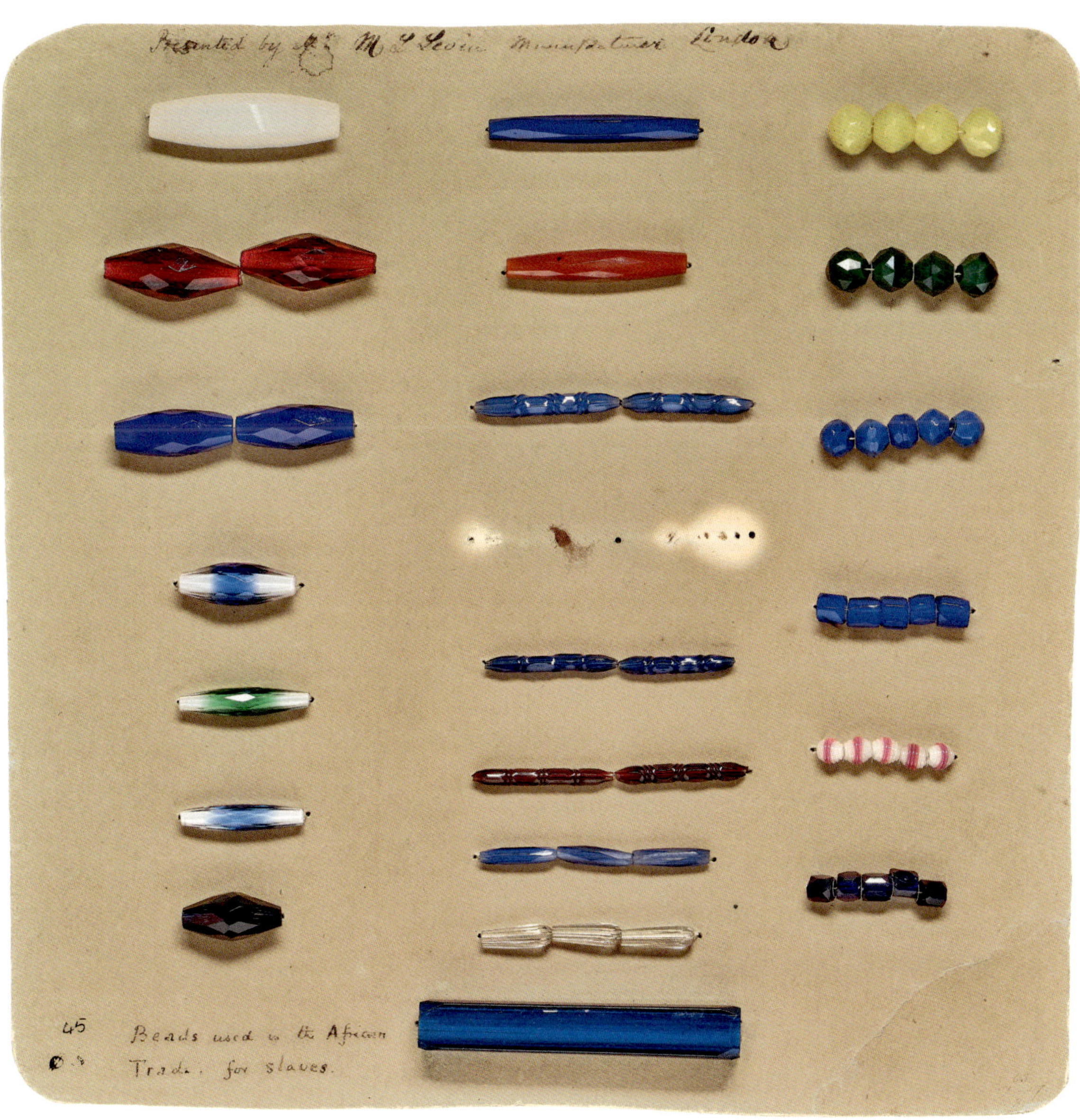

The British Empire often represented itself as a benefactor, aiding and protecting its colonies. Seals can tell us about how Britain viewed itself and the territories in its dominion. These seals represent just six of the many territories that were at one point under British imperial rule. They were selected for their iconography, with ships symbolising trade and subject peoples symbolising the subservience of colonies to the British crown. While the imagery speaks to Britain's self-fashioning across its colonial territories, the objects also stand in for the wider system of power these seals represented and how they were transported and used across the globe. Images of supplicant or seated Indigenous figures often recur, often facing Britannia or the British sovereign.

"I've used replicas of seals in my work for a long time. A seal has a historic aspect to it, an official nature. These few seals were chosen from many in the Museum for specific reasons. The Seal of British Guyana features boats. The Nova Scotia seal also has ships in it – it's about trade and conquest. The one for the Leeward Islands has a ship and a pineapple, a symbol of exoticism and the reach of empire. I also like the seal for South Australia – the image of Britannia reaching her hand out to an Indigenous person. It's about who's in charge: they're not on equal footing and the benign image belies the violence behind what was actually going on. It's the same with Sierra Leone – a 'native' person, which is what they called them, is sitting down with a hand outstretched as a ship arrives." HL

"Seals are the legal expression of a sovereign's power. They tell the viewer 'We're in charge of you – we run things.'"

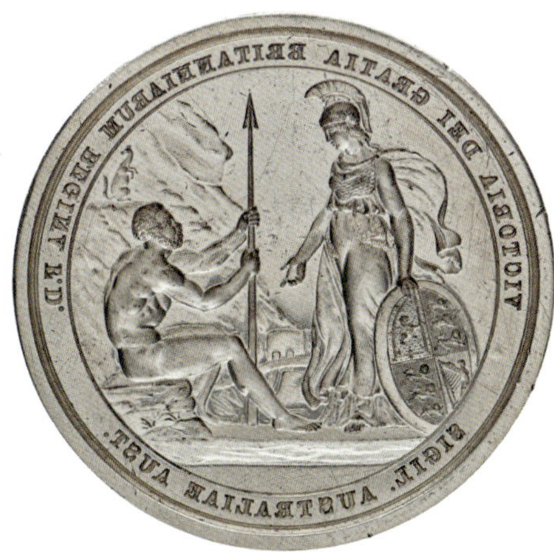

Joseph Shepherd Wyon, seal-die for South Australia, *c.* 1858–73.

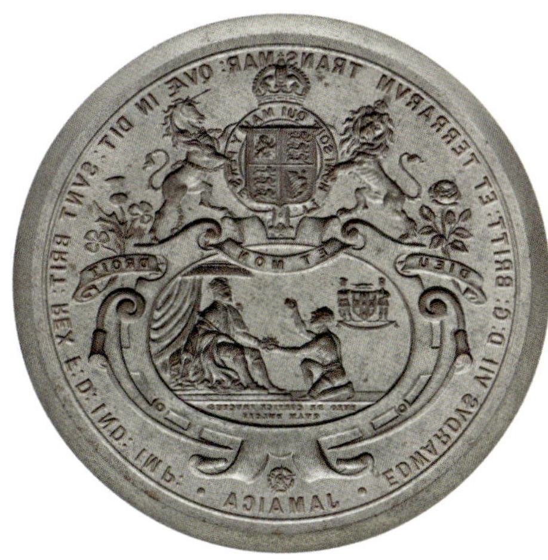

The Royal Mint, seal-die for Jamaica, 1901–10.

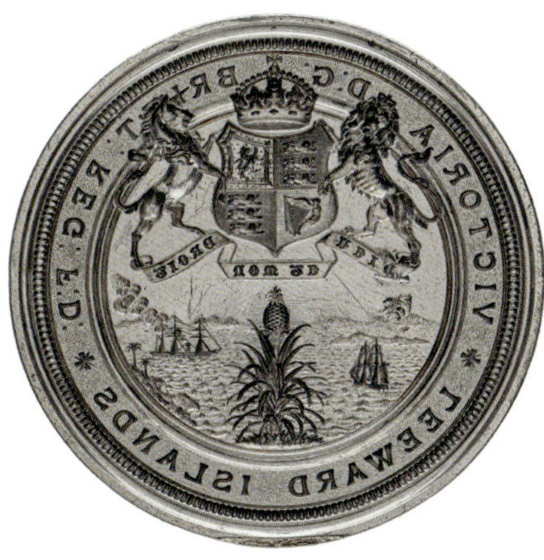

Joseph Shepherd Wyon and Alfred Benjamin Wyon, seal-die for the Leeward Islands, 1872–3.

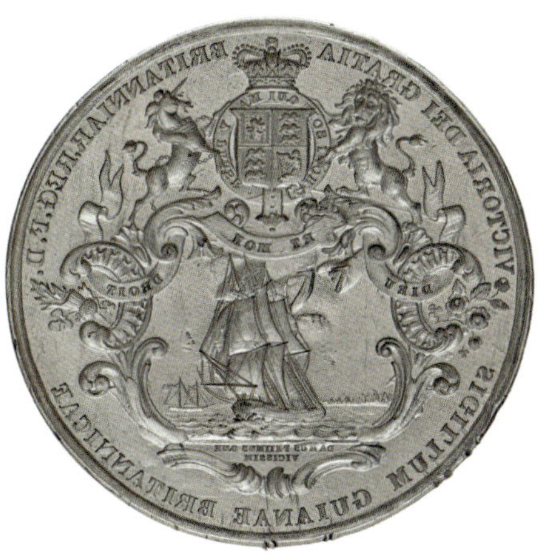

Benjamin Wyon, seal-die for British Guiana, 1839–40.

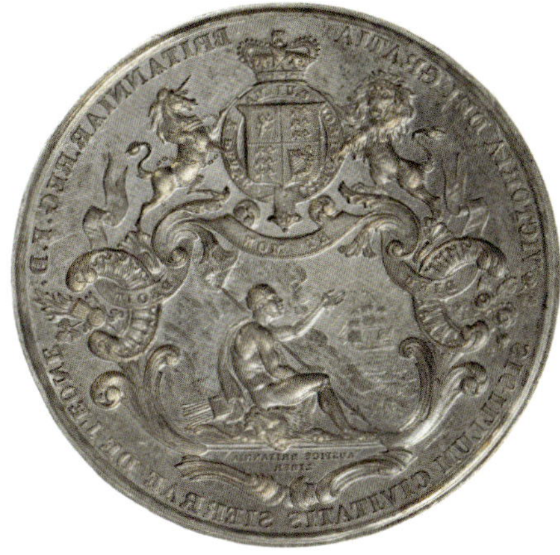

Benjamin Wyon, seal-die for Sierra Leone, 1838–9.

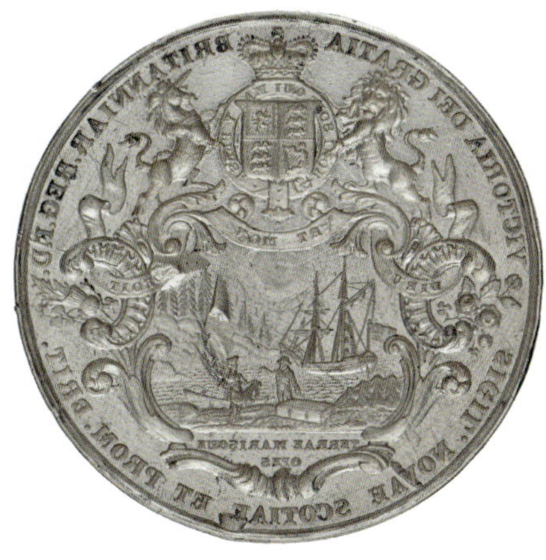

Benjamin Wyon, seal-die for Nova Scotia, 1838–9.

In 1877 Queen Victoria was the first British royal to be proclaimed Empress of India in a lavish ceremony known as a Durbar – an invented tradition drawing on Mughal precedents. The print opposite was produced for Queen Victoria's Golden Jubilee in 1887 and imagines a scene in which a painting of her is carried through the streets by Indian people.

In total there were three Imperial Durbars. The second, in 1903, marked the proclamations of King Edward VII and Queen Alexandra. The third Delhi Durbar of 1911, was the only one that was attended in person by the monarchs being proclaimed – both King George V and Queen Mary were present and all governors and princes of India were in attendance. The ceremonies served to emphasise the legitimacy of British rule over India and were also demonstrations of military force.

George and Mary sat under a richly decorated *shamiana* (canopy), which is visible in recordings made during the occasion. It shielded them from the sun while governors and princes of the Indian states came to acknowledge them. After the Durbar, the *shamiana* was cut up and reused to adorn the throne room at Buckingham Palace, where it still hangs (p. 56). The drawings for the *shamiana* (pp. 56–7) were prepared at the Mayo School of Arts, founded by the British Crown in Lahore in 1876.

"Queen Victoria's legacy is interesting. Her love affair with Albert is highly romanticised, so is her learning Urdu. I'm thinking, hang on a second. She was the head of the British Empire. She may have been a figurehead, but she was the top of the pyramid, and she allowed a lot of things to happen under her watch. She's not innocent at all." HL

"When you rule an empire, you've got to constantly remind people of your power."

"This print is absurd. It's not presented as allegorical, but as bloody literal! But then, if you're Indian at that time and you see this image, it's not necessarily so funny because you're being shown where power truly lies. You can go to the temple, you can go to the mosque … But this is who you should really be venerating." HL

The quotation from a poem by Alfred Lord Tennyson at the bottom of the print includes the lines:

… May you rule us long,
And leave us rulers of your blood
As noble to the latest day!
May children of our children say,
'She wrought her people lasting good …'

After Godefroy Durand, *The Jubilee in the East*, 1887.

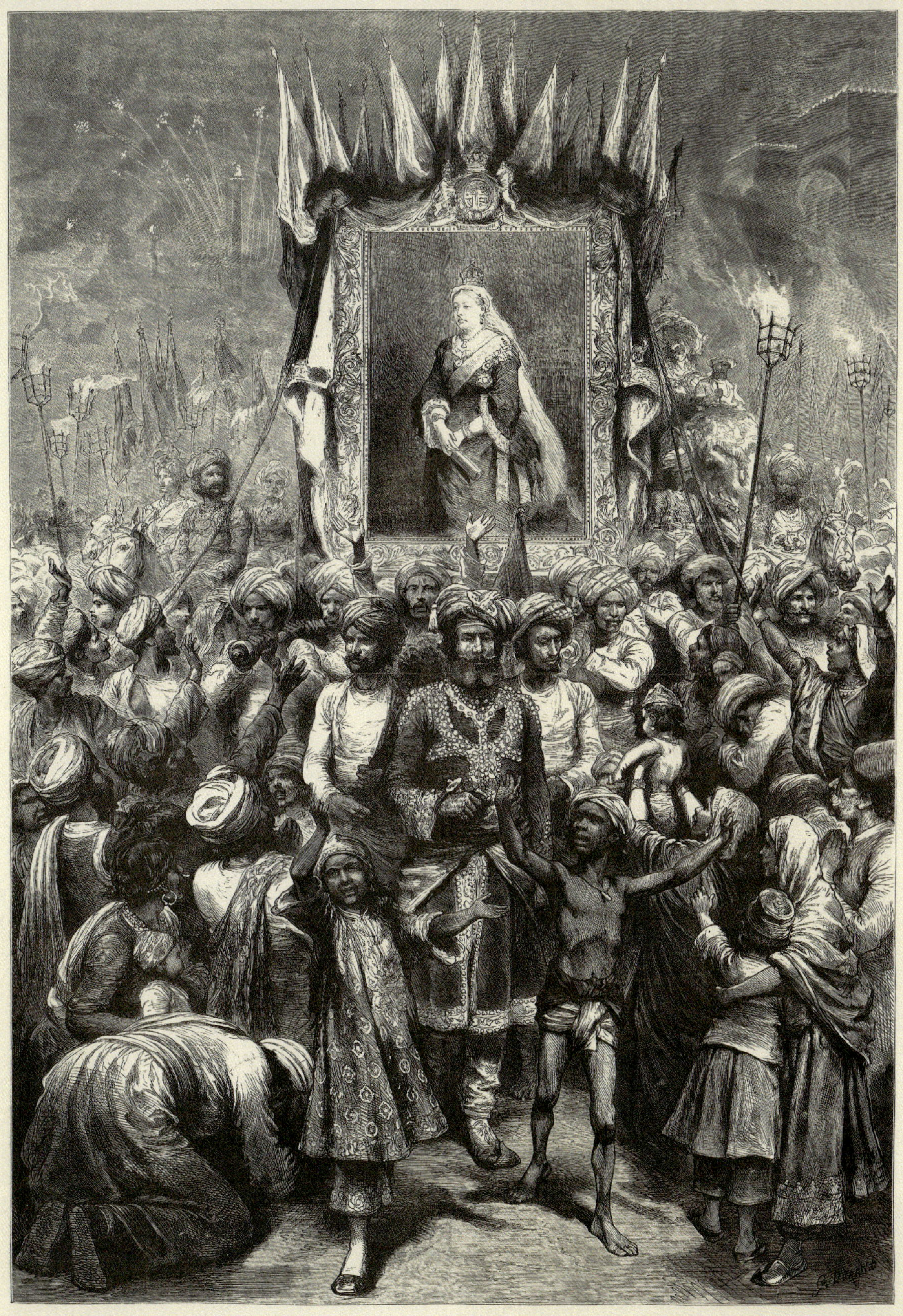

. . . . . May you rule us long,
And leave us rulers of your blood
  As noble to the latest day!
  May children of our children say,
" She wrought her people lasting good;

" Her court was pure; her life serene;
  God gave her peace; her land reposed;
  A thousand claims to reverence closed
On her as Mother, Wife, and Queen;

" And statesmen at her council met
  Who knew the seasons when to take
  Occasion by the hand, and make
The bounds of freedom wider yet.

" By shaping some august decree,
  Which kept her throne unshaken still,
  Broad-based upon her people's will,
And compassed by the inviolate sea ! '
                              TENNYSON.

THE JUBILEE IN THE EAST—AN ALLEGORY:
VICTORIA, EMPRESS OF INDIA

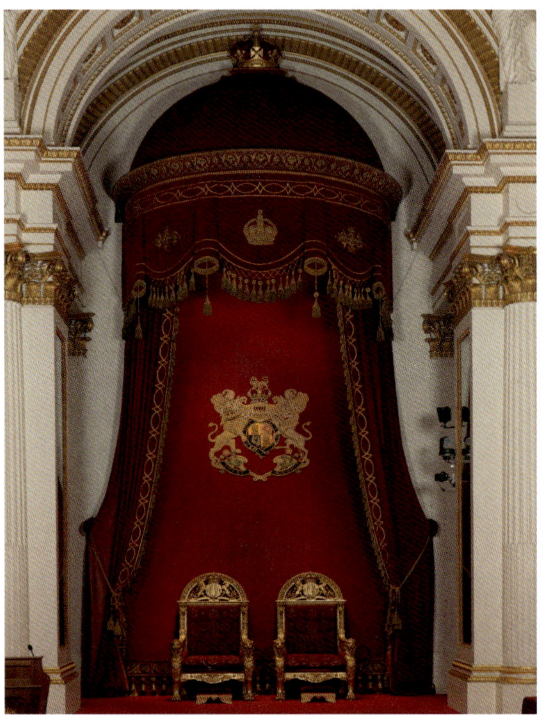

Mayo School of Arts and Sir Edwin Landseer Lutyens, throne canopy, Buckingham Palace, 1911–16.

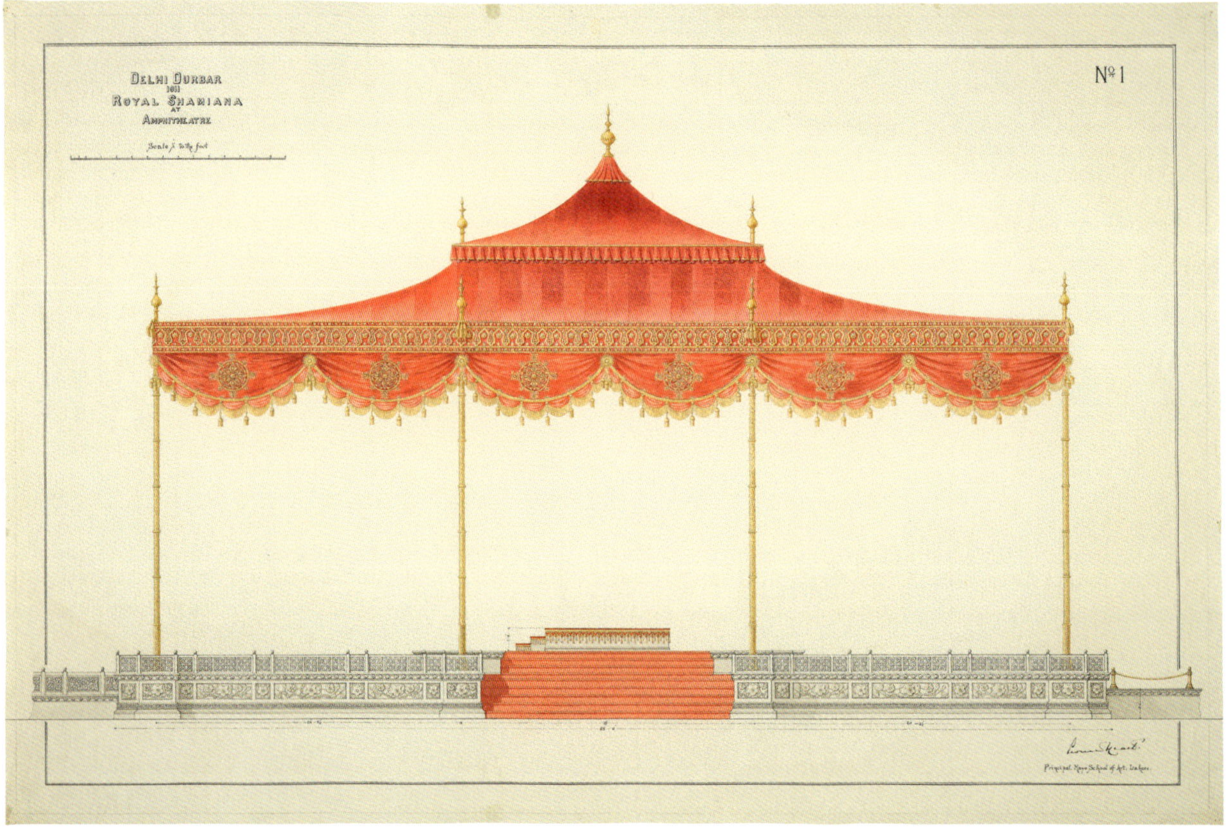

Mayo School of Arts, drawing of the Royal Shamiana, 1911.

Detail, Mayo School of Arts, drawing of the Chandoa, hanging interior of the canopy roof, 1911.

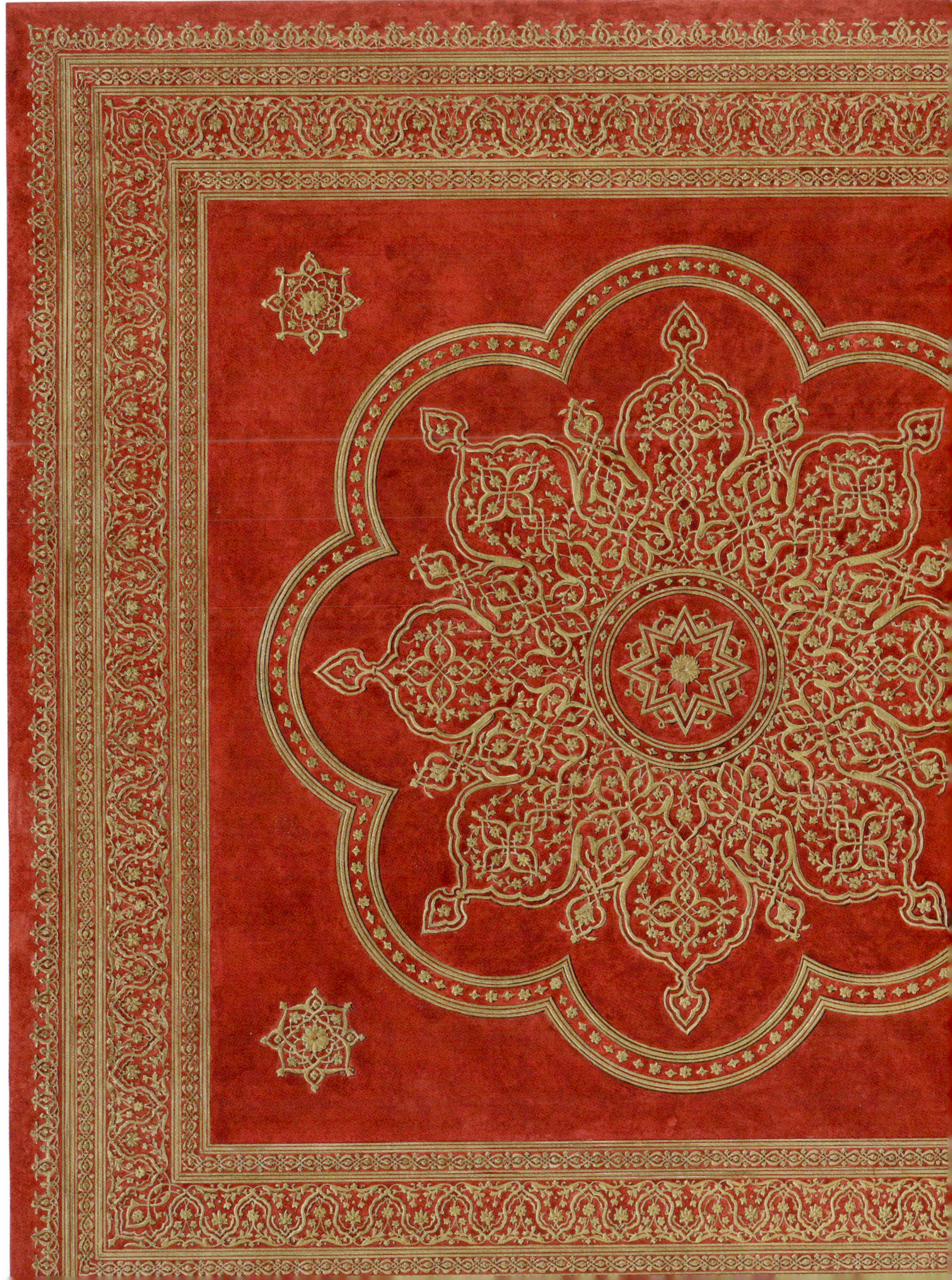

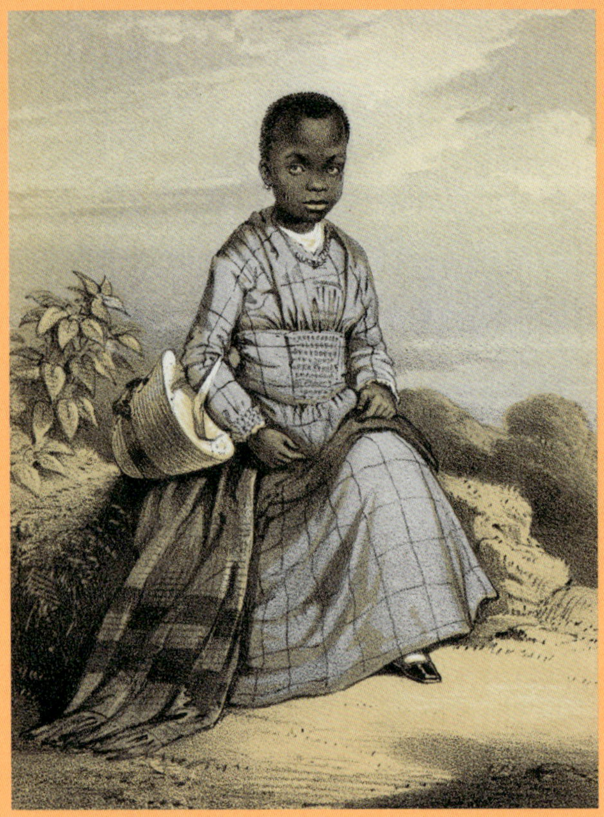

M. & N. Hanhart, after Frederick E. Forbes, *Sarah Forbes Bonetta: The African Captive*, 1851.

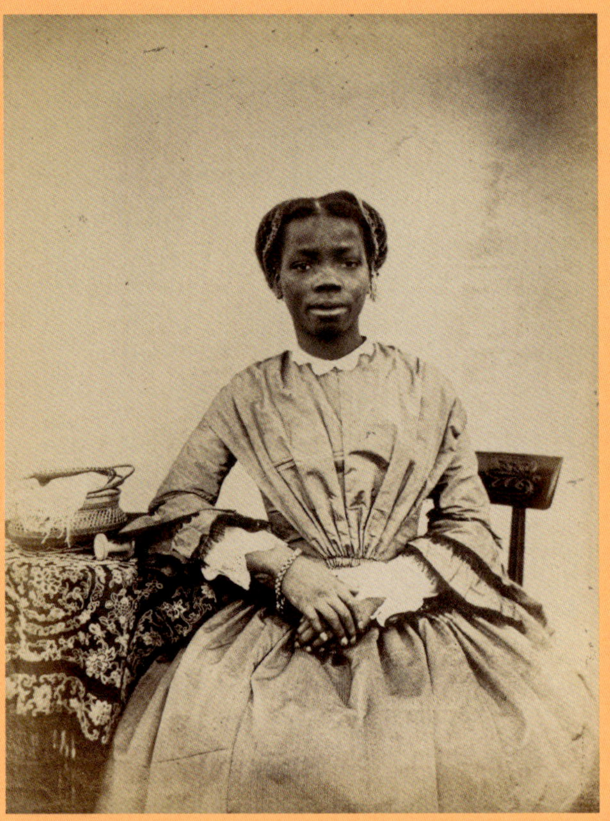

William Bambridge, *Sally [Sarah] Forbes Bonetta*, 1856.

"You can look at these stories a different way – that Queen Victoria collected these children and had a very complicated relationship with them. At first Duleep Singh accepted his position, and then slowly as he got older, he realised what was going on and what he'd lost. For Sarah Forbes Bonetta, somebody has saved her life, whereas for Alemayehu – the world he came from was completely destroyed." HL

"I suppose Queen Victoria was like a lot of people. She felt bad for her godchildren. But ultimately she was the head of this thing – this thing called the British Empire."

As an expression of Queen Victoria's role as the humanitarian 'Mother of Empire', she was godmother to several children displaced or orphaned by colonial wars (pp. 58, 60–3). While some of these children benefited from Victoria's support, others suffered under the spotlight of the royal court. Several were forcibly removed from their homes or countries of birth and became casualties of diplomatic schemes.

Sarah Forbes Bonetta (*c.* 1843–1880) was born as the Yoruba princess Omoba Aina in southern Nigeria and later enslaved by the King of Dahomey. She was presented as a 'gift' to Captain Frederick E. Forbes (1819–1851) and taken to England on the HMS *Bonetta* (Forbes Bonetta became her English surname). Sarah impressed at court with her talents in music and languages. Victoria became her godmother, gave her a pension and later arranged her marriage to Captain James Pinson Labulo Davies, a Yoruba businessman. She died of tuberculosis before the age of 40.

Victoria Gouramma was born in Varanasi (Benares), India, daughter of Chikka Virarajendra, the last ruler of Coorg before he was deposed by the British. Virarajendra left her in Queen Victoria's care when he travelled to England to ask for his wealth to be returned to him. There, she was baptised with the name 'Victoria'. Against other people's wishes, she married Lieutenant Colonel John Campbell (1753–1784), 30 years her senior. They had a daughter before Victoria died in 1864 of tuberculosis, aged just 23.

Duleep Singh was the last maharaja of the Sikh Empire, deposed at the age of 10 by the East India Company. He was forced to surrender the Koh-i-Noor, one of the world's largest cut diamonds, to Queen Victoria (see p. 98). An English education was imposed on him and he converted to Christianity by the age of 15, after which he was sent to England in 1854. At first, he was on good terms with Victoria, who found him handsome and charming, and even spent time with her children, as depicted in her intimate sketches. Later their relationship soured; he was censored as he tried to re-establish contact with his mother in Kathmandu and forbidden from travelling home to India. He eventually re-converted to Sikhism and died in Paris, aged 55. His wish for his body to be returned to India was never honoured.

Prince Alemayehu of Ethiopia was the son of Emperor Tewodros II. He was orphaned after his father died by suicide during the British invasion of Maqdala in 1868 and his mother, Empress Tiruwork Wube, died of illness and stress on the journey to England. He travelled under the guardianship of Captain Tristram Speedy (see p. 148), with whom he was photographed in Ethiopian dress (p. 63, see p. 62 for Alemayehu's necklace). His presentation at court, aged 7, moved Queen Victoria, and she promised him a pension. Alemayehu went to boarding school but was reportedly miserable there. He died of pleurisy at the age of 18, without ever going home to Ethiopia.

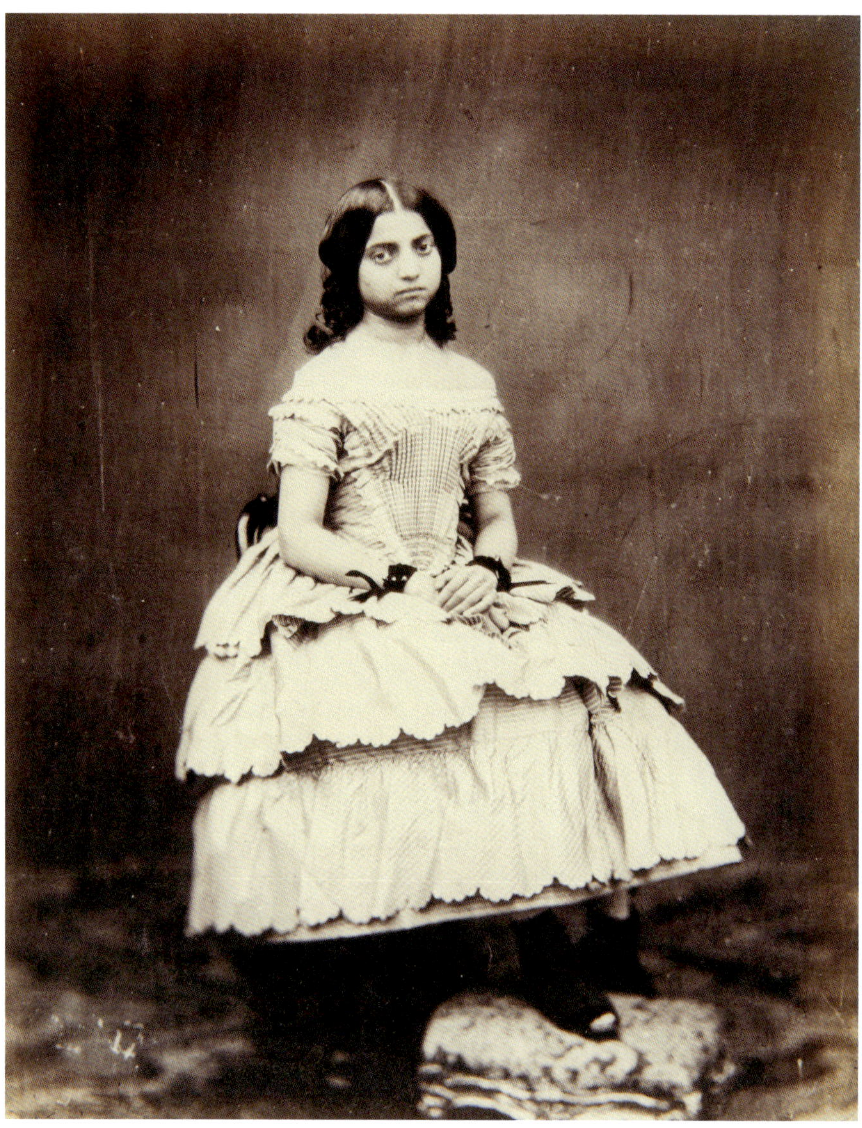

Roger Fenton, *Princess Victoria Gouramma of Coorg*, 1854.

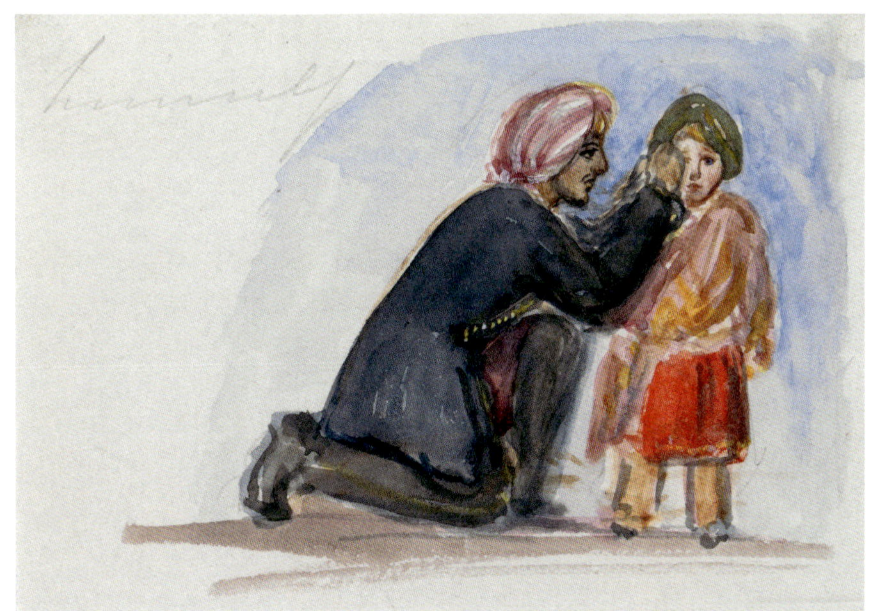

Queen Victoria, *Maharaja Duleep Singh dressing Prince Arthur in Indian costume, c.*1854.

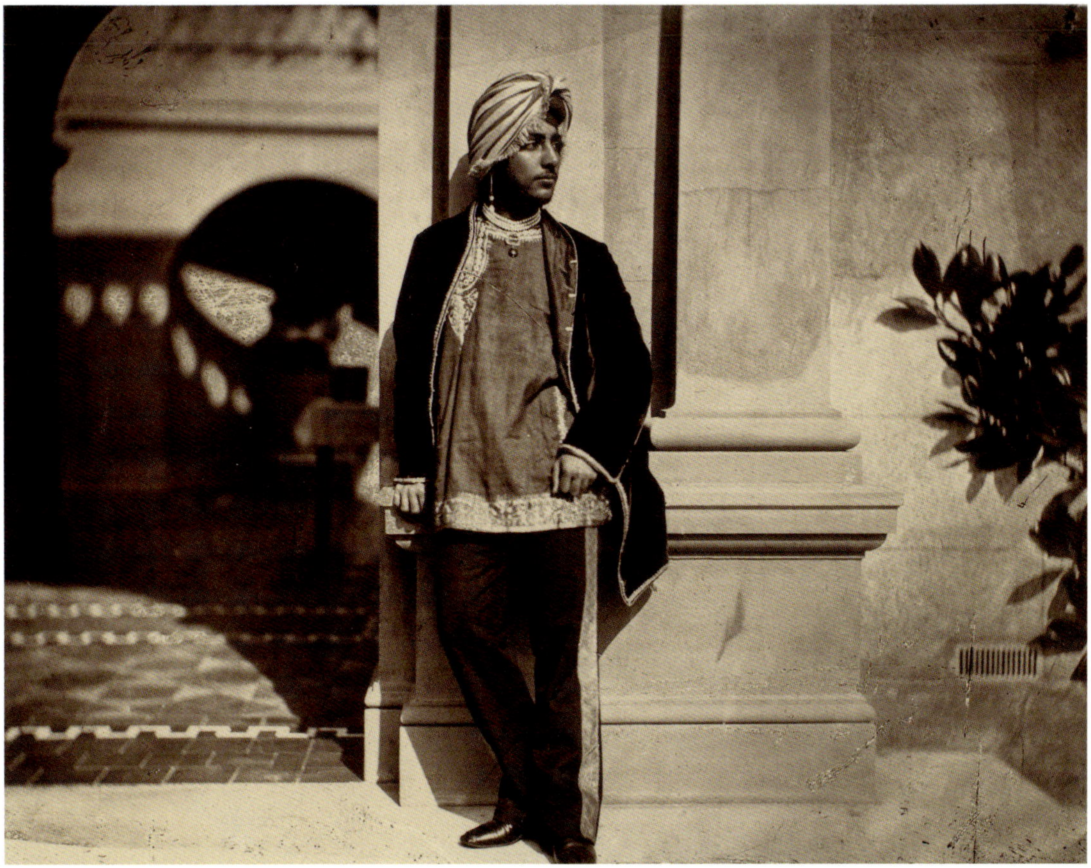

Ernst Becker, *Maharaja Duleep Singh of Lahore*, 1854.

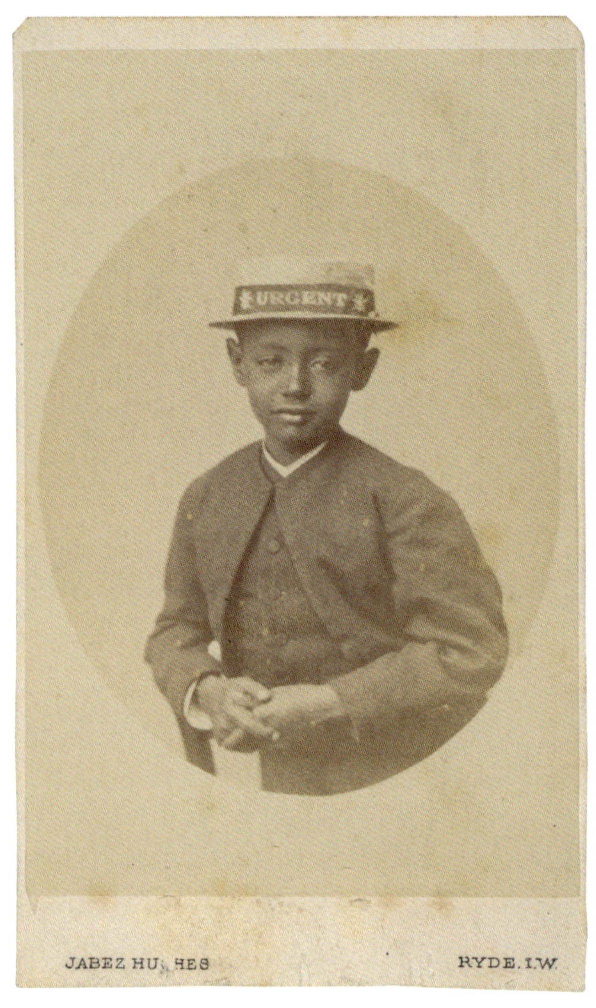

Cornelius Jabez Hughes, carte de visite of Prince Alemayehu, 1868.

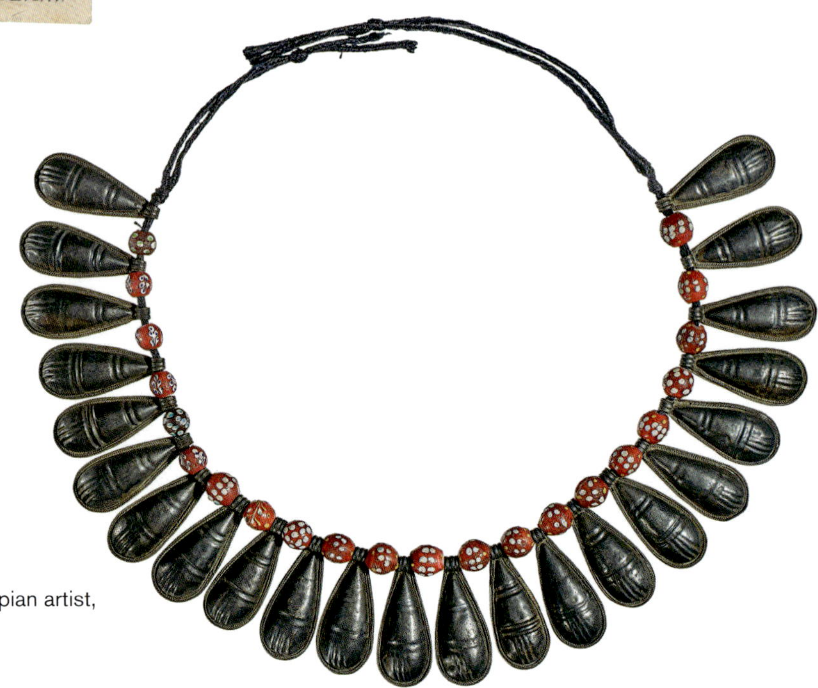

Unrecorded Ethiopian artist, necklace, 1800s.

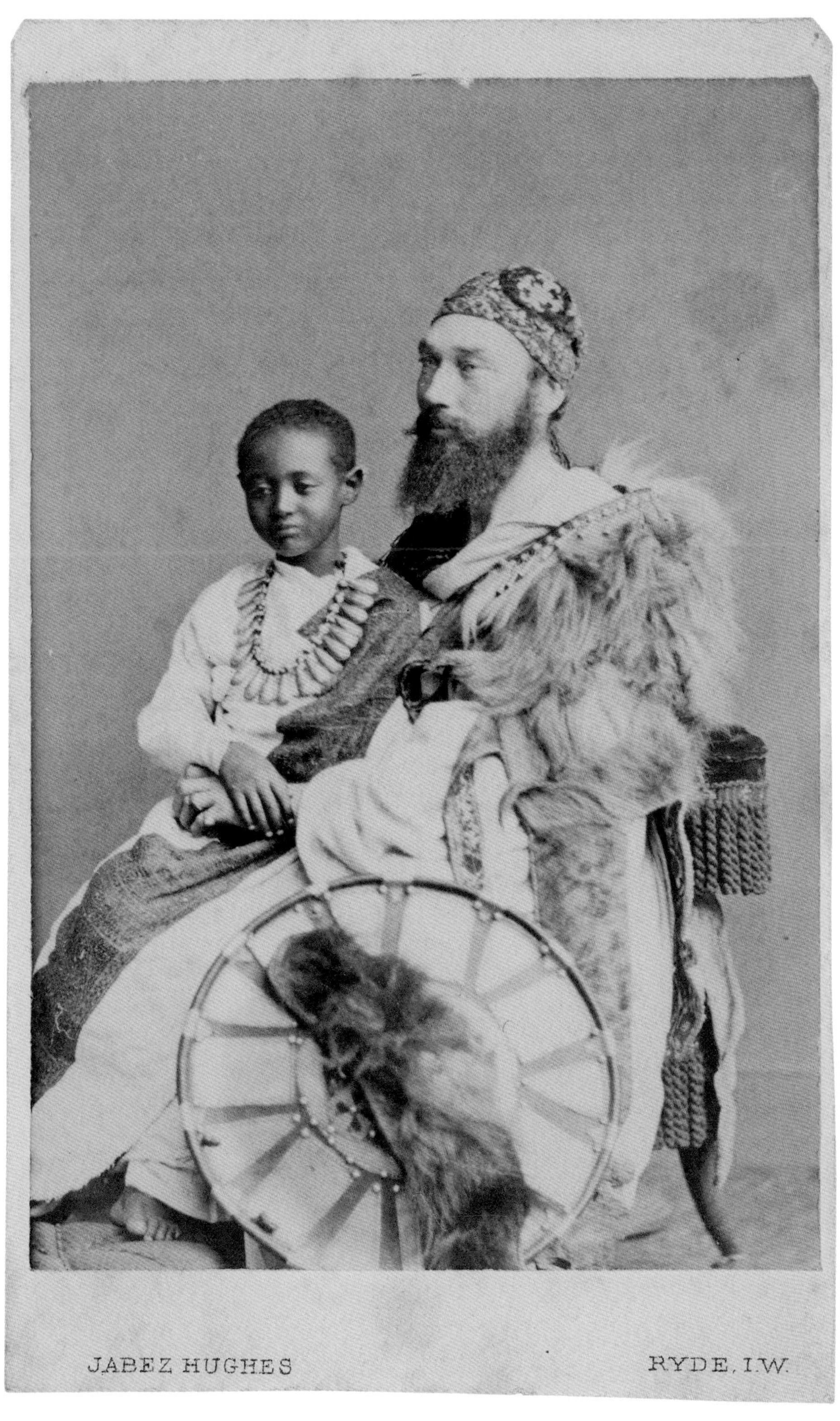

Cornelius Jabez Hughes, carte de visite of Prince Alemayehu and Captain Speedy, 1868.

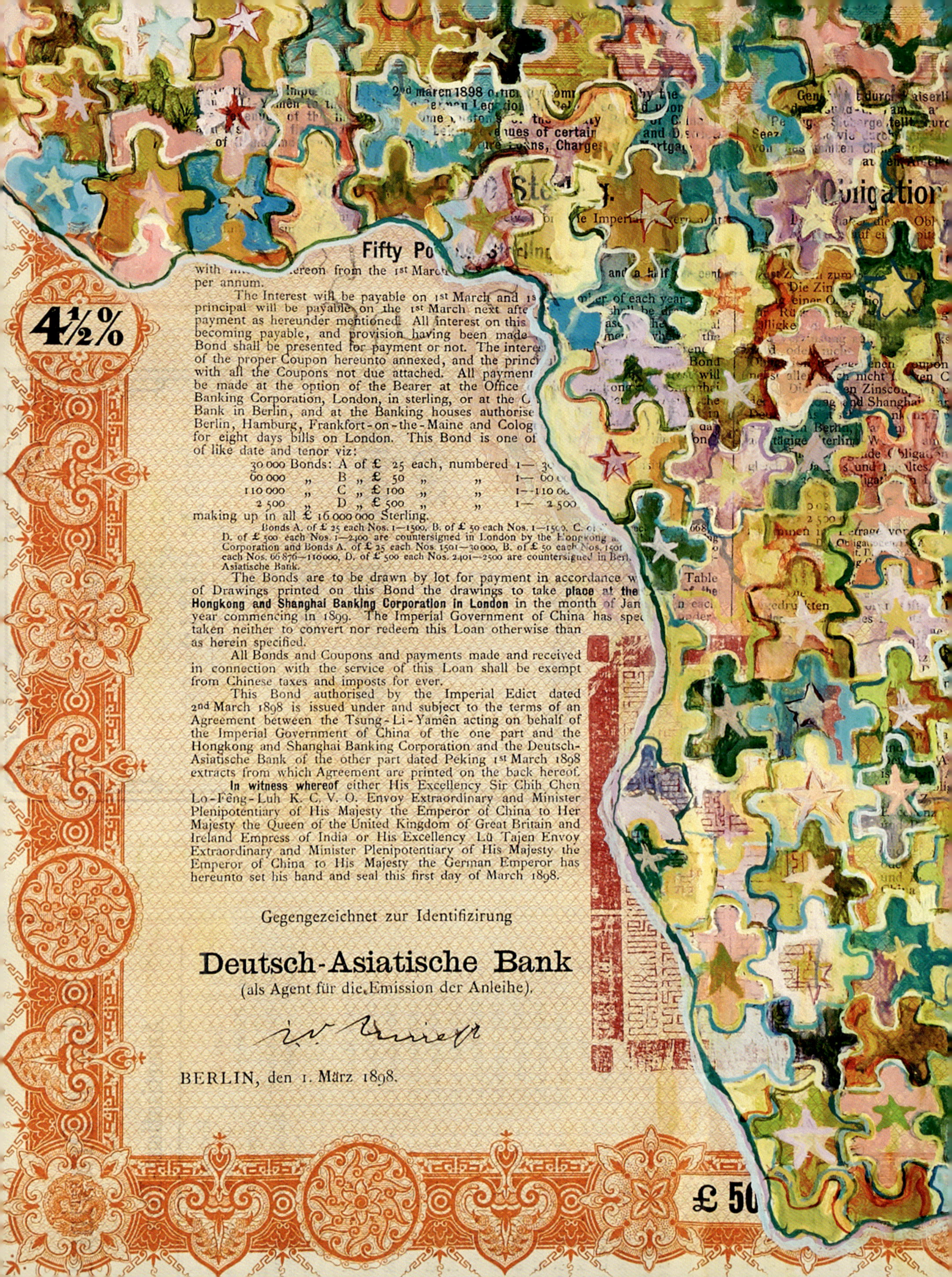

4½%

Fifty Po[unds] Sterling

Obligation

with inte[rest] [th]ereon from the 1st March ... and a half ... cent
per annum.

The Interest will be payable on 1st March and 1s[t ...] principal will be payable on the 1st March next afte[r] payment as hereunder mentioned. All interest on this [...] becoming payable, and provision having been made [...] Bond shall be presented for payment or not. The intere[st ...] of the proper Coupon hereunto annexed, and the princi[pal] with all the Coupons not due attached. All payment[s ...] be made at the option of the Bearer at the Office [...] Banking Corporation, London, in sterling, or at the C[...] Bank in Berlin, and at the Banking houses authorise[d ...] Berlin, Hamburg, Frankfort-on-the-Maine and Colog[ne ...] for eight days bills on London. This Bond is one of [...] of like date and tenor viz:

30 000 Bonds: A of £ 25 each, numbered 1— 30[...]
60 000   „   B „ £ 50 „   „   1— 60[...]
110 000   „   C „ £ 100 „   „   1—110 00[...]
2 500   „   D „ £ 500 „   „   1— 2 500

making up in all £ 16 000 000 Sterling.
Bonds A. of £ 25 each Nos. 1—1500. B. of £ 50 each Nos. 1—1500. C. of [...] D. of £ 500 each Nos. 1—2400 are countersigned in London by the Hongkong a[nd ...] Corporation and Bonds A. of £ 25 each Nos. 1501—30000, B. of £ 50 each Nos. 150[...] each Nos. 66 876—110000, D. of £ 500 each Nos. 2401—2500 are countersigned in Ber[lin ...] Asiatische Bank.

The Bonds are to be drawn by lot for payment in accordance w[ith ...] of Drawings printed on this Bond the drawings to take place at the [...] Hongkong and Shanghai Banking Corporation in London in the month of Jan[uary ...] year commencing in 1899. The Imperial Government of China has spe[cially under]taken neither to convert nor redeem this Loan otherwise than as herein specified.

All Bonds and Coupons and payments made and received [...] in connection with the service of this Loan shall be exempt from Chinese taxes and imposts for ever.

This Bond authorised by the Imperial Edict dated 2nd March 1898 is issued under and subject to the terms of an Agreement between the Tsung-Li-Yamên acting on behalf of the Imperial Government of China of the one part and the Hongkong and Shanghai Banking Corporation and the Deutsch-Asiatische Bank of the other part dated Peking 1st March 1898 extracts from which Agreement are printed on the back hereof.

In witness whereof either His Excellency Sir Chih Chen Lo-Fêng-Luh K. C. V. O. Envoy Extraordinary and Minister Plenipotentiary of His Majesty the Emperor of China to Her Majesty the Queen of the United Kingdom of Great Britain and Ireland Empress of India or His Excellency Lü Tajen Envoy Extraordinary and Minister Plenipotentiary of His Majesty the Emperor of China to His Majesty the German Emperor has hereunto set his hand and seal this first day of March 1898.

Gegengezeichnet zur Identifizirung

Deutsch-Asiatische Bank
(als Agent für die Emission der Anleihe).

BERLIN, den 1. März 1898.

£ 50

The first European travellers to reach Benin by sea were Portuguese explorers in the 15th century. They established a successful trading relationship with the Oba, offering new luxury goods as well as weapons such as cannons. In the late 1400s the Oba hired Portuguese mercenary soldiers. The two sculptures on p. 67 depict the kind of mercenaries that often fought in his army. Other representations of Europeans featured in the plaques on the courtyard columns of the palace in Benin City. The display of these figures symbolised the Oba's monopoly over trade with Europe.

"I used to go to the Museum of Mankind [where the British Museum ethnography collections were held from 1970 to 1997] to draw sculptures like these soldiers (p. 67). I would spend a day drawing a single object. It was a thing you did in art school at that time. He is a representation of power. The firepower he's holding – today it would be a Kalashnikov." HL

The jug on p. 66 was made in England in the 1390s, possibly for King Richard II, but later travelled to West Africa, ultimately entering the Asante royal court in modern-day Ghana. How the jug made its way to Africa is unknown – it was probably traded over long distances, either as a diplomatic gift or as war booty. It might have arrived via trans-Saharan trade, or, more likely, via early European maritime sea journeys to the West African coast. In the photograph, the jug can be seen in the courtyard of an Asante royal palace with a second European medieval jug, now in York Army Museum.

"This photograph is extraordinary (p. 66). What's the jug doing there? How did this thing end up in Ghana? We can speculate on how it got to the Asante court but we know that it got there and that it was a prized object. Thinking about how foreign objects become symbols of British power – here, in a mirrored way, European objects become a symbol of African power." HL

These objects point to early modern connections that precede later imperial relationships and a period of prosperous trade between kingdoms in West Africa and Europe. The soldier figures and jug both came to Britain in the late 1800s as loot from colonial wars. A similar story is told by the Portuguese cannon made in Lisbon in the 15th or 16th century (pp. 66–7). The royal coat of arms of Portugal is visible on the barrel. It was looted from Benin during the 1897 Expedition (see p. 140) with three other cannons.

"What's the jug doing there? How did this thing end up in Ghana?"

"The cannon being stored in the Museum is interesting. It's normally too big to be on display. Why did I choose this? It's so big and awkward. It's a very old piece that was traded or gifted by the Portuguese. The different European powers they were getting arms and mercenaries from later became the people who destroyed their whole world [laughs]. 'We're gonna loan this piece to you for a few hundred years, but then we're coming back with a vengeance!' This show is all about colonial power and loot." HL

Detail, Hew Locke, *Chinese Imperial Gold Loan 11*, 2017 (see p. 70).

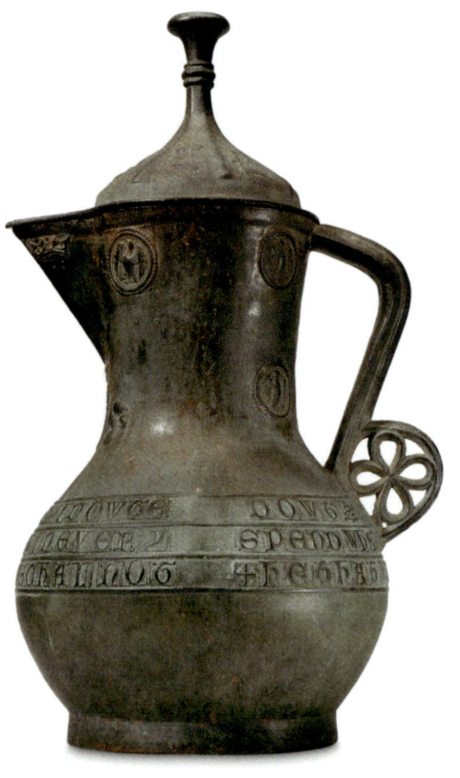

Unrecorded English artist,
the Asante Jug, 1390s.

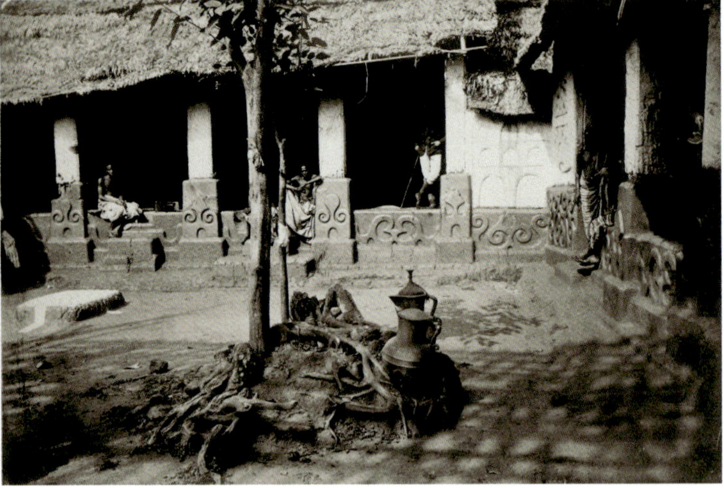

Frederick Grant, the Asante Jug in a courtyard associated
with royal buildings in Kumasi, Ghana, 1884.

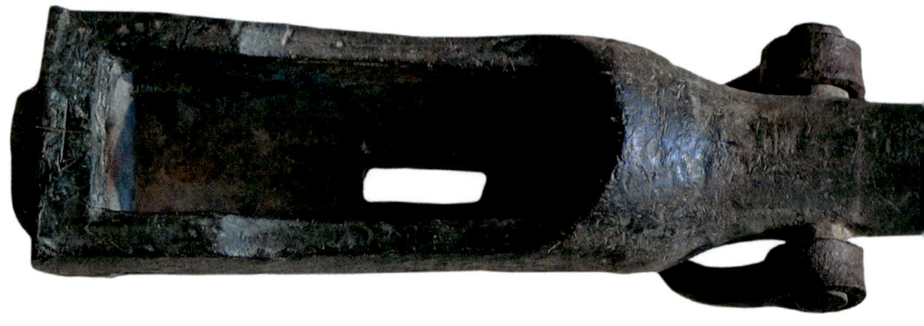

Francisco Alvares, Portuguese cannon, *c.* 1540.

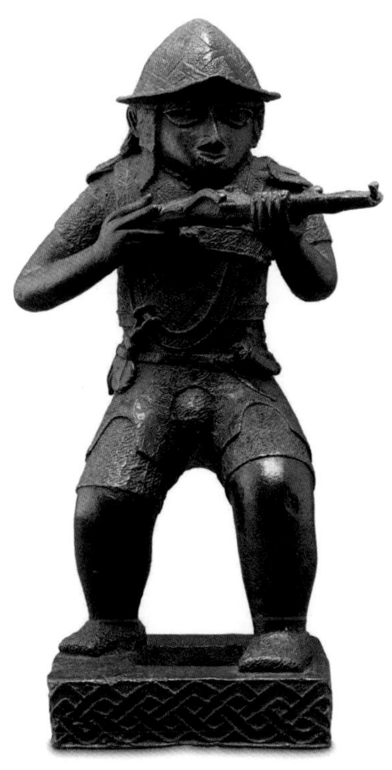

Unrecorded Edo artist, Portuguese soldier,
late 1600s to early 1700s.

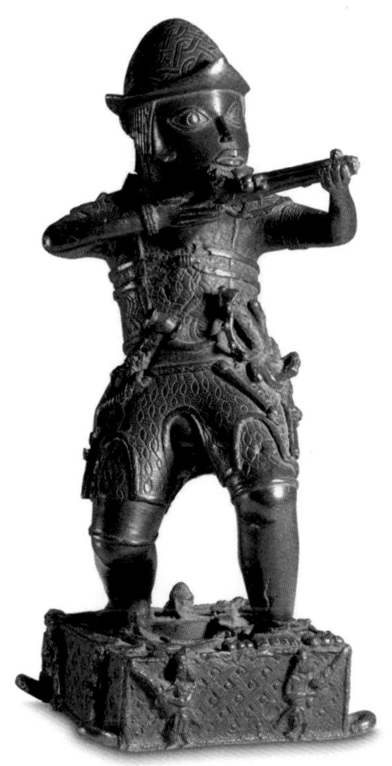

Unrecorded Edo artist, Portuguese soldier,
late 1500s to early 1600s.

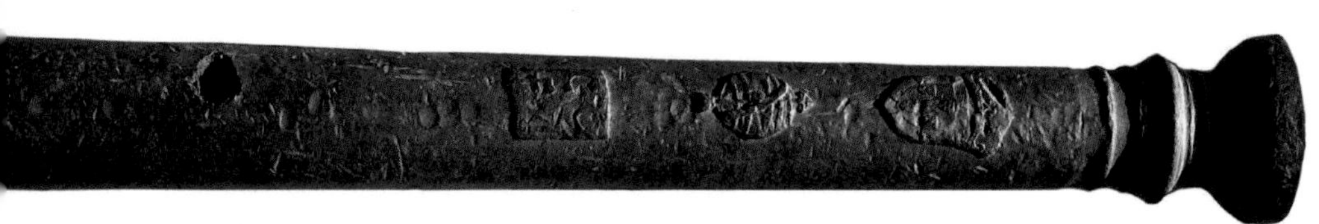

"These share certificates are a reminder of the history of power. The tail end, the hangover, from colonial relationships."

The Royal African Company (see p. 46) moved more enslaved people across the Atlantic than any other institution during the history of the 'triangular trade'. Trade routes had already been established in West Africa for millennia; gold, ivory, salt, cloth and eventually people were moved and exchanged.

The Akan drum (opposite) was made in West Africa and taken to North America, probably by an enslaver. It may have been used to force enslaved people to exercise on the boats, a grim practice known as 'dancing'.

Hew Locke's *Share* series draws on historical share certificates from companies that have since foundered. In his *Chinese Imperial Loan* shares, Locke takes shares from the 1800s – when the Chinese emperor sought to raise funds using European banks – and overpaints them with jigsaw puzzle maps of Africa that point to China's current investment in African infrastructure (pp. 70–1).

The Asante Kingdom in West Africa was rich in gold deposits that were traded along the trans-Saharan routes. As a result, gold dust was the currency of the Asante Kingdom. From the 1400s, Akan makers cast European brass and bronze into gold-weights. The earliest examples were geometric in shape, but from the 1600s more figurative forms evoked the proverbs of Akan society (pp. 72–3). Gun-shaped weights reflected the importance of European firearms to the expansion of Asante territory. The use of diverse currencies exploded with the profitability of slavery (pp. 74–5). Cowrie shells had been used as currency since at least the 1300s but Europeans introduced huge numbers of Maldivian shells in the 1700s. Gold beads in the shape of cowries were worn by high-status Akan people to symbolise their wealth; this one was relinquished by Asantehene Kofi Karikari (*c.* 1837–1884) as part of the indemnity paid at the end of the Third Anglo-Asante War (1873–4). Golden guineas were introduced to British coinage by George I and stamped with the RAC's symbol, an elephant; they were made using gold from 'Guinea', then a general term for West Africa. While referencing pre-existing artistic traditions within West Africa, brass manillas, many made in Birmingham, were taken to West Africa by the Portuguese and the British and widely used as part of the trade. Birmingham produced various other brass objects for export to Africa. Though these bells appear to be almost identical (pp. 76–7), one was made in the Lower Niger area before 1500 and the other is a much later copy made in Birmingham to fulfil demand.

"Enslaved people weren't allowed to have their own drums in America; that's a part of the dehumanising process. There was a ban on drums in many plantations as they contain potential for resistance. Like a censorship programme. You can't have people remembering where they came from – you need them to forget their past." HL

"Gold-weights can take different shapes, but we've chosen several weapons because, as in most societies, the threat of violence is at the back of power relationships. Even if you don't actually use the violence, it's always there." HL

"If you compare the Birmingham bell and the Forcados bell, you have what is essentially a British imitation of an African form. It was made for a particular market that valued them." HL

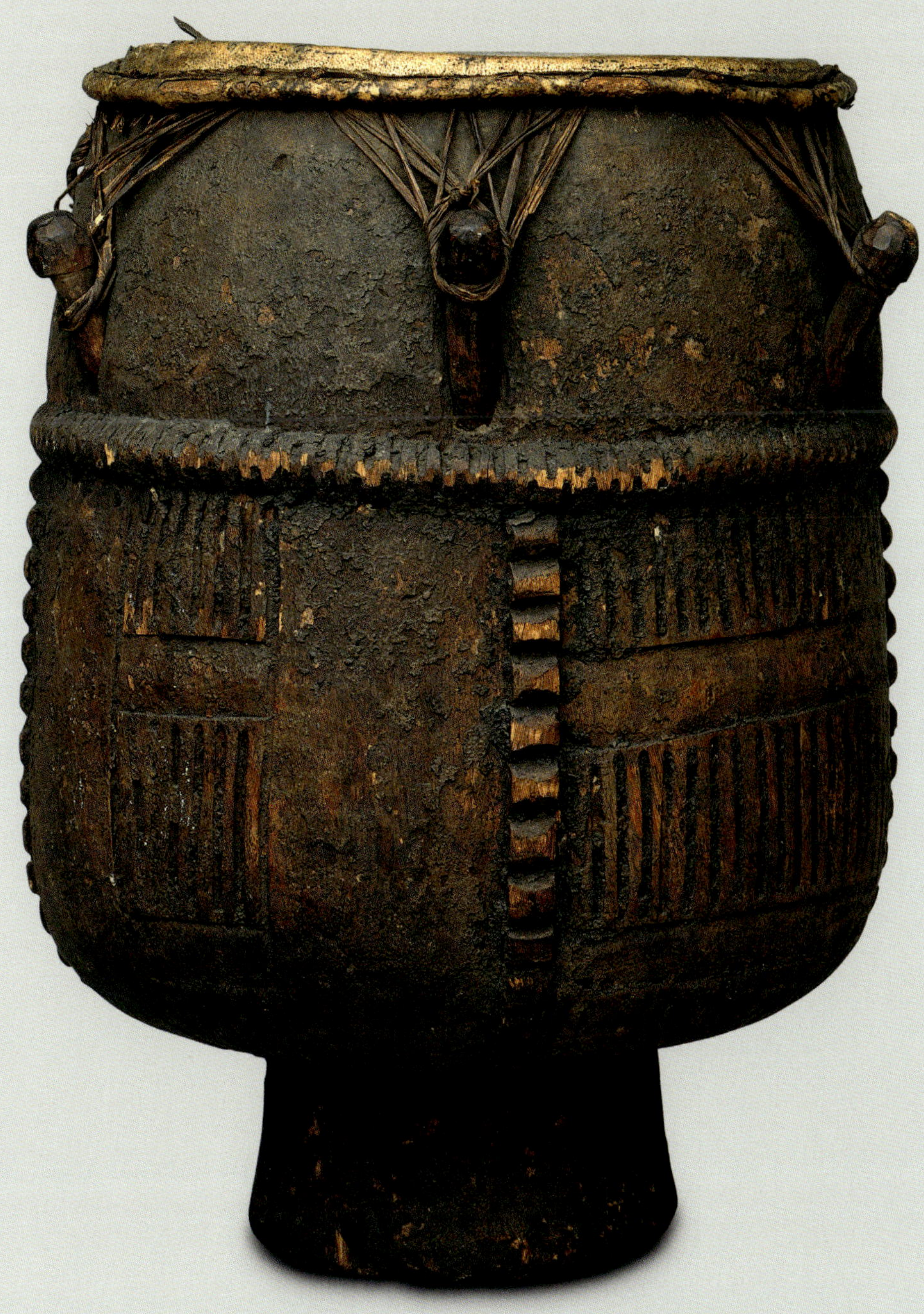

Unrecorded Akan artist, drum, early 1700s.

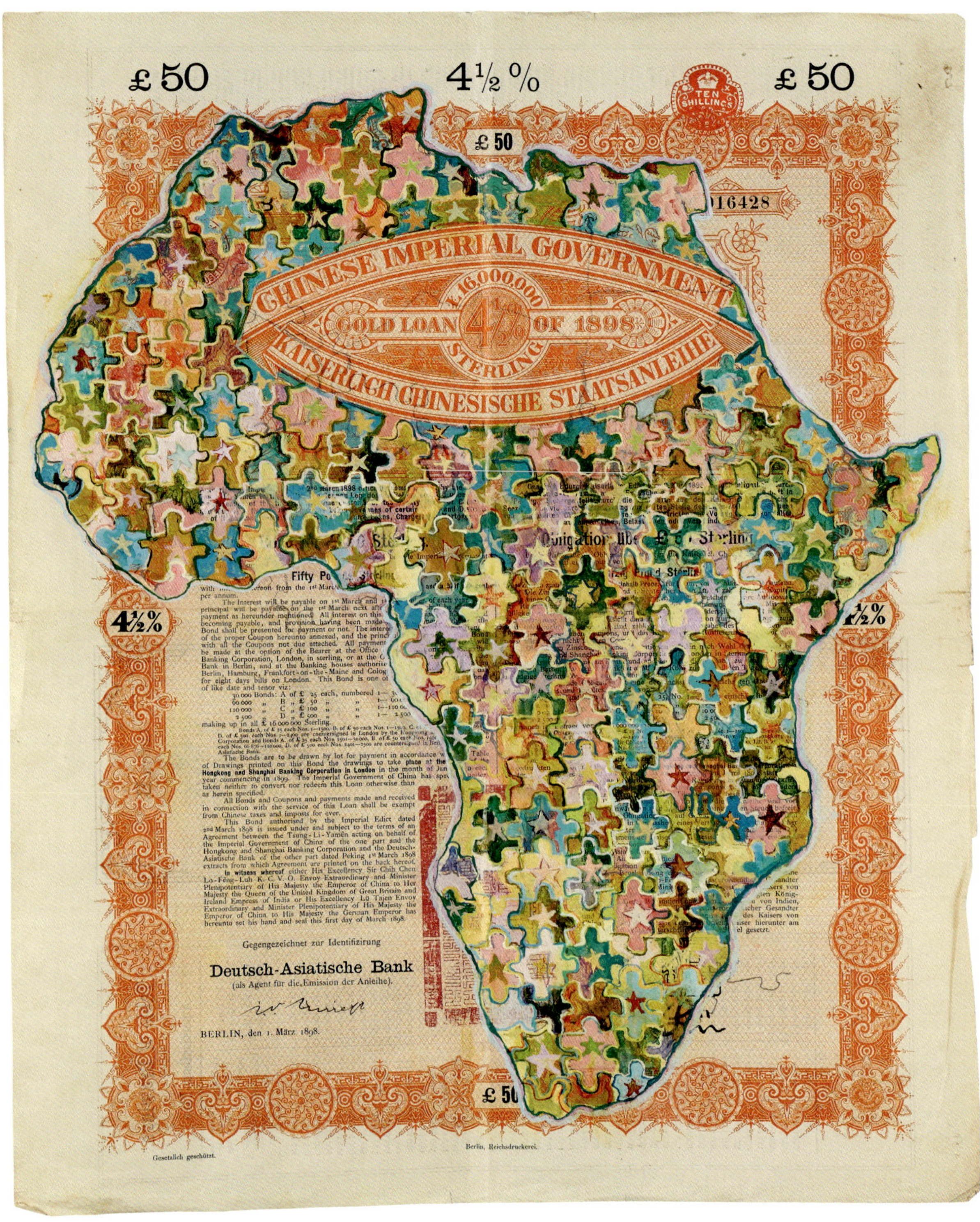

Hew Locke, *Chinese Imperial Gold Loan 11*, 2017.

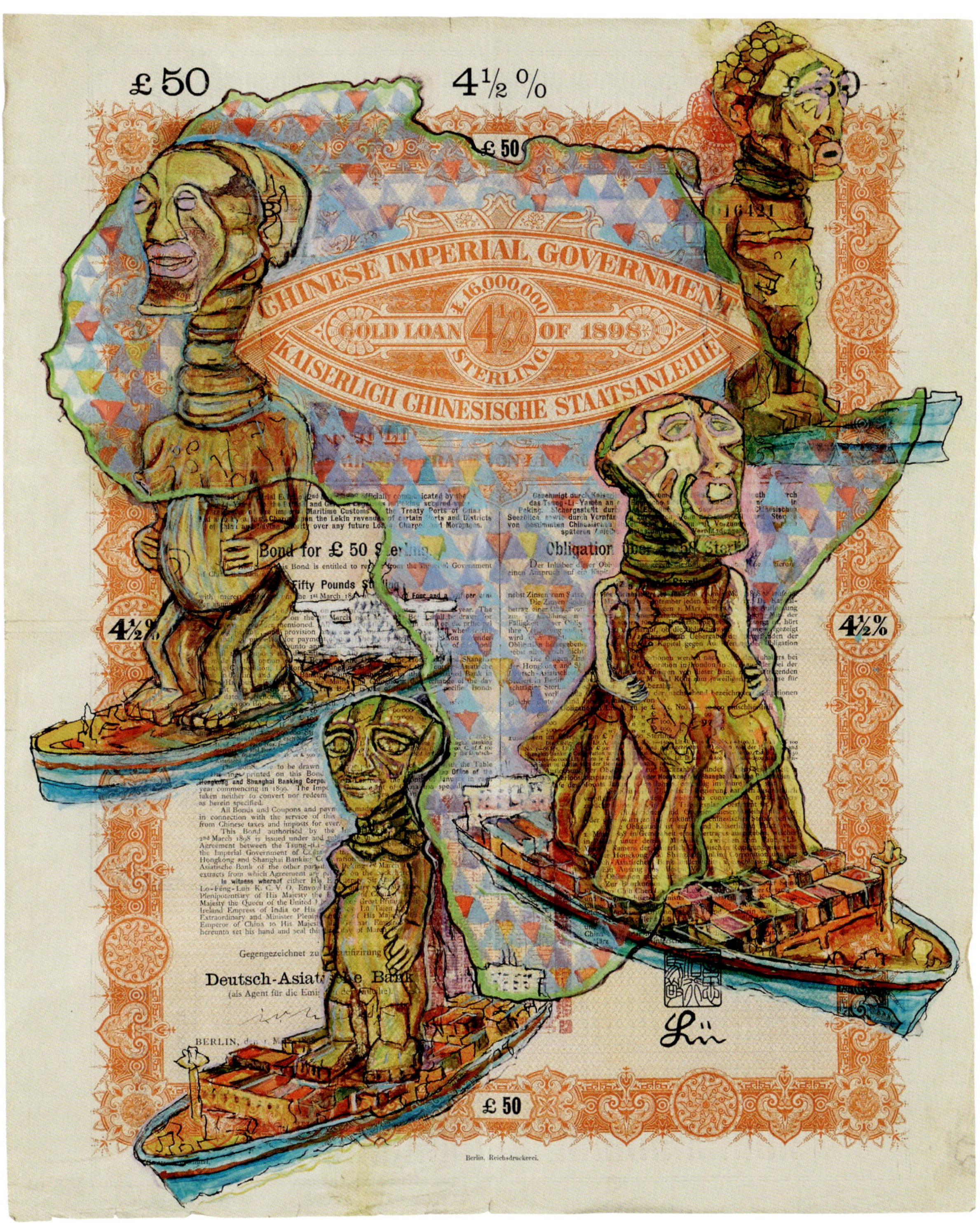

Hew Locke, *Chinese Imperial Gold Loan 14*, 2019.

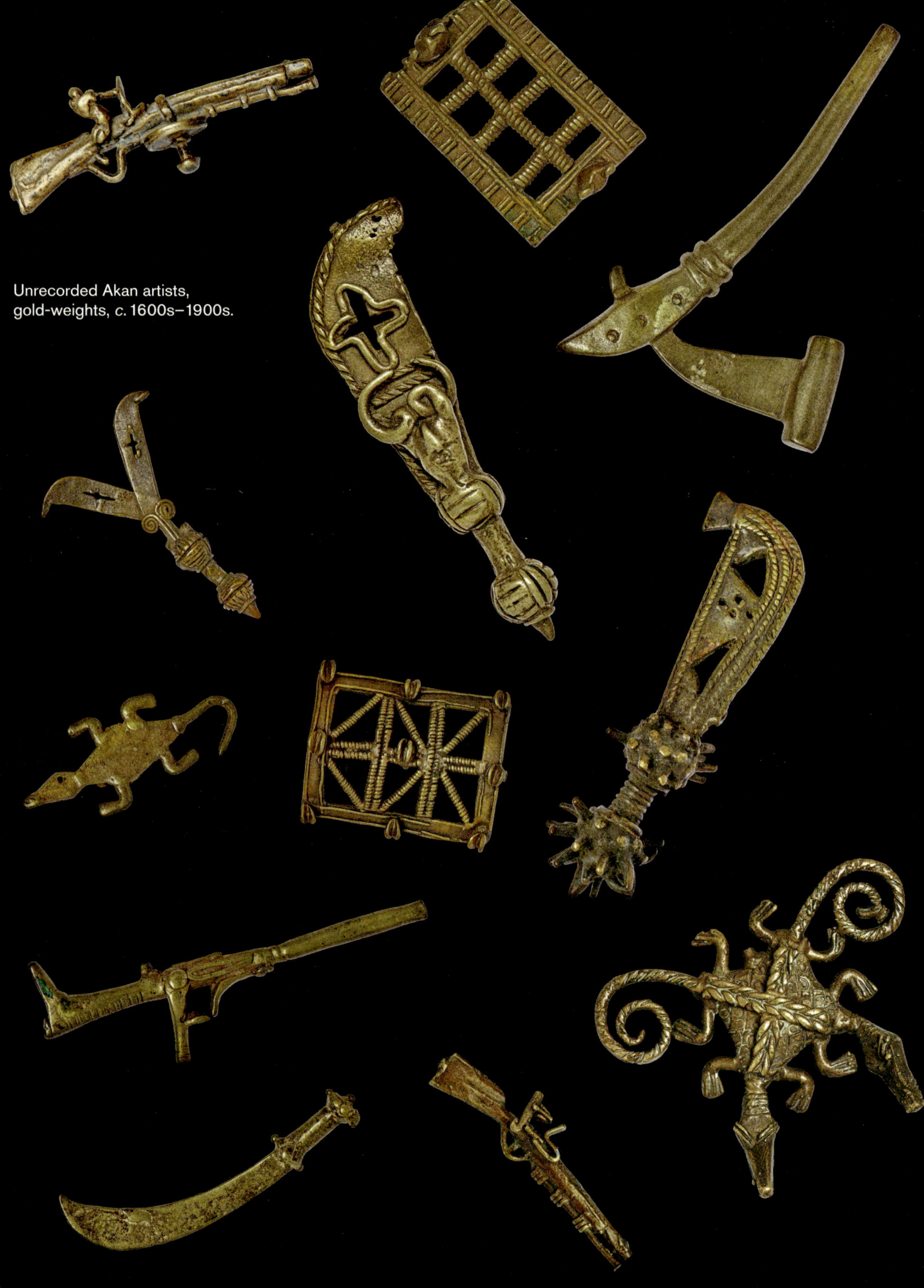

Unrecorded Akan artists,
gold-weights, *c.* 1600s–1900s.

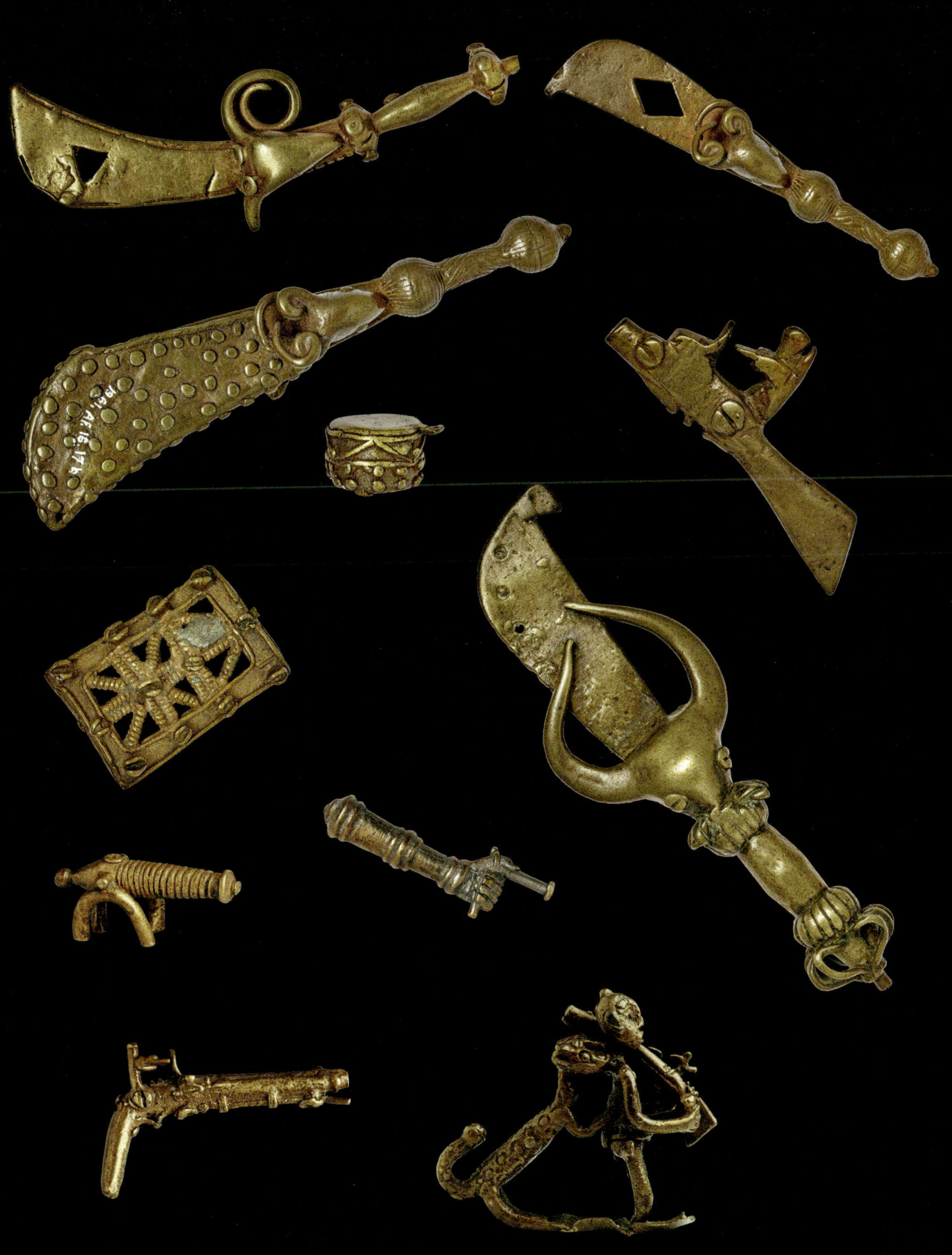

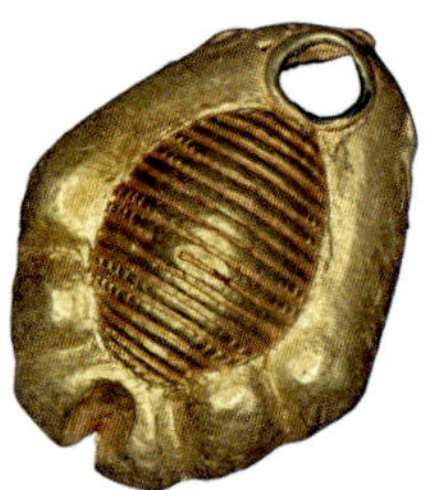

Unrecorded Akan artist, bead in the shape
of a cowrie shell, early 1800s.

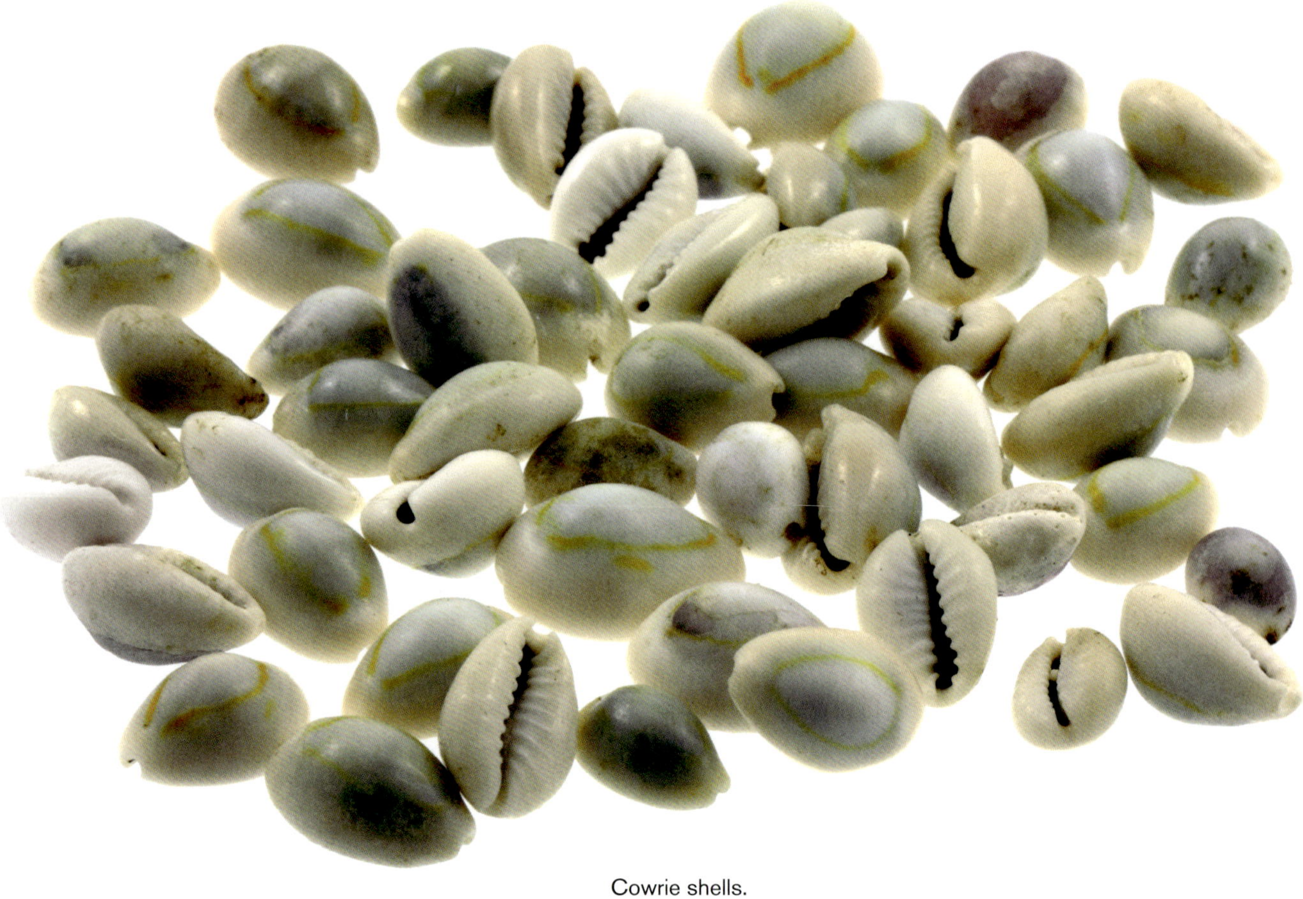

Cowrie shells.

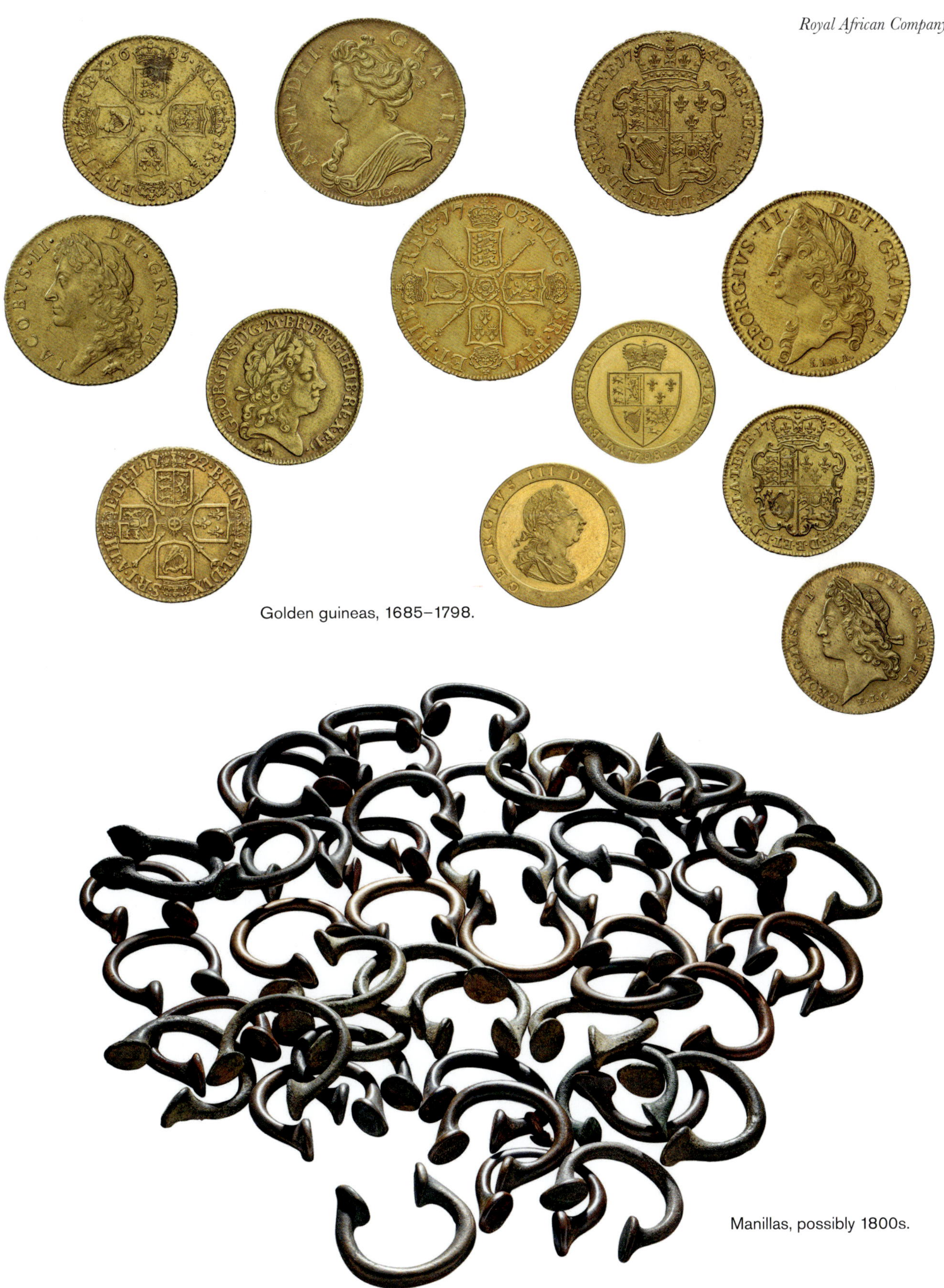

Golden guineas, 1685–1798.

Manillas, possibly 1800s.

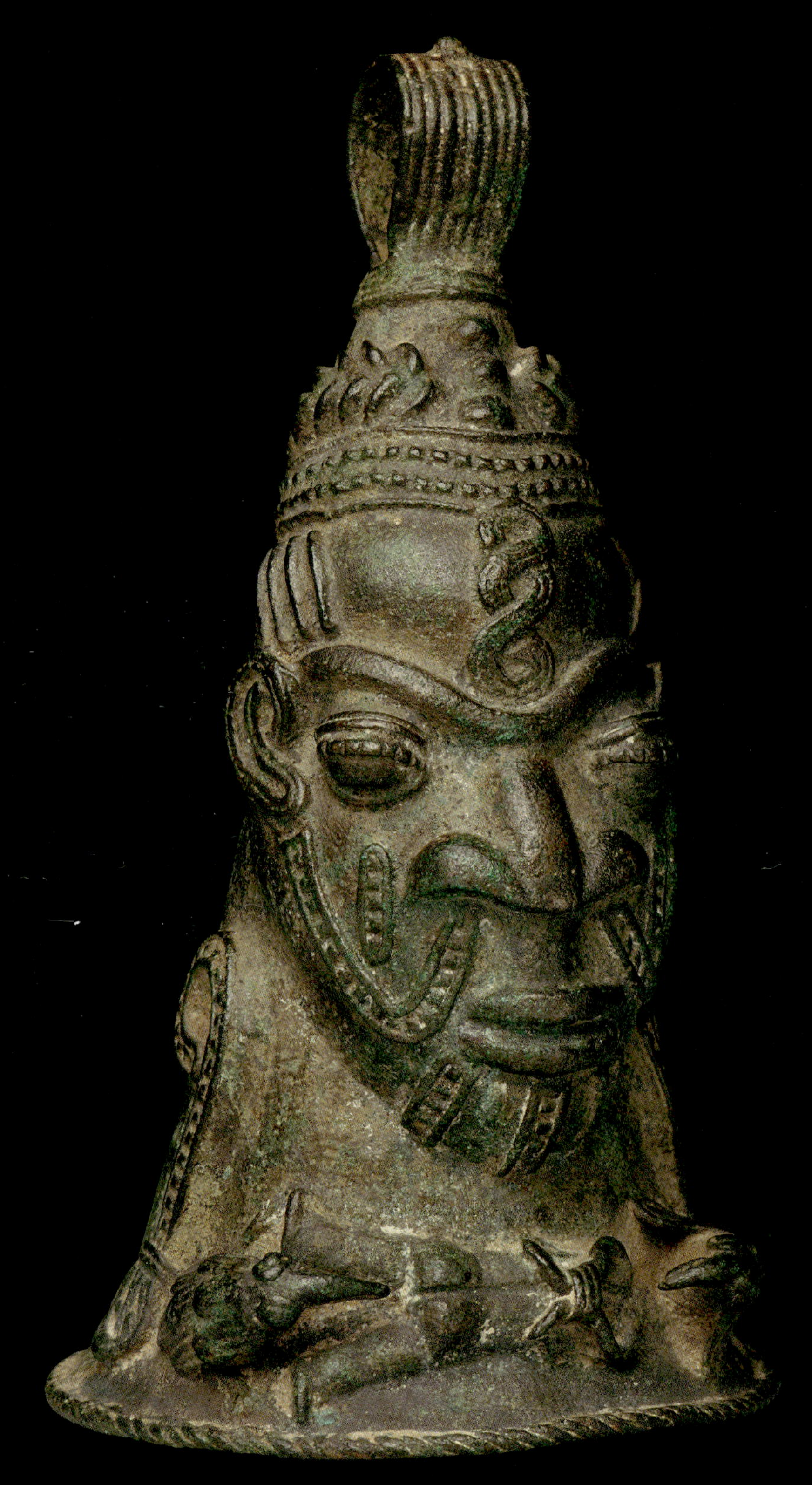

Unrecorded artist, Lower Niger Bronze Industries bell, 900–1500.

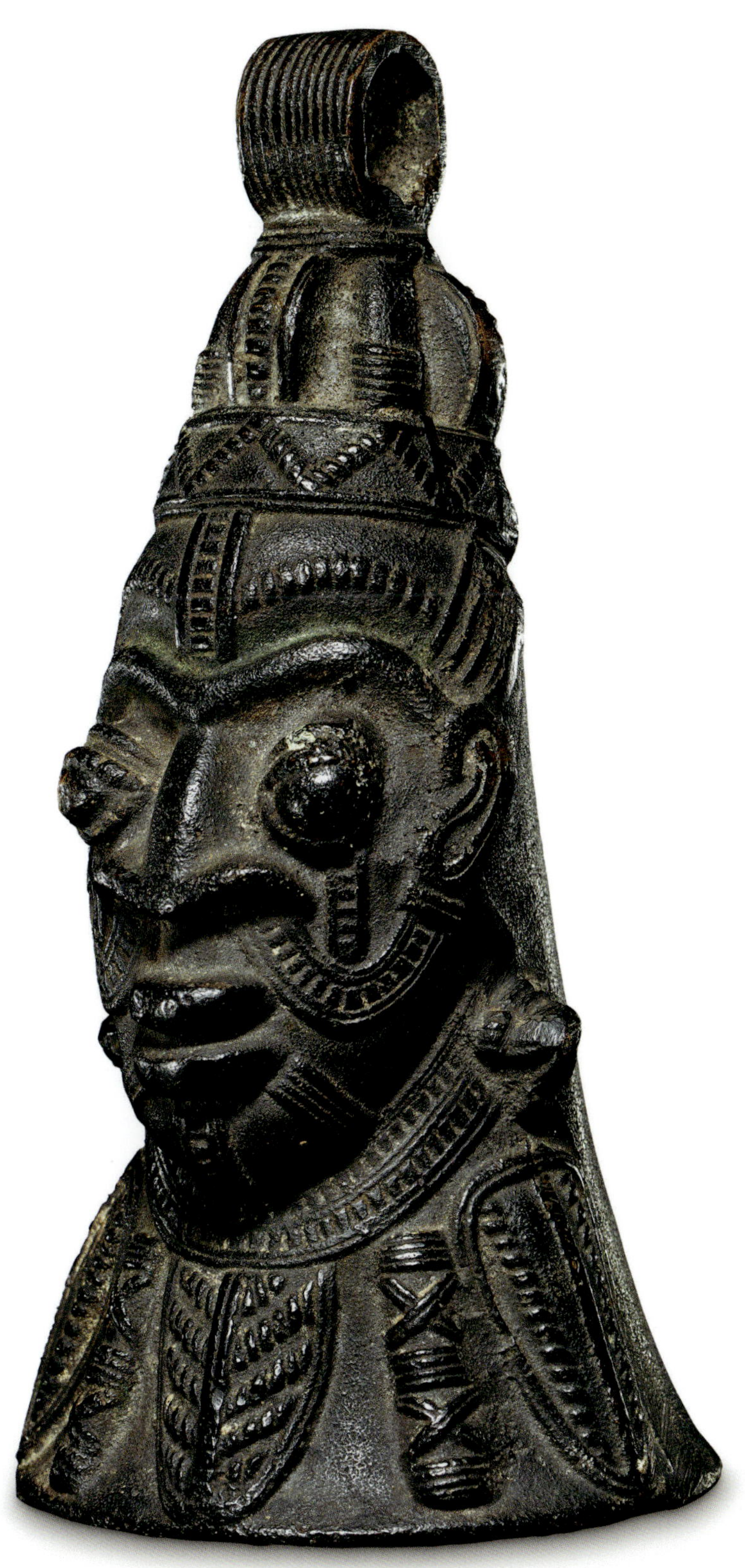

Unrecorded Birmingham artist, bell, 1892.

The violent ubiquity of enslavement in the Caribbean was reflected in art and material culture. The Italian painter Agostino Brunias worked mostly in Dominica and took commissions from plantation owners (pp. 79–81). His work highlights racial hierarchies, both between plantation owners and workers, and between free people. The British artist Augustus Earle (1793–1838) provides a sanitised view of planters inspecting enslaved people at a market in Rio de Janeiro (p. 83). Markets like this took place across the Caribbean, South America and the South of the USA.

The 'Barbados Penny' (p. 82) was commissioned by plantation owner Sir Philip Gibbes. Its design combines an English translation of the motto of the Prince of Wales – 'I Serve' – with the head of an enslaved African man, suggesting a satirical intention. This anti-abolitionist print (p. 82 and detail opposite) by Richard Newton (1777–1798) was published within six weeks of William Wilberforce's first motion for abolition. It imagines enslaved people merrily dancing before a seemingly happy crowd. In the foreground, an abolitionist concedes: 'I reform abroad those cruelties my own wild imagination has formed.' Another man responds, 'I have seen this repeatedly with my own eyes – they are a happy people.'

In 1833 Parliament abolished slavery within the British Empire and agreed to compensate enslavers for their 'loss' (p. 84), an estimated £20 million (around £16.5 billion in today's money). The 'medal for good conduct' (p. 83), struck after abolition, was designed to motivate workers to continue working on Henry De la Beche's Jamaican plantation. An 1863 carte de visite produced by an educational charity shows Rebecca Huger, who was emancipated aged 11 during the American Civil War, and evokes the lives of newly freed people (p. 85). Its caption still starkly states 'A Slave Girl from New Orleans.'

"It's a sick joke."

"The Caribbean has been described as a pigmentocracy – the lighter your skin, the higher up the tree you go. But it's more complex than that – class and religion come into it. These etchings talk about this complexity (pp. 79–81). The way people's hair is wrapped, the way they're dressed says something about their status. The image of the market in Rio is documentary (p. 83). It's what's both interesting about it, and truly horrible about it – it's so very casual. It's just an everyday slave market scene. 'No drama, nothing horrible, just everyday business.'

After slavery was abolished, slave owners didn't have a sudden change of conscience. They had to be bought off. Slave owners were able to claim compensation from the British government for the loss of their property – because enslaved people were property. The claim on p. 84 is from Guyana. Guyanese people have always known that the land is soaked in blood. Objects like the 'good conduct' medal are also horrendous (p. 83). The mere fact that somebody felt they had to produce an object of such quality says a lot about how horrific slavery was, and what you needed to do to persuade people to work for you after abolition.

The final objects in this section (p. 85) are a letter describing a runaway enslaved woman and a carte de visite featuring Rebecca Huger. When I went to New Orleans, I got fascinated by the history of quadroons and octoroons – people classified as one-quarter or one-eighth Black. To outsiders, this girl could 'pass' as white – but in a small society like New Orleans, everybody would know what her ancestry was. This shows how insidious racism is, how it lingers." HL

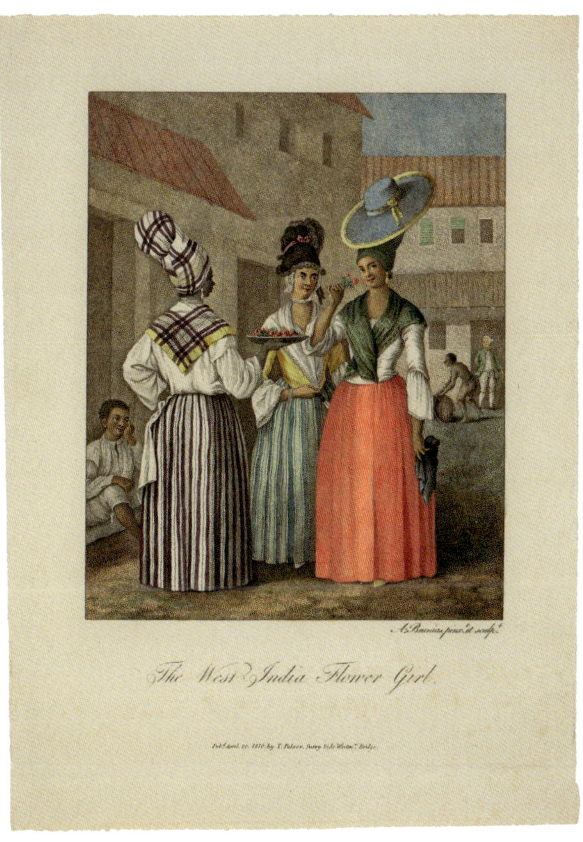

Agostino Brunias, A West Indian flower girl and two free West Indian women, 1810.

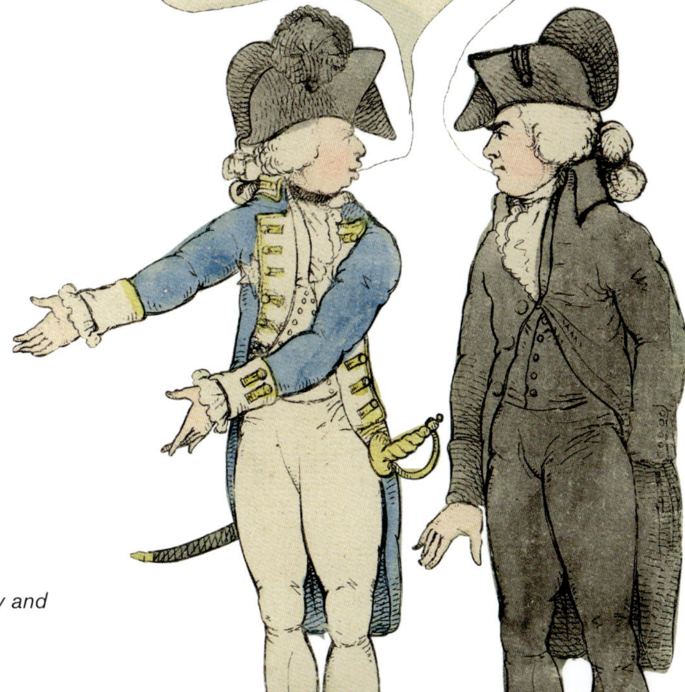

Detail, Richard Newton, *Cruelty and Oppression Abroad*, 1792.

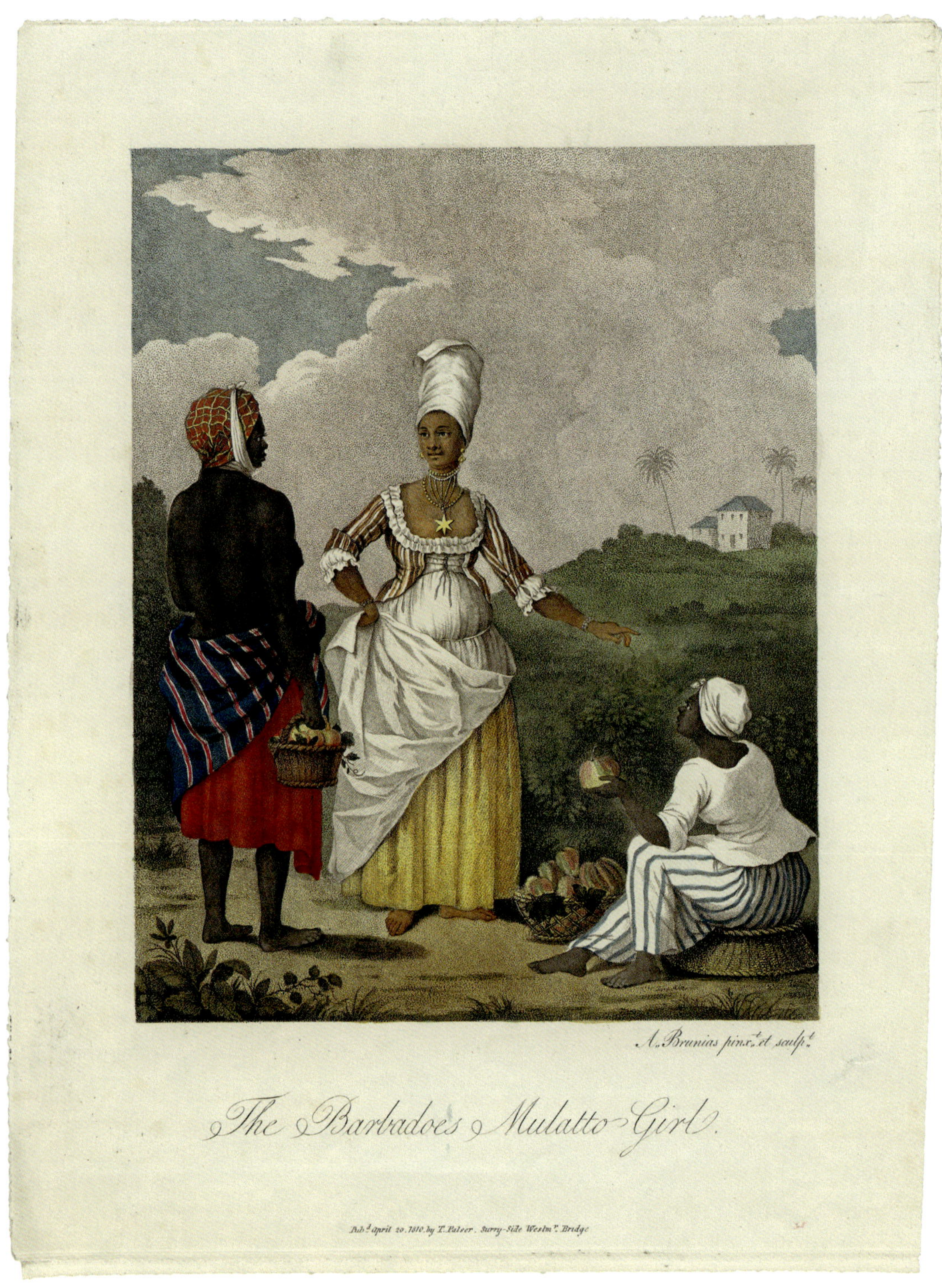

Agostino Brunias, Three West Indian women on Barbados, 1810.

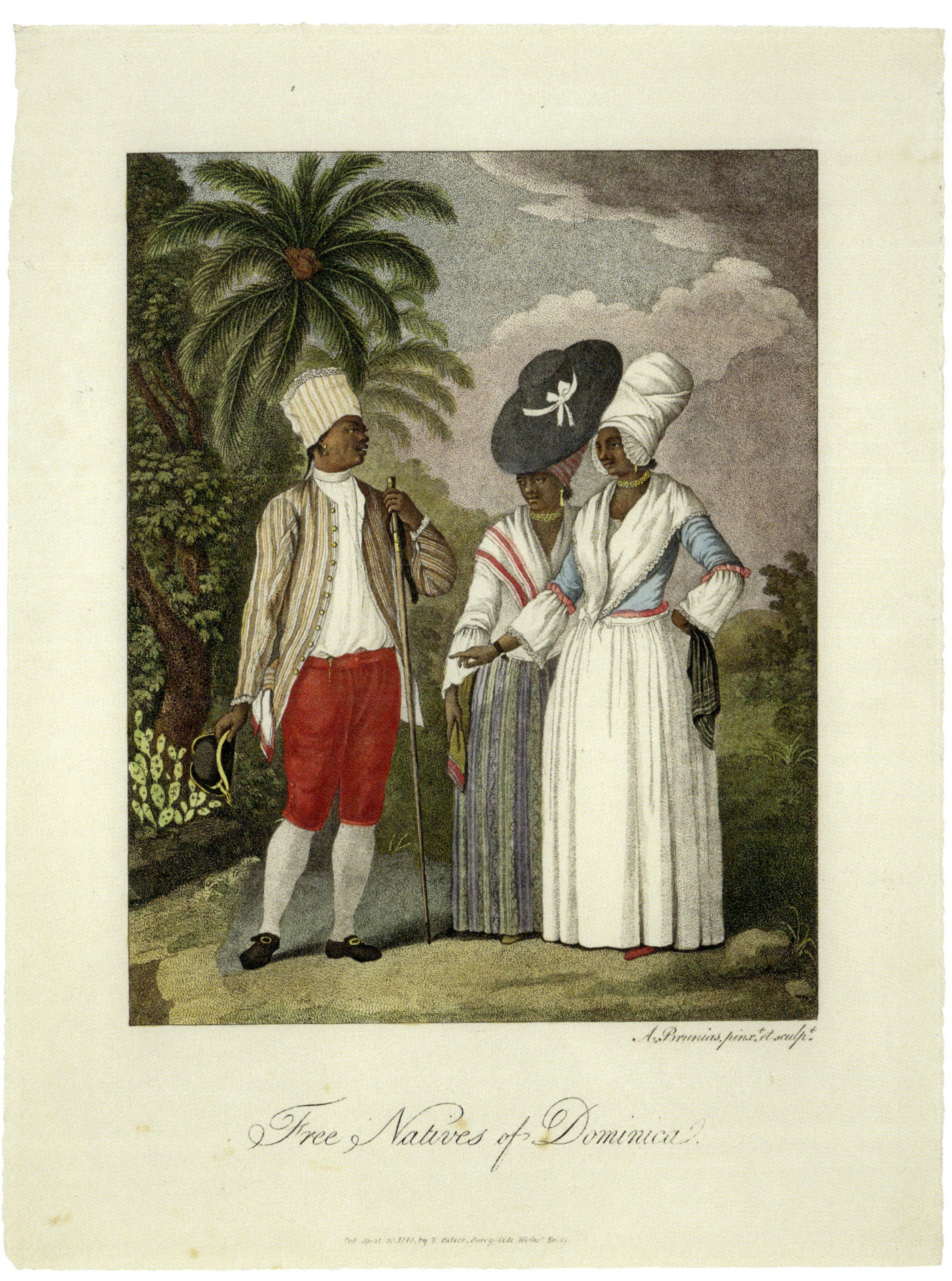

Agostino Brunias, Free West Indian Dominicans, 1810.

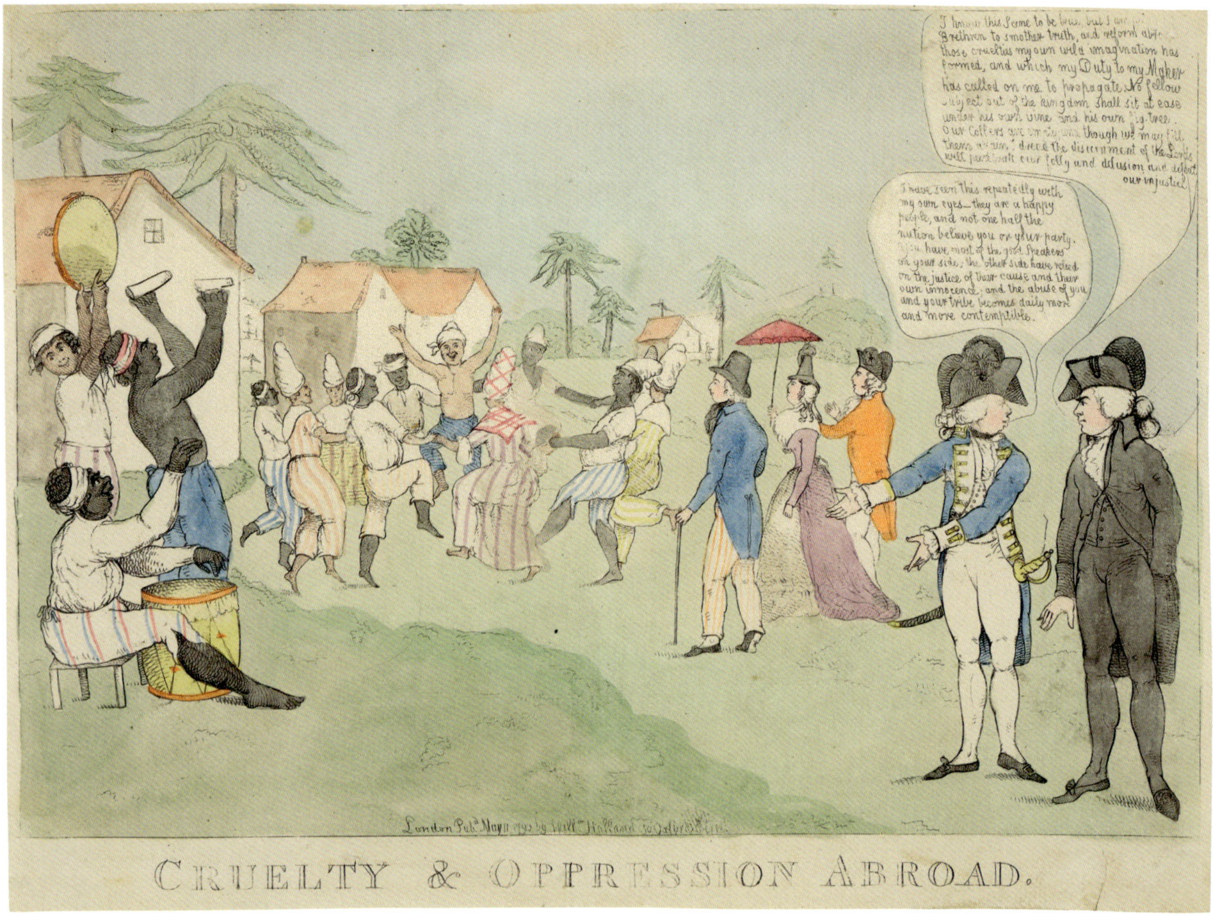

Richard Newton, *Cruelty and Oppression Abroad*, 1792.

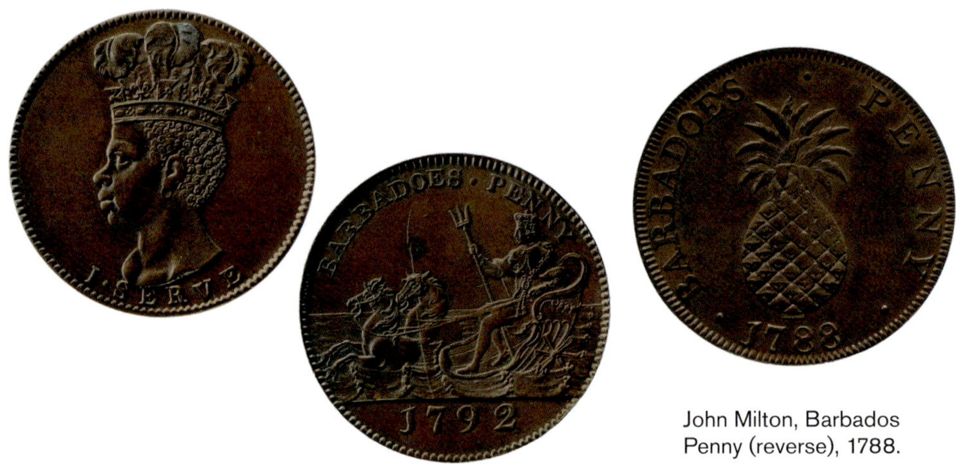

John Gregory Hancock Sr, Barbados
Penny (obverse and reverse), 1792.

John Milton, Barbados
Penny (reverse), 1788.

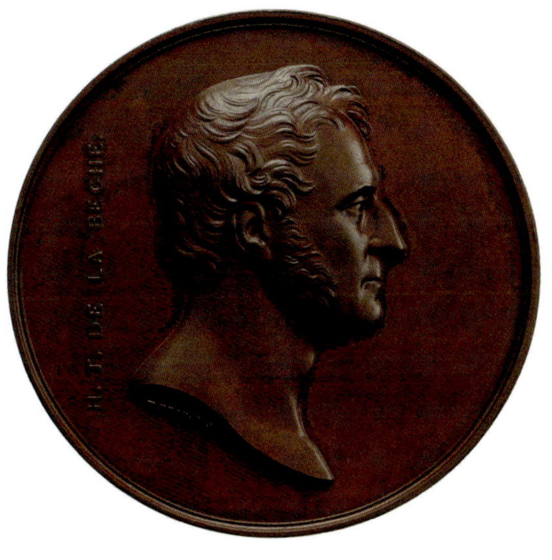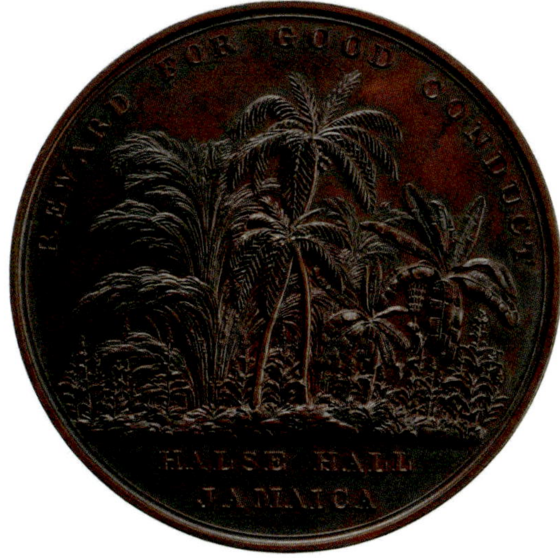

William Wyon, medal for good conduct, 1842.

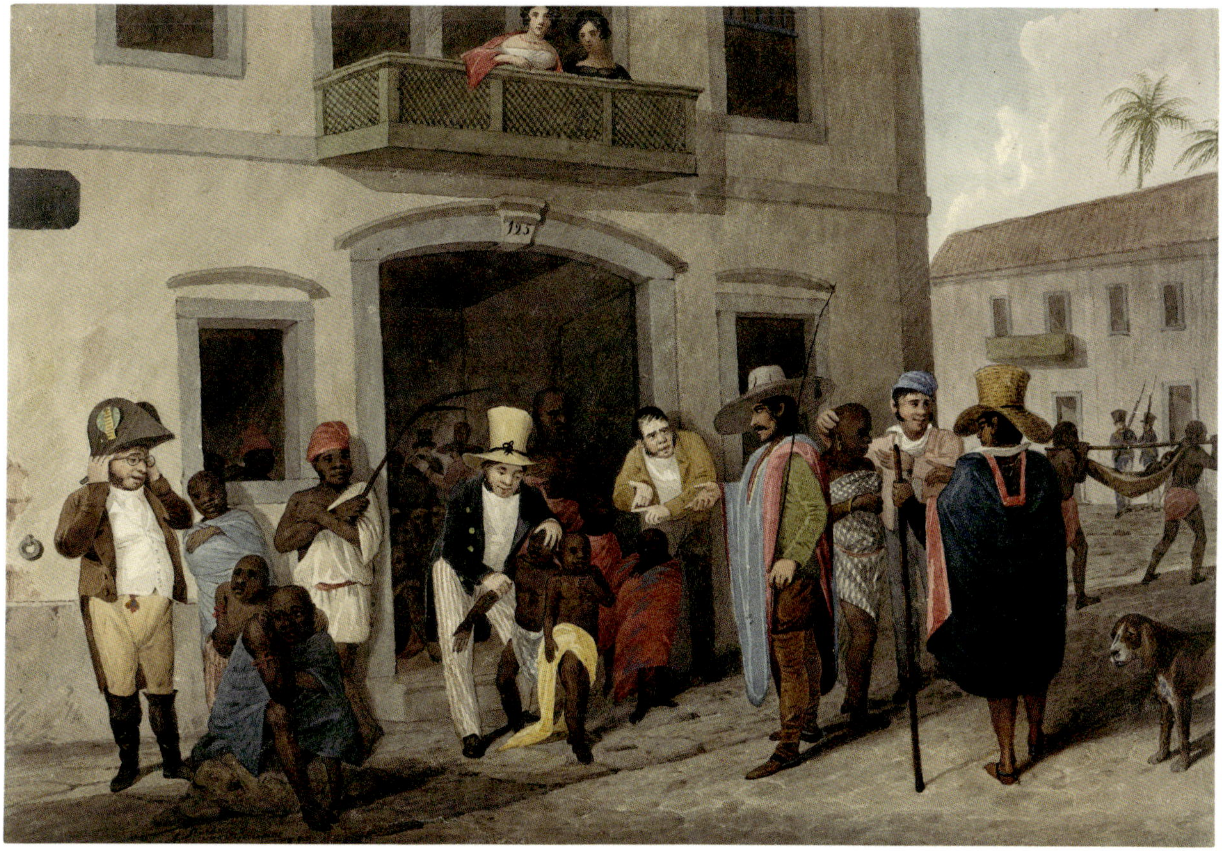

Augustus Earle, *Slave Market at Rio Janeiro*, c. 1823.

<table>
<tr><td rowspan="2">Name of Estate,
or
Domicile of Slaves.

Taymouth Manor

Essequebo</td><td colspan="6">*Guiana*

RETURN

Of the Number of Slaves and Estimated Value thereof, in each Class, in possession of *Thos. Daniel & Sons of Bristol by their*
on the 1st day of August, 1834.
Att^y. Chas. Bean</td><td colspan="1">N^o *2355*</td></tr>
</table>

TOTAL NUMBER of SLAVES						*185*

DIVISIONS.	No.	CLASSES.	Male.	Female.	Number.	Value in Sterling.
Prædial attached	1	Head People	—	—	*9*	*2070*
	2	Tradesmen	—	—	*2*	*36 0*
	3	Inferior Tradesmen	—	—	*3*	*300*
	4	Field Labourers	—	—	*112*	*19.14 0*
	5	Inferior Field Labourers	—	—	*37*	*3.5 30*
Prædial unattached	1	Head People				
	2	Tradesmen				
	3	Inferior Tradesmen				
	4	Field Labourers				
	5	Inferior Field Labourers				
Non-Prædial	1	Head Tradesmen				
	2	Inferior Tradesmen				
	3	Head People employed on Wharfs, Shipping, or other Avocations }				
	4	Inferior People of the same description				
	5	Head Domestic Servants				
	6	Inferior Domestics				
Children under Six Years of Age on 1st of August, 1834				—	*11*	*550*
Aged, Diseased, or otherwise Non-effective				—	*11*	*330*
					185	*26.280*

Claim for compensation, 1834.

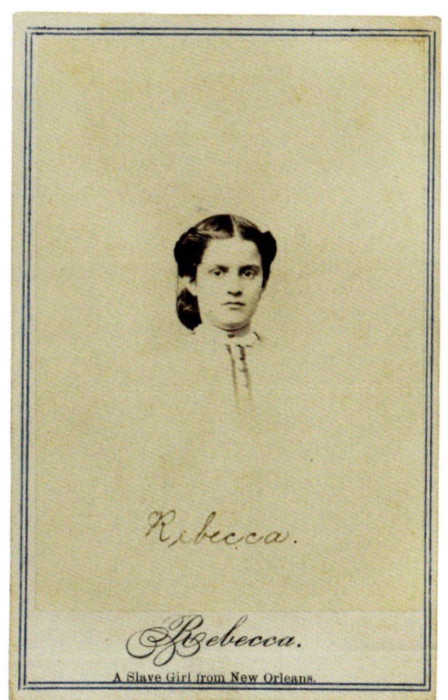

J.E. McClees, carte de visite of Rebecca Huger, 1863.

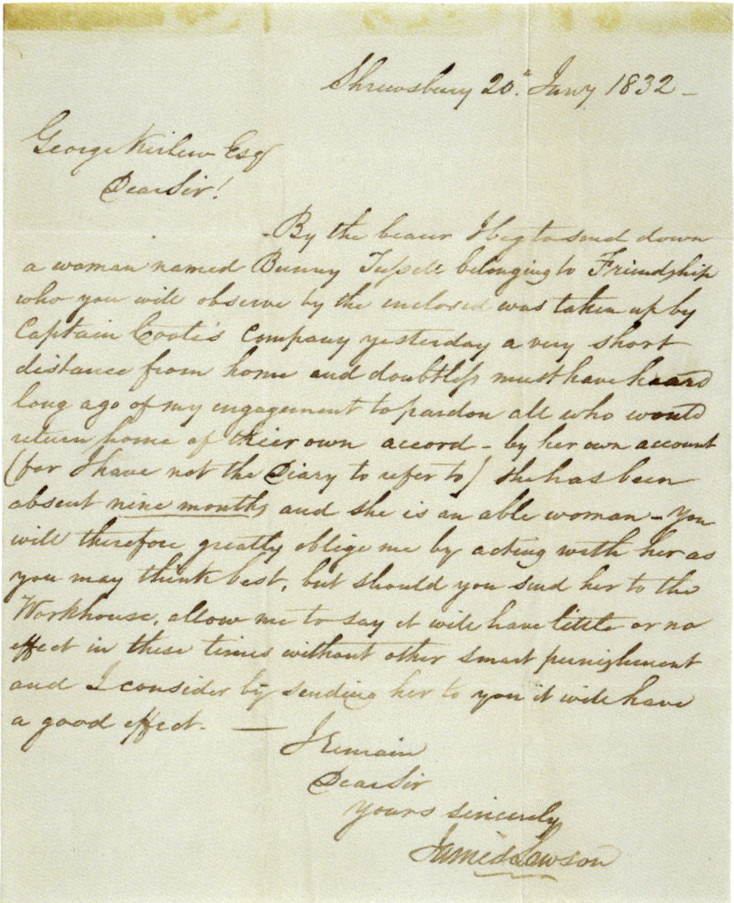

Letter describing the punishment of a runaway enslaved woman, 1832.

Shrewsbury 20 Jan 1832
George Kirlew Esq.

'Dear Sir! By the bearer I beg to send down a woman named Bunny Tussele belonging to Friendship who you will observe by the enclosed was taken up by Captain Coates' company yesterday a very short distance from home and doubtless must have heard long ago of my engagement to pardon all who would return of their own accord — by her own account (for I have not the diary to refer to) she had been absent <u>nine months</u> and she is an able woman — you will therefore greatly oblige me by acting with her as you may think best, but should you send her to the workhouse, allow me to say it will have little or no effect in these times without other smart punishment and I consider by sending her to you it will have a good effect.

I remain Dear Sir, yours sincerely,
James Lawson'

"This is like Heathrow and Harwich and Rotterdam all rolled into one. There was space in the East India Docks for 84 ships of 800 tonnes each, so that gives you an idea of the scale. These two docks encapsulate the whole Empire. These images (opposite) are missing the noise, the shouting and the calls. There was a quay nicknamed 'Blood Alley' by the workers, from people having to carry the sugar sacks, which took the skin off their backs and irritated them because of how sticky and sharp they were." HL

Commerce in London had nearly trebled during the 1700s, making up around three-fifths of the nation's trade, much of it flowing in via the Indian Ocean and the West Indies. East India Company ships transported tea, spices and textiles from Bengal and China, while West Indies imports included tobacco, sugar, rum, cotton and mahogany. These two prints (opposite) present a sanitised, peaceful image of the new West India and East India Docks in what is now the Isle of Dogs and Canary Wharf in London. The docks are bathed in morning light, emphasising their order and rationality, while ignoring the cost to people producing these commodities across the Empire and to those working in the docks.

"These two docks encapsulate the whole Empire."

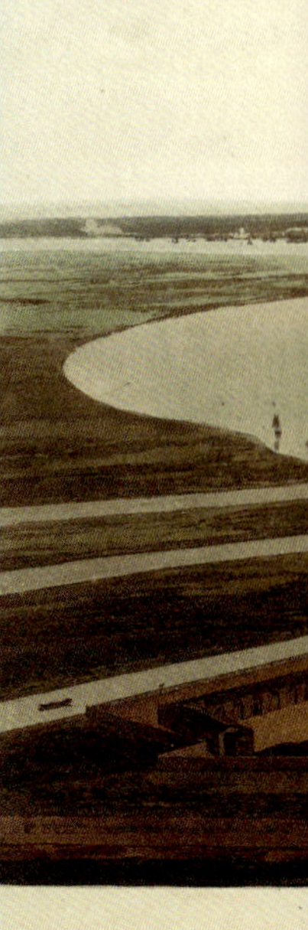

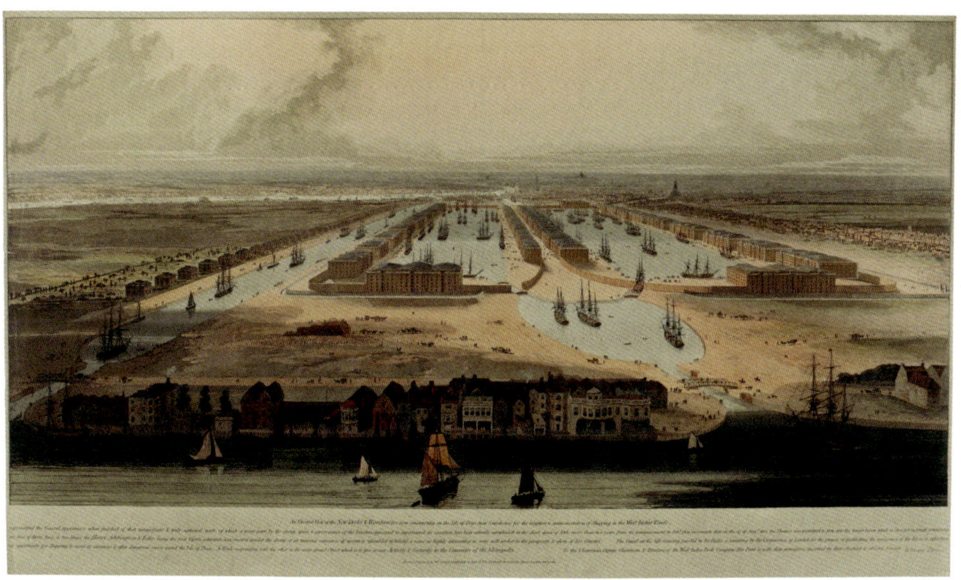

William Daniell, *An Elevated View of the New Docks & Warehouses now constructing on the Isle of Dogs near Limehouse for the reception & accommodation of Shipping in the West India Trade*, 1802.

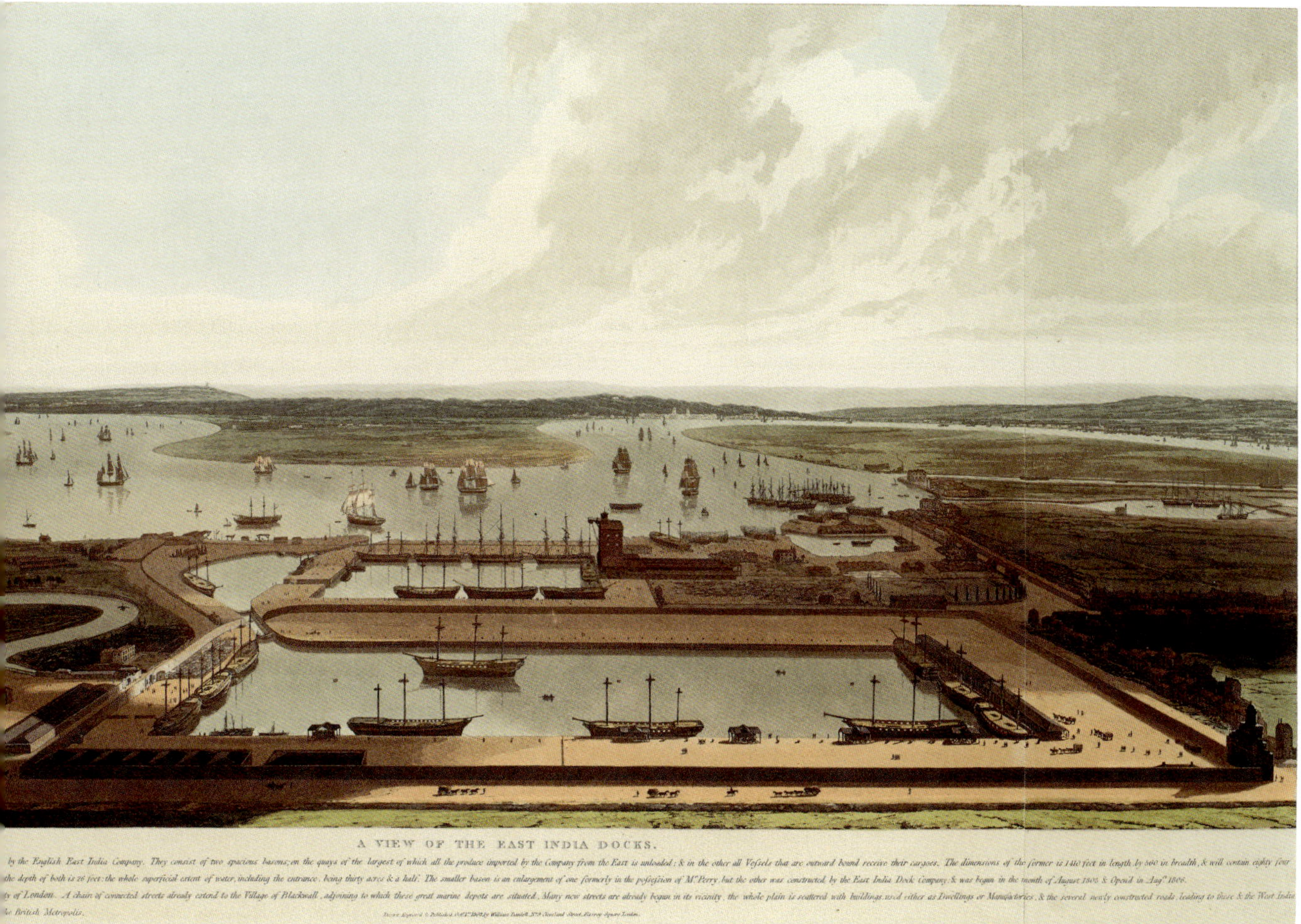

William Daniell, *A View of the East India Docks*, 1808.

Founded in 1600, the East India Company (EIC) traded from South Africa to India and all the way to eastern China and Australia. It colonised large parts of India and Southeast Asia and became the foundation for the British Empire in India. The objects in this section speak to the profiteering and bureaucracy of the EIC (p. 89) but also its quasi-regal self-image (pp. 96–7). This is echoed in two paintings of EIC commander Sir John Dalling (*c.* 1731–1798) and his officers watching a *nautch* (Indian dance) and being carried on raised beds in a military procession (p. 94).

In 1672 the EIC launched the Bombay Mint. At first, its currency had to compete against regional ones such as Mughal coins, but by the time of the Indian Uprising in 1857–8, it had taken over all local currencies. One British Indian quarter anna (p. 89) was equal to one sixty-fourth of an Indian rupee (p. 91). People could invest in the EIC by buying shares (p. 89). At its height the EIC was the largest corporation of its kind, dominating global trade between Europe, South Asia and the Far East, trading in and transporting commodities including salt and spices (p. 90), tea, cotton, silk, diamonds (p. 91) and opium. The seal-die on p. 97, inscribed in Persian, commemorates the EIC's 1765 Treaty following its victory over the Mughal Emperor Shah Alam II (1728–1806), which forced him to allow the EIC to collect taxes from territories such as Bengal, India's wealthiest province.

Several pieces in Hew Locke's *Share* series, such as his work *Middleton & Tonge Cotton Mill*, respond to events during British colonial rule of India (pp. 92–3, 95). In 1929 the Indian National Congress called for a boycott of British cotton goods, which were flooding their market.

"An empire within an empire."

"By 1803 [when it took down the Mughal Empire] the EIC had a private military force twice the size of the British army. The EIC essentially functioned as a sovereign state for a long time before it was finally dismantled. Financial documents show the extent of this economic extraction. The numbers that are involved here, it's hundreds of thousands of pounds. That's tens of millions in today's money. Somebody described the EIC as an empire within an empire … India was the richest country in the world before they got involved and they just gutted the economy. India is an economic powerhouse today, but the history of the EIC still rankles … When Indians think of the EIC, they don't think of nice romantic costume dramas.

The portrait of Jonathan Duncan at his desk is an Indian miniature by a Mughal-trained artist (p. 89). I wanted to include this because it shows the bureaucracy of Empire. Something so casual and small, almost banal, but it's crucial because it shows somebody plotting how to be in charge; it's about control. The maps and documents signify his administrative power over nearly 600 princely states. His job was to keep these 'natives' in line.

The *Share* certificates include navigation and railways companies, with bulk carriers and cargo ships, to talk about the trade that India supplied, even after Independence. People say, 'Oh, but the British gave India Shakespeare and the railway,' but the railway was created to move troops and goods around, not to benefit Indians. The Steel Corporation of Bengal was a British company meant to rival Tata Steel, run by local employer Jamsetji Tata. History flips around, and Tata Motors eventually bought the British company Jaguar and the old British Steel plant in Port Talbot." HL

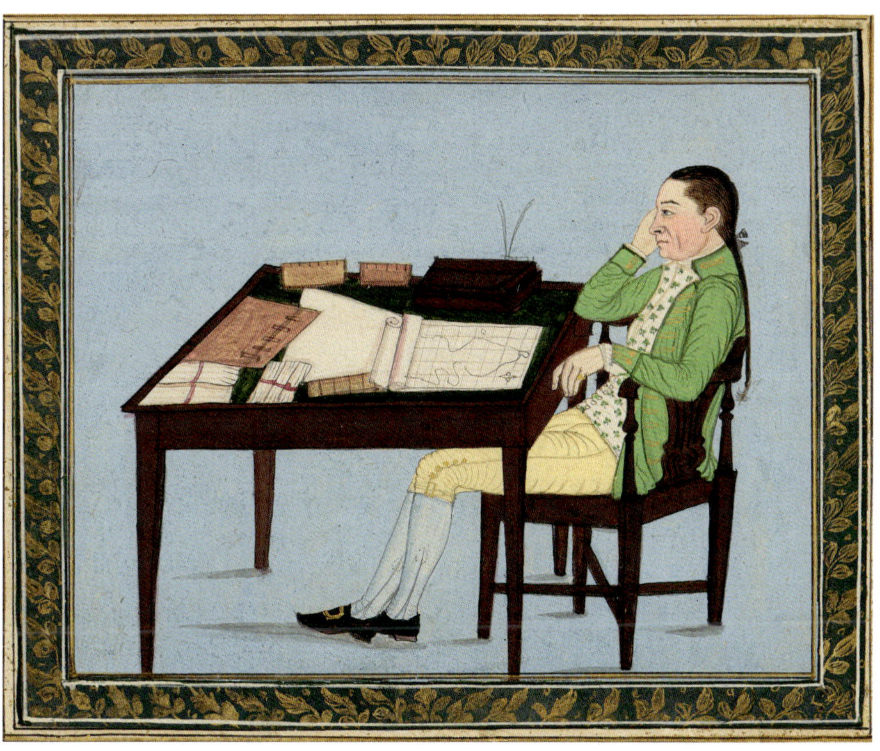

Unrecorded Indian artist, *Portrait of Jonathan Duncan*, c. 1800.

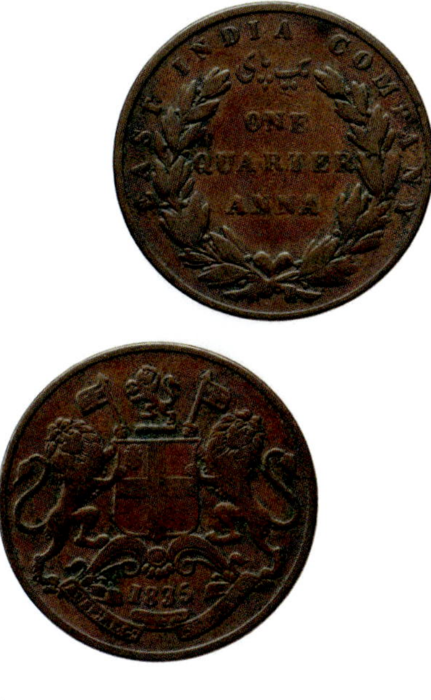

Quarter anna coin, 1835.

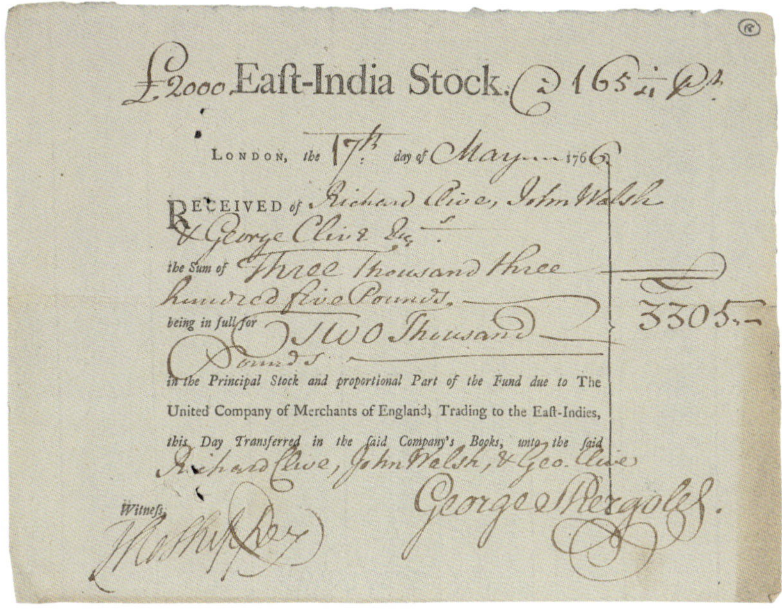

East India Company share certificate, 1766.

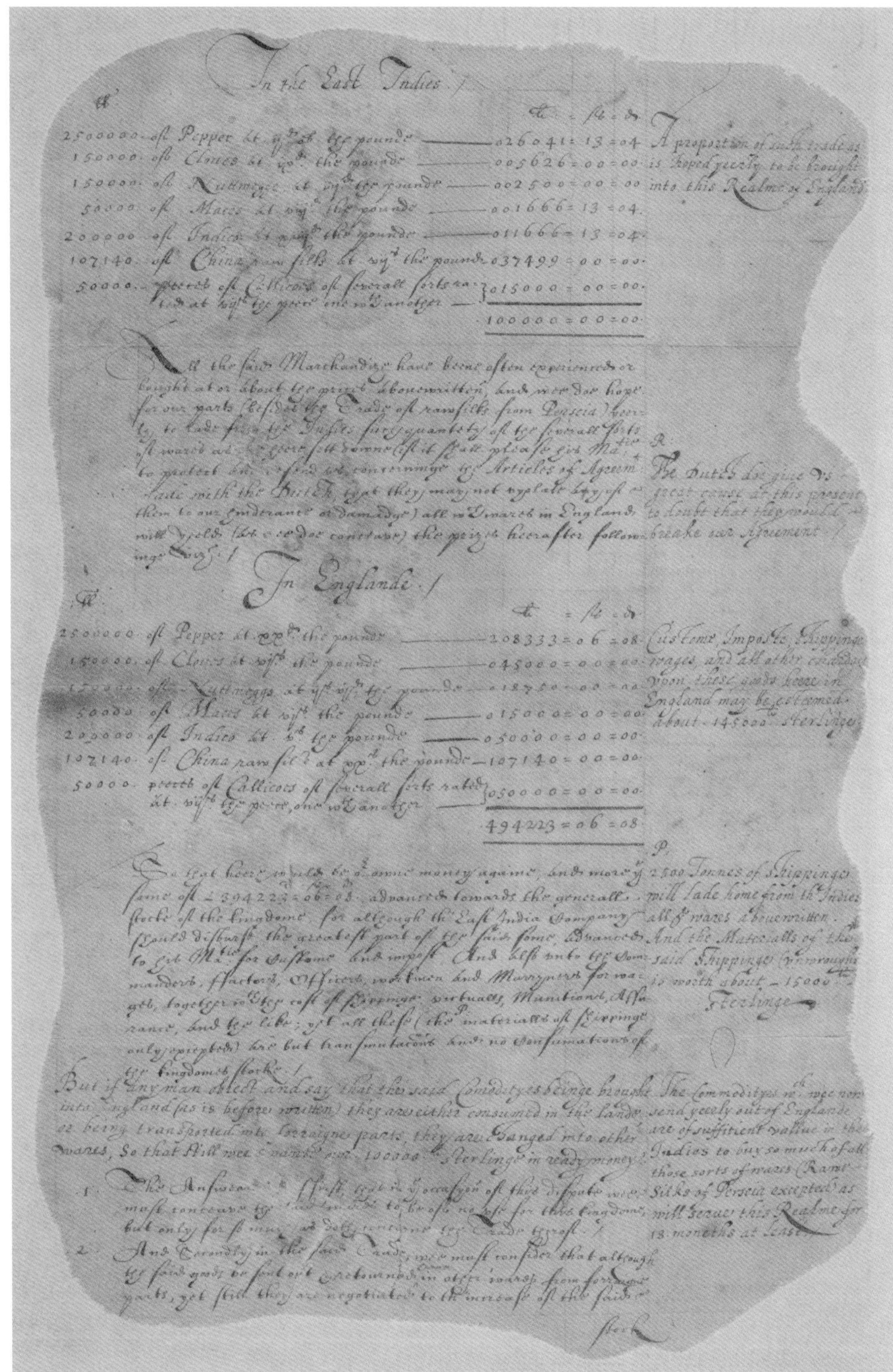

 East India Company estimate of trade in spices, textiles and indigo, 1621.

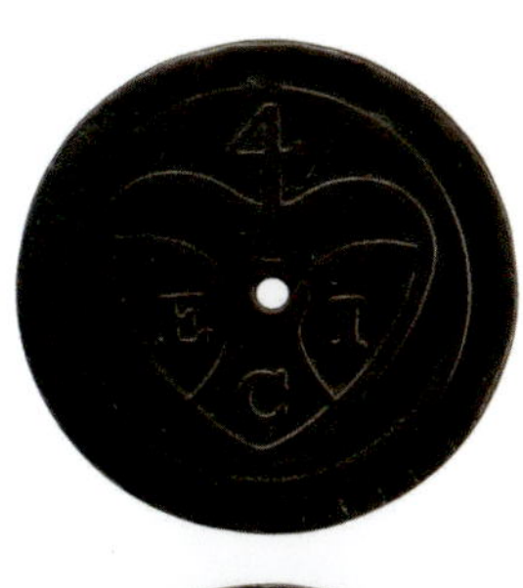

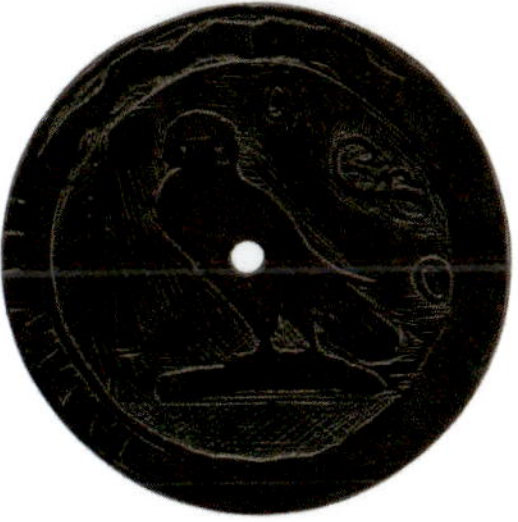

Engraved East India
Company coin, 1786.

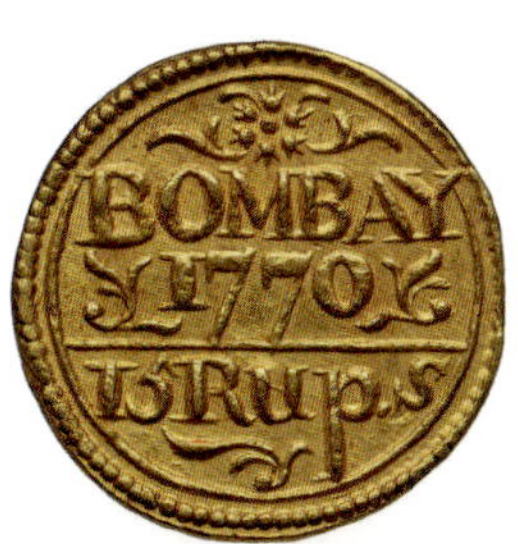

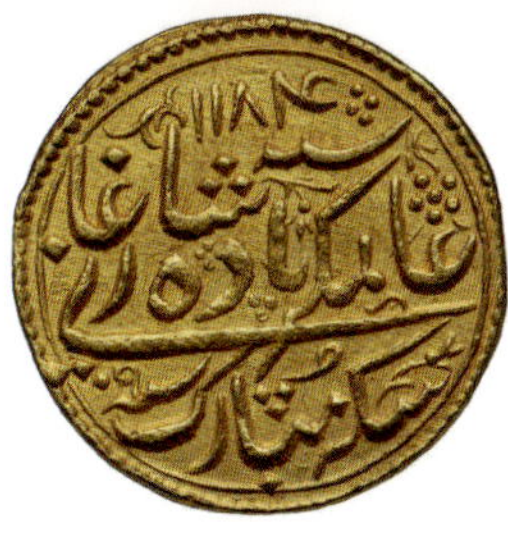

15-rupee coin, 1770.

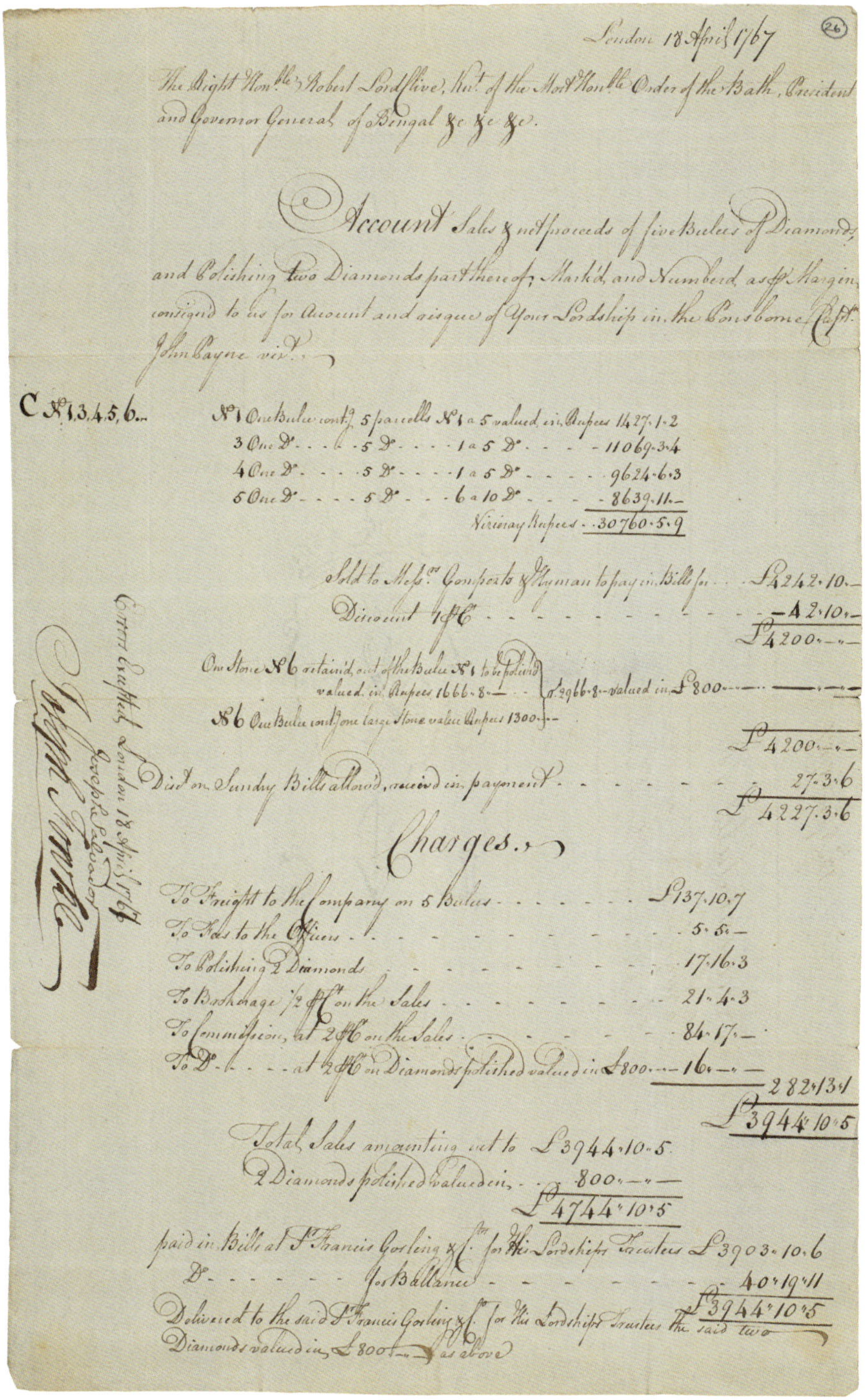

Accounts for diamonds imported by Lord Clive, 1767.

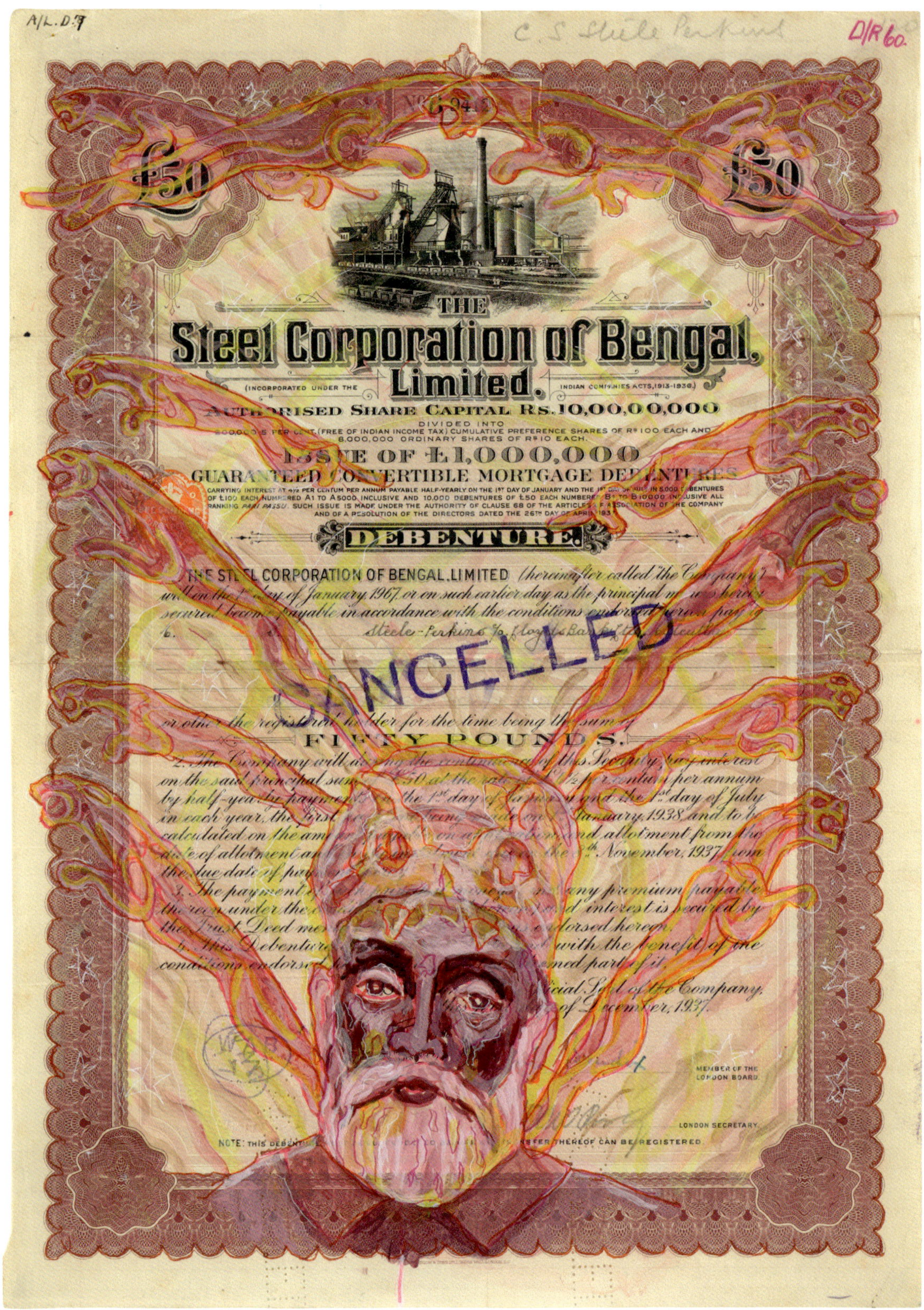

Hew Locke, *Steel Corporation of Bengal 1*, 2009.

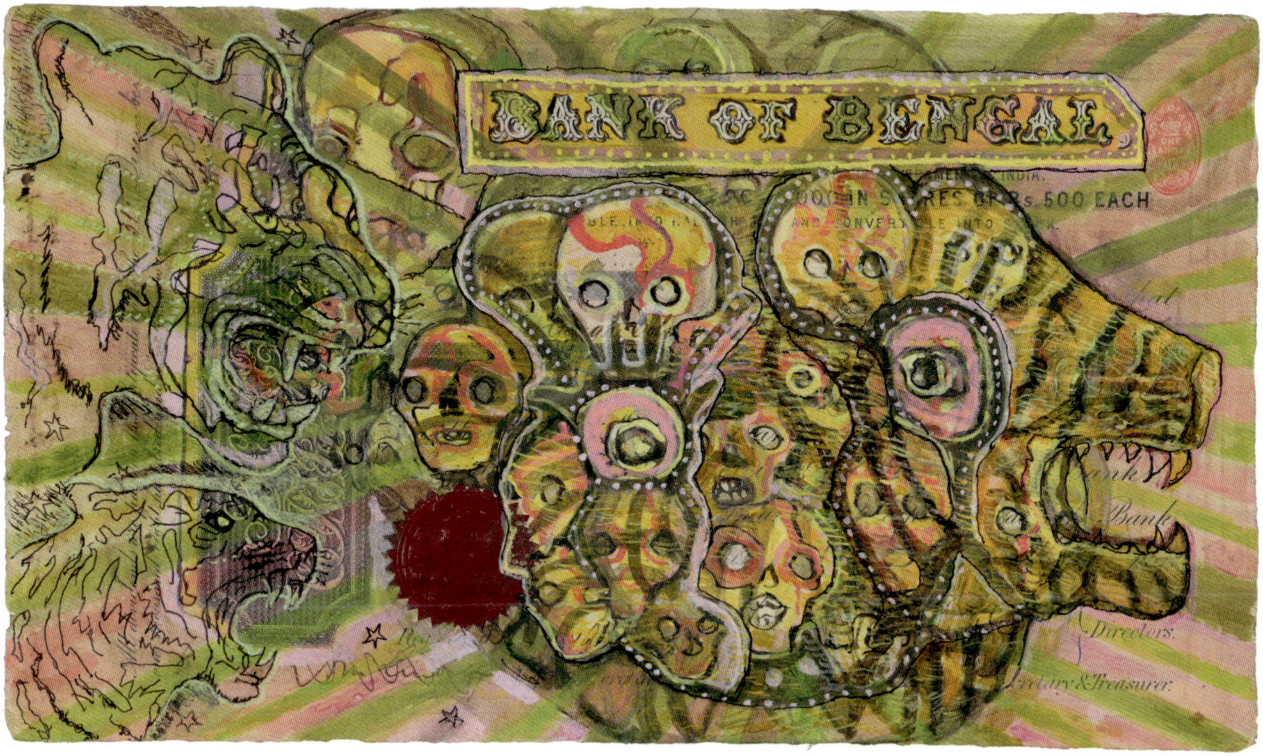

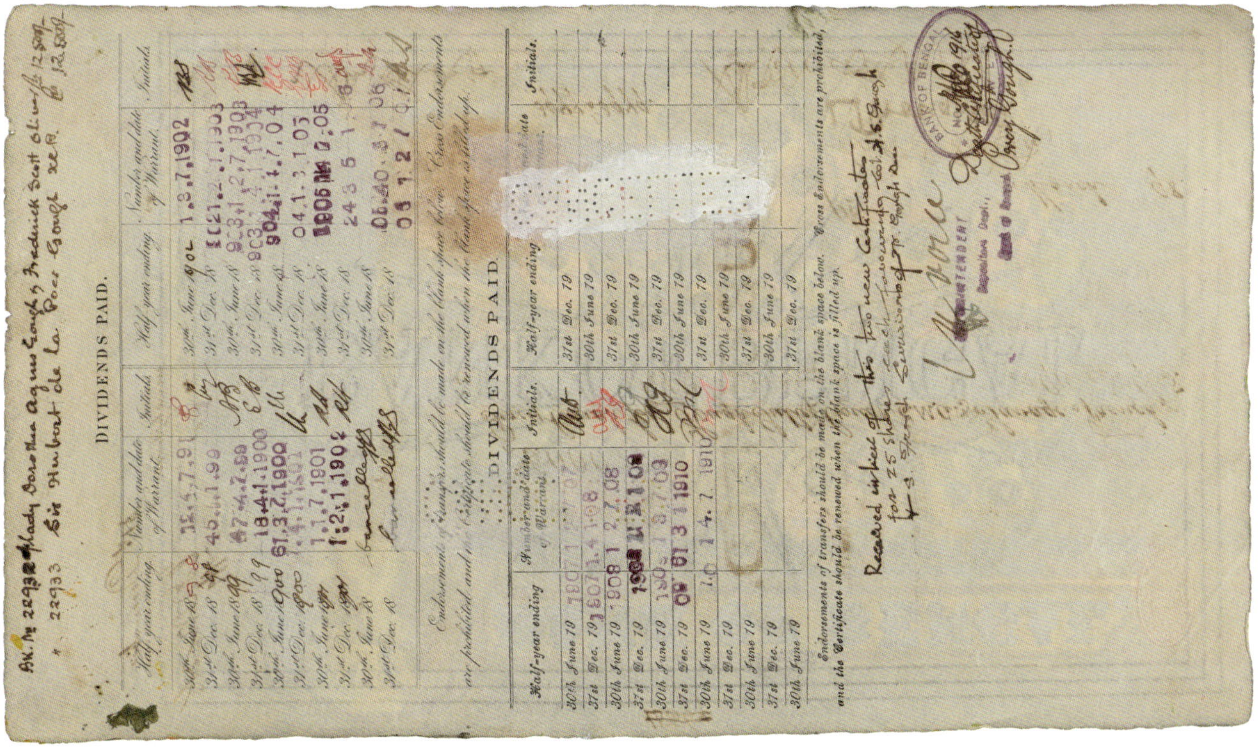

Hew Locke, *Bank of Bengal* (front and reverse), 2012–24.

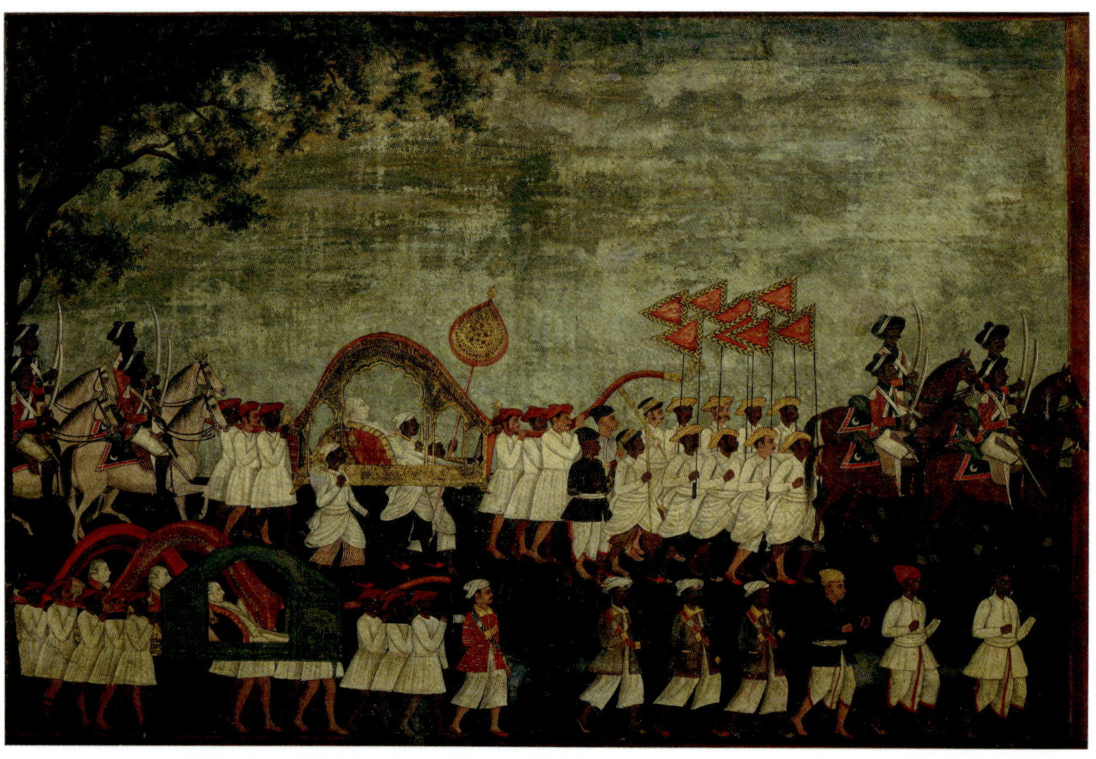

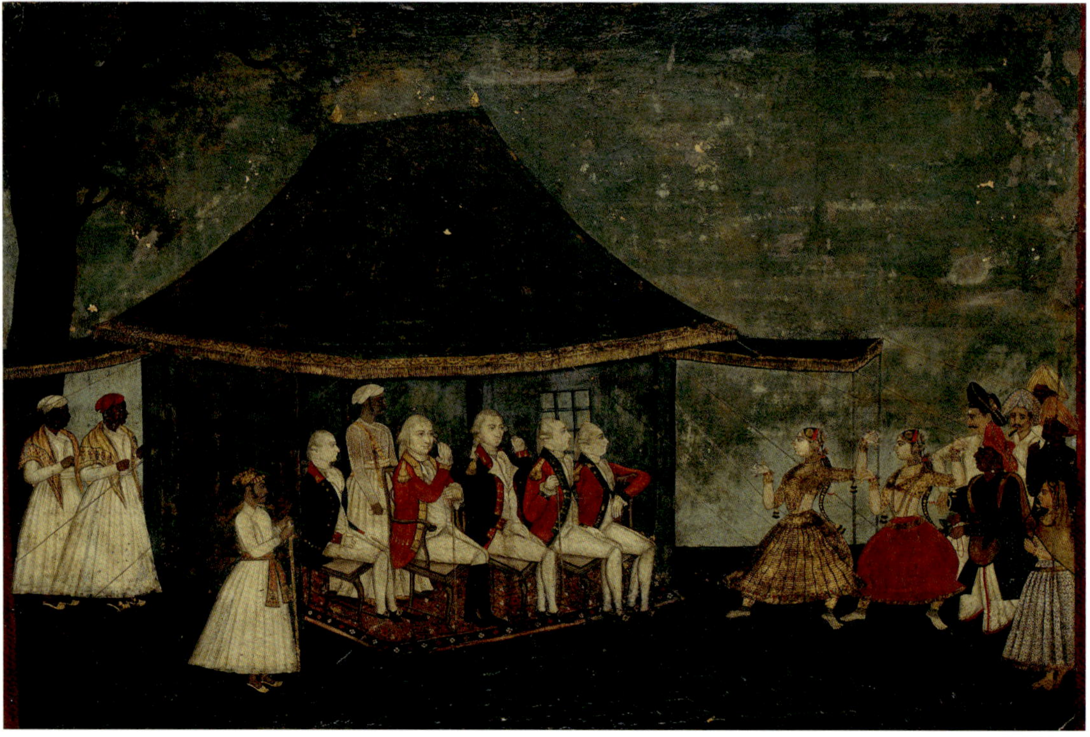

Unrecorded Company School artist, Sir John Dalling and fellow officers, *c.* 1785−6.

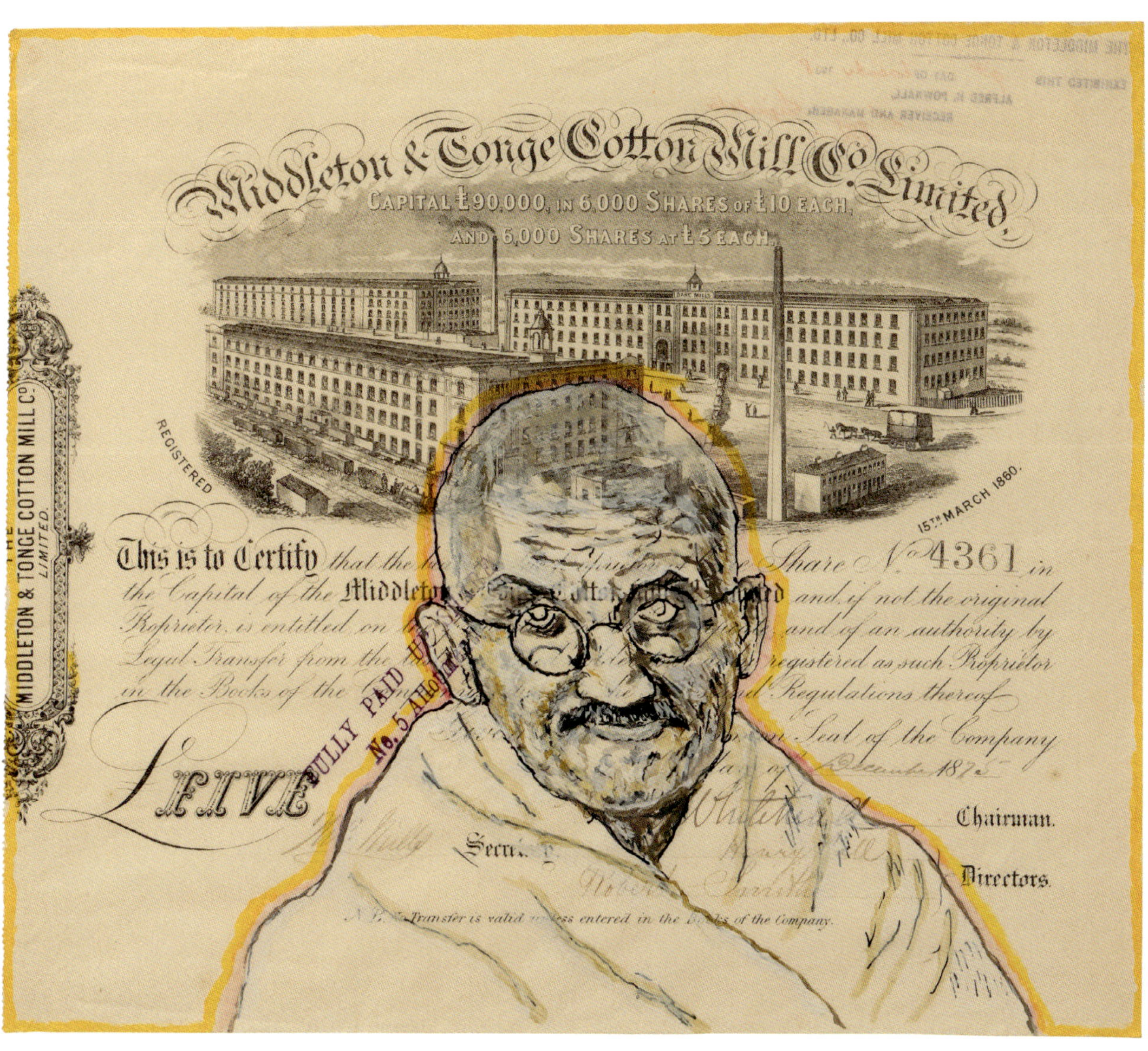

Hew Locke, *Middleton & Tonge Cotton Mill*, 2023.

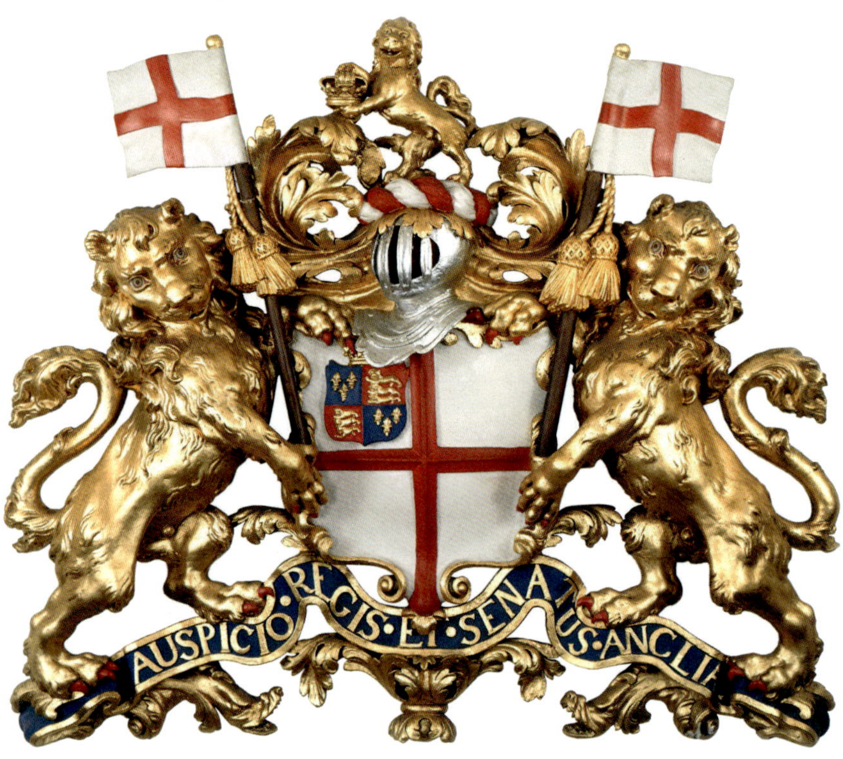

Unrecorded artist, coat of arms of the East India Company, *c.* 1730.

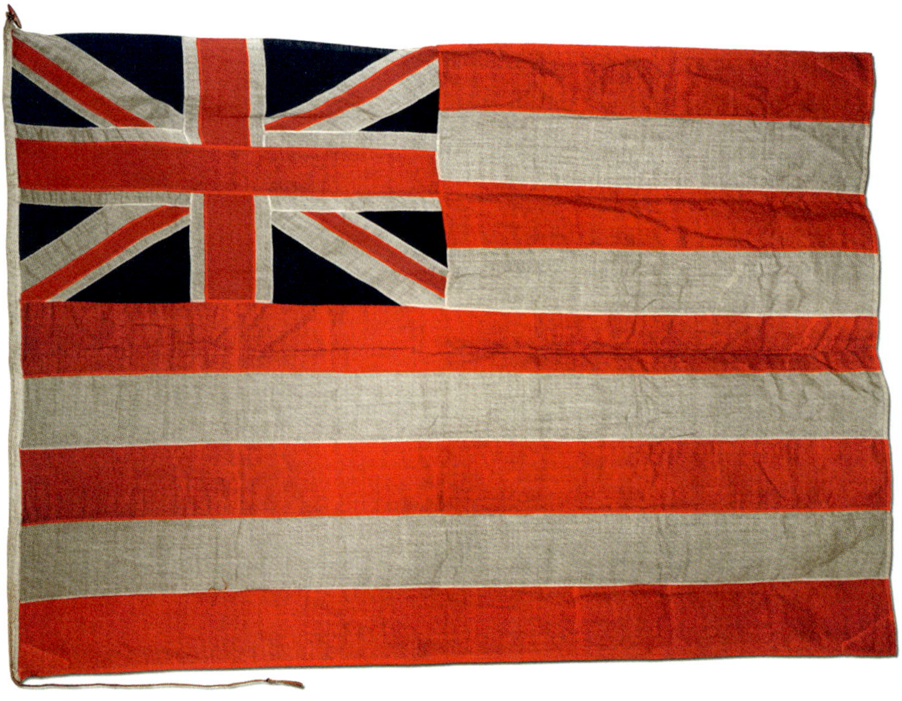

Honourable East India Company ensign, *c.* 1911 (modern copy).

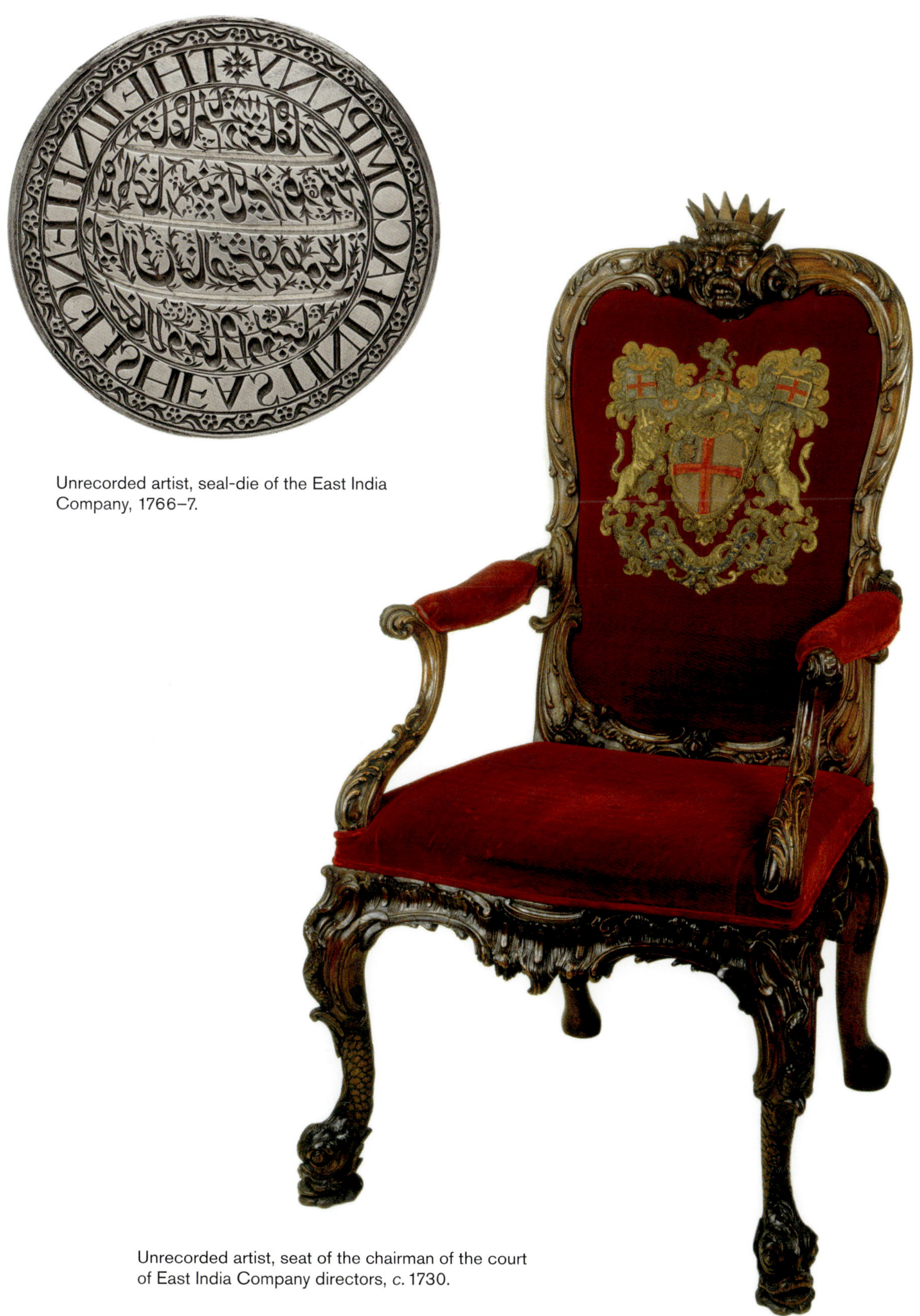

Unrecorded artist, seal-die of the East India
Company, 1766–7.

Unrecorded artist, seat of the chairman of the court
of East India Company directors, *c.* 1730.

The Koh-i-Noor is one of the largest cut diamonds in the world. It has long been a symbol of power and status and has changed hands many times, often as a result of violence and conquest. Several countries have laid claim to the Koh-i-Noor, including India, Pakistan, Iran, Afghanistan and the United Kingdom. The earliest known owner is Shah Jahan I (1592–1666), the fifth emperor of Mughal India. When the Iranian ruler Nader Shah invaded and captured Delhi in 1739, his troops looted the city and carried off Shah Jahan's Peacock Throne, which the diamond was set into. It is said that when Nader Shah saw the diamond, he exclaimed 'Koh-i-Noor!', the Persian for 'mountain of light'. After the collapse of Nader Shah's Empire, the diamond was passed on to the Durrani Afghan Empire before being possessed by Ranjit Singh – the first maharaja of the Sikh Empire – who was paranoid that it might be stolen. According to legend, he would transport it in a pannier on a camel, followed by a convoy of camels with identical panniers – a decoy to confuse potential attackers. The diamond would end up with his youngest son, Duleep Singh (see p. 59), and after the Last Treaty of Lahore (1849) following the end of the First Anglo-Sikh War, it was surrendered to Queen Victoria.

The diamond was shown in the Great Exhibition at Hyde Park in 1851, and the following year, Prince Albert decided to have it polished into a brilliant cut, decreasing its weight by around 42 per cent. When Victoria showed the newly cut Koh-i-Noor to Duleep Singh, he is said to have handed it back to her, after a long silence, saying, 'It is to me, Ma'am, the greatest pleasure thus to have the opportunity, as a loyal subject, of myself tendering to my Sovereign – the Koh-i-Noor!' After Victoria's death, the diamond became part of the Crown Jewels and was set into successive crowns; it is currently part of the crown of Queen Elizabeth, the Queen Mother, on display at the Tower of London. It was not worn by Queen Elizabeth II (1926–2022) and has not been worn by Queen Camilla (b. 1947).

"As with lots of things in history, it's complicated."

"Any big gemstone has its problems but this one has a *world* of problems. It's been through lots of different hands so it's not as simple as saying 'it should go back' – where should it go back to? But is that question playing into the hands of people who want it to stay here? As with lots of things in history, it's complicated. I don't think the diamond will stay here forever. Empires fall." HL

WHO OWNS THE KOH-I-NOOR DIAMOND?

Six countries currently have a claim to the Koh-i-Noor diamond: India, Pakistan, Bangladesh, Iran, Afghanistan and the UK. Now on display in the Tower of London, it has been owned by a succession of rulers across South Asia, Central Asia and Great Britain. A selection of past owners is presented below.

Mughal dynasty (modern-day India, Pakistan and Bangladesh), 1526–1857

In 1628 Shah Jahan I commissions the jewel-encrusted Peacock Throne, which includes the Koh-i-Noor diamond.

| Shah Jahan I | Aurangzeb | Muhammad Azam Shah **Killed in battle** | Bahadur Shah I | Jahandar Shah **Beheaded** | Farrukhsiyar **Blinded and executed** |
| Rafi ud-Darajat **Suspicious death** | Shah Jahan II | Muhammad Shah **Overthrown** | | | |

Afsharid dynasty (modern-day Iran), 1736–1796

In 1739 Nader Shah sacks Delhi and takes the diamond.

| Nader Shah **Assassinated** |

Durrani dynasty (modern-day Afghanistan), 1747–1856

In 1751 Nader Shah's grandson gives the diamond to Ahmad Shah Durrani in return for his support.

| Ahmad Shah Durrani | Timur Shah Durrani **Killed in battle** | Zaman Shah Durrani **Blinded and deposed** | Mahmud Shah Durrani **Deposed** | Shah Shuja Durrani **Exiled** |

Sikh Empire (modern-day India and Pakistan), 1799–1849

In 1813 Shah Shuja Durrani is forced into giving the diamond to Ranjit Singh in return for asylum, reportedly after seeing his son being tortured.

| Ranjit Singh | Kahrak Singh **Overthrown and poisoned** | Nau Nihal Singh **Killed** | Maharani Chand Kaur **Deposed and murdered** | Sher Singh **Assassinated** | Duleep Singh **Deposed** |

Houses of Hanover, Saxe-Coburg-Gotha and Windsor (Great Britain), 1714–

In 1849 Duleep Singh surrenders the diamond to Queen Victoria. Prince Albert has the diamond cut and it is later mounted as part of the British Crown Jewels.

| Queen Victoria and Prince Albert | King Edward VII and Queen Alexandra | King George V and Queen Mary | King George VI and Queen Elizabeth (the Queen Mother) | Queen Elizabeth II and Prince Philip | King Charles III and Queen Camilla |

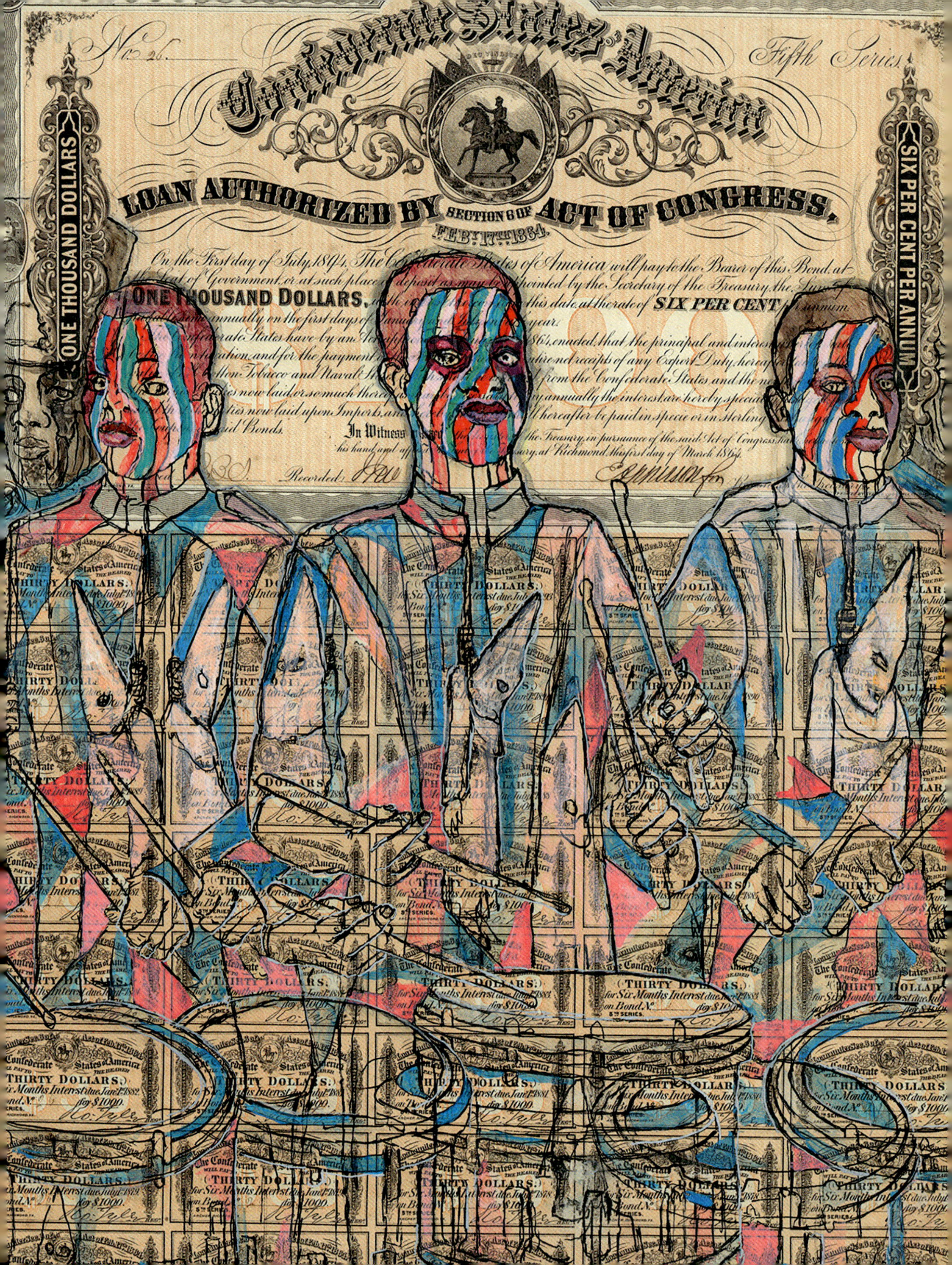

No. 26.
Confederate States of America
Fifth Series
LOAN AUTHORIZED BY SECTION 6 OF ACT OF CONGRESS,
FEBY. 17TH. 1864.
ONE THOUSAND DOLLARS
SIX PER CENT PER ANNUM
On the First day of July, 1894, The Confederate States of America will pay to the Bearer of this Bond, at
the seat of Government, or at such places deposit as may be appointed by the Secretary of the Treasury, the sum of
ONE THOUSAND DOLLARS, with the interest accruing from this date, at the rate of SIX PER CENT per annum.
ONE THOUSAND DOLLARS
SIX PER CENT PER ANNUM
In Witness
Recorded:
THIRTY DOLLARS.
$1000

In 1492 Christopher Columbus sailed across the Atlantic in search of India and instead encountered a continent largely unknown to Europeans. His travels opened up the American continents for Europeans to settle on and exploit local resources while Indigenous peoples and their ancient civilisations were decimated or violently altered. This exhibition poster (p. 102) quotes from Columbus's journals, detailing his thoughts about the Indigenous people. The T-shirt (p. 103) shows a photo of Apache leader Geronimo (1829–1909) with three warriors who resisted colonisation of their lands. In the years following the 1846–8 Mexican–American War and the annexation of Texas by the United States, the US army forced Apache peoples to re-settle on 'Indian Reservations'. Geronimo led many breakouts and raids from these reservations to protect the Apache lands and ways of life. The T-shirt is a wry reimagining of the current US Department of Homeland Security, with white colonisers cast as the original terrorists, starting with Columbus.

The narrative of the 'discovery' of the 'New World' erases the diverse Indigenous peoples with complex histories and cultures who had inhabited the continents of North and South America, sometimes for thousands of years. Made from dense tropical hardwood, the sacred carved forms on pp. 104–5 depict and house two *cemís* – powerful deities or ancestral spirits, representing crop-watering rain and fertility. They were made by Taíno people, a name used for different Indigenous Caribbean groups at the time of Columbus's arrival. Although once considered extinct, Taíno heritage is now reclaimed by many people across the Caribbean. The cemís were found in a cave in Carpenter's Mountains, Jamaica, in 1792, and bequeathed to the Museum by Isaac Alves Rebello between 1799 and 1802.

Further works from Hew Locke's *Share* series are drawn on Confederate government bonds that financed their operations during the American Civil War (pp. 106–7). The Confederate States seceded from the Union in 1860–1 over their right to uphold a plantation economy dependent upon enslavement.

"These things become a symbol of collective memory, a myth, an idea of nationhood."

"People still celebrate Columbus Day. What he did was crazy, sailing into nowhere not knowing what you're going to hit. Growing up in Guyana, we were given the feeling that this guy was a noble explorer. He was an exploiter. The provenance of an object is what makes something very ordinary and boring actually very important. This brick was supposedly brought as ballast in Columbus's ship on his second voyage and then used to build the church on the island of Hispaniola (p. 103). It's almost like a ready-made conceptual piece. It's a souvenir of an empire beginning.

When working on the *Share* series, I found out I could get hold of Confederate share certificates. The bonds were issued during the American Civil War and feature George Washington on horseback because, as the first president and as a slave owner, he was an icon for the Confederacy. There's a direct link between that Columbus journal entry – 'We can do what we want to the people here' – and the system of enslavement that developed. But these shares are about the survival of Afro-Caribbean people in general, survival against the odds.

What I find fascinating about the Taíno objects is that they're made of wood. Something of this age in the Caribbean is special – even the hardest woods don't survive the climate. They have become a symbol of collective memory, a myth, an idea of Jamaican nationhood." HL

Hew Locke, *Confederate States of America Loan 4*, 2018.

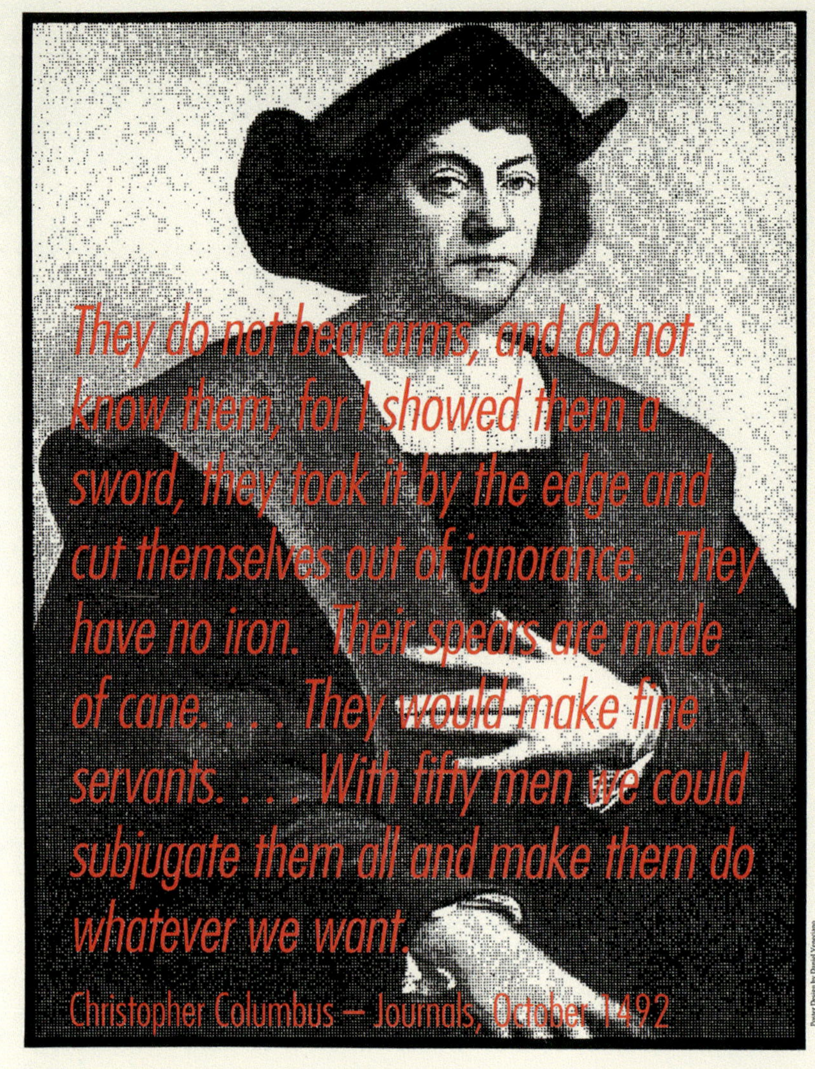

Daniel Veneciano, *500 Years Since Columbus: the Legacy Continues*, 1992.

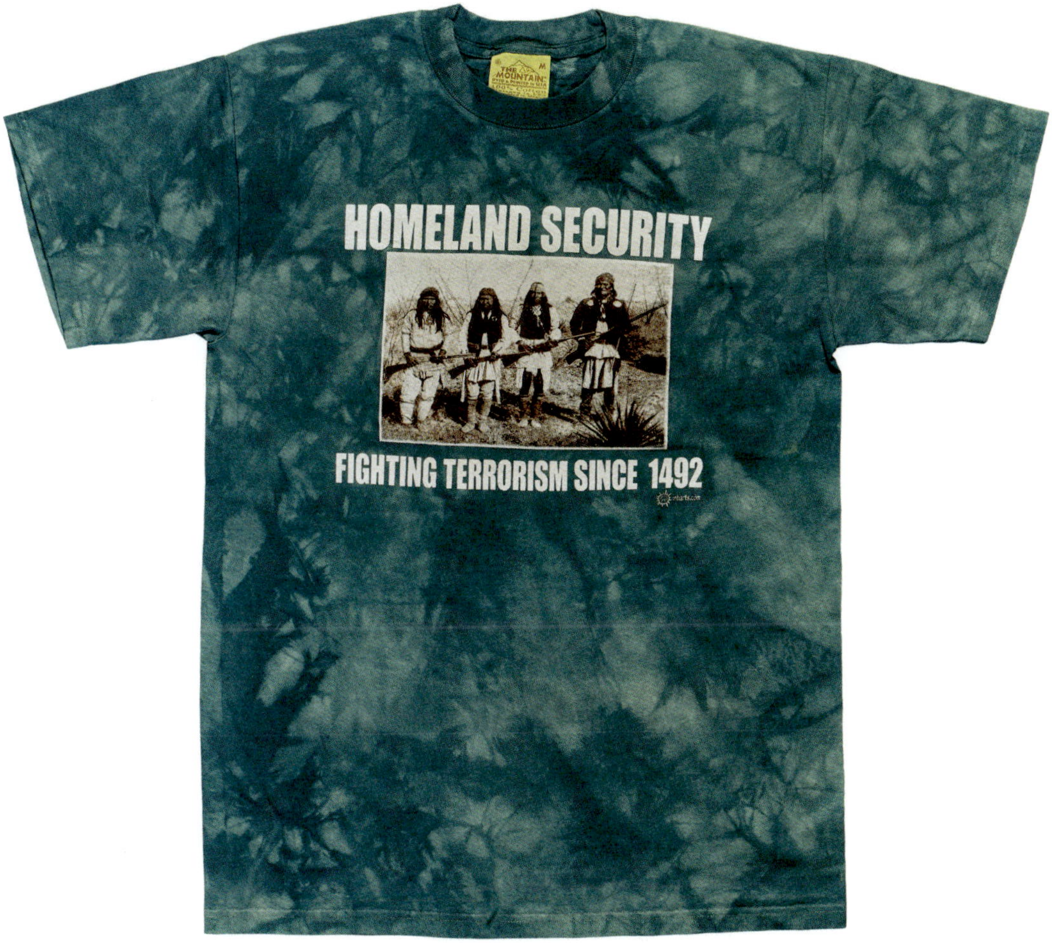

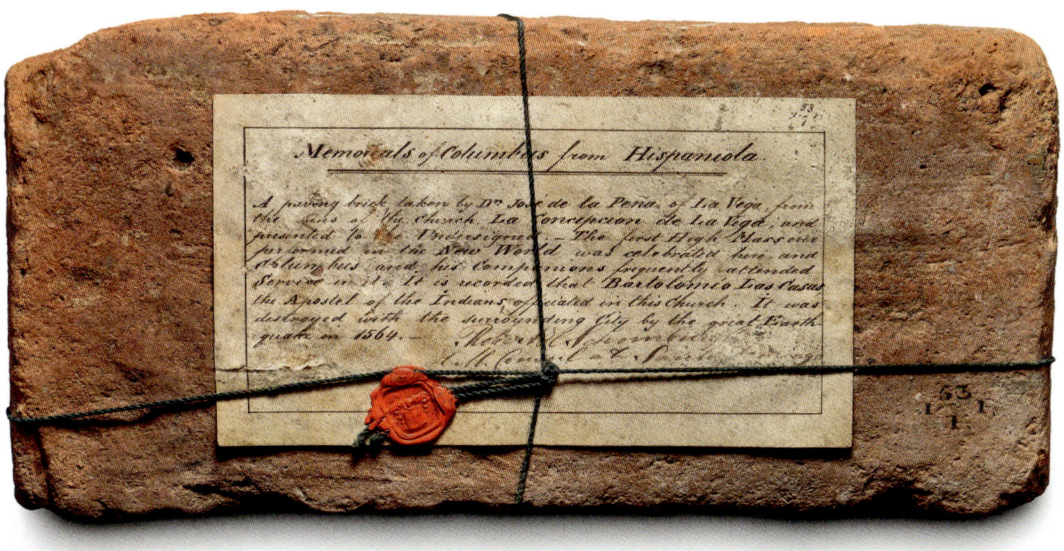

T-shirt, *c.* 2000–10.

Brick, possibly made in Hispaniola after 1492.

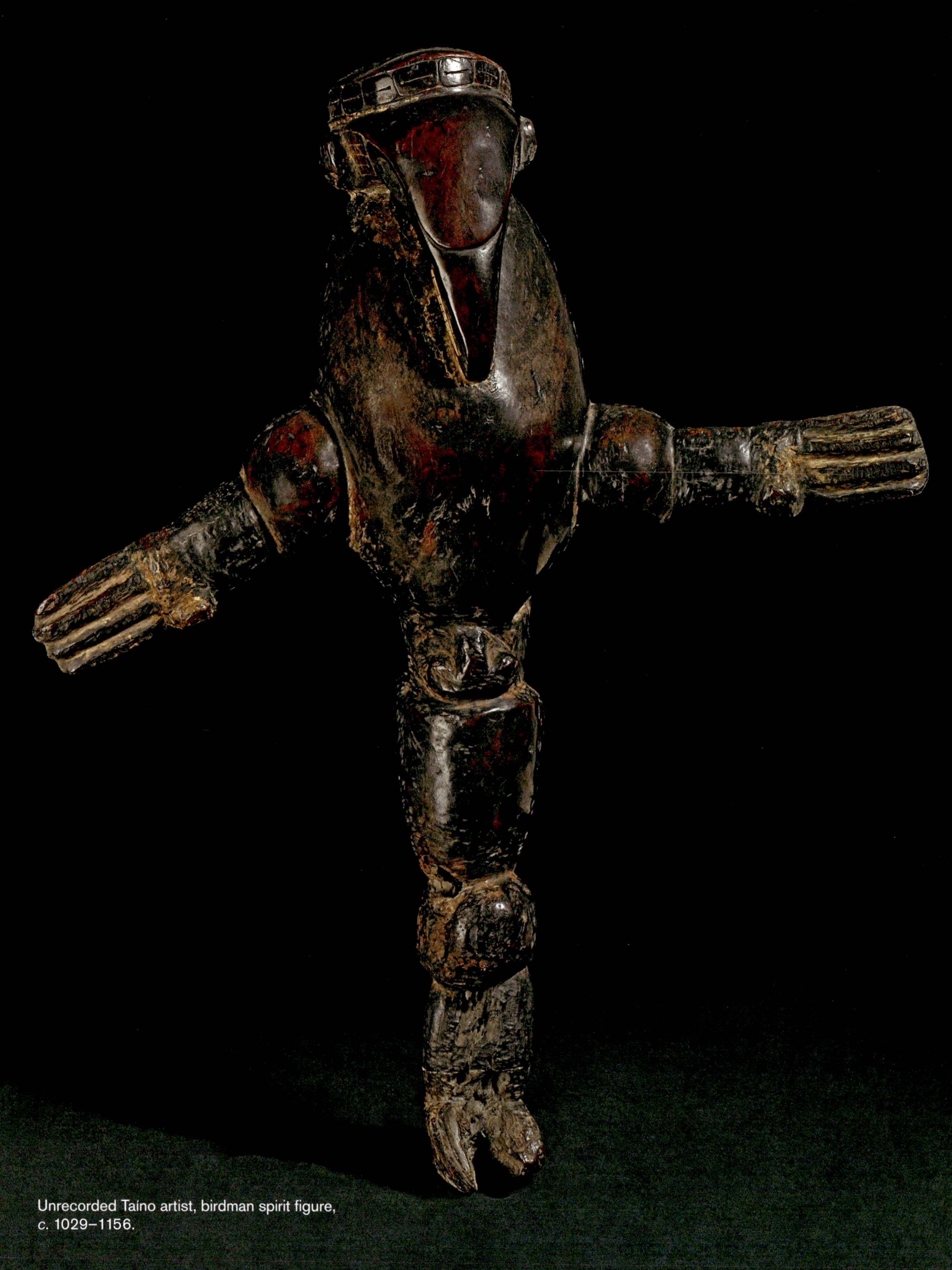

Unrecorded Taíno artist, birdman spirit figure,
c. 1029–1156.

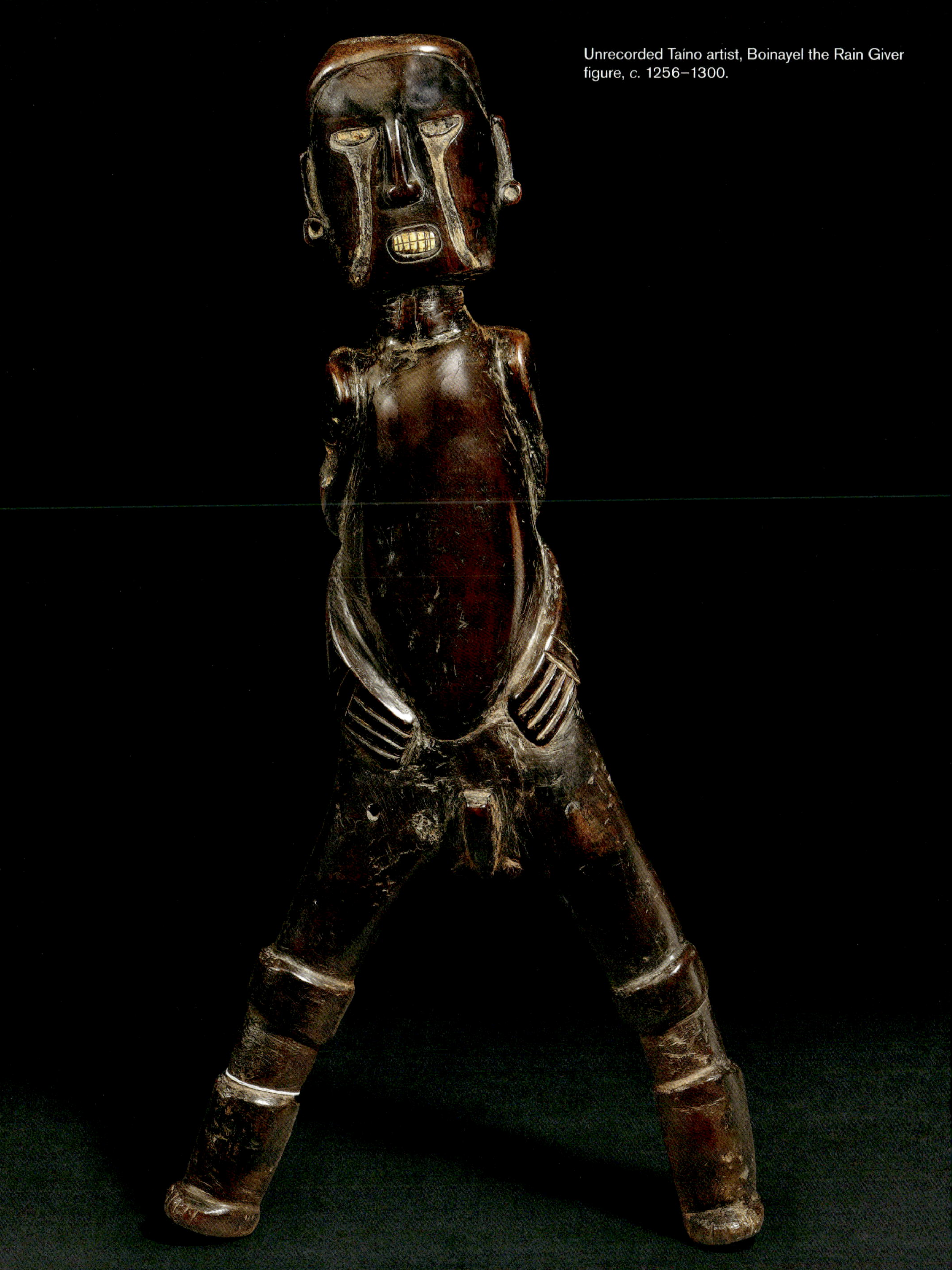

Unrecorded Taíno artist, Boinayel the Rain Giver figure, *c.* 1256–1300.

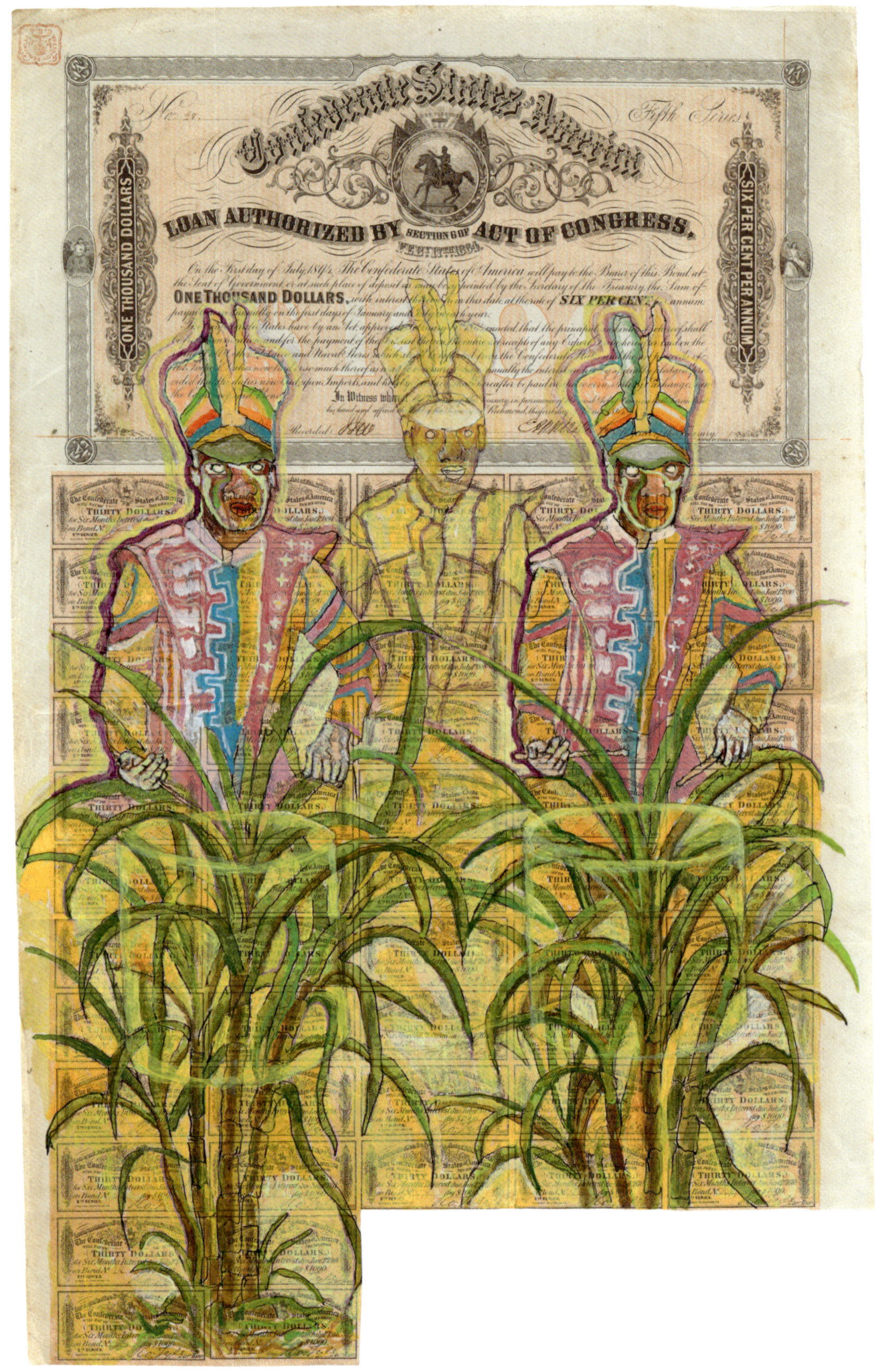

Hew Locke, *Confederate States of America Loan 14*, 2023.

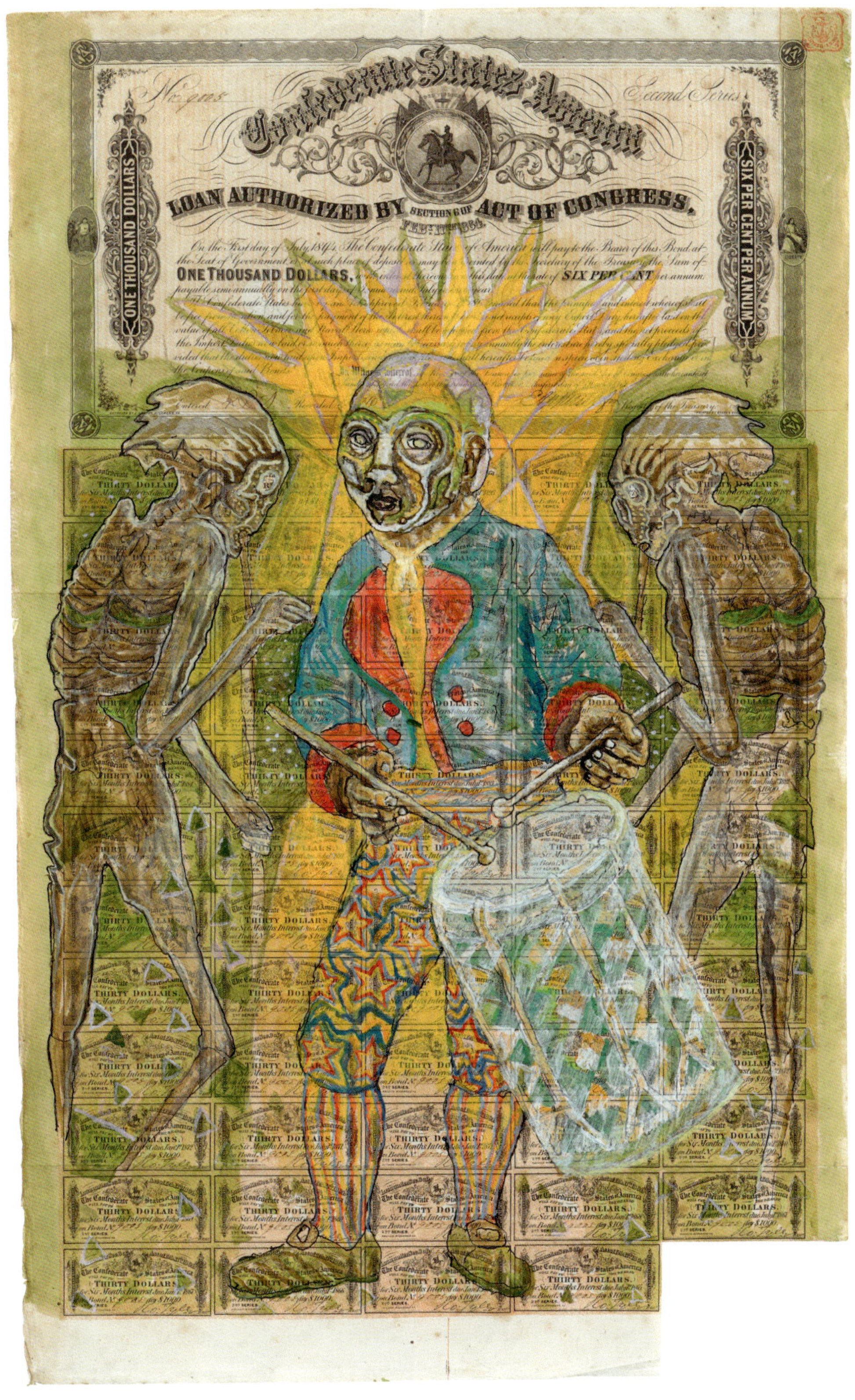

Hew Locke, *Confederate States of America Loan 16*, 2024.

John White (fl. 1585–93) was a governor of the Roanoke colony in Virginia; his watercolours and drawings are among the earliest depictions of Indigenous Americans by a European artist (pp. 109–11). His quasi-ethnographic depictions of the Algonquian people were also intended to advertise new markets for trade, enticing potential colonists.

Gold, birds' feathers and iridescent insect wings were among the commodities that became highly sought-after in Europe. Their origin and perceived exoticism conveyed the owner's status. This tiara, necklace and earrings were made from 46 green weevils from Brazil and Argentina (p. 112). In 1884 a British-Portuguese treaty gave Portugal ownership of the mouth of the Congo River while allowing Britain navigation rights. According to Granville family tradition the Portuguese ambassador gave these weevils to Lady Granville (1785–1862), the foreign secretary's wife, who had them mounted in a design borrowed from Egypt, a territory that had become a British Protectorate in 1882. The 1884 treaty was so inflammatory to other European powers that it led to the Berlin Conference of 1884–5 and was abandoned before the conference began. A necklace with seven stuffed hummingbirds also exemplifies this trend of exoticism (p. 113). The eyes have been replaced with tiny gemstones, and the beaks with golden points. Hummingbird specimens first reached Europe in the 1820s, causing significant excitement. Empress Eugénie (1826–1920), the wife of Napoleon III (1808–1873), and Princess Alexandra were notable figures who adorned themselves with hummingbird-feather accessories. By the mid-1870s, campaigns against the mass killing of birds for fashion began, leading to eventual legal control over feather imports after the First World War.

The Indigenous peoples of Guyana's interior include the Akawaio, Arekuna, Patamona, Wai Wai, Makushi and Wapishana. This Akawaio feather headdress and Wai Wai feather hair tube represent some of the kinds of featherwork Hew Locke saw growing up in Guyana (p. 114).

"The fish jump out of the water into your boats. They're people we can do business with."

"John White's drawings are extraordinary (pp. 109–11). They're so reproduced and copied and have a big impact on the European imagination and idea of Indigenous Americans. They're filtered through a classical European mindset; the poses are taken directly from antiquity. That's the beginning of hundreds of years of depictions of Amerindian people in that way: the 'noble savage'. They were also an advertisement for colonists – come, the natives are nice, they're handsome, good-looking people and with plenty of land, you know, the fish jump out of the water into your boats. They're people we can do business with. Some elements of these drawings seem reasonably accurate, but this is also about selling an image to the audience back home. It was successful. Nobody in Europe would have seen anything like this. But it also has a lens or filter of European values or expectations.

As for the hummingbird necklace … Who the hell thought this up? Today they're collected as quirky objects. A stuffed bell jar full of bird specimens is one thing, it's honest in its exploitation. As a child, I knew many spectacular Amerindian feather headdresses still made and worn today by different groups in the Amazon. But the Western feather trade was a different operation, it was mass exploitation. Once, when I was a teenager, I travelled on this steamer coming out of the interior of Guyana. It was full of cages of birds. Macaws, parakeets – anything that looked pretty. Hundreds and hundreds of birds, shipped for the exotic pet trade. Every morning, somebody would go through the cages and toss out the dead birds." HL

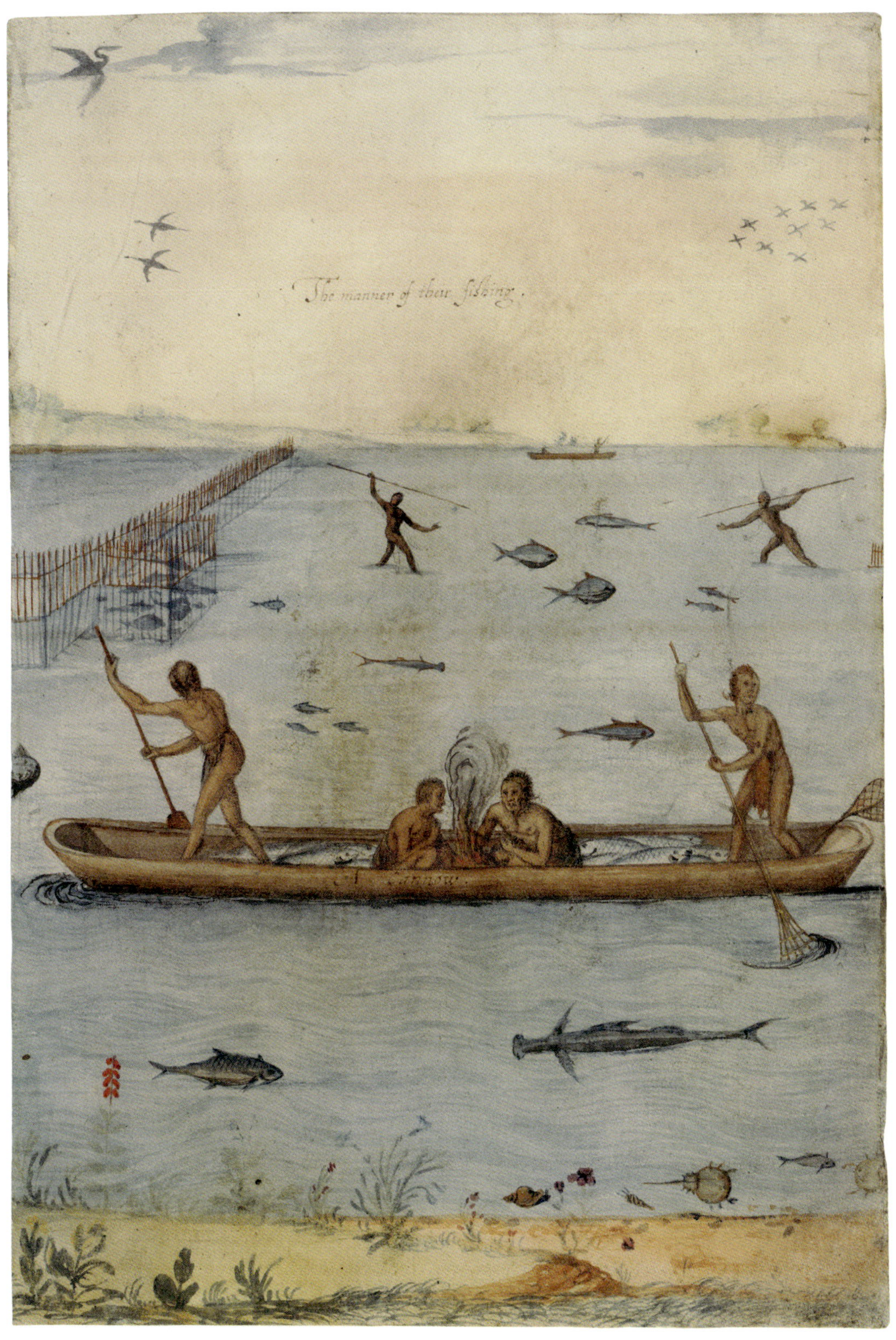

John White, *North Carolina Algonquian people fishing*, c. 1585–90.

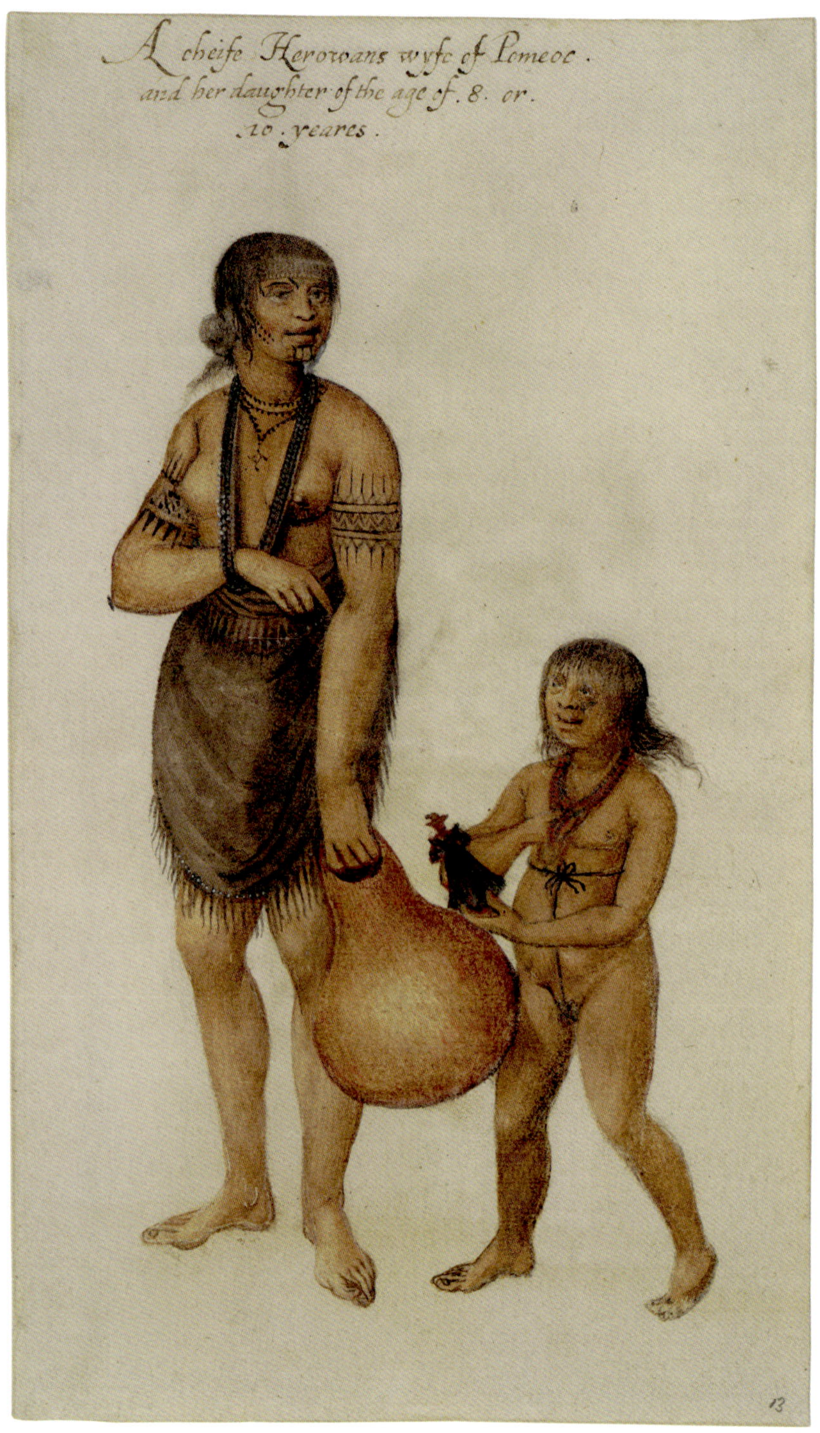

John White, *A North Carolina Algonquian woman (wife of a* werowance *or leader)
and her daughter, c.* 1585–90.

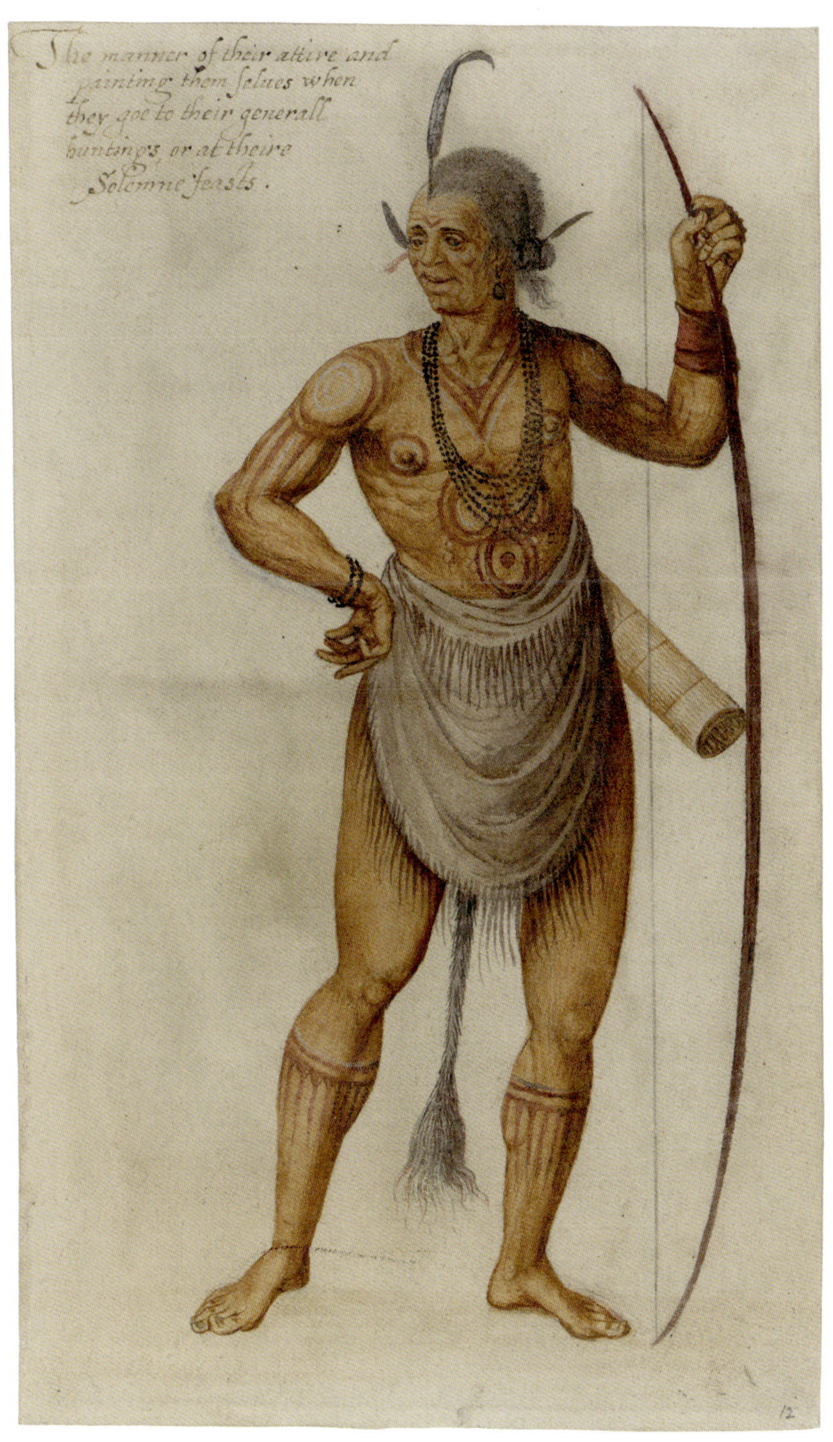

John White, *A North Carolina Algonquian* werowance *(leader)*, c. 1585–90.

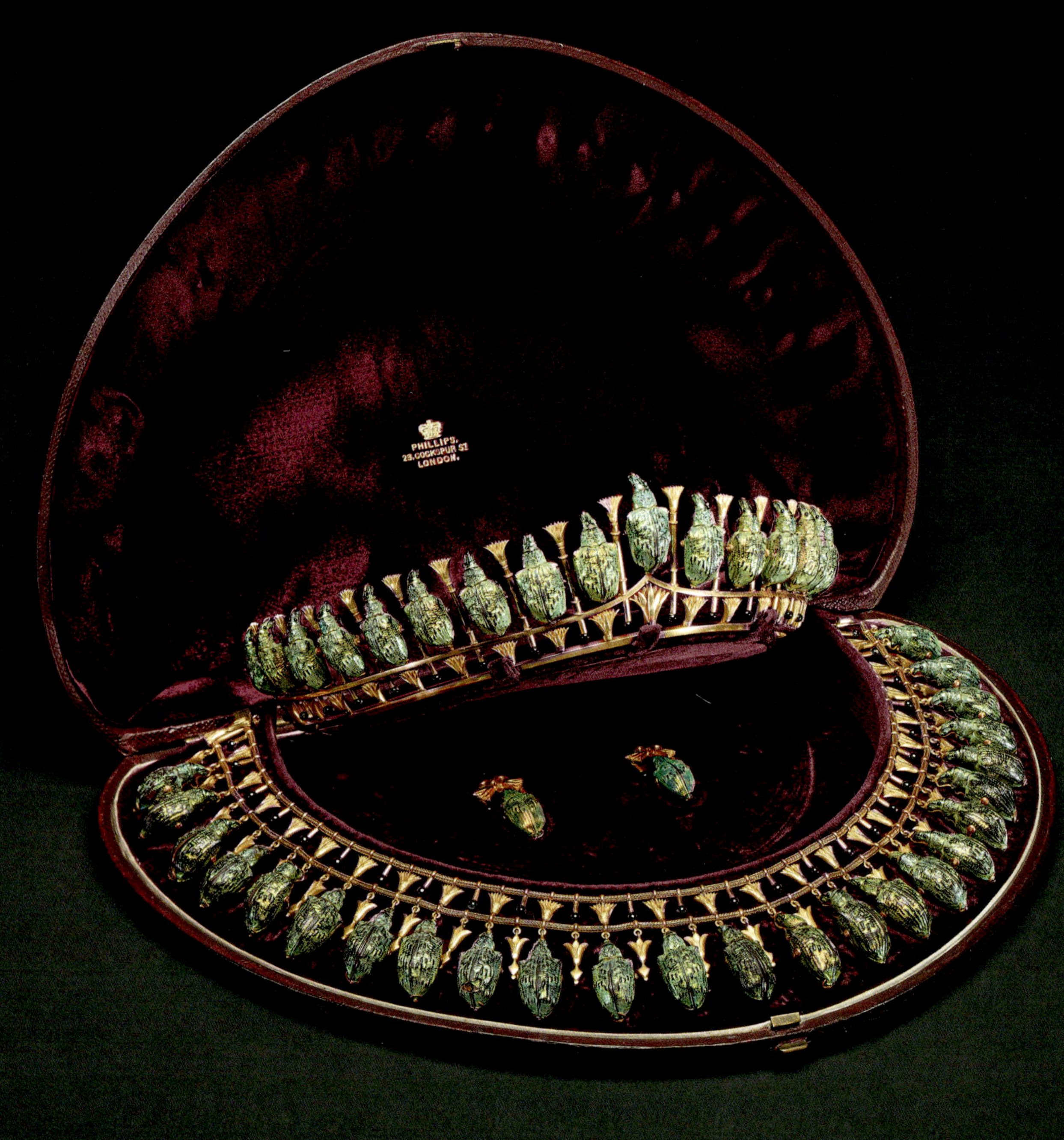

Phillips Brothers, beetle tiara, necklace and earrings, 1884–5.

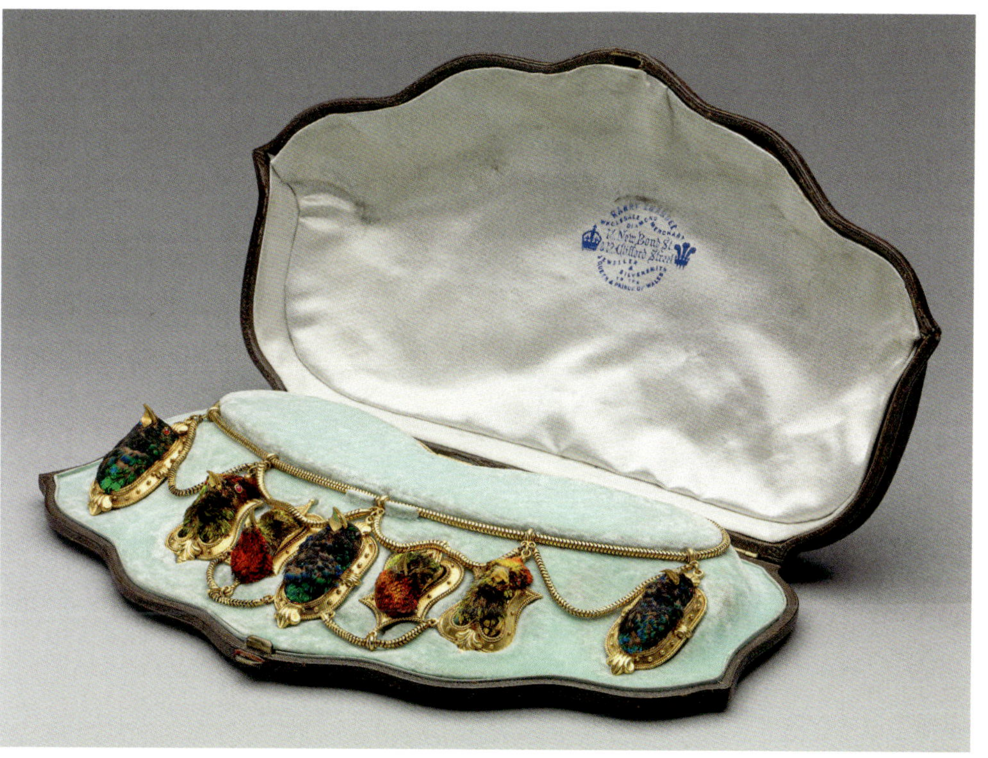

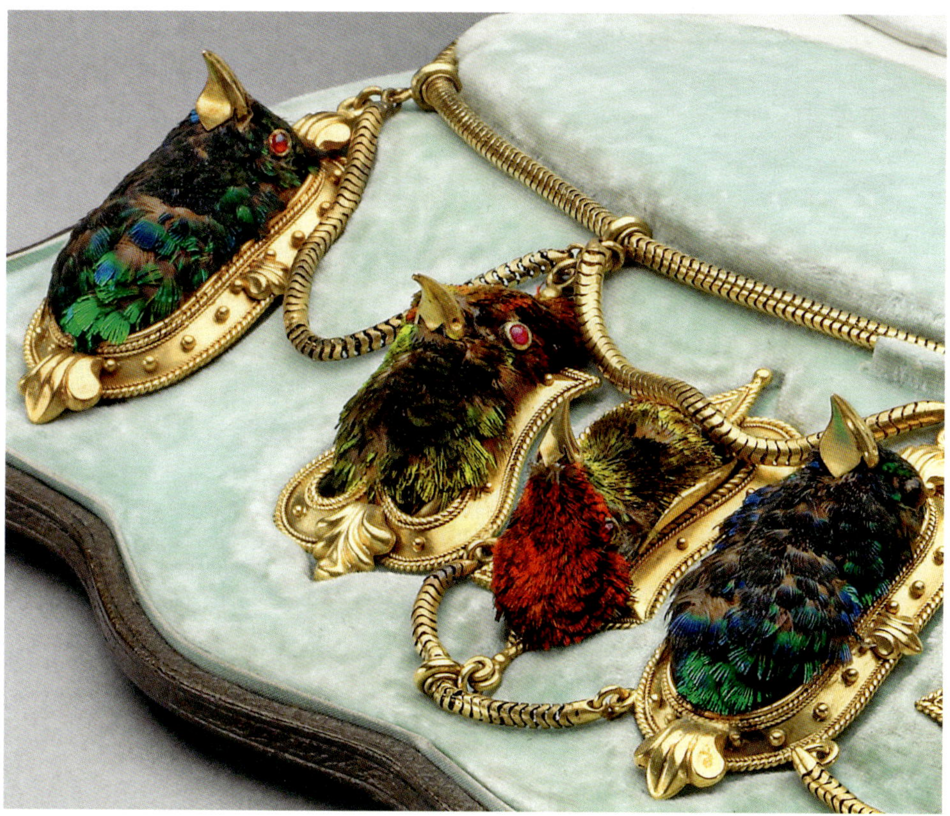

Harry Emanuel, hummingbird necklace, 1865, and detail.

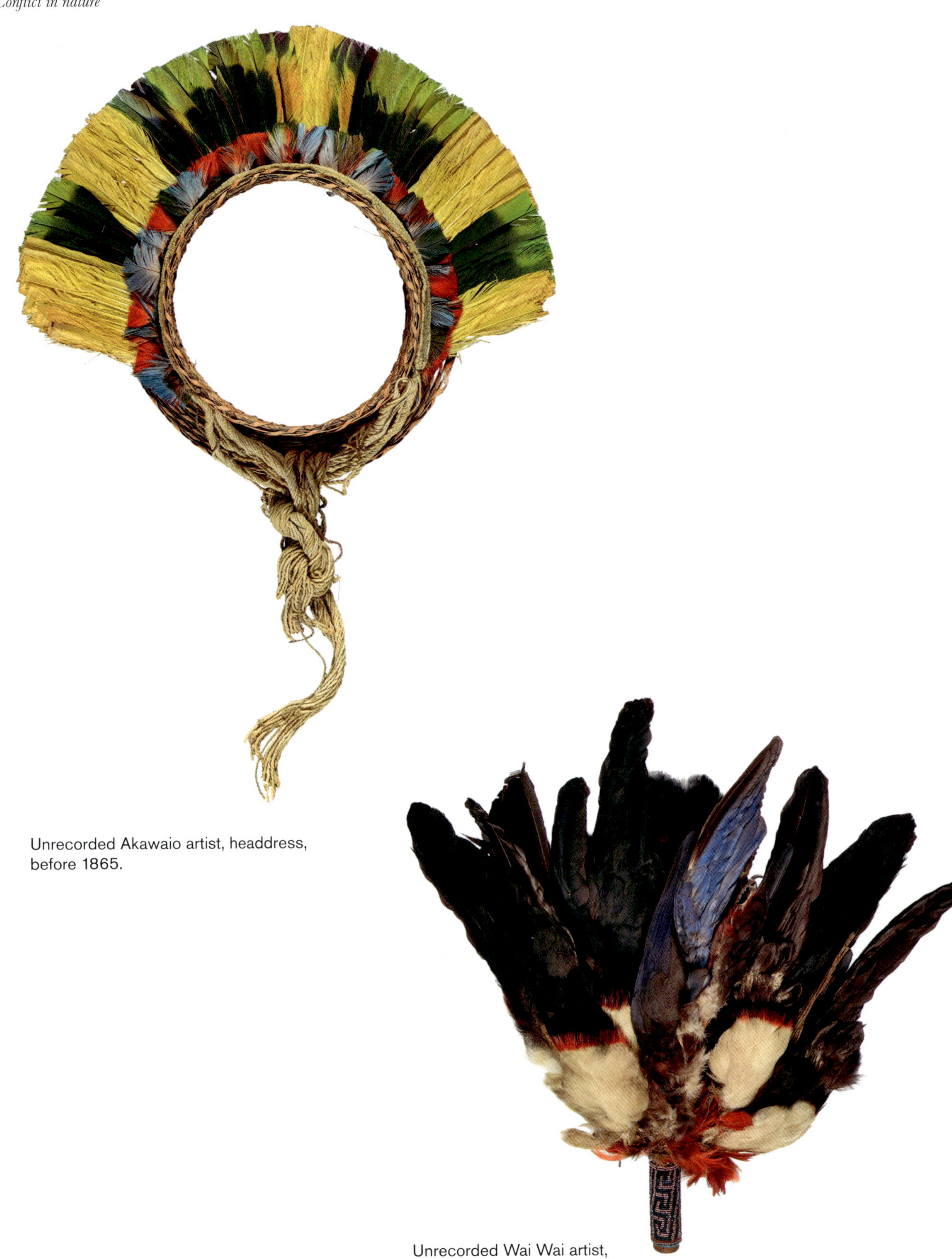

Unrecorded Akawaio artist, headdress,
before 1865.

Unrecorded Wai Wai artist,
hair-tube, before 1865.

The German naturalist Maria Sibylla Merian (1647–1717) was a skilful botanical and zoological artist. From 1699 to 1701, she made a self-funded journey to the Dutch colony of Suriname on the equatorial northeast coast of South America, accompanied by her daughter Dorothea Maria Graff (1678–1743). Merian's drawings were the first to depict the native fauna and flora of Suriname in such detail. Assisted by enslaved African and local Indigenous people, Merian and Graff recorded Indigenous names and uses for the plants and animals, presenting them in a lavishly illustrated book.

Almost a century later, the Dutch-Scottish soldier John Gabriel Stedman's (1744–1797) *Narrative, of a Five Years' Expedition, Against the Revolted Negroes of Surinam* (1796) described many of the brutalities perpetrated during the suppression of a major rebellion against plantation owners, and was illustrated with engravings by the artist William Blake (1757–1827).

"These drawings are beautiful, but they have a perverse, violent side to them."

"These objects are grouped together because they demonstrate artists' responses to life under colonialism (pp. 116–17). I saw a television programme about forgotten women artists and one of them was Maria Sibylla Merian. I always thought – how could she have been forgotten? Well, we all know. But I thought the images were extraordinary. They seem to be made up of many different studies from life but also stories that have been told to her: 'this bird did this. I once saw a toucan eating a bird.' But Merian was in Dutch Guiana (Suriname) when it was a slave colony. To me, the images are metaphors for what was going on there – the crocodile eating the snake, the toucan eating the bird.

On the other hand, Blake's images from Stedman's book are very famous, especially the ones I use in my own work of enslaved people being punished. But they're all poetic pictures of struggles. Blake's image of an enslaved person with a hook through his ribs has been reproduced many times. It's like the graphic of the Brooks ship. I'm trying to find a fresh way of processing this situation. I've chosen not to show explicit images of brutality, though they do exist. Other artists of colour feel the same about not wanting to see broken Black bodies. Imagination is a powerful thing. We need to think about what was happening there. It's a really brutal system and it's perverse to make it look pretty. Plantation owners have power of life and death over their subjects, they can do what they want – and they did. The image of a dead man I've included shows someone who tried to resist. They failed, but you have to try – the alternative was unthinkable.

I have placed it with the images painted by Merian and her daughter because I find the contrast interesting. These women accepted the situation they were in. They didn't approve of slavery but they didn't resist it. They came from Amsterdam to an extreme society and they must have witnessed the extremes of punishment. It doesn't take a psychologist to examine this work and see it as a metaphor for what they're seeing – well, I think so anyway." HL

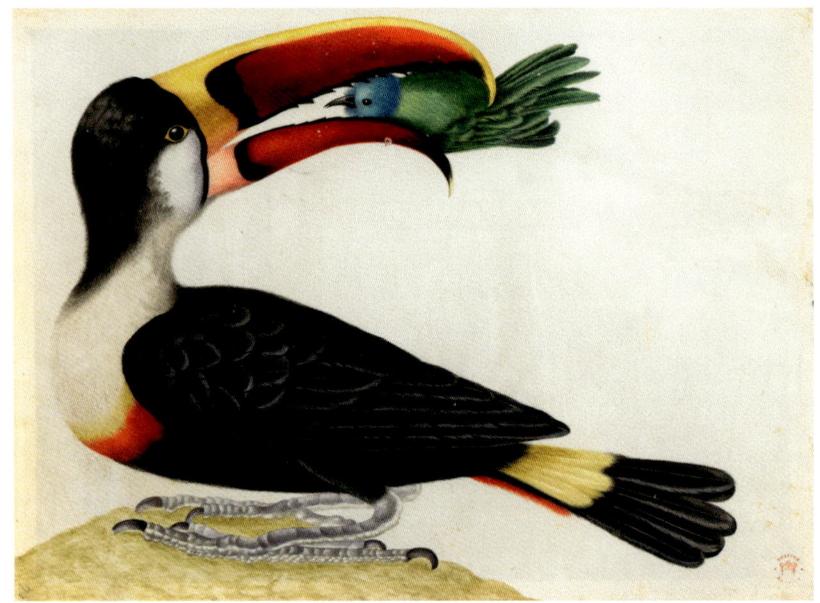

Maria Sibylla Merian, *Toucan eating a small bird*, c. 1701–5.

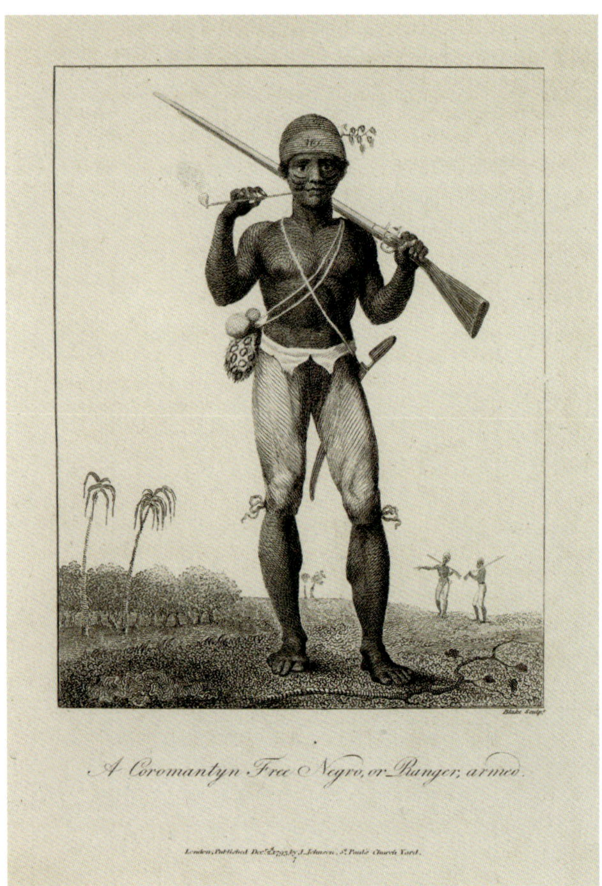

William Blake, after John Gabriel Stedman,
An armed Coromantyn Free Ranger, 1793.

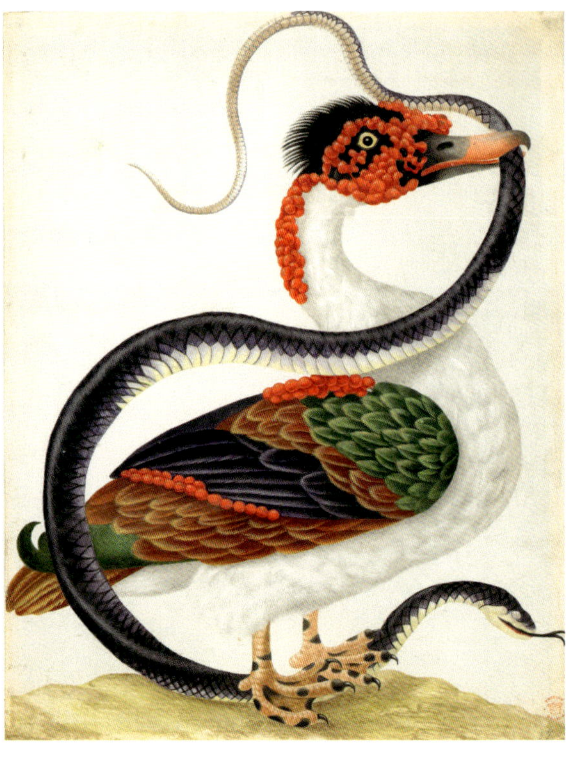

Maria Sibylla Merian, *Muscovy duck wrestling with a snake*, c. 1701–5.

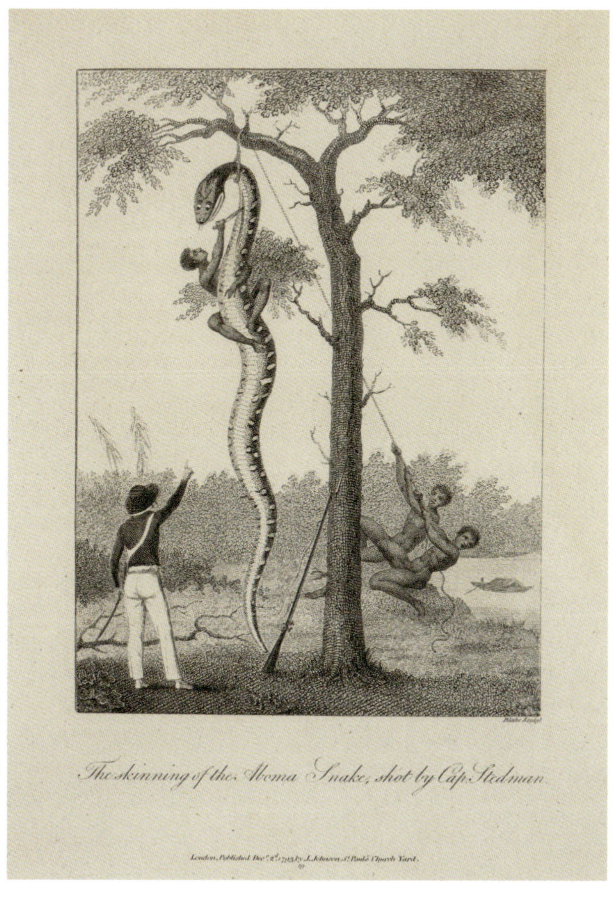

William Blake, after John Gabriel Stedman, *The skinning of the Aboma Snake, shot by Captain Stedman*, 1793.

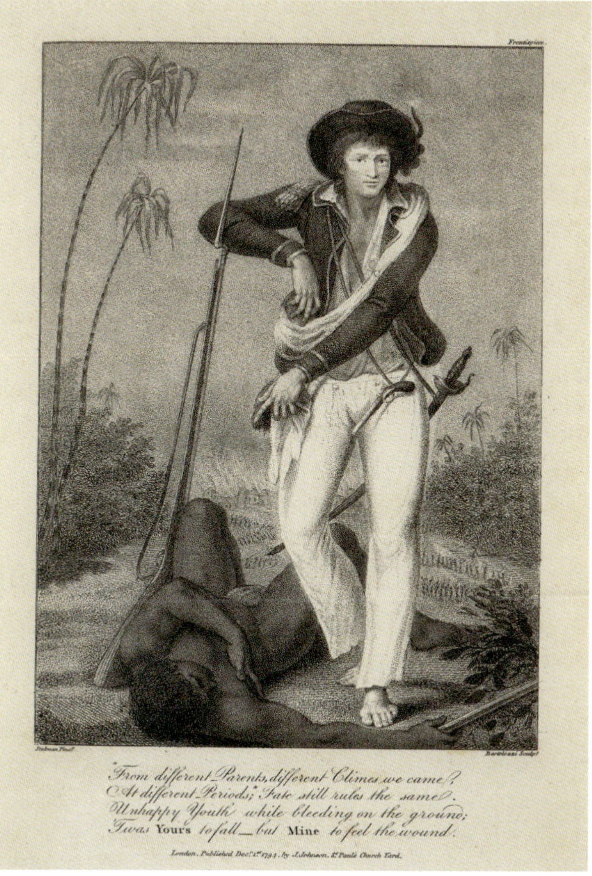

Francesco Bartolozzi, after John Gabriel Stedman, *Frontispiece for Stedman's Narrative*, 1794.

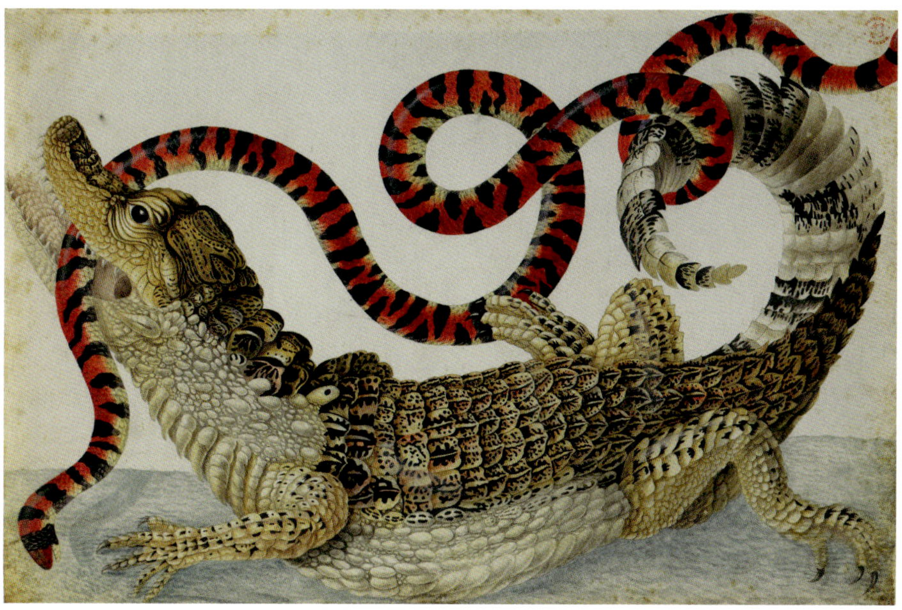

Attributed to Dorothea Graff, *Caiman wrestling with a snake*, c. 1701–5.

"Clubs are symbols of resistance. To me they are also very beautiful. One of the clubs was collected by Robert Schomburgk, who I learned about growing up because he delineated the boundary between Guyana and Venezuela. This thing is personal for me because there is current tension around the border. The activities of the past during Empire are affecting my present in an existential way. It's a whole country I know and love, it's a highly emotionally charged object.

Henri Christophe modelled himself after a Roman emperor (p. 120), just as King George III did. Haitian revolutionary leaders understood that to be taken seriously by Western powers, you had to be depicted in a certain way.

For European artists, a view *had* to be an idyllic, classical landscape. This print (p. 124) shows the moment before a Maroon ambush. Maroons are hailed as heroes who kept the British at bay. Tragically, they had to agree to hand back runaway slaves in exchange for being allowed to live freely. People learn forms of resistance though. Dance and music can be used to pass on messages, to keep yourself fit, or to practise martial arts under the noses of the white planters (p. 124). Humour is another form of resistance; plantation owners laughed at the enslaved people in the carnival outfits that copied their white 'betters', but they didn't pick up that the joke was on them. The image from the Port of Spain (p. 125) is after emancipation and now these former enslaved people are free and they're twice as scary in their edgy exuberance.

My works on pp. 122–3 relate to New World companies in the Caribbean and South America. The rubber boom in Brazil was a get-rich-quick scheme, forcing locals to find and harvest rubber. It was like the Congo – really bad. I took the Brazilian and Amerindian imagery from ceramics found on the island. 'West India Improvement Co' – I always liked that name. They're improving things, but only for themselves. It was an American company manoeuvred out by the British. I have included images of the main crop, bananas, and one of the Taíno figures. These documents are all records of failure." HL

This Guyanese club (opposite, right) was collected by the German-born explorer Robert Schomburgk (1804–1865), who was commissioned by Britain to survey British Guiana in 1840, resulting in the 'Schomburgk Line', border markings that were disputed by Venezuela. An international arbitration panel resolved the dispute in 1899, though Venezuela revived its claim in the 1960s and 2010s, rekindled by the discovery of oil reserves in Guyanese waters. In 2018 Guyana applied to the International Court of Justice to validate the 1899 award.

On the island of Hispaniola, a revolution involving more than 100,000 enslaved African people against the armies of France, Spain and Britain resulted in the creation of the world's first Black-led Republic in 1804: the Republic of Haiti. Toussaint Louverture (p. 120), born enslaved but emancipated in 1776, was a leading revolutionary figure. He considered himself French and believed in Enlightenment thinking, which saw all men as equals.

Anti-slavery prints, such as this collaged example showing a mother threatening to jump overboard with her child (p. 121), were designed to draw sympathy from Europeans and encourage support for abolitionism. The prints on pp. 124–5 provide a selective view of life in the Caribbean during the colonial period and after emancipation. Jewish Jamaican artist Isaac Mendes Belisario (1795–1849) provides the first known depiction of Jonkonnu (or John Canoe), the Afro-Jamaican masquerade performed by enslaved people during holidays (p. 125).

"Carnival today is still considered by many participants as an expression of resistance."

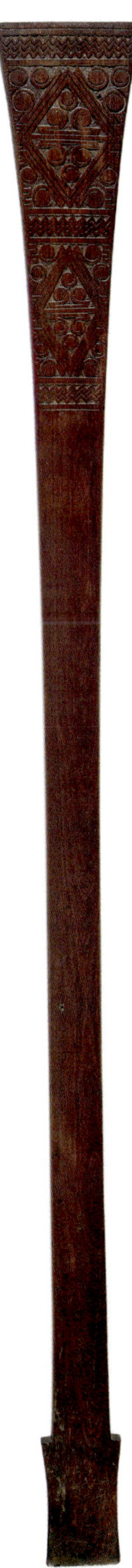

Unrecorded Guyanese artist, club,
c. 1600–50.

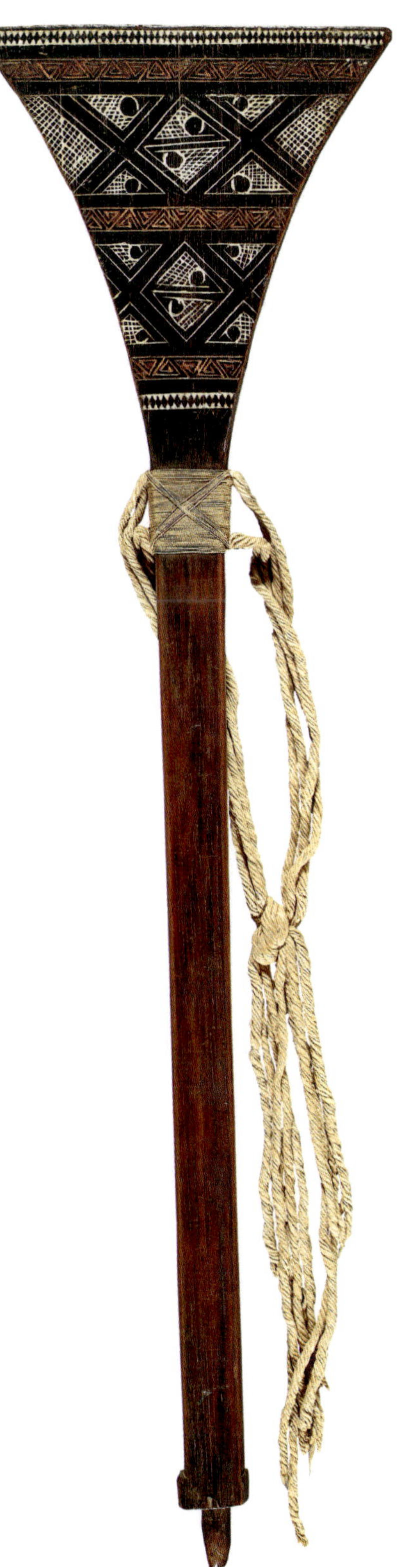

Unrecorded Guyanese artist, club,
before 1836.

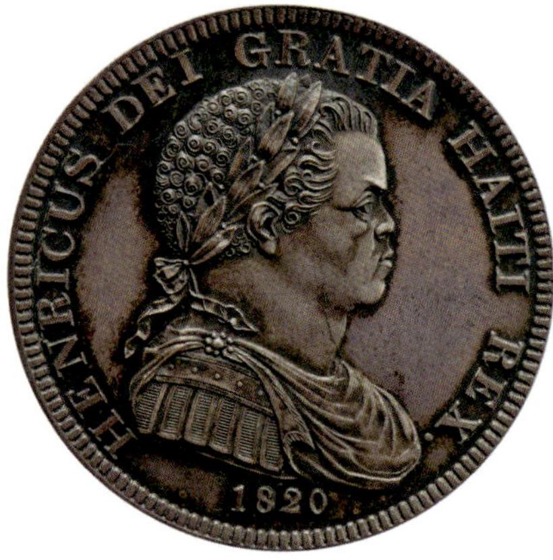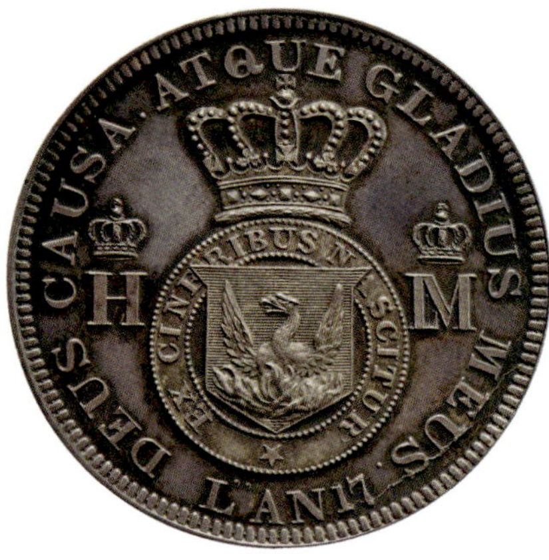

Coin of Henri Christophe, President and King of Haiti, 1820.

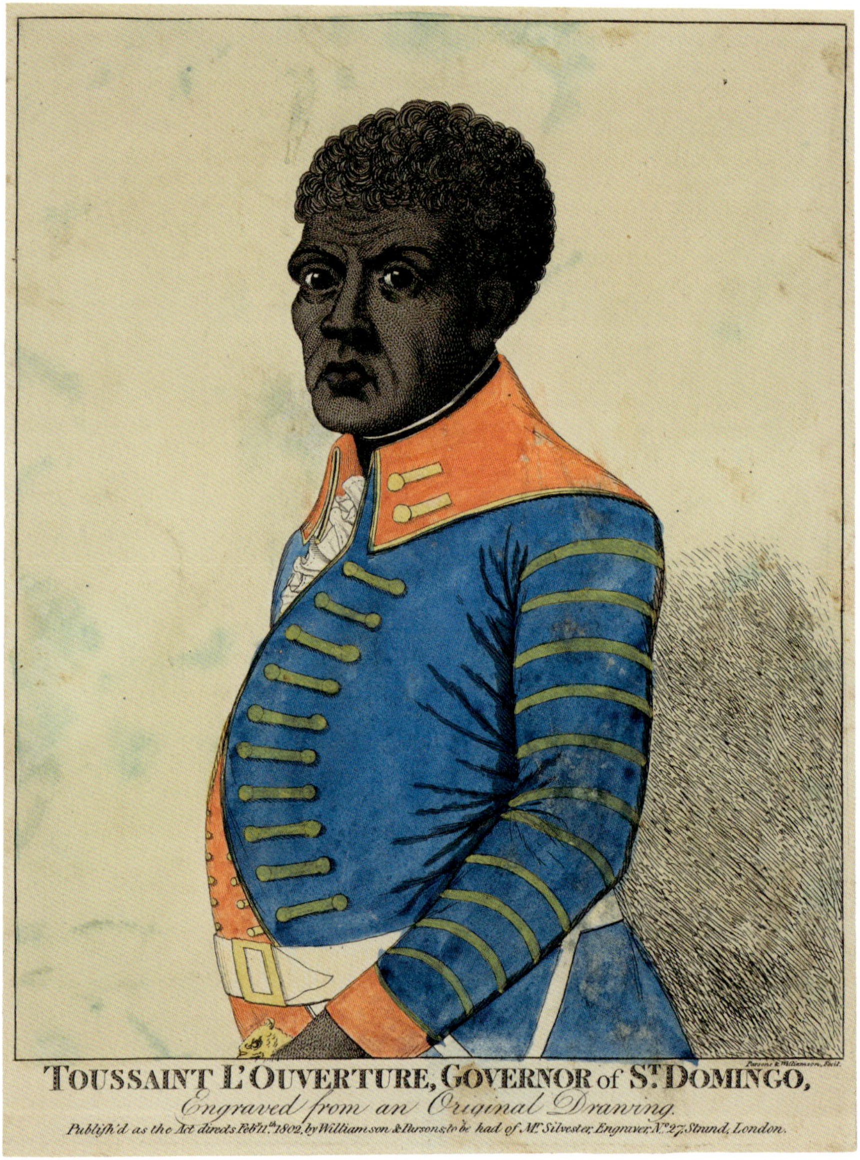

Williamson & Parsons, *Toussaint L'Ouverture, Governor of St. Domingo*, 1802.

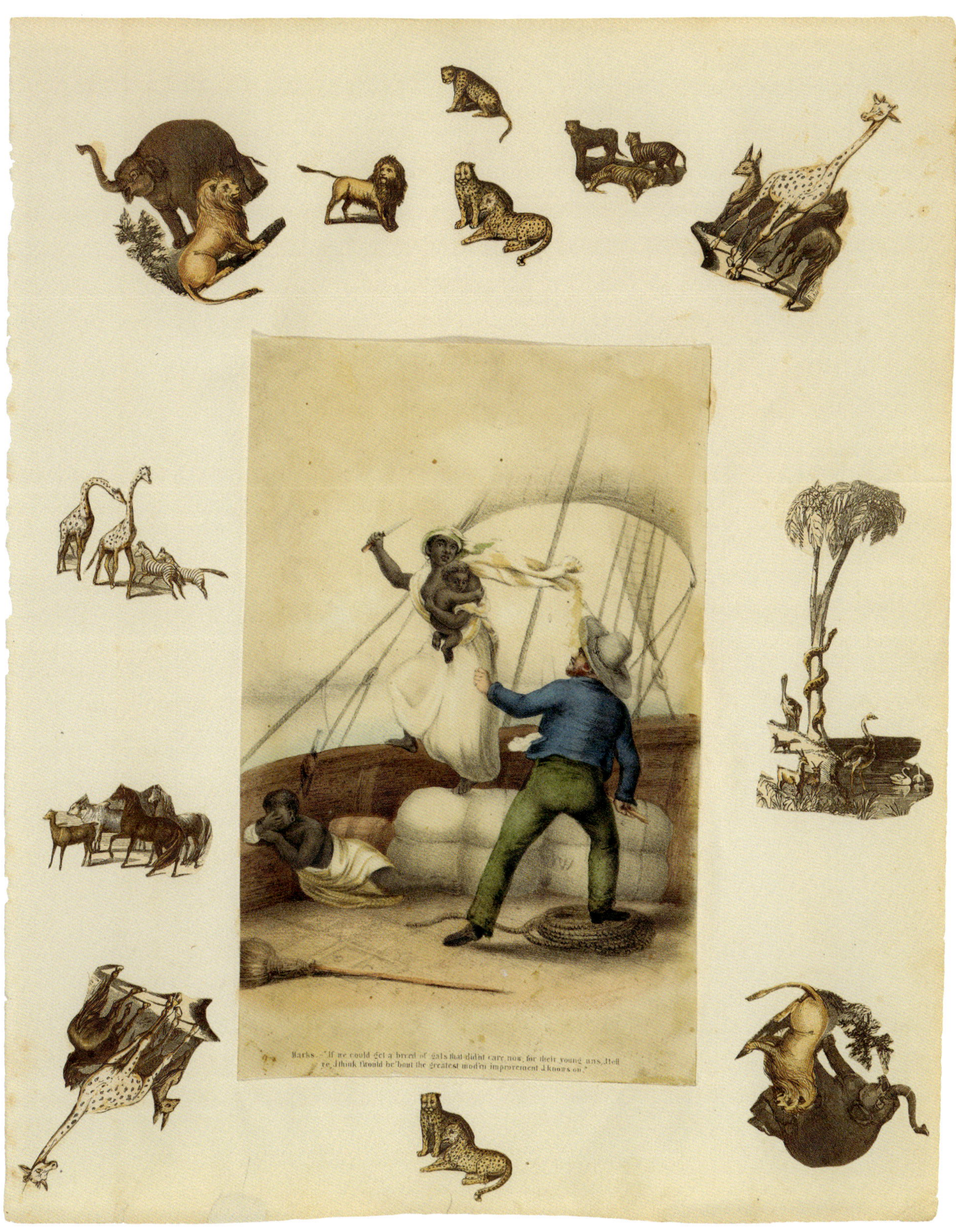

Unrecorded British artist, print showing a mother threatening to jump overboard with her child, *c*. 1850.

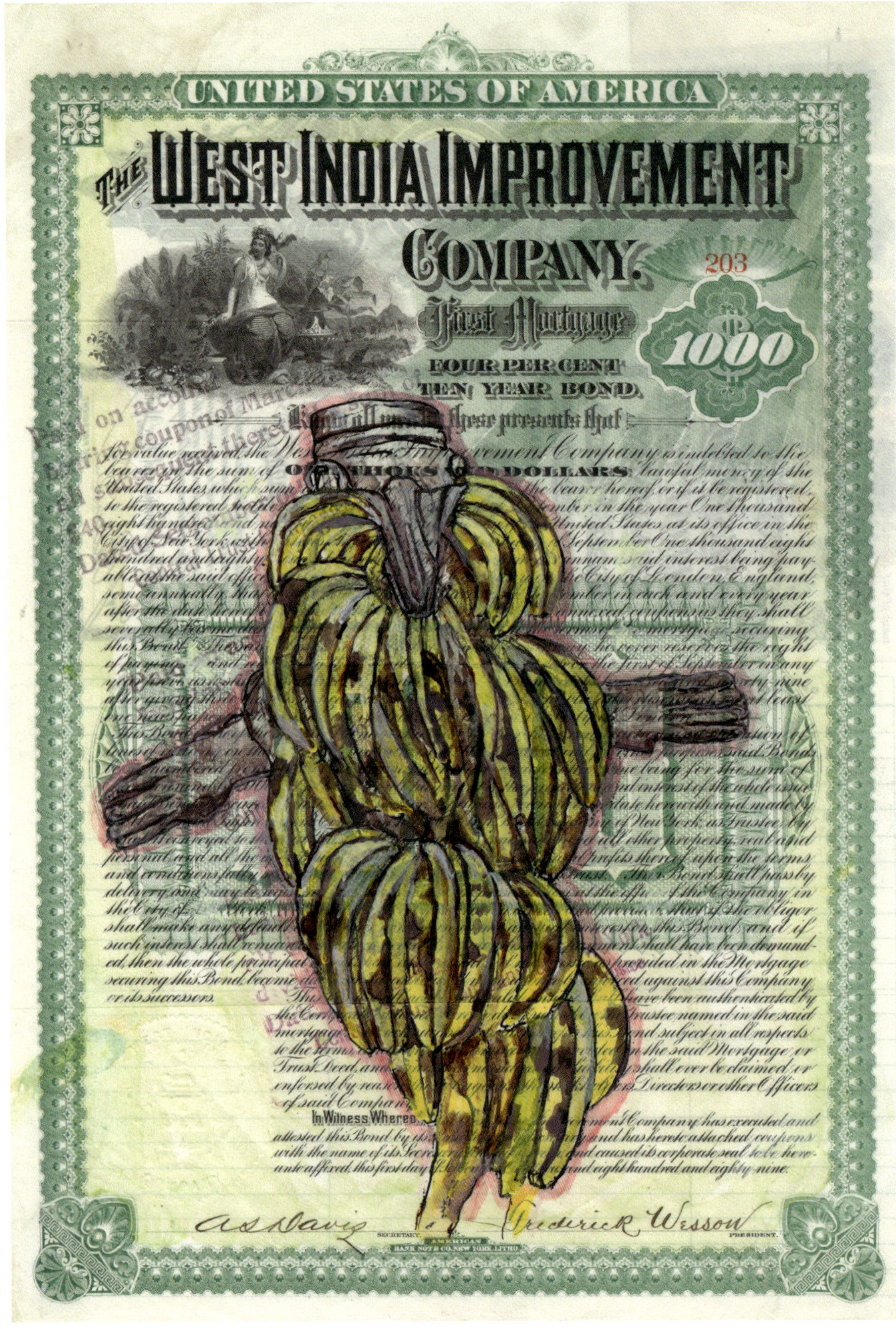

Hew Locke, *West India Improvement Company 1*, 2021.

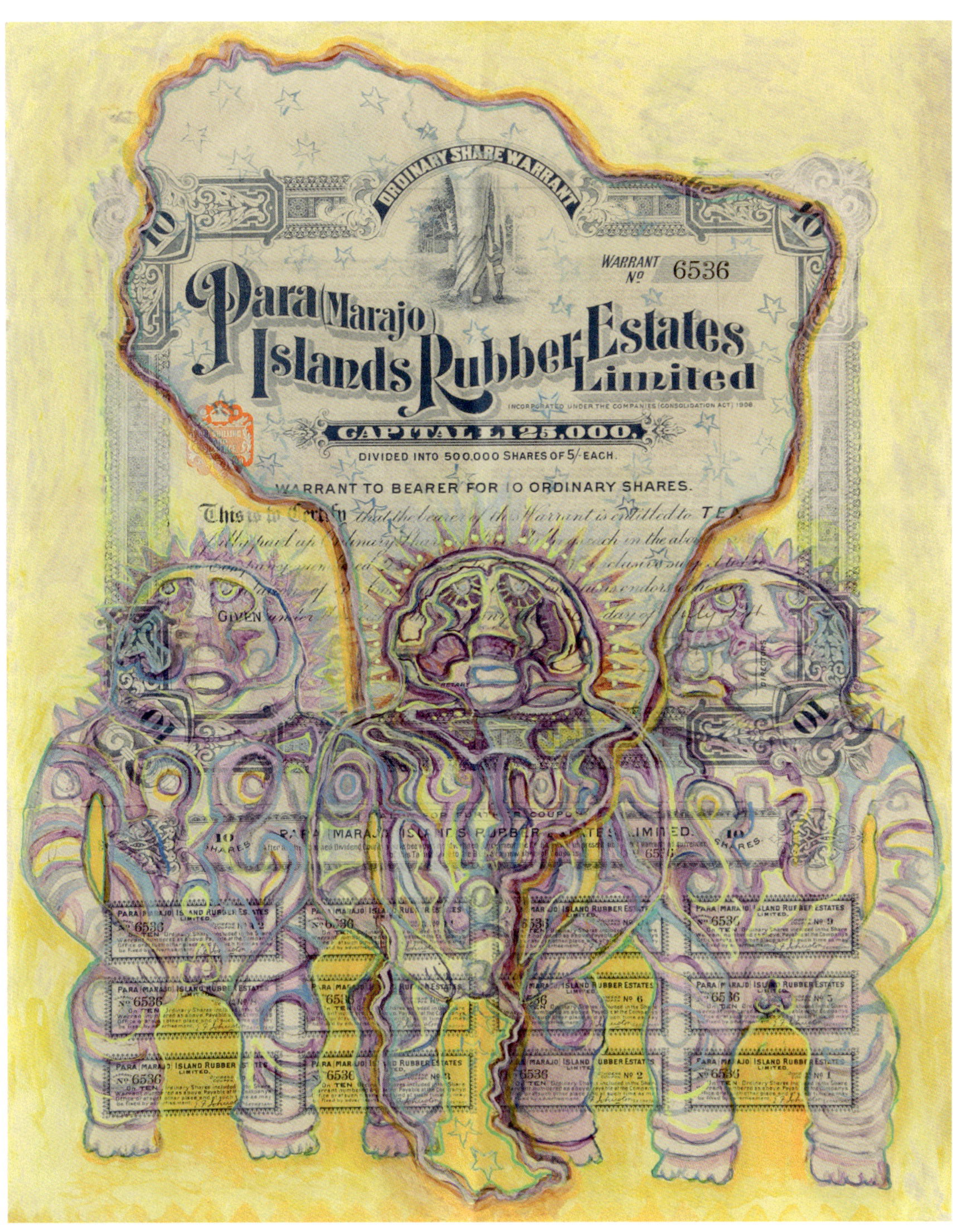

Hew Locke, *Para (Marajo) 3*, 2013.

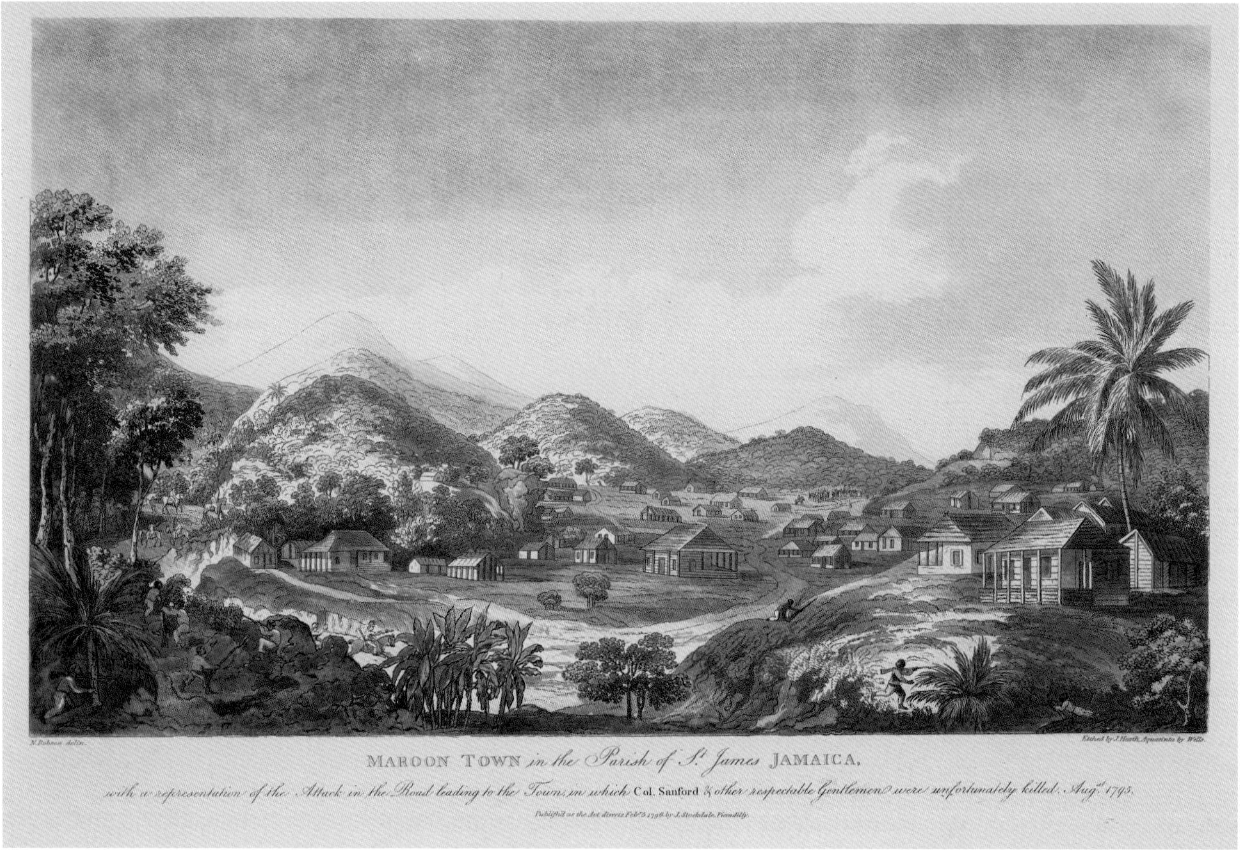

James Heath, *Maroon Town in the Parish of St James Jamaica*, 1796.

Agostino Brunias, A Cudgeling Match between English and French West Indians on the Island of Dominica, 1779.

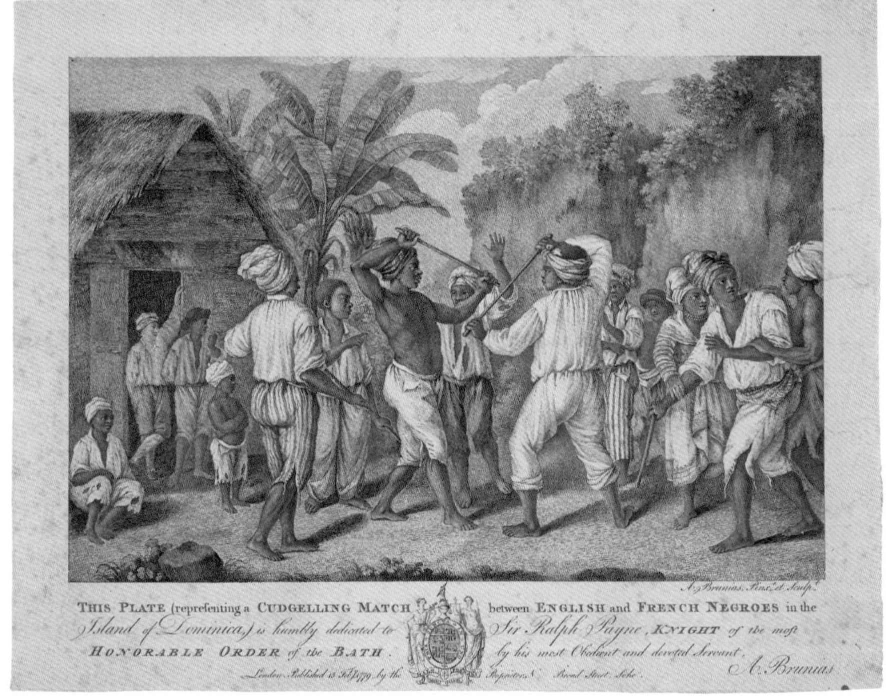

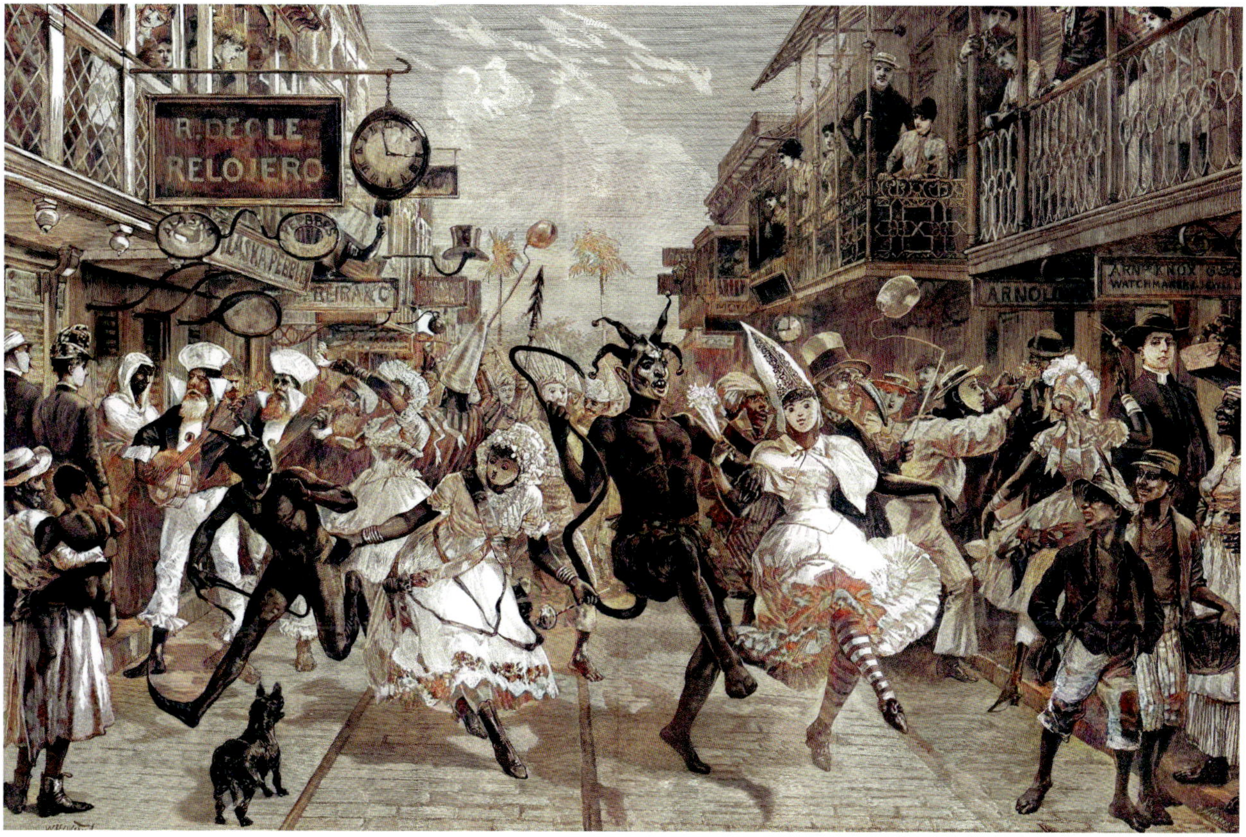

William Heysham Overend, after Melton Prior,
Carnival in Port of Spain, Trinidad, 1888.

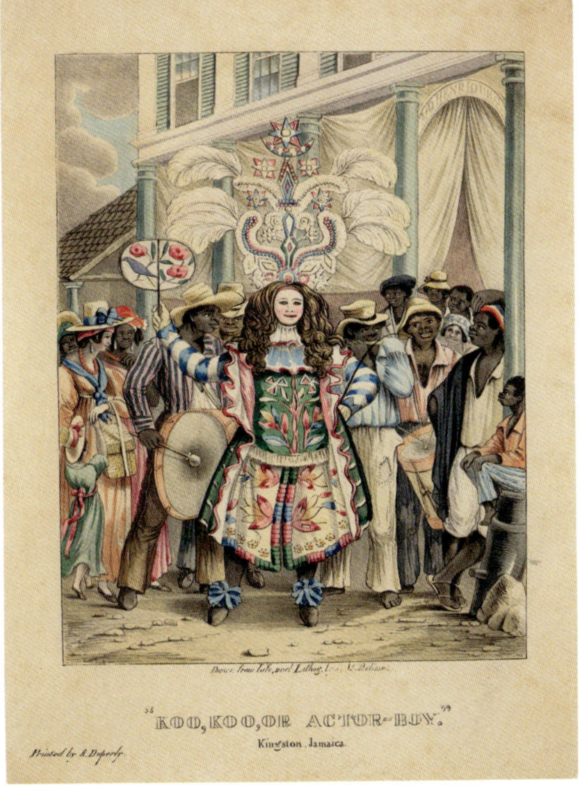

Isaac Mendes Belisario, *Koo, Koo,
or Actor-Boy*, 1837–8.

The East India Company (EIC) had been gaining territory in India in the 1700s through a series of brutal battles. After years of resistance, Tipu Sultan – the ruler of the Kingdom of Mysore in South India – was defeated during the siege of Seringapatam (Srirangapatna) in 1799. A commemorative war medal shows Tipu, also known as the 'Tiger of Mysore', defeated by the 'Lion of England' (p. 127). As the British broke the walls of his fortress and his advisors encouraged him to escape, Tipu is claimed to have said that it was 'better to live one day as a tiger than a thousand years as a sheep'. Many of his personal possessions were taken, including his ring and sabre, as well as a tiger's head from his throne (p. 128). Tipu had commissioned the throne in 1787 in the form of a *howdah* (platform) carried by a tiger. With precious stone inlay, a canopy decorated with pearls and its gilded wooden structure illuminated with Arabic verses, it was a powerful image of Indian sovereignty. When Srirangapatna fell, the British seized the throne and broke up its ornaments. Many, including the tiger's head finial, are now in British public and private collections. Tipu's final defeat was recreated as a 36-metre-wide panoramic painting by Sir Robert Ker Porter (1777–1842) and exhibited in London. A print made after *The Storming of Seringapatam* (p. 129) represents the moment British troops identified the body of the fallen Tipu.

In 1857 a military mutiny against the EIC escalated into the nationwide Indian Uprising (1857–8) against British rule in India. Though the rebellion was eventually brutally suppressed, it saw the end of Company rule and paved the way for later independence. The Rani of Jhansi, Lakshmibai Newalkar (1828–1858), was a leading figure of the Indian Uprising, and became a national hero. In this souvenir booklet for the iconic 1953 film, she is depicted riding a horse into battle (p. 130).

During the uprising British soldiers looted and destroyed the Qaisar Bagh palace in Lucknow. Charles Canning, Governor-General of India, chose a white marble kiosk from the palace to present to Queen Victoria. The collage opposite imagines it installed in the East Terrace Gardens of Windsor Castle. The queen instead placed it in her private gardens at Frogmore Cottage, where it remains in use today.

"Tipu Sultan has always fascinated me. He was mythologised even while he was still alive."

"Tipu Sultan has always fascinated me. He was mythologised even while he was still alive. He was one of the last people holding out against the EIC. His troops were trained by the French and he allied himself with them. The desire to keep the French out of India and Mysore under British control was the EIC's motivation for the wars. Tipu's ring (p. 128) is important because it was something very personal to him, something that he touched and used. The tiger was Tipu's symbol so he put it everywhere – on his weapons, his throne (pp. 128–9). The British did the same with the lion.

The Rani of Jhansi is another symbol of resistance (p. 130). According to the story, when her castle was taken, she got on her white horse and leapt off the battlements with her baby son tied to her back, escaped, and joined the resistance army. When they eventually lost, she broke up her pearl necklace and gave a pearl to each soldier." HL

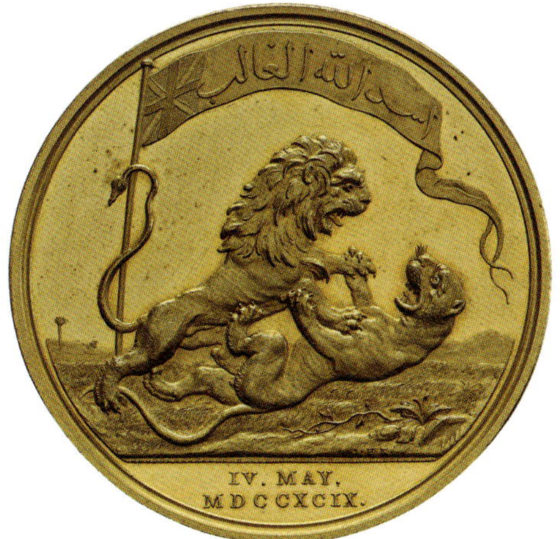

Conrad Heinrich Küchler,
Seringapatam medal, 1799.

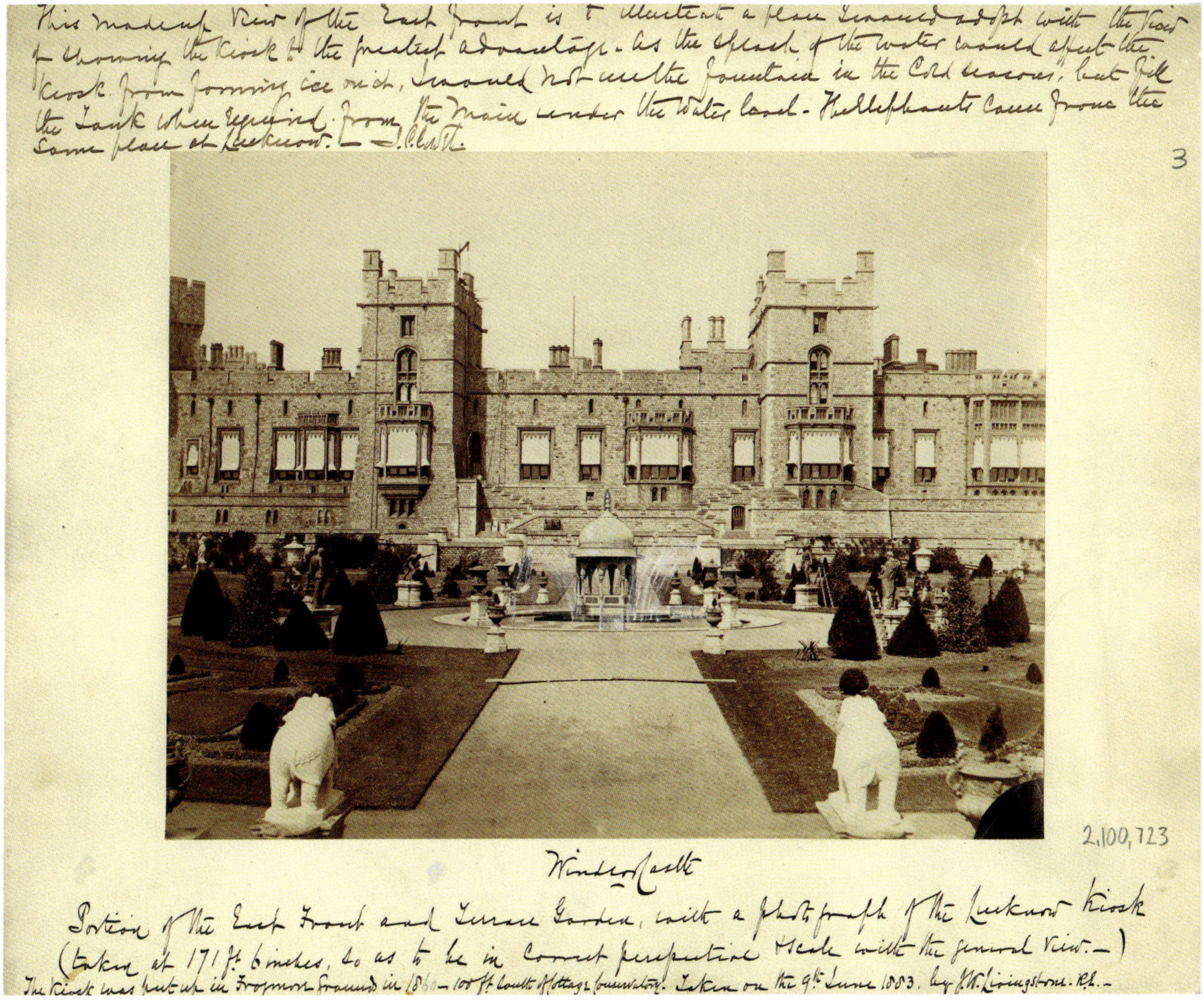

John Wesley Livingston, *Windsor Castle: Proposal for the East Terrace Gardens*, 1883.

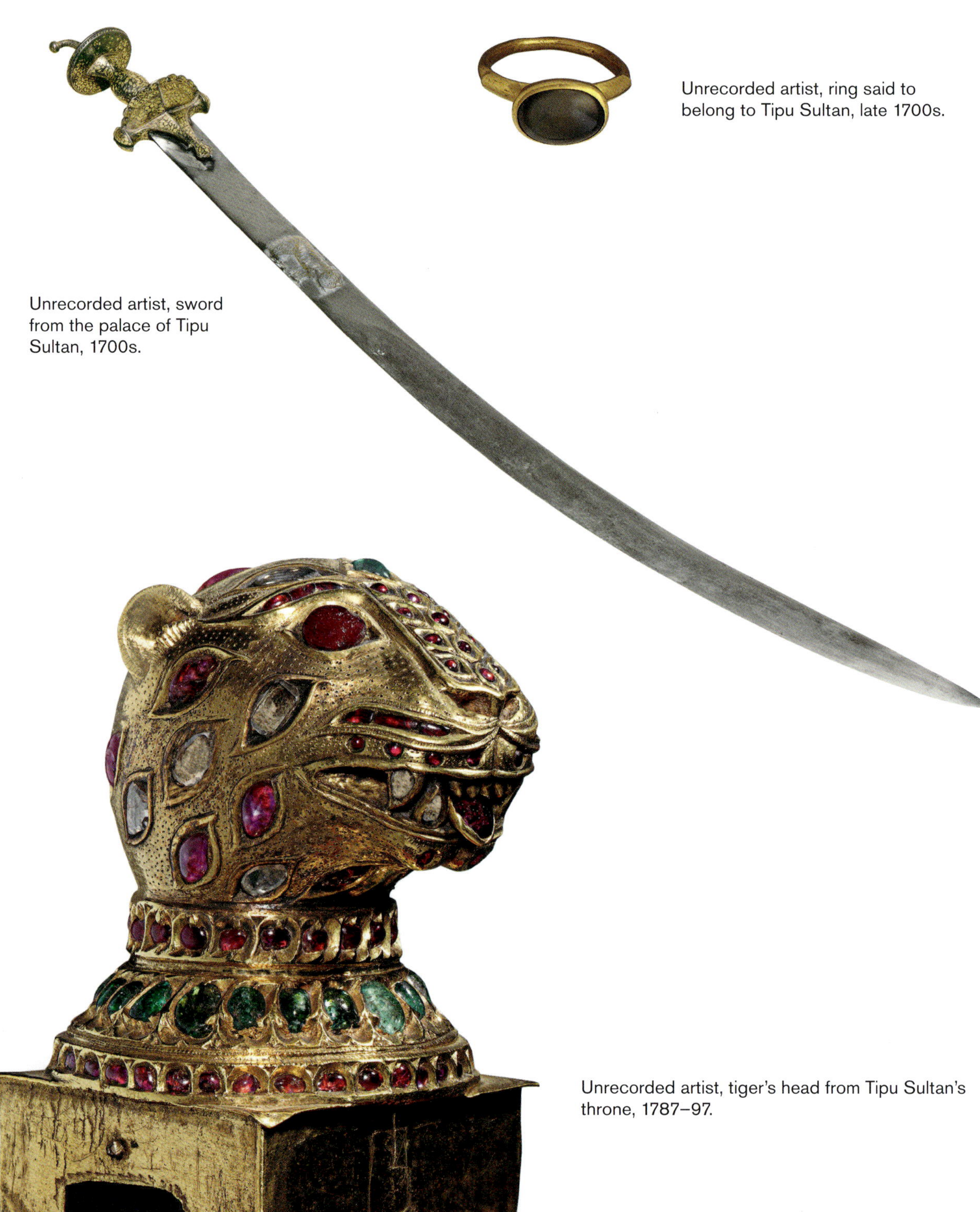

Unrecorded artist, ring said to belong to Tipu Sultan, late 1700s.

Unrecorded artist, sword from the palace of Tipu Sultan, 1700s.

Unrecorded artist, tiger's head from Tipu Sultan's throne, 1787–97.

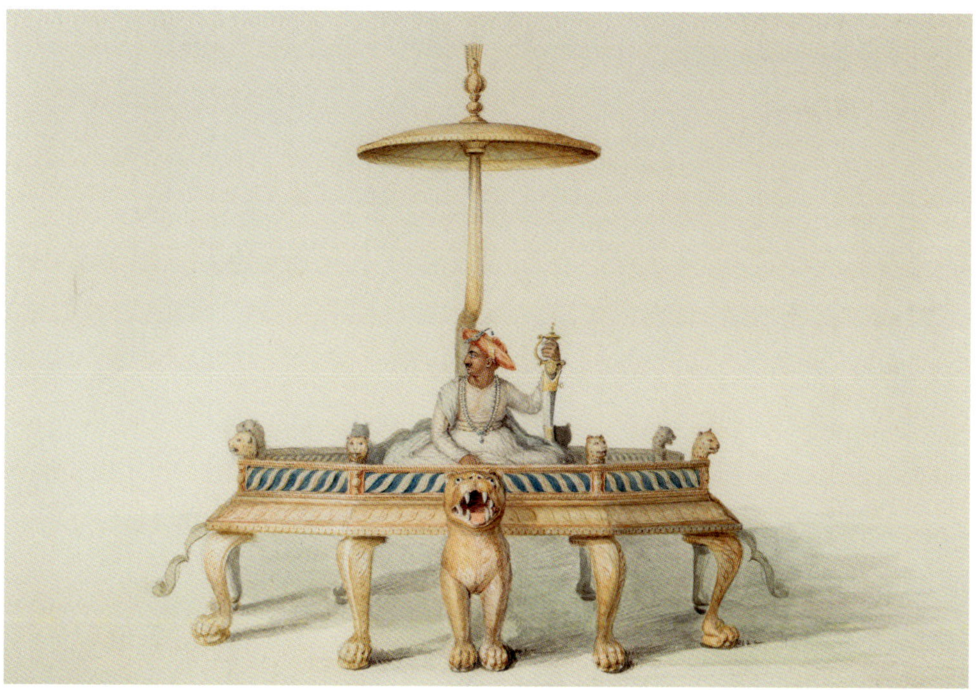

Anna Tonelli, *Tipu Sultan enthroned*, 1800.

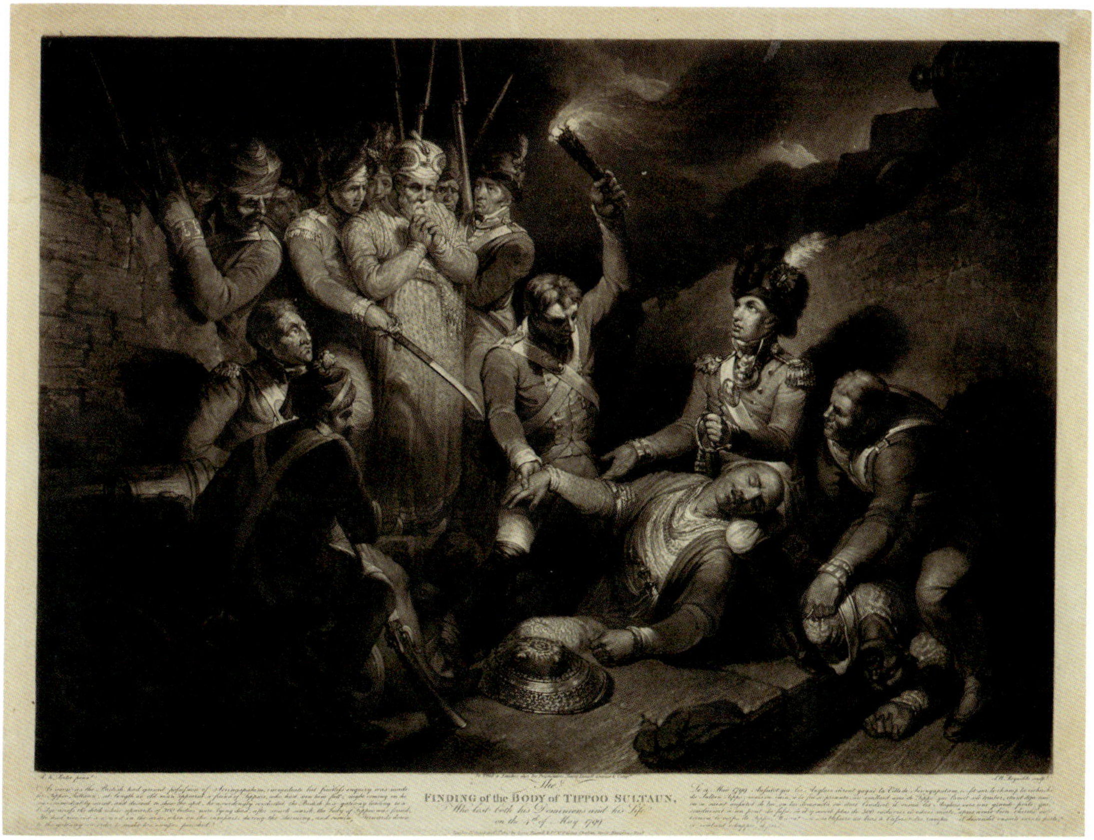

Samuel William Reynolds I, after Sir Robert Ker Porter, *The finding of the body of Tipu Sultan*, 1800.

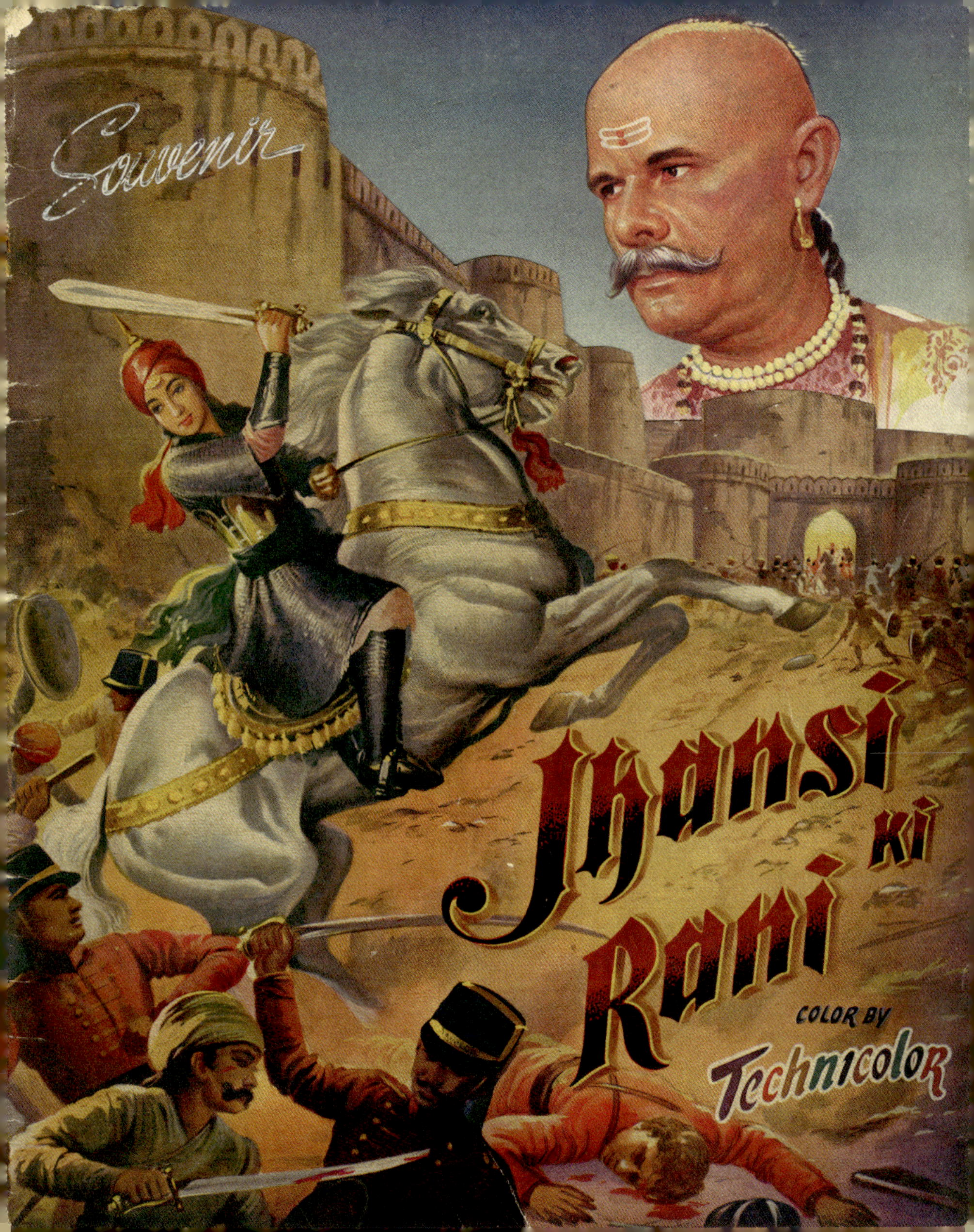

Souvenir
Jhansi Ki Rani
COLOR BY
Technicolor

In the late 1800s Britain, along with other European powers, violently seized territory across the African continent in what became known as the 'Scramble for Africa'. Colonial wars and occupations, including invasions routinely called 'expeditions', were met with fierce resistance. Named after its maker, the engineer Hiram Maxim (1840–1916), this machine gun (p. 133) gave the British a weapon that allowed them to carry out massacres with few casualties on their side. Used from the late 1880s in Africa, it became an effective and violent way to ensure colonial administration of territory, such as in the Second Boer War (South Africa, 1899–1902). The prolific use of the Maxim gun was retrospectively erased from visual history; representations of battles generally focused on hand-to-hand combat and acts of individual heroism. The sheer number of military campaigns throughout Africa during this period is evidenced by commemoration medals presented to soldiers, each with a new bar representing a different conflict (p. 132). The bars on the South African War medal list battles and sieges fought during the Second Boer War. The Anglo-Asante War medal shows an image of hand-to-hand combat, both sides armed with rifles.

In the 1950s Gikuyu Kenyans organised themselves into groups known as the Mau Mau and targeted military bases to fight back against colonial land grabs. Their handmade firearms were formed of everyday materials such as door bolts, rubber bands and irrigation piping (p. 134). Though probably very unsafe to fire and perhaps used as blunt weapons, they were an important symbol of anti-colonial authority.

In 1878 Sir Henry Bartle Frere (1815–1884), High Commissioner for the British Empire in South Africa, initiated the invasion of Zululand. These horns were engraved by a Zulu artist (p. 135) with European soldiers holding rifles and musical instruments, and travelling by train and on a penny-farthing, as well as Zulus with spears and shields. The war lasted from January to July 1879, with a British victory eventually leading to the annexation of Zululand in 1887. The Sudanese Kaskara sword, the Edo crossbow and ceremonial sword from Benin (p. 134) are all examples of the types of weapons that would be collected by European soldiers and colonial officers at the end of battles, both as trophies of war and as ethnographic curiosities.

"Violence underpins the enlargement of any state – even if you don't use it, the threat is there."

"I am interested in these medals (p. 132) because similar ones were handed out to the troops who took part in the Benin Expedition (1897). Because there were so many conflicts in Africa, they didn't design a new one for each conflict – they put a small bar on it. The idea of Pax Britannica was a lie. Someone would rebel and they would have to be suppressed. The Maxim gun represents industrialised killing, basically. The gun that won an empire. Weaponry is a strong feature of this book as violence underpins the enlargement of any state; even if you don't use it, the threat is there. There's something cold and mechanical about it.

If anyone's seen the 1964 film *Zulu*, it depicts their battle formation in the shape of horns against the Red Coats. In the 80s and 90s, at Christmas you'd sit down and watch *Dam Busters* followed by *Zulu*. It's part of that continuation of the myth of empire past the point where the empire exists anymore." HL

Cover of a souvenir booklet for the film *Jhansi Ki Rani*, 1952.

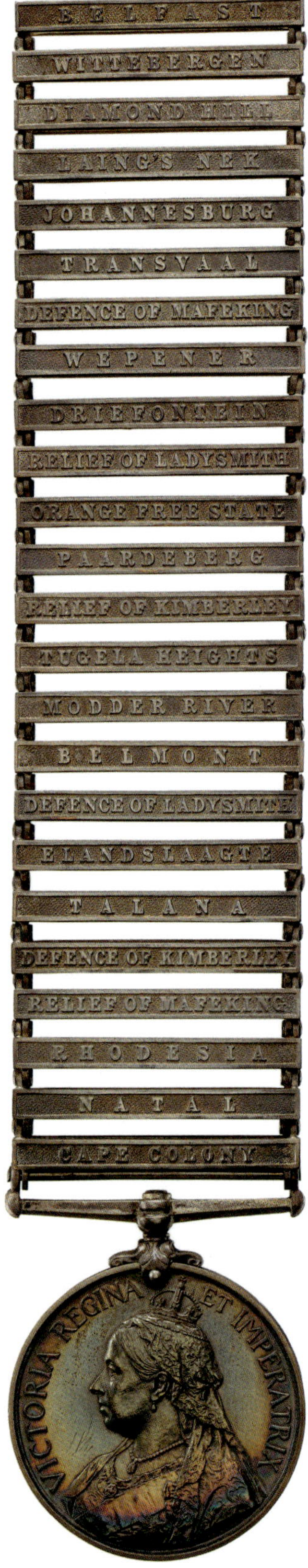

South African War medal, 1910.

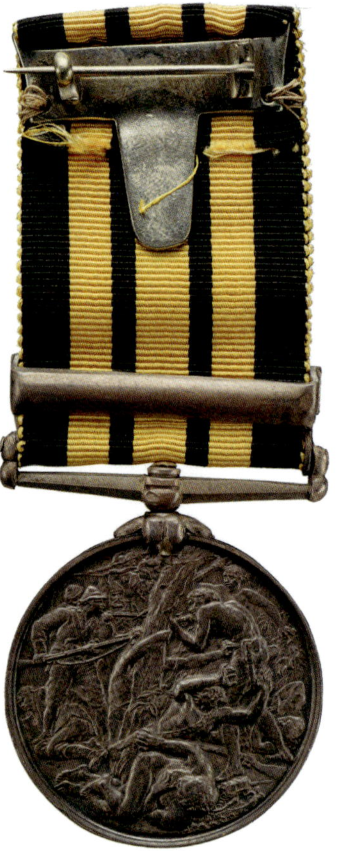

Anglo-Asante War medal, 1874.

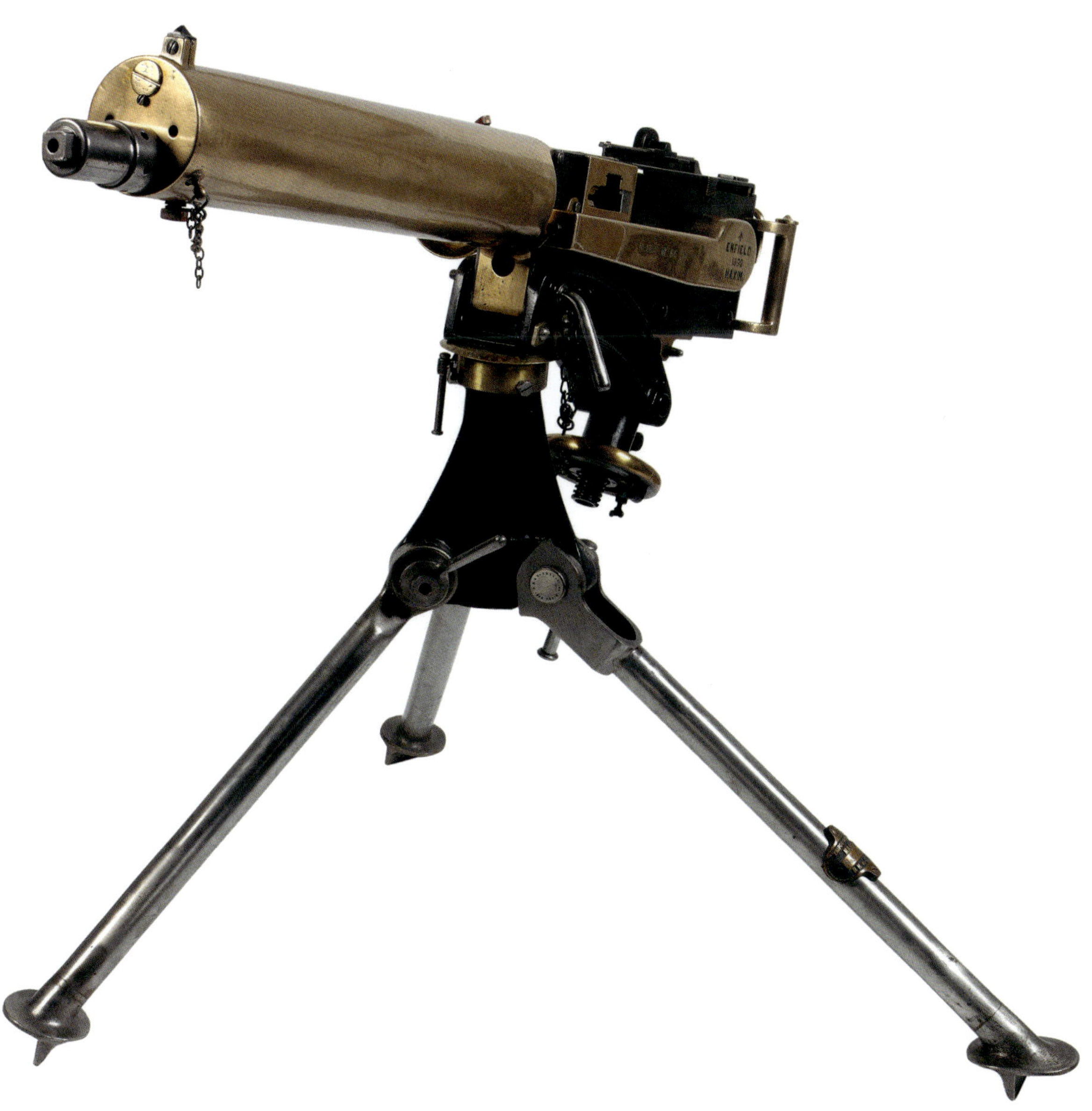

Maxim machine gun, 1892.

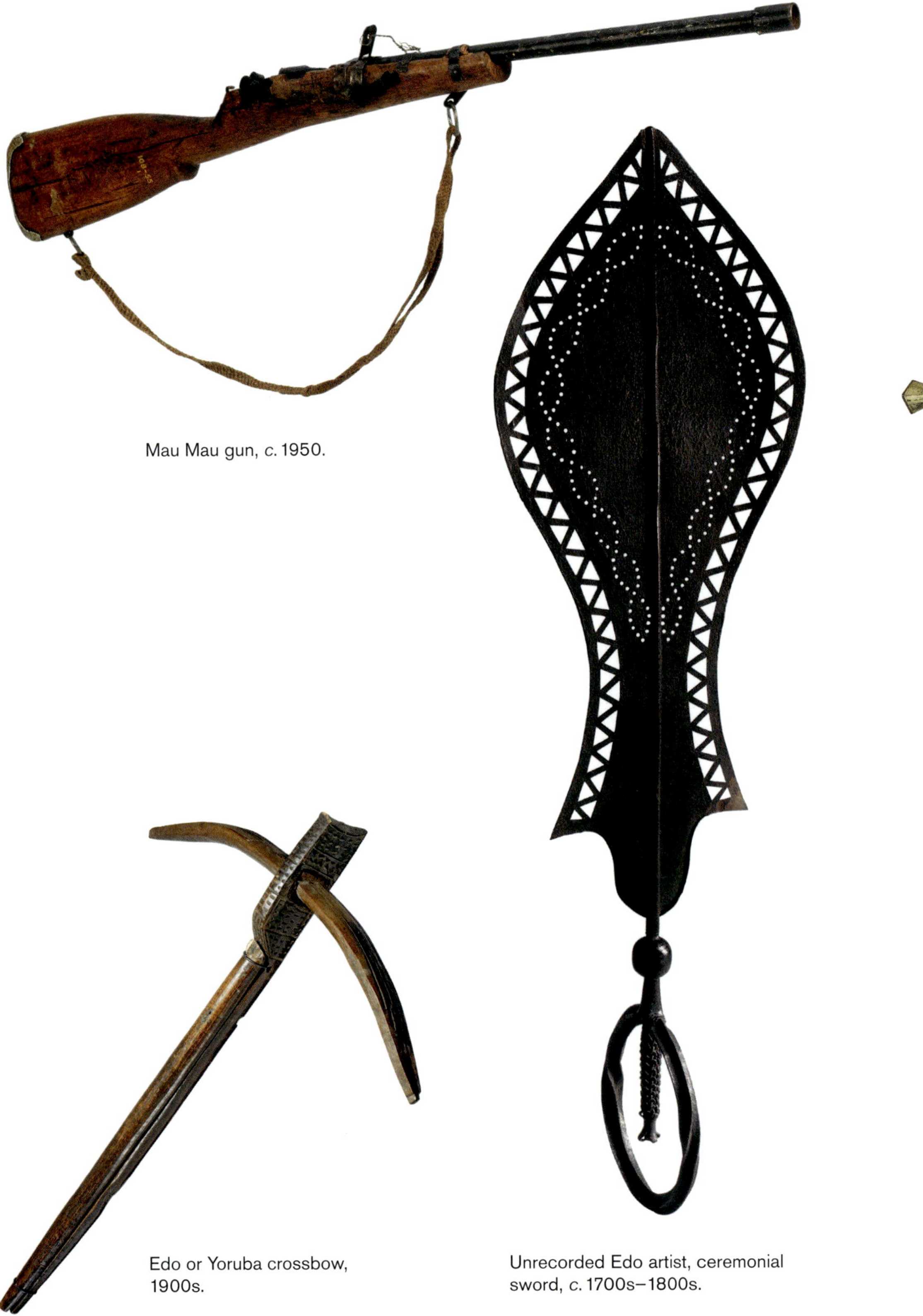

Mau Mau gun, *c.* 1950.

Edo or Yoruba crossbow, 1900s.

Unrecorded Edo artist, ceremonial sword, *c.* 1700s–1800s.

Unrecorded artist, Kaskara sword, *c.* 1900–6.

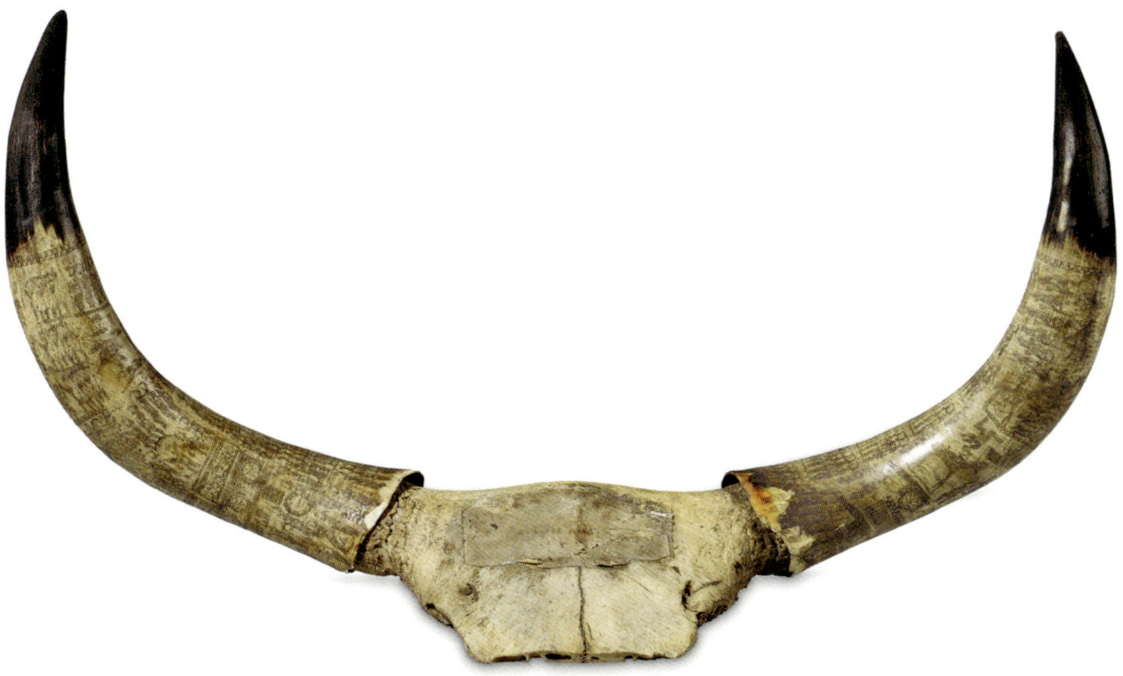

Unrecorded Zulu artist, engraved cattle horns,
c. 1879–99, and detail below.

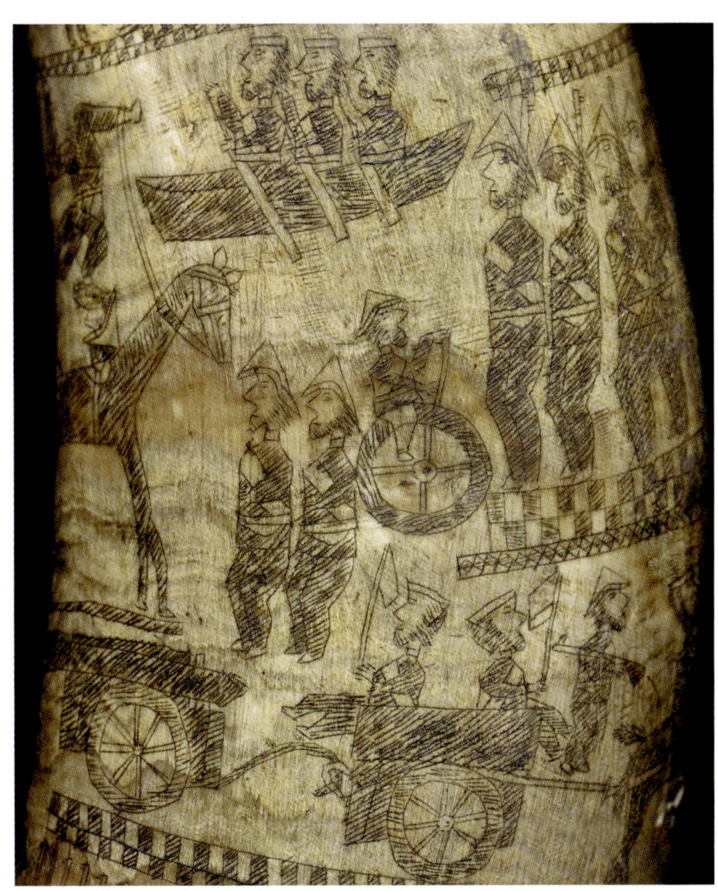

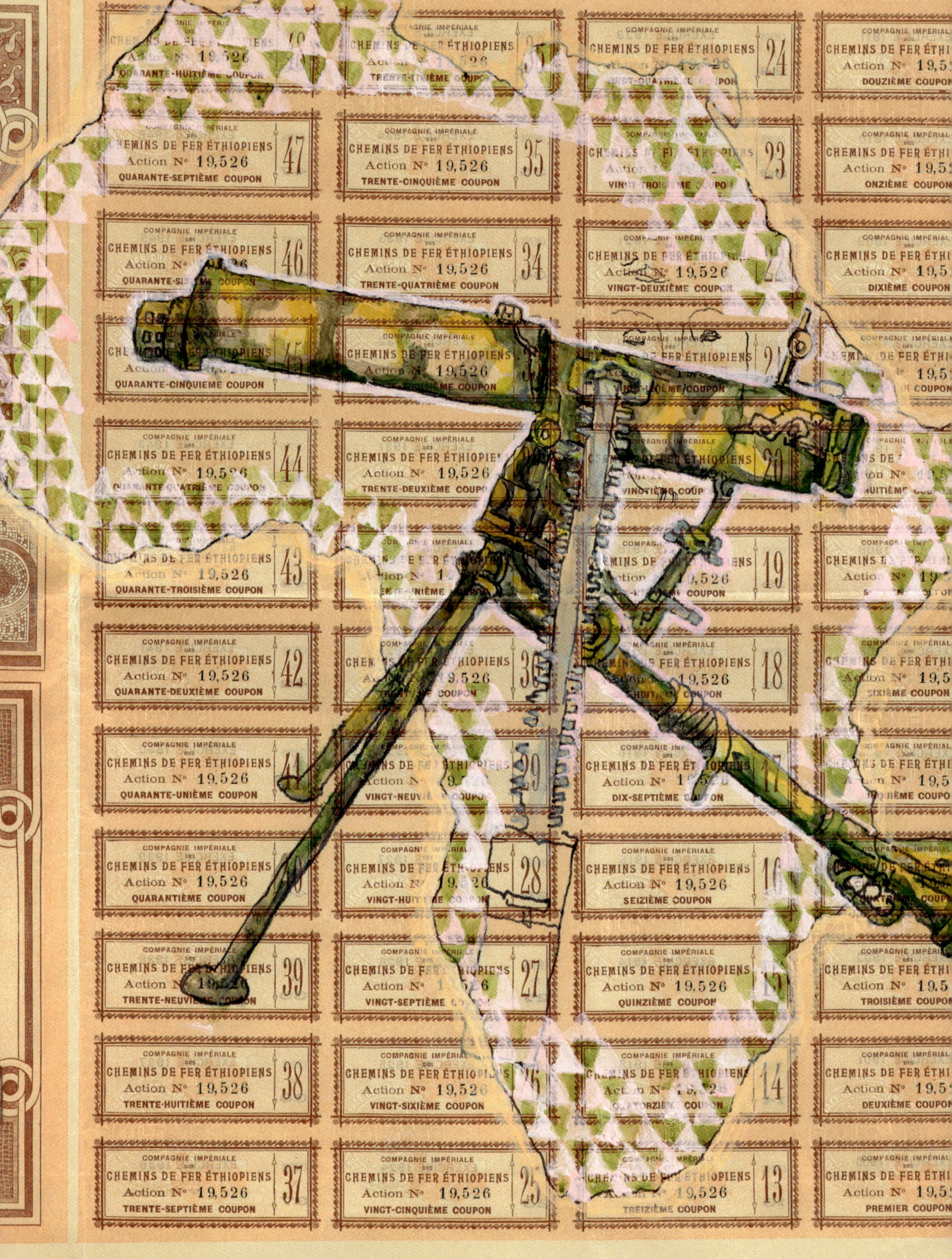
COMPAGNIE IMPÉRIALE DES CHEMINS DE FER ÉTHIOPIENS
Action N° 19,526
QUARANTE-HUITIÈME COUPON 48
TRENTE-SIXIÈME COUPON 36
VINGT-QUATRIÈME COUPON 24
DOUZIÈME COUPON 12
QUARANTE-SEPTIÈME COUPON 47
TRENTE-CINQUIÈME COUPON 35
VINGT-TROISIÈME COUPON 23
ONZIÈME COUPON 11
QUARANTE-SIXIÈME COUPON 46
TRENTE-QUATRIÈME COUPON 34
VINGT-DEUXIÈME COUPON 22
DIXIÈME COUPON 10
QUARANTE-CINQUIÈME COUPON 45
TRENTE-TROISIÈME COUPON 33
VINGT-UNIÈME COUPON 21
NEUVIÈME COUPON 9
QUARANTE-QUATRIÈME COUPON 44
TRENTE-DEUXIÈME COUPON 32
VINGTIÈME COUPON 20
HUITIÈME COUPON 8
QUARANTE-TROISIÈME COUPON 43
TRENTE-UNIÈME COUPON 31
DIX-NEUVIÈME COUPON 19
SEPTIÈME COUPON 7
QUARANTE-DEUXIÈME COUPON 42
TRENTIÈME COUPON 30
DIX-HUITIÈME COUPON 18
SIXIÈME COUPON 6
QUARANTE-UNIÈME COUPON 41
VINGT-NEUVIÈME COUPON 29
DIX-SEPTIÈME COUPON 17
CINQUIÈME COUPON 5
QUARANTIÈME COUPON 40
VINGT-HUITIÈME COUPON 28
SEIZIÈME COUPON 16
QUATRIÈME COUPON 4
TRENTE-NEUVIÈME COUPON 39
VINGT-SEPTIÈME COUPON 27
QUINZIÈME COUPON 15
TROISIÈME COUPON 3
TRENTE-HUITIÈME COUPON 38
VINGT-SIXIÈME COUPON 26
QUATORZIÈME COUPON 14
DEUXIÈME COUPON 2
TRENTE-SEPTIÈME COUPON 37
VINGT-CINQUIÈME COUPON 25
TREIZIÈME COUPON 13
PREMIER COUPON 1

FESTAC '77 was an international festival held over the course of a month in Lagos, Nigeria, celebrating pan-African culture. The festival organisers requested the loan of the Queen Mother Idia pendant mask from the British Museum. The reply stated that the mask was too fragile to travel and instead the Museum offered to produce and lend a replica (p. 138). In response, the Nigerian government commissioned several artists to create their own replicas of the mask. Joseph Alufa Igbinovia carved an ivory version based on a postcard of the original and Erhabor Emokpae created the seminal poster, plastering Queen Mother Idia's image all over Lagos (p. 139).

FESTAC was a watershed moment in Black cultural history. Around 500,000 people from over 50 countries attended. The decision to place the mask of Queen Mother Idia front and centre highlighted its looting from Benin by the British during the 1897 expedition. There are five known ivory masks of a similar style and date; four are held at the British Museum, The Metropolitan Museum of Art, The Al Thani Collection and the Seattle Art Museum. Another was kept in the Linden Museum until 2022 when it was restituted to Nigeria. The openwork carving around Idia's head represented heads of Portuguese men, often associated with ivory. The title of Iyoba (Queen Mother) was specifically created for Idia when she helped her son Esigie to become the Oba. She was a highly respected authority and advisor, and was recorded as providing medicines and charms for her son in battle.

"This is the African equivalent of the *Mona Lisa*."

"I remember talking to [Guyanese artist] Aubrey Williams (1926–1990) about FESTAC. He was talking about how extraordinary it felt to be there. It was such a refreshing thing to go to something happening in Africa. It gave him a real boost – living in England for a Black artist wasn't easy back then and it was the same for my dad [artist Donald Locke, 1930–2010]. Aubrey also told me about Nigeria not being able to borrow the Queen Idia ivory mask, and that was the first time I'd heard about the piece. For FESTAC, the idea was that the mask wasn't safe to travel to its country of origin. At the end of our show, by contrast, there's a replica of an Ife head (p. 175) – while the real one is back in Africa.

It's about how you make something stolen iconic – the empty space. This festival and its poster made the mask famous. In a world where we're having debates about authenticity and virtual art, this is fascinating. The mask itself is the African equivalent of the *Mona Lisa*. It's a clichéd shorthand symbol for the heights of culture from sub-Saharan Africa. I've used it sometimes as a trope. But I've underestimated its beauty. It's a clichéd image, like Botticelli's *Birth of Venus*, but at the same time it's very special." HL

Detail, Hew Locke, *Company of the Imperial Railway of Ethiopia 5*, 2024 (see p. 149).

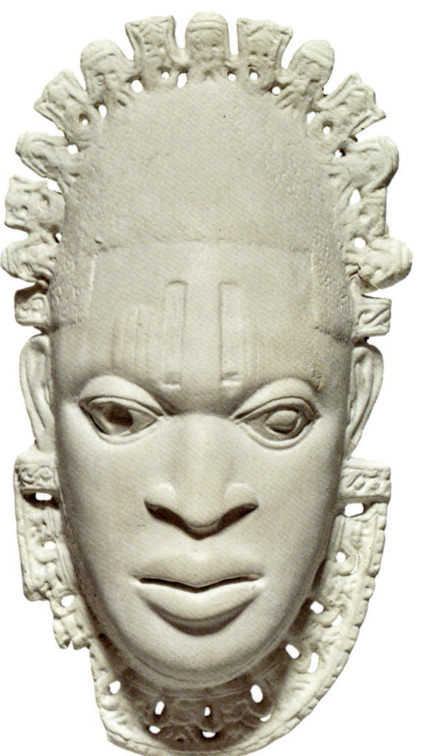

Unrecorded British artist, pendant mask cast, cast *c.* 1940–58, original 1500s.

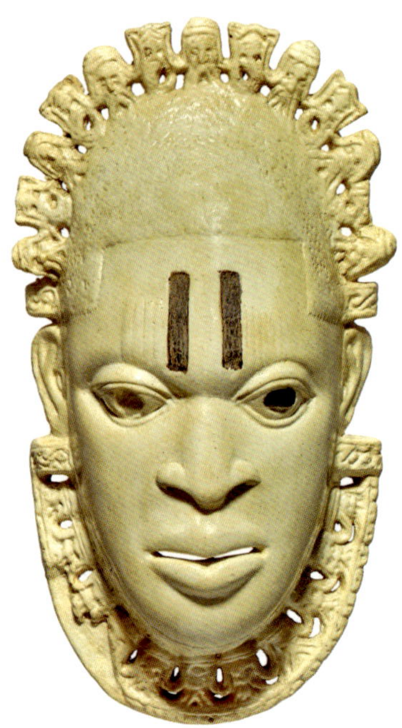

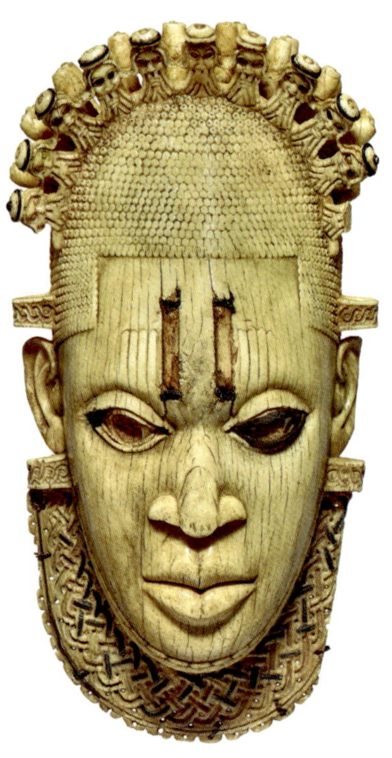

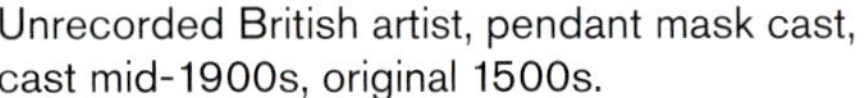

Unrecorded British artist, pendant mask cast, cast mid-1900s, original 1500s.

Derrick C. Giles, pendant mask cast, cast 1977, original 1500s.

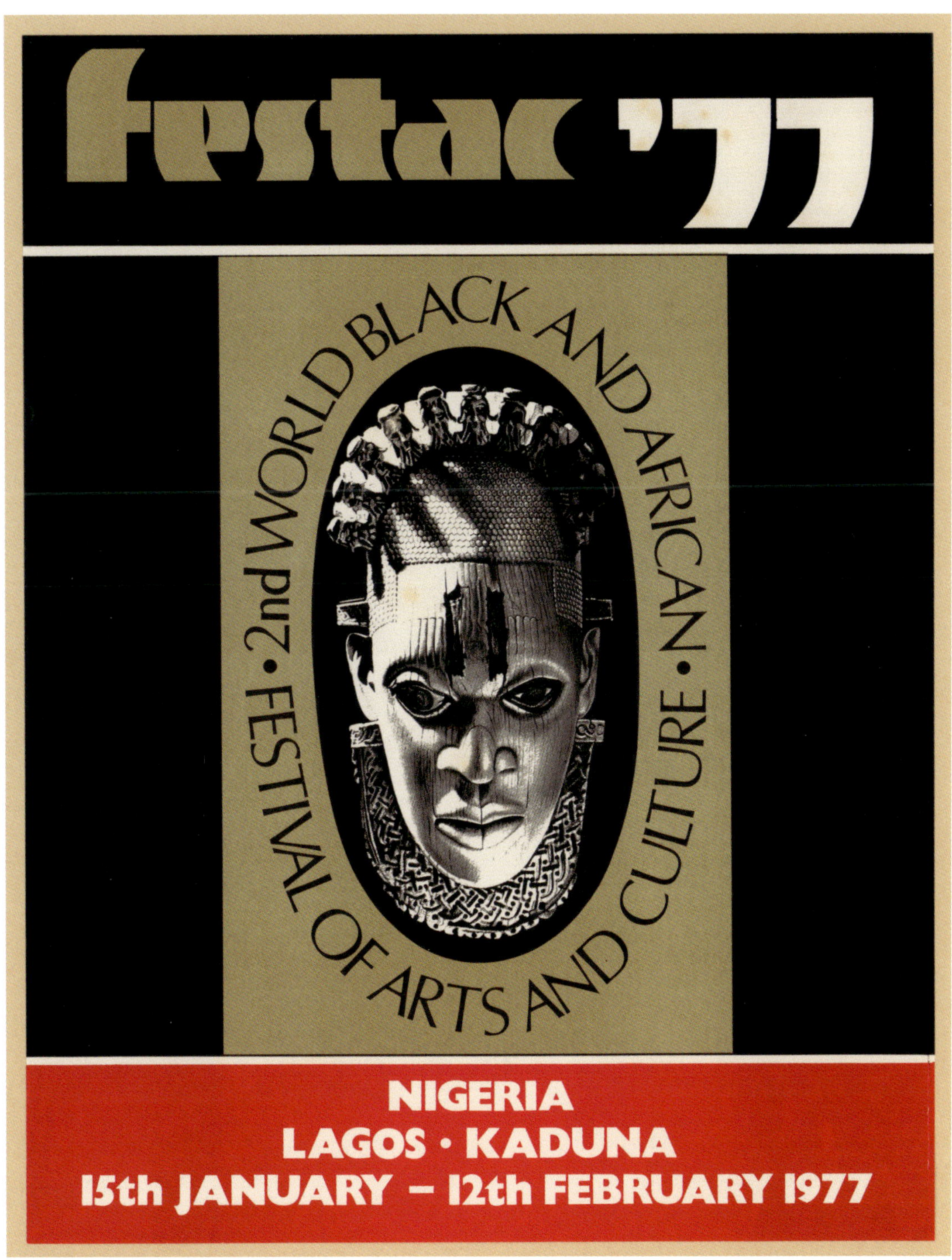

Erhabor Emokpae, FESTAC '77 poster, 1977.

The gradual expansion by the British into territory neighbouring the Kingdom of Benin, and an increasing reluctance to accept Benin's trading conditions, created an atmosphere of distrust and animosity between the two powers. In January 1897 an allegedly peaceful but clearly provocative British trade mission was attacked on its way to Benin City, leading to the deaths of 7 British delegates and 230 of the mission's African carriers. This triggered large-scale retaliation, and in February 1897 Benin City was captured.

"These objects have symbolic and ritual importance, but they are also personally directly linked to the Oba. He would have worn these things, held these things."

Benin suffered a bloody and devastating occupation. No exact figure can be given for the number of its population killed but accounts suggest many casualties. Benin City saw widespread destruction and pillaging by British forces, including the burning of the Royal Palace and other monuments. These discs from the palace, which incorporate images of European men, show evidence of fire damage likely caused during the invasion (p. 145). Thousands of objects of ceremonial and ritual value were taken to the UK as official 'spoils of war' or distributed among members of the expedition according to their rank, as evidenced by photographs taken at the time (p. 146).

Oba Ovonramwen Nogbaisi (r. 1888–97) exercised a monopoly over trade in Benin, and until the 1897 Expedition, he had been largely independent from British rule. His coral regalia (p. 144), symbolic of his power and status, was looted by British forces. The Nigerian photographer Jonathan Adagogo Green (1873–1905) photographed the Oba aboard the SS *Ivy* – the British ship taking the Oba into exile in Calabar, Nigeria (pp. 141–3). Traditionally, the Oba was depicted seated when everyone else was standing. Here, his dress is elegant, but his bare head and shackled feet betray his status as prisoner. Green's photographs were published in British newspapers but his name rarely appeared in print; he marked the reverse of his photos with his studio stamp 'J.A. Green, Artist Photographer', which can be seen on this Christmas card featuring his architectural photographs (p. 147).

"I wonder who directed the scenarios in Green's photographs (pp. 141–3). Was it Green, was it the officer in charge? The expression on the Oba's face is interesting. In one image he's smiling, a wry moment of noting what has changed – well, that's my interpretation. I don't think you'd have got that smile if it hadn't been an African photographer. It might be one person acknowledging to another, 'see what things have come to.' Green must have known this commission was one of the most important moments of his career; the weight of history is in these images.

I hadn't come across the discs from the Royal Palace before (p. 145) and wanted to draw them out. A whole civilisation was boxed up and shipped out. Beautiful things like this became minutiae. They're beautiful, of course, but the physical damage shows evidence of conflict, like the Second World War bombing damage at the V&A Museum or Tate Britain. As for the Oba's regalia (p. 144), the coral tradition continues today, you can go to shops selling African fabric and you'll see fake plastic or real bits of coral. It is a legacy from this time." HL

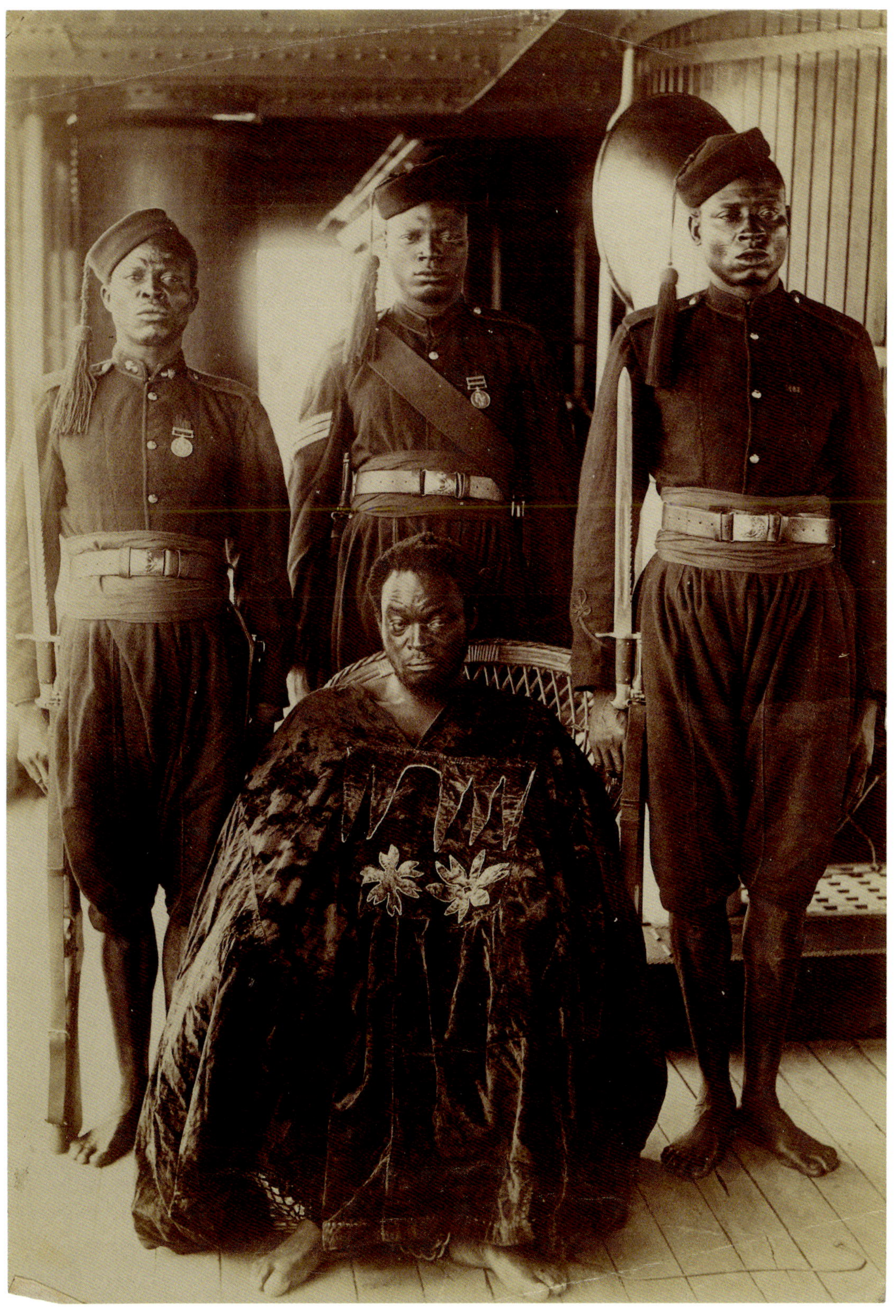

Jonathan Adagogo Green, Oba Ovonramwen Nogbaisi on-board the SS *Ivy* with soldiers, 1897.

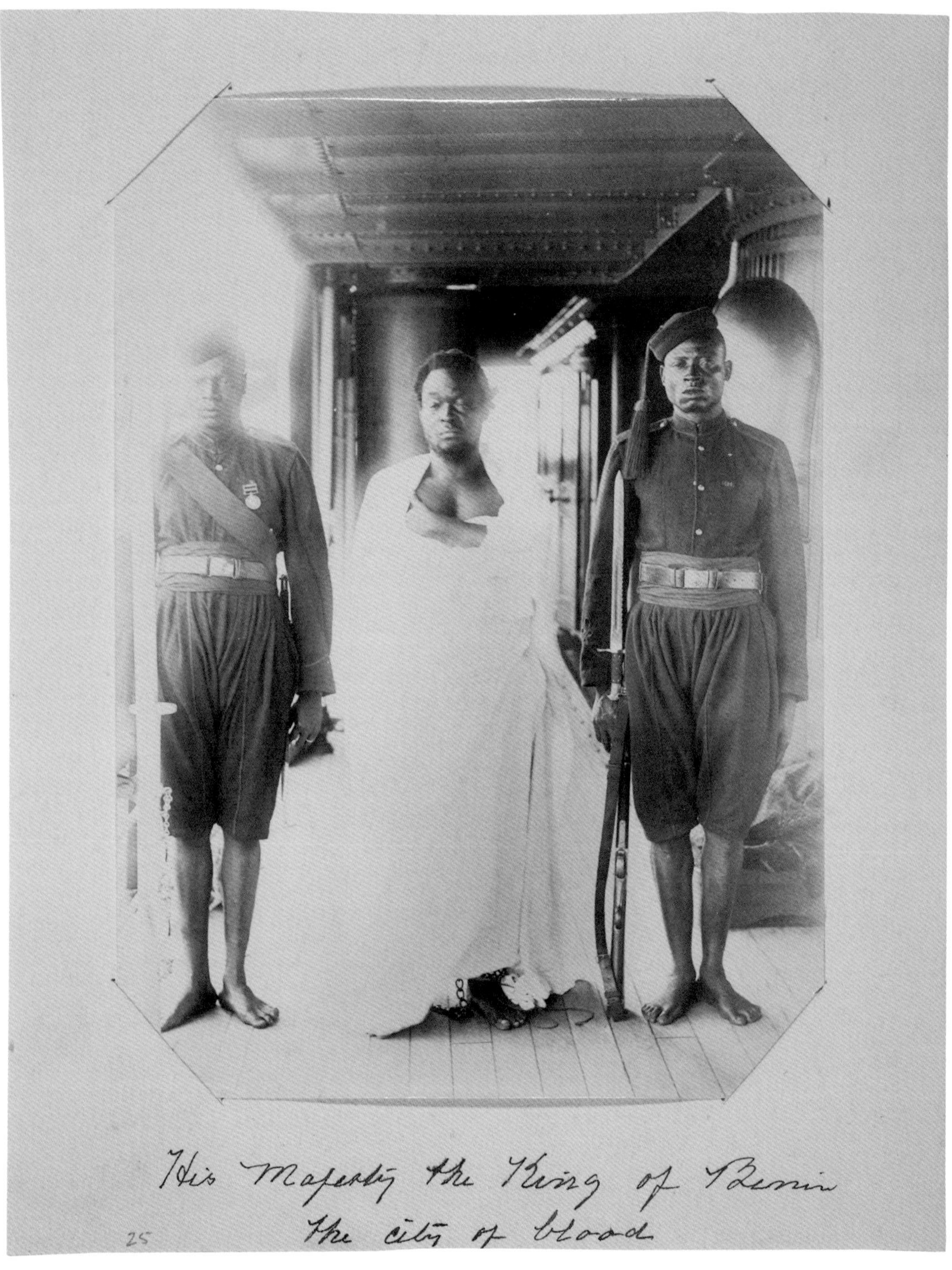

Jonathan Adagogo Green, Oba Ovonramwen Nogbaisi on-board the SS *Ivy* with soldiers, 1897.

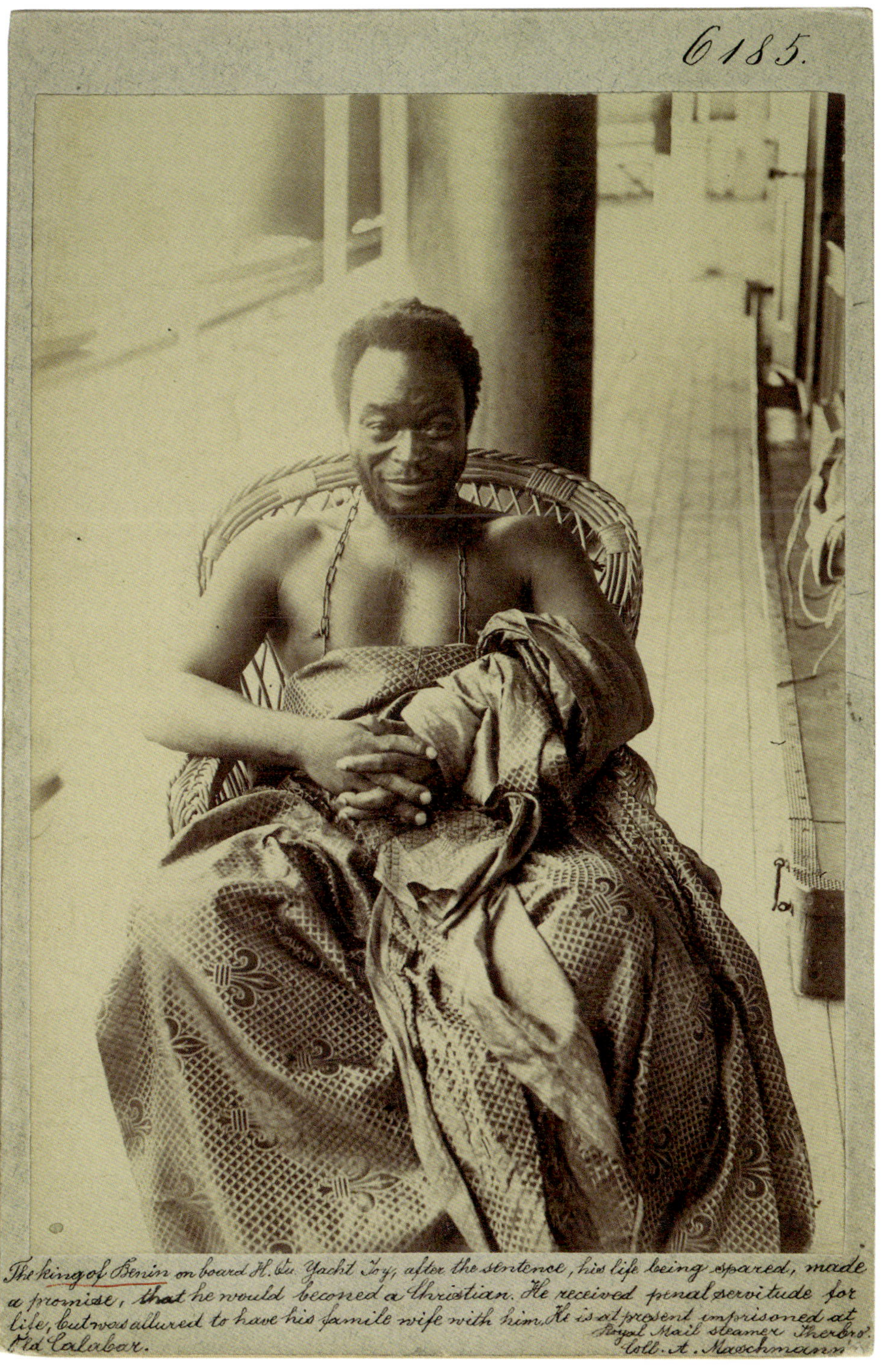

Jonathan Adagogo Green, Oba Ovonramwen Nogbaisi on-board the SS *Ivy*, 1897.

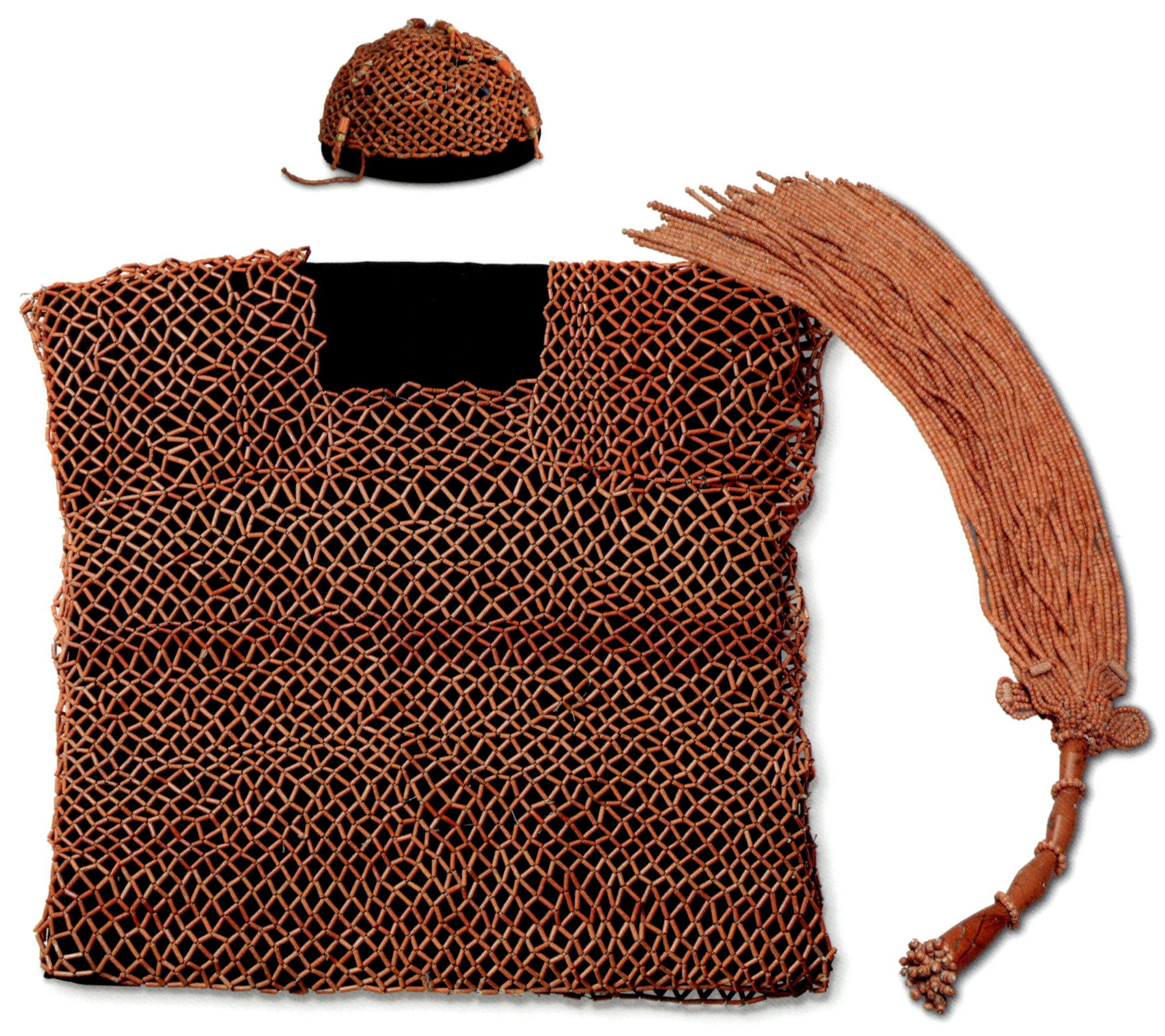

Unrecorded Edo artist, ceremonial crown,
corslet and flywhisk, *c.* 1700s–1800s.

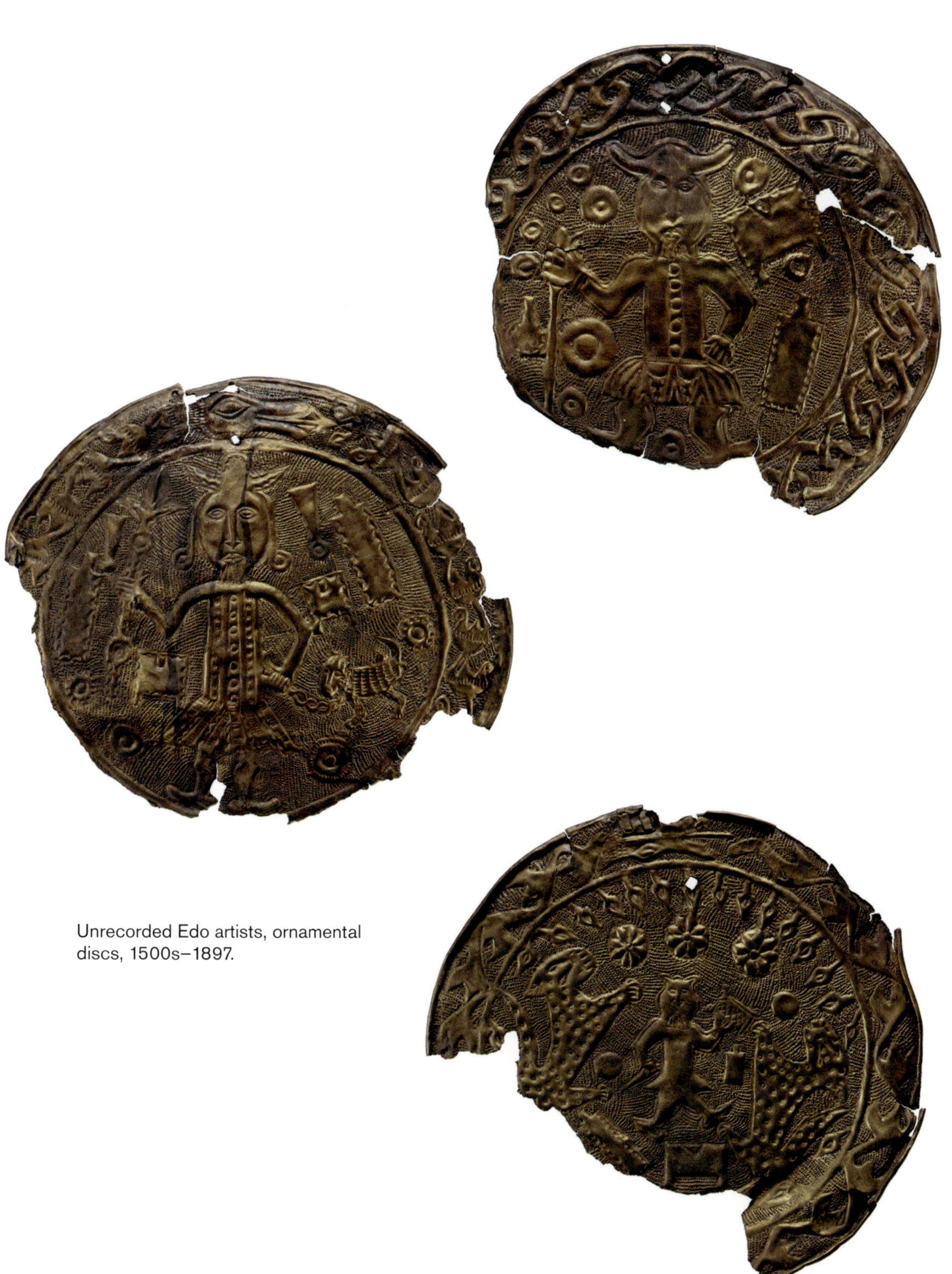

Unrecorded Edo artists, ornamental discs, 1500s–1897.

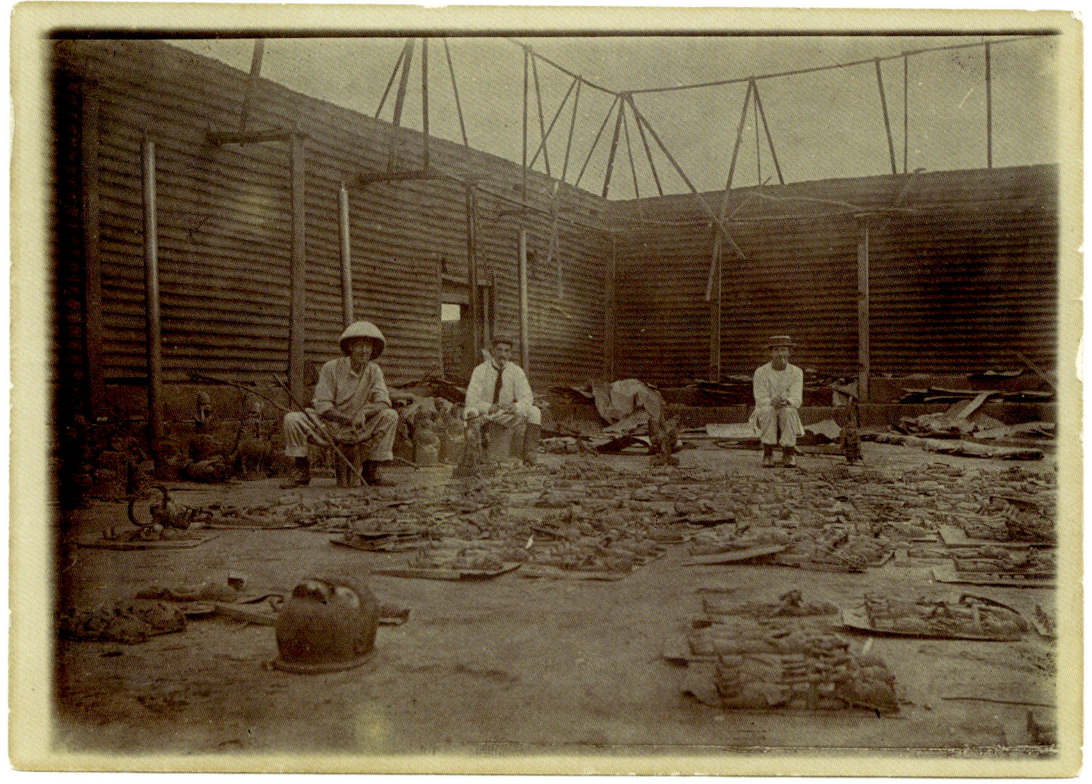

Reginald Kerr Granville, British soldiers posing with Benin artefacts in the
Oba's compound, 1897.

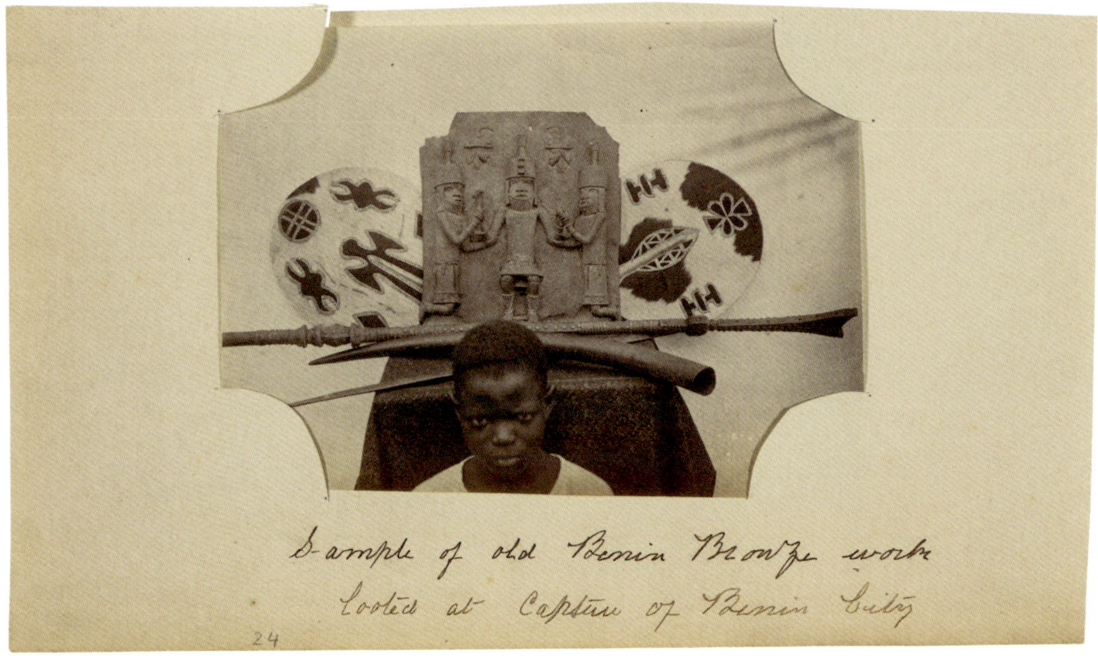

Unrecorded photographer, *Sample of old Benin Bronze work looted at Capture
of Benin City*, 1897–1905.

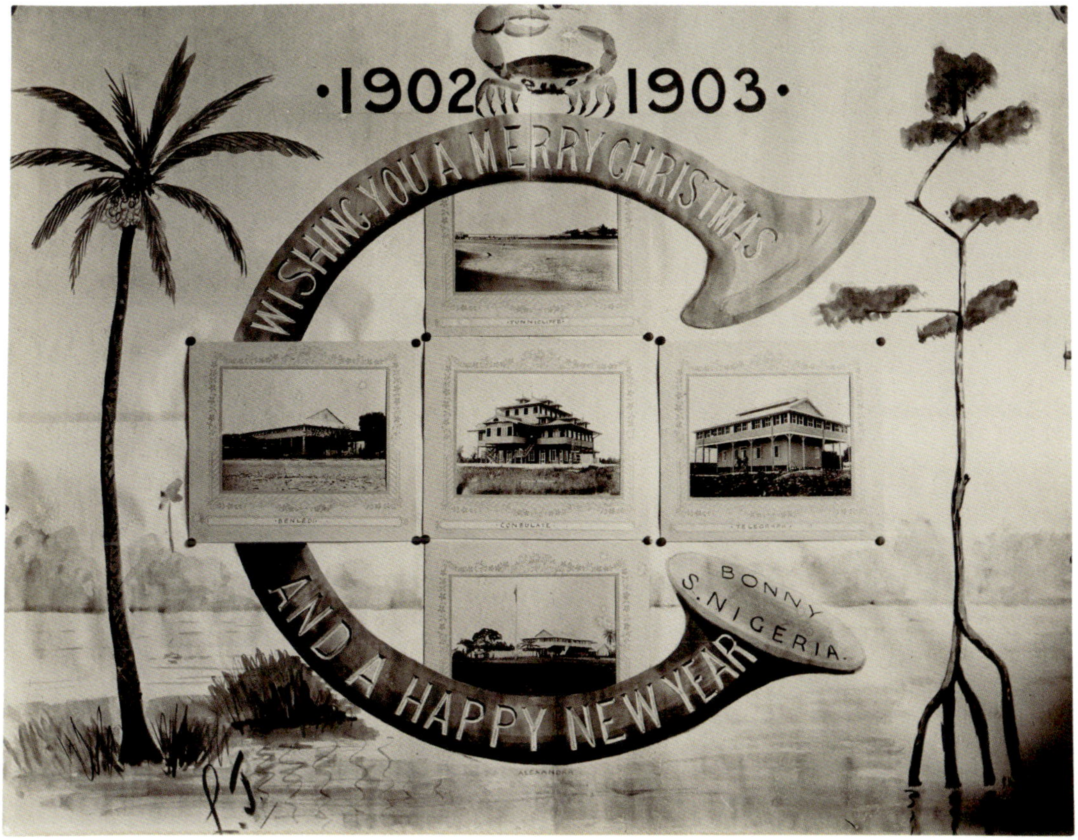

Jonathan Adagogo Green, Christmas card, 1902–3,
and detail of reverse below.

"Captain Speedy sounds like he's a fictional character, the sort of swashbuckling military hero who brings home these prizes and photographs. He wore traditional Ethiopian dress, which is a trope sometimes derogatorily referred to as 'going native'. Speedy was playing a role, a persona, but he also had a relationship with Emperor Tewodros prior to 1868. He spoke the local language and acted as an ambassador but he was also part of the Expedition. By the time Tewodros came to power he had amassed a lot of loot for himself, taken from churches. So when the British arrived, it was already in one spot. Part of the reason why the invasion of Maqdala was so scandalous at the time was because Ethiopia was a Christian country and they were essentially looting religious items from a church. Britain is generally a Christian country and yet that didn't stop them from looting Christian items. Many Indian troops fought [for the British] at the battle of Maqdala – over a dozen regiments from the Bengal Cavalry to the Bombay Native Infantry, including the Corps of Madras Sappers and Miners. Because this is a colonial army, it is made up of the colonised … I suppose you could put it that way." HL

Relations between Tewodros II of Ethiopia and Britain began to deteriorate in the 1860s. When Britain ignored his request for military support, he took several European hostages, including the British Consul. In response, an army led by Lord Napier launched an expedition in 1867, invading Tewodros's mountain-top fortress, Maqdala, in 1868. During the expedition, hundreds of Tewodros's soldiers were killed and many thousands injured. Tewodros chose to die by suicide rather than be taken prisoner. His son Prince Alemayehu (see p. 59), aged seven, was taken by the British officer and interpreter Captain Tristram Speedy to England. Speedy was already familiar with Ethiopia and the royal court, having been employed by Tewodros to train his army, but their relationship ended as the situation became increasingly hostile. A sword and shield may have belonged to Speedy before this breakdown – the shield came with a note inscribed 'gift from Theodore', the Anglicised version of Tewodros's name (pp. 150–1). They can be seen in the photograph of Speedy on p. 151, in which he wears Ethiopian clothing.

Looting was widespread as part of this expedition: the treasury, church and royal household were plundered by British troops. Much of the material was reassembled by an Army Prize Committee and sold at an auction of loot on the nearby Delanta Plain (20–21 April 1868). An intricate bronze and gold sacred processional cross with engravings depicting the life of Saint George (the patron saint of Ethiopia) was purchased by Napier (p. 152). Richard Rivington Holmes, an official representative from the British Museum, had joined the expedition as an archaeologist and participated directly in the plundering of the city (p. 153). Holmes purchased objects at the auction on behalf of the British Museum, as well as taking items for himself, including the Kwer'ata Re'esu icon (*c.* 1520), a painting of Christ from Iberia or Flanders, that was highly venerated in Ethiopia. Even at the time, the plunder of Maqdala drew fierce criticism, notably from the British prime minister William Gladstone who regretted the seizure of church property.

"I've always found the term 'expedition' really perverse."

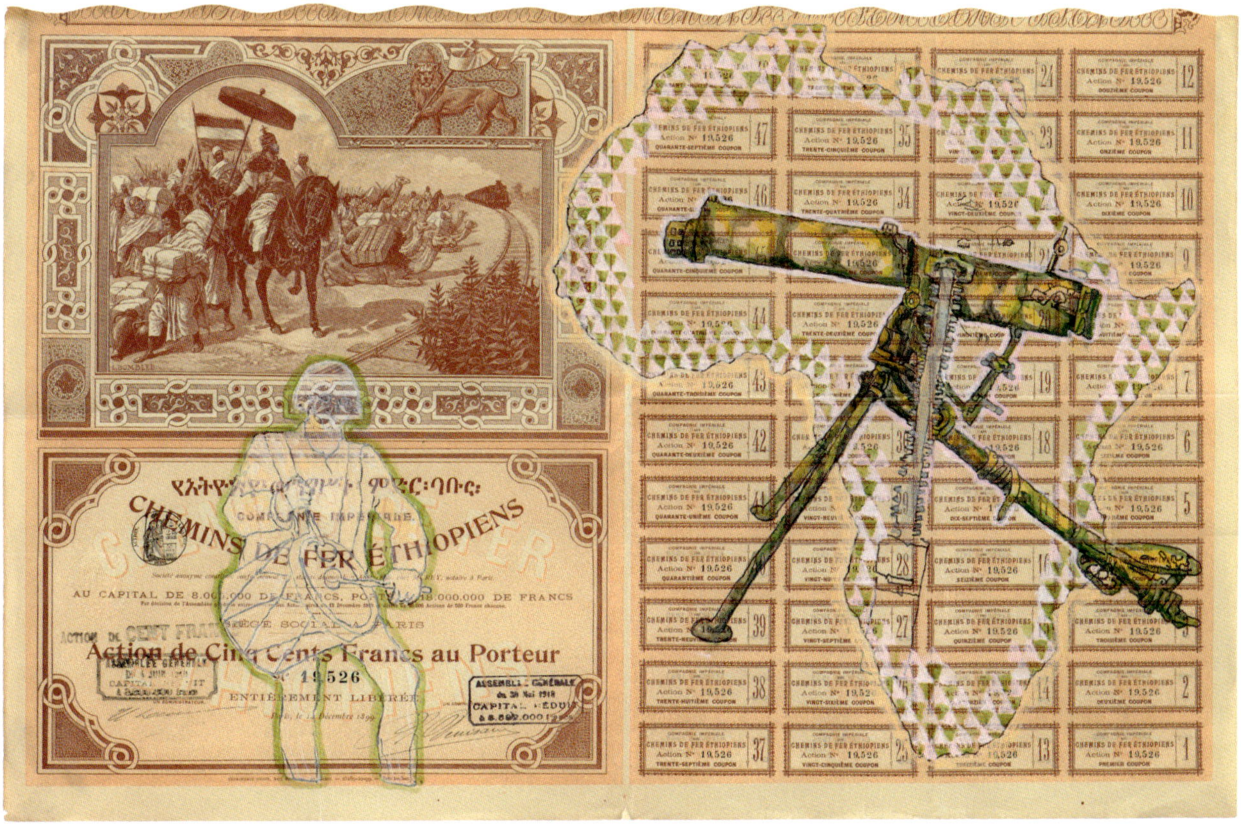

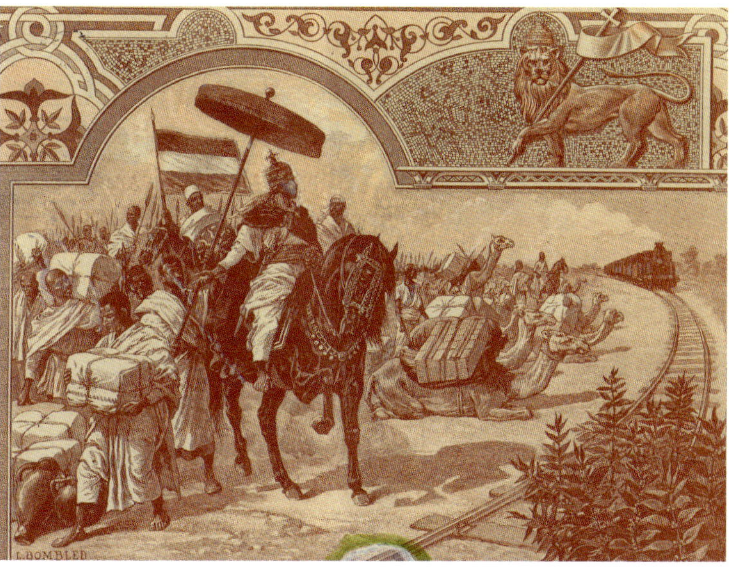

Hew Locke, *Company of the Imperial Railway of Ethiopia 5*, 2024,
and detail of Emperor Menelik II inspecting the railway.

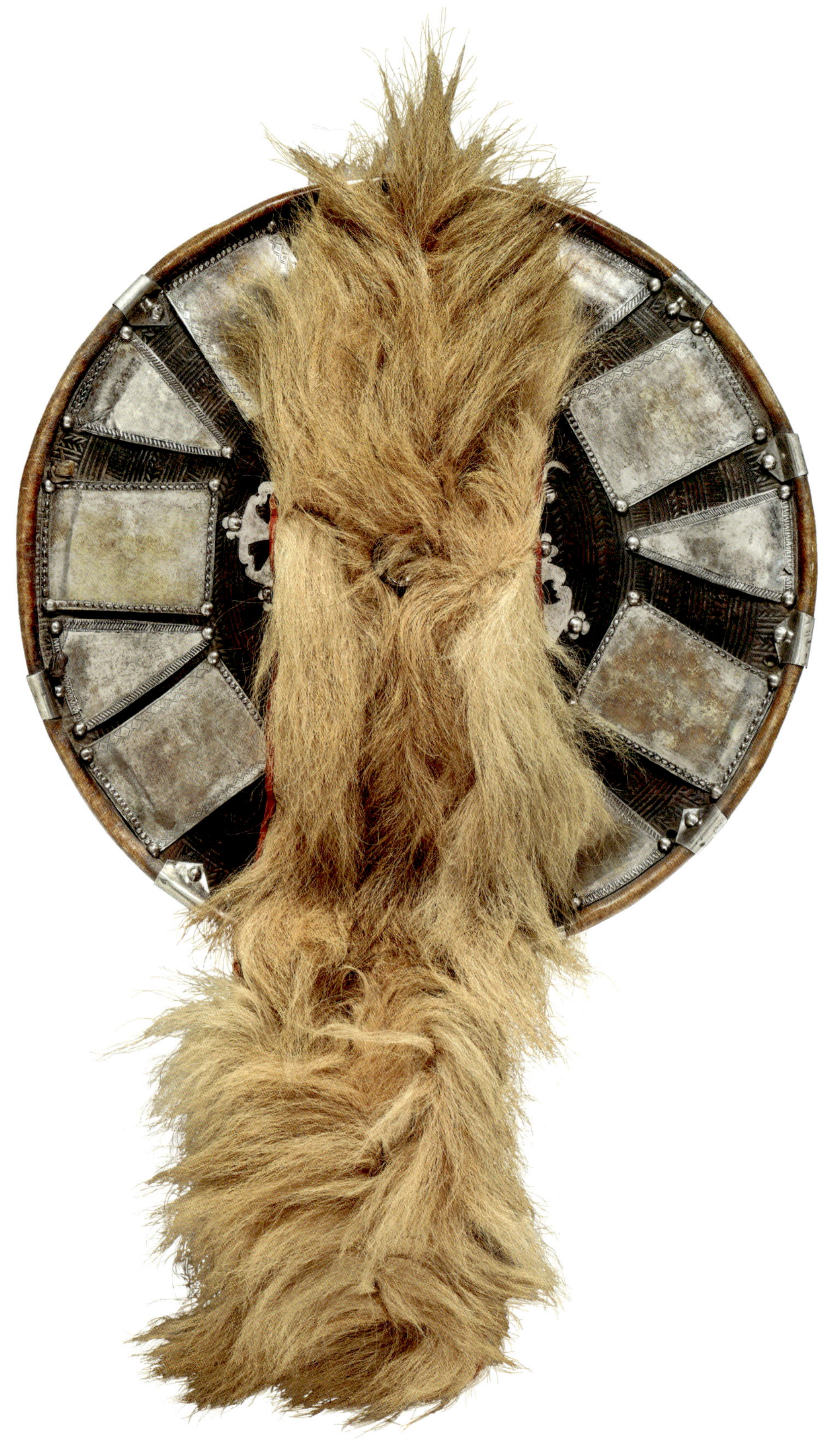

Unrecorded artist, Ethiopian shield, mid-1800s.

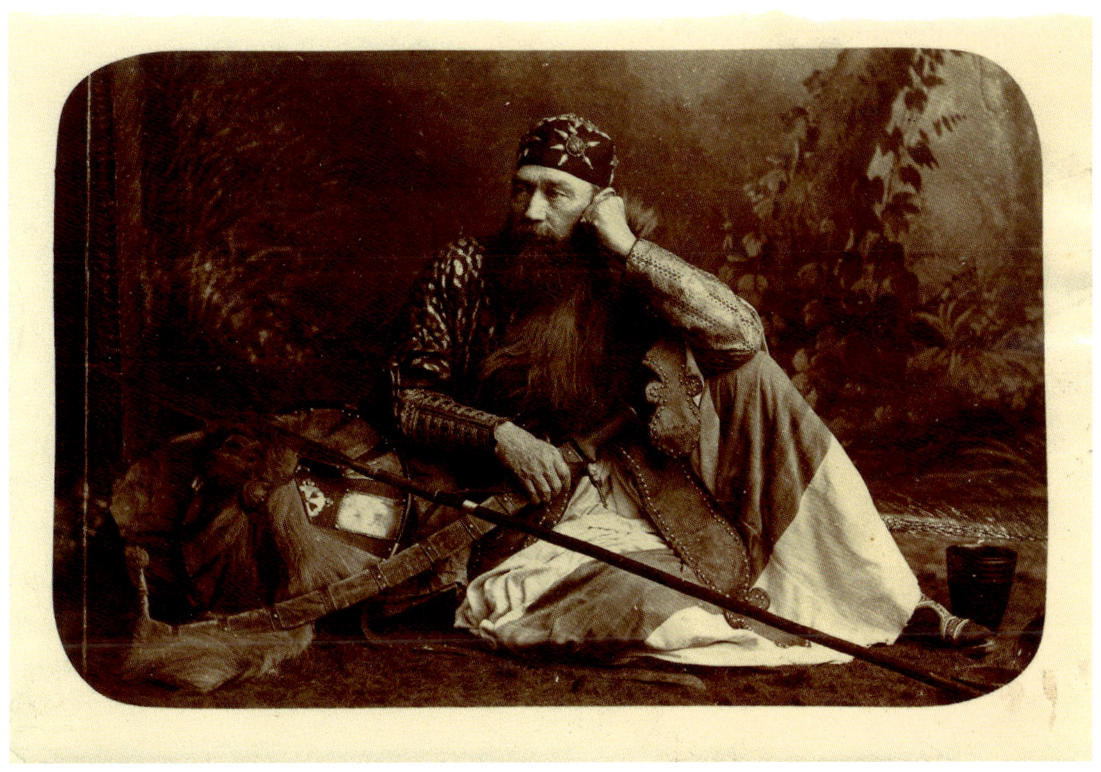

Lawrence Lowe, portrait of Captain Speedy, late 1800s.

Unrecorded Ethiopian artist,
sword and sheath, mid-1800s.

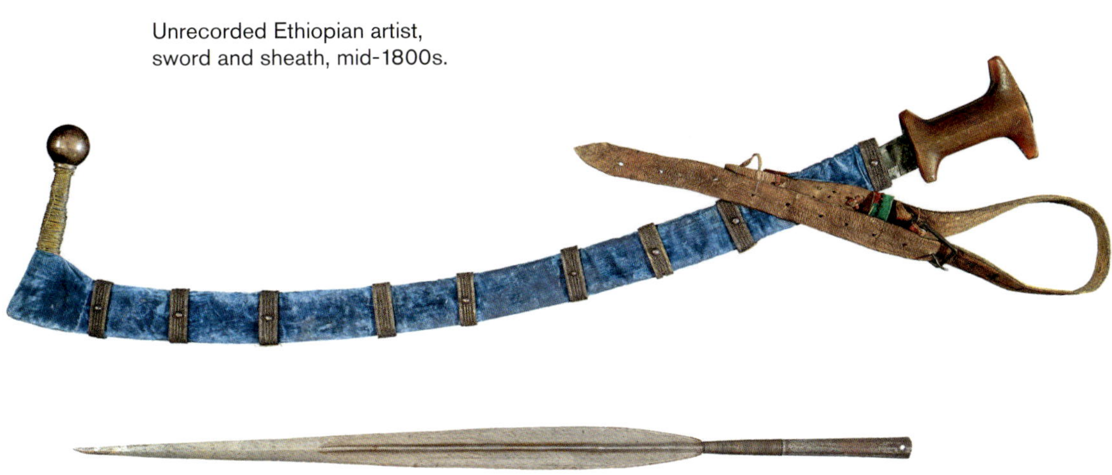

Ethiopian spear, mid-1800s.

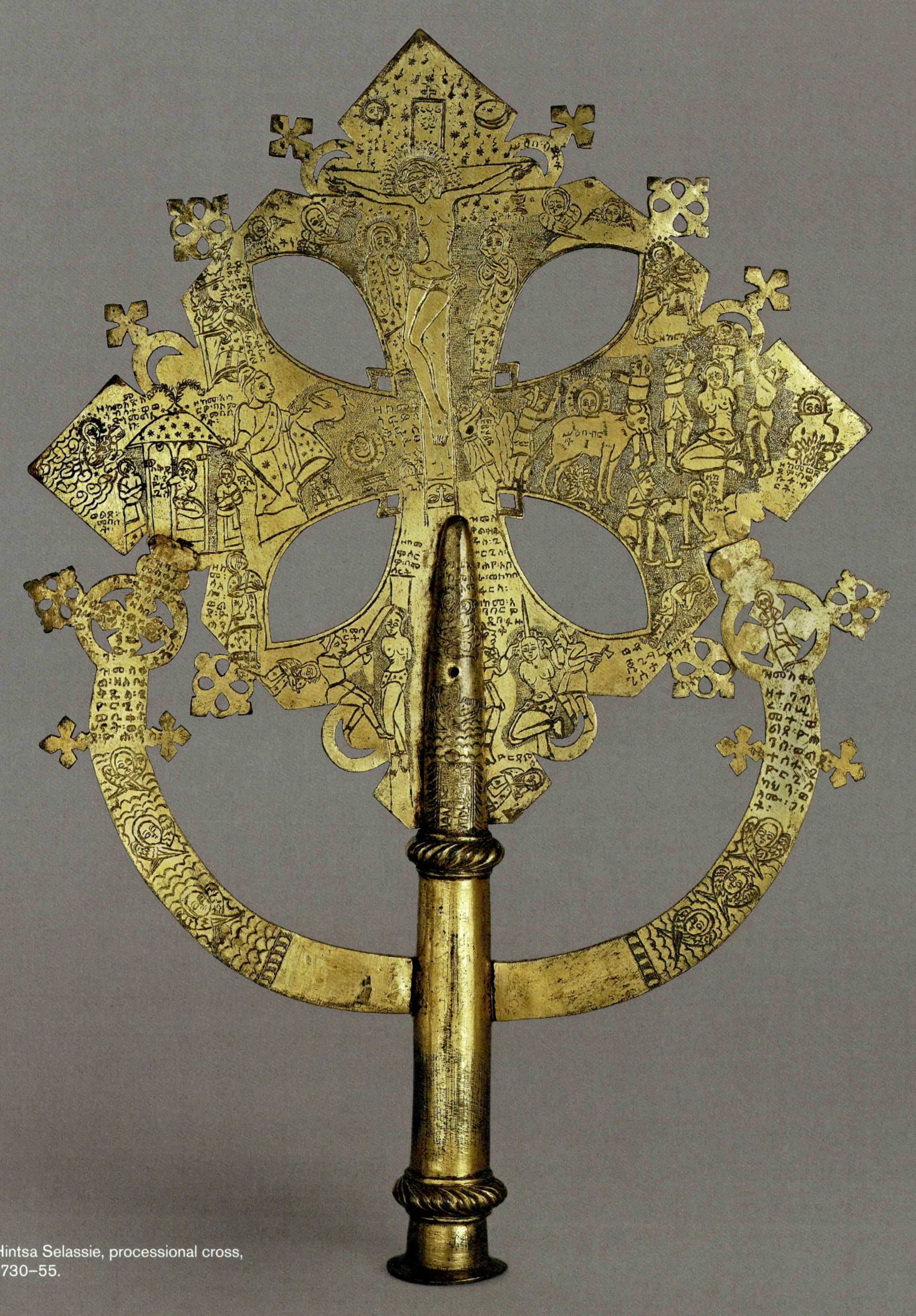

Hintsa Selassie, processional cross,
1730–55.

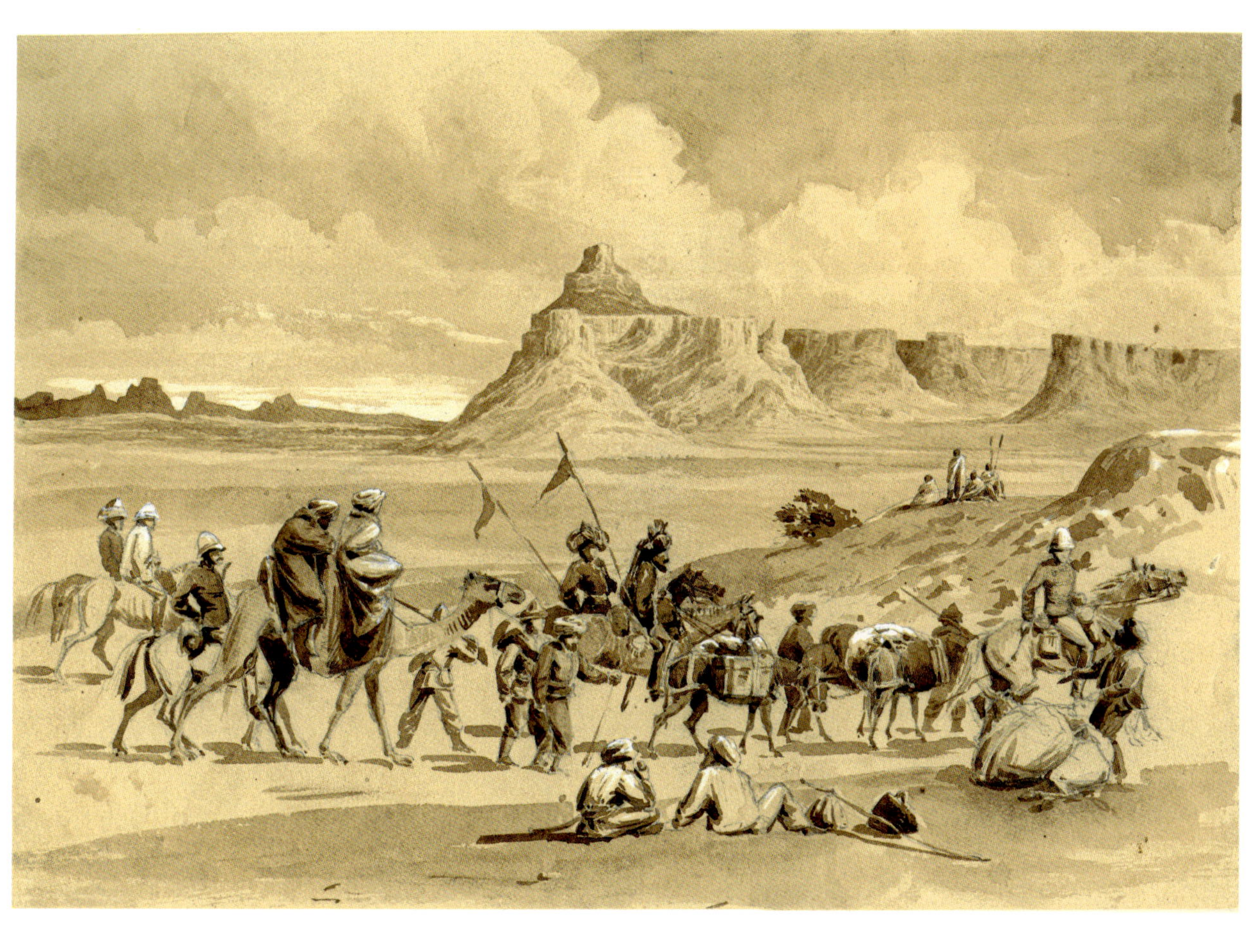

Richard Rivington Holmes, drawing of the Maqdala expedition force, 1868.

In 1903–4, due to tensions between the British and Russian empires over control of Central Asia, the British invaded Tibet. Headed by Francis Younghusband (1863–1942), the invading soldiers killed between 2,000 and 3,000 Tibetans and looted objects from monasteries and homes. Two representatives for the British Museum – Lawrence Augustine Waddell and Perceval Landon – were instructed to collect books and manuscripts for the Museum. Items included objects of religious significance that Tibetans were unlikely to have sold willingly to the British. The items on pp. 155–7 were all purchased by the Museum in 1905 from Major Herbert Augustus Iggulden (1861–1937), the Chief Staff Officer on the expedition. The chalice and amulet would have been taken as examples of 'curios', and the wicker shield was likely taken from a *gonkhang* (protective space near a shrine) and not worn in battle. The figure represents Tibetan Buddhist monk Dolpopa Sherab Gyeltsen (1292–1361), also known as 'the Buddha from Dolpo'. He was the head of the Jonang tradition of Tibetan Buddhism. This copper and golden seated figure of Dolpopa (p. 156) shows him holding rosary beads and a cloak for meditation. It is believed to have been taken from Tsechen Monastery in Gyantse, which was used by Tibetan troops as a base to resist the British advance before it was finally sacked, looted and burnt on 28 June 1904.

"The Tibetans were armed with swords against Maxim guns – they just had no chance."

"I didn't know much about the Younghusband Expedition, which is less talked about than it should be. They killed so many people, to the point where some officers stopped shooting because it became obscene. They left with 400 mules laden down with treasure, and there was a lot of anxiety among the officers about this damaging the British self-image. I'm fascinated by the fact that some of these Tibetan items have turned up in the media in recent years. Sometimes they're found in people's attics, their descendants. A decade ago, a silver teapot and five other items were sold on the BBC show *Flog It!* for £140,000. The auction house expert then described the find, saying that 'anything to do with the Younghusband Expedition to Tibet is incredibly collectable.' That says it all." HL

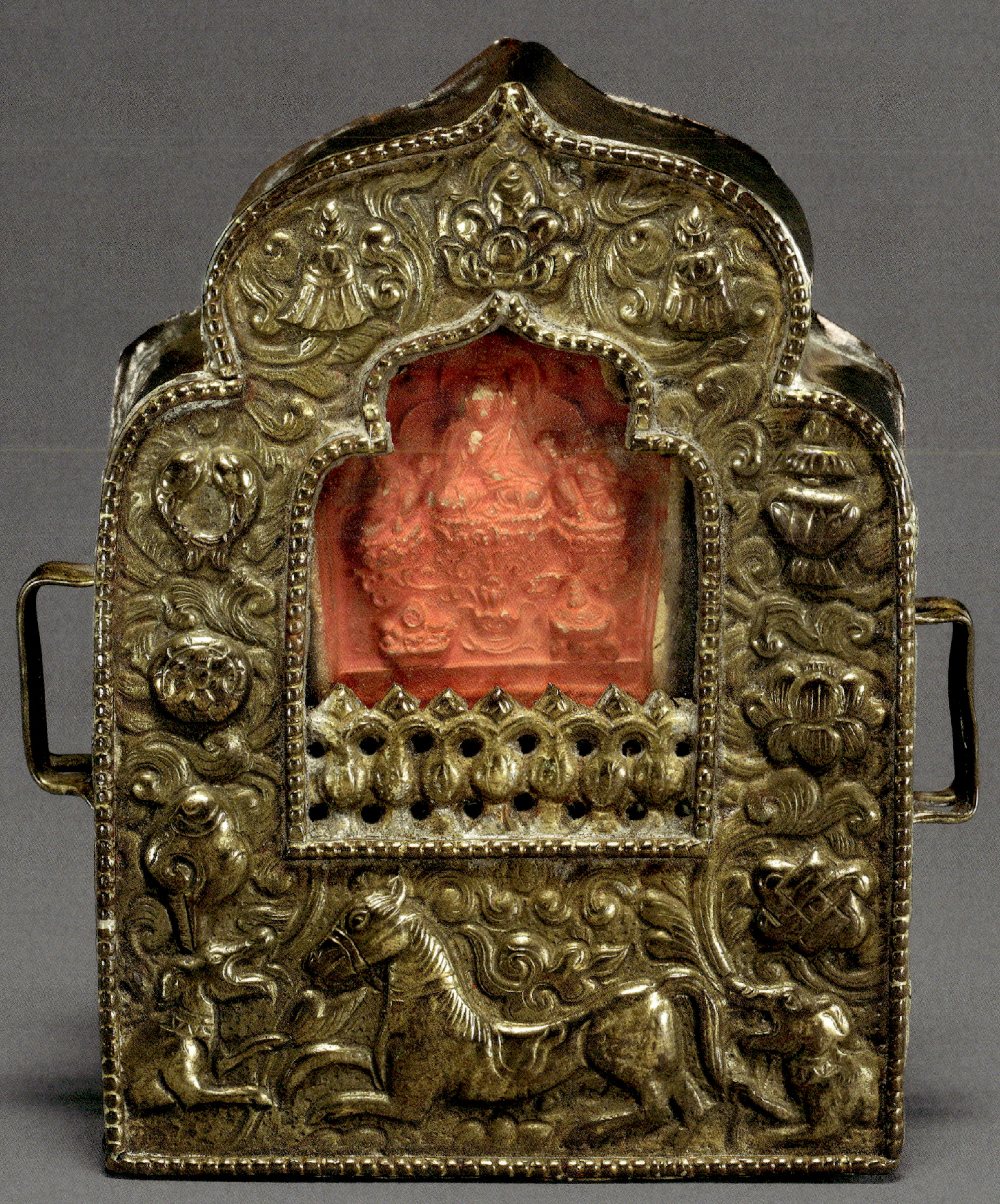

Unrecorded artist, Ts'a-t's'a amulet, 1800s.

Unrecorded artist, lama figure, 1400s.

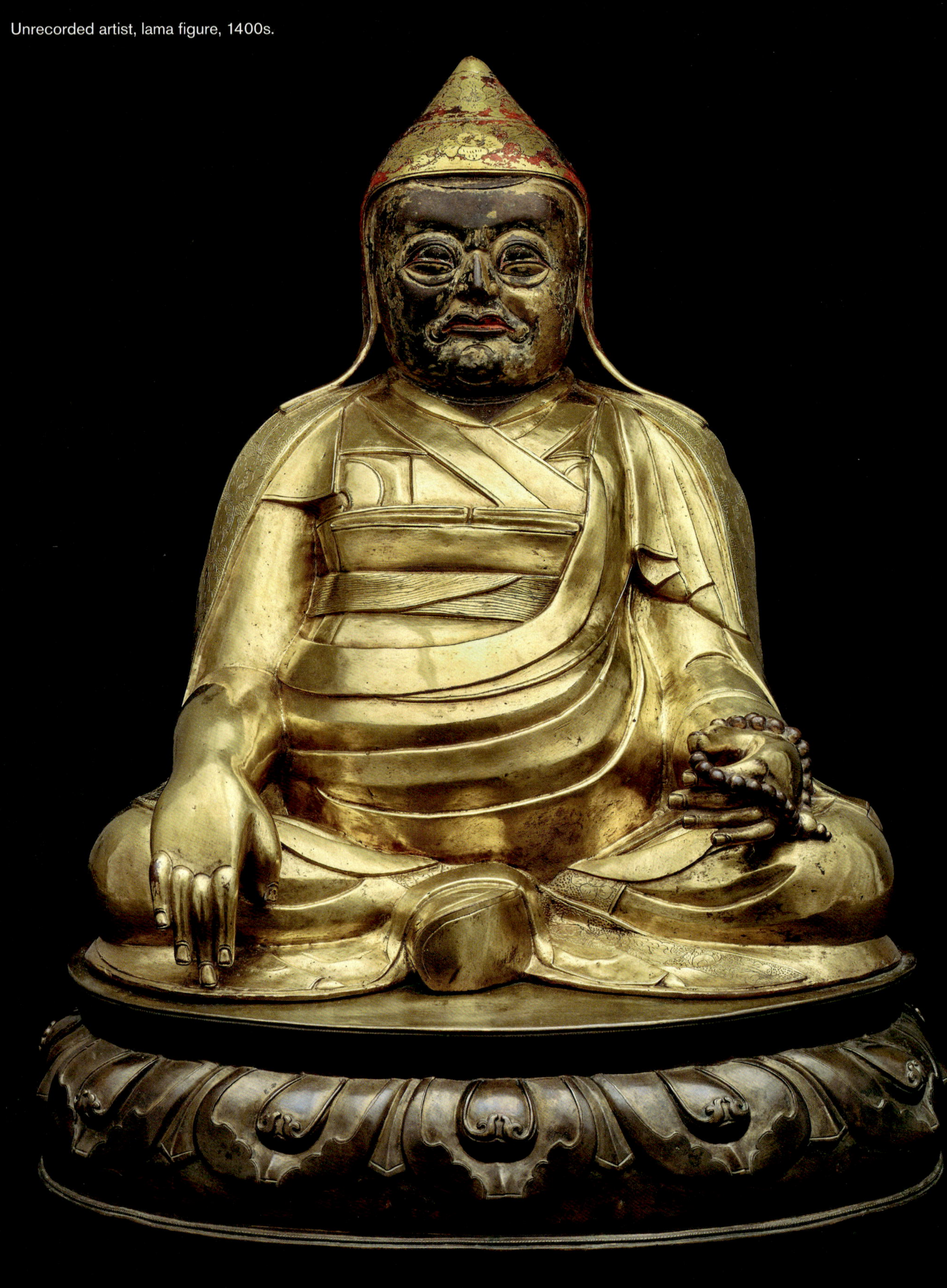

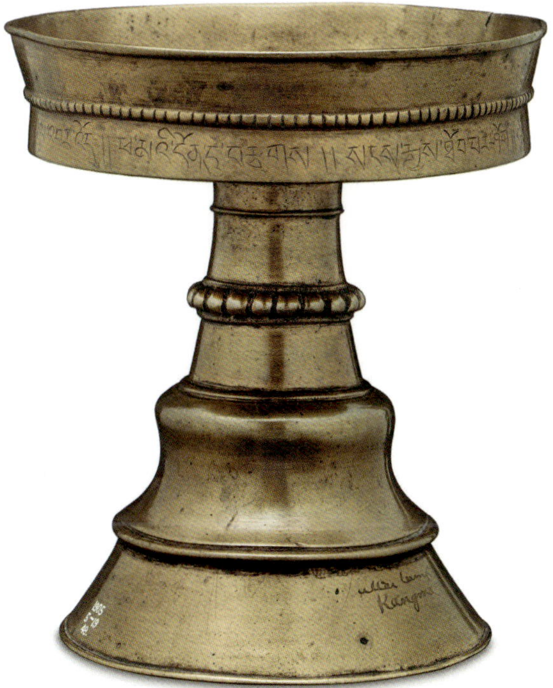

Unrecorded artist, chalice, *c.* 1700s–1800s.

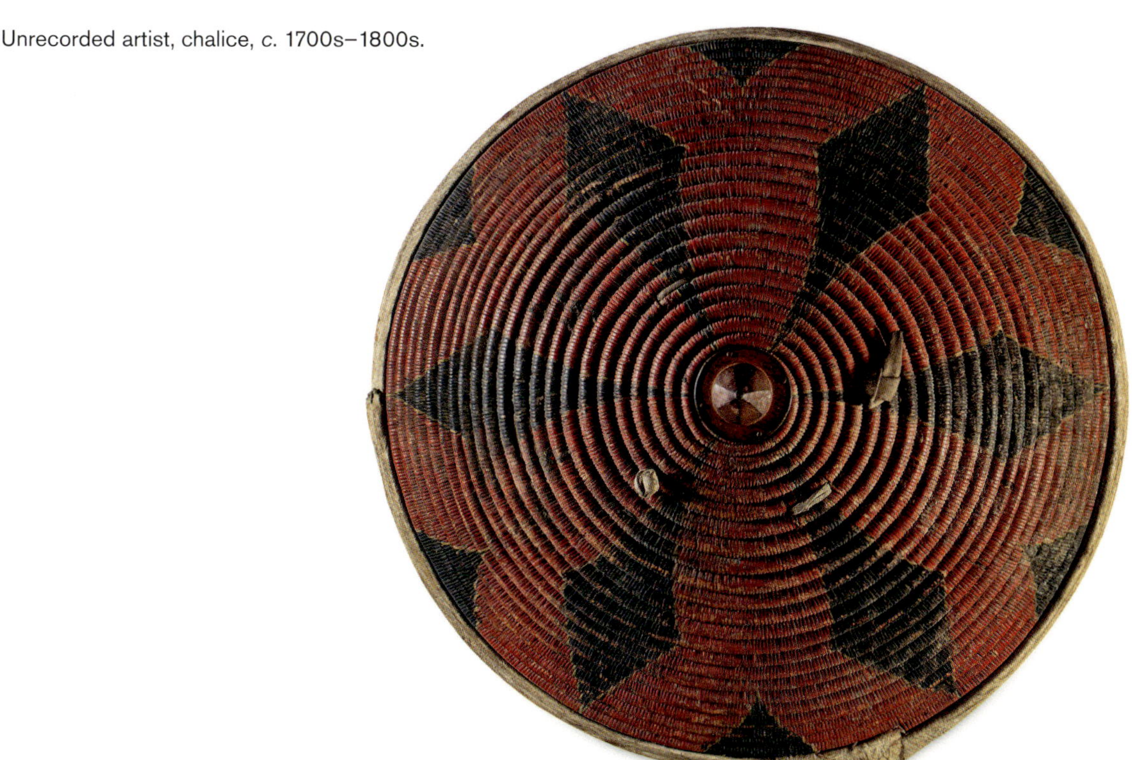

Unrecorded artist, wicker shield,
c. 1700s–1800s.

While some of the golden objects taken during British wars and other actions were melted down, others made their way into museum collections. In the 1800s a series of wars was waged between the British Empire and the Asante Empire. During the Third Anglo-Asante War, the Asantehene (king) Kofi Karikari attempted to prevent the invasion of the capital Kumasi, but General Garnet Wolseley (1833–1913) and his troops demolished the palace with explosives in February 1874.

The centre of this dish (opposite) is a pendant (*awisiado*) belonging to a soul priest. Similar discs were used by members of the Asantehene's court in rituals that purified and replenished his vital powers (pp. 160, 162–3). Taken during the Third Anglo-Asante War, the pendant was set in a silver-gilt dish by the Victorian jewellers Garrard & Co. in 1874, in a design that echoes that of the central pendant. The engraving on the back of the dish says: 'The gold ornament in the centre of this dish is a portion of the indemnity paid by the Ashanti King Coffee Calcalli [Kofi Karikari] to Her Majesty's forces under the command of Major Genl Sir Garnet Wolseley, January 1874.'

The three gold discs were said to have been taken 'from the cross on the altar at Magdala [Maqdala]' (p. 161). The use of solid gold like this was rare and exclusive to royalty. The discs depict Christian images: one shows the Crucifixion, with a Roman soldier wounding Jesus on the cross with a spear and another offering him a sponge soaked in vinegar. A second disc shows an angel with crossed arms, perhaps grieving, and the third depicts the Virgin Mary with the infant Jesus in her lap as they bless a recumbent person. The conical armlet (p. 164), a Bitäwa, was collected in the 1840s by an envoy in Ethiopia; it entered the Museum in 1866, two years prior to the Maqdala looting. Bitäwa were exclusively worn by warriors; they were gifts from the ruler to recognise bravery in battle. The other objects on pp. 164–5 were taken or purchased by Richard Rivington Holmes (see p. 148) following the looting of Maqdala. The silver cup is a highly luxurious vessel used for fermented honey wine; the gold and silver anklets were only worn by high-ranking Christian women with the emperor's permission.

"African gold, that's what people have been seeking for centuries. That's the thing, that's the ideal kind of loot."

"The dish (opposite) looks like a European thing. The original Asante object, the aesthetic of it, has been ensnared within a European design. It ignores its function completely, and it's just there as a trophy. It traps it and it kills it at the same time. It reminds me of the Koh-i-Noor being damaged to fit a European aesthetic (see p. 98). It's about how you display your trophy – make it even bigger than it is. I wanted to include it for that reason. It's been taken because it's gold but it is important to see it alongside Asante gold discs of the same sort. This arrangement reminds me so much of going to the old Museum of Mankind where you'd have a case full of stuff, like a Wunderkammer – a cabinet of curiosities." HL

The final pages (pp. 166–7) show anthropomorphic Tolima pendants surrounding a Yotoco breastplate — all early objects from Colombia that were purchased by the Museum in the early 1900s as examples of exquisitely manufactured gold.

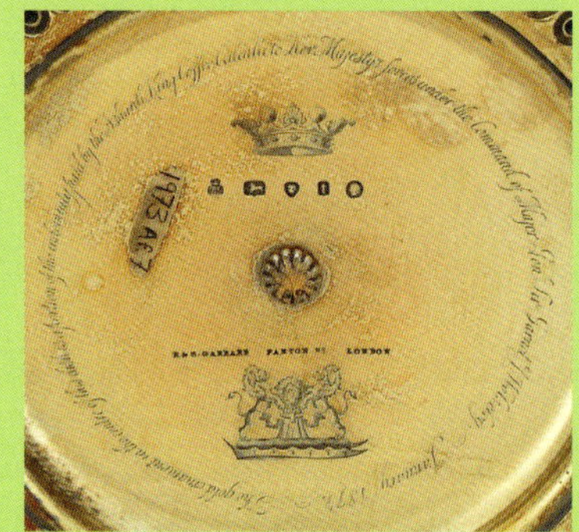

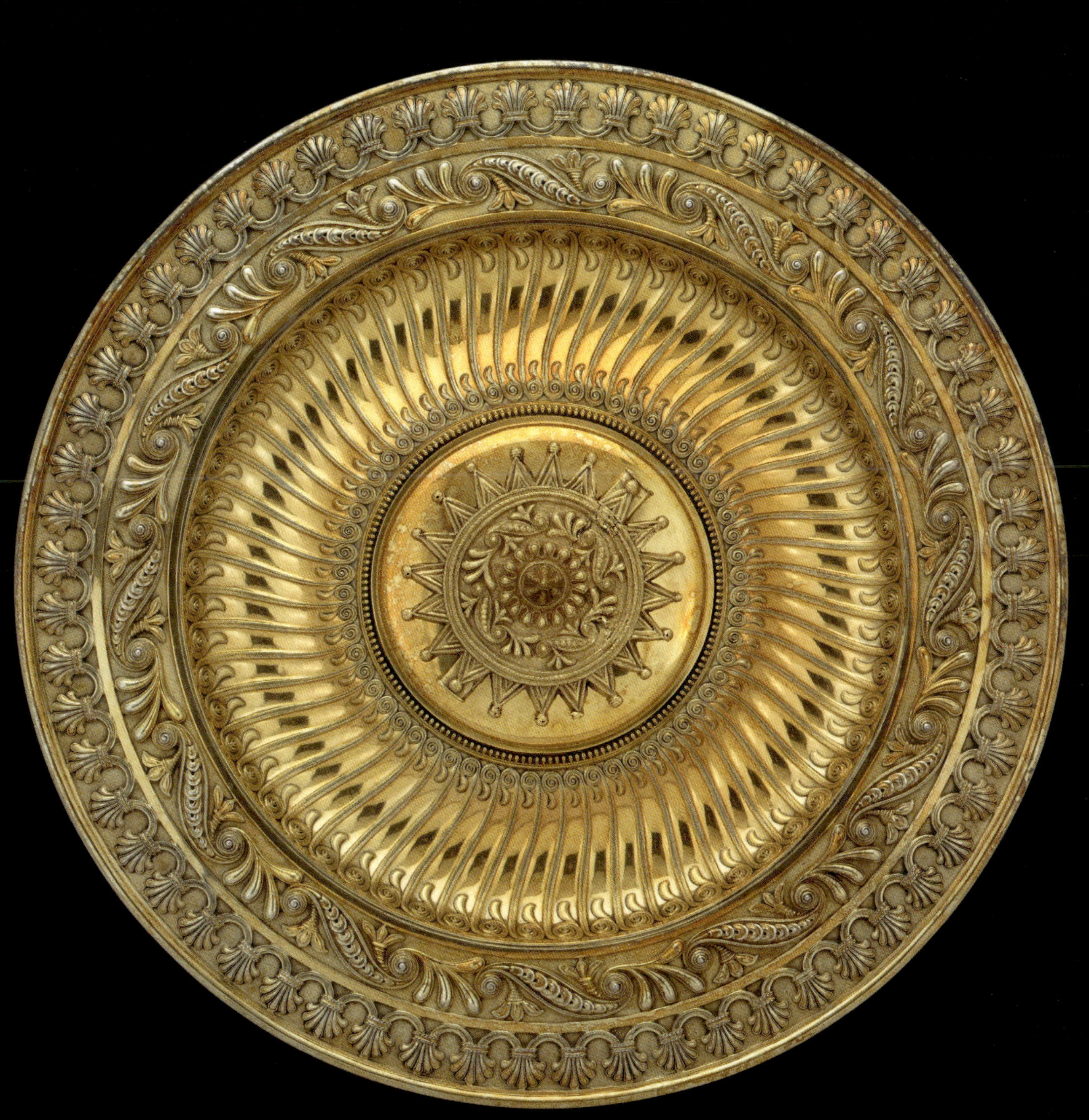

Unrecorded Asante artist and Garrard & Co., pendant, 1850–70,
dish, 1874, and detail of reverse opposite.

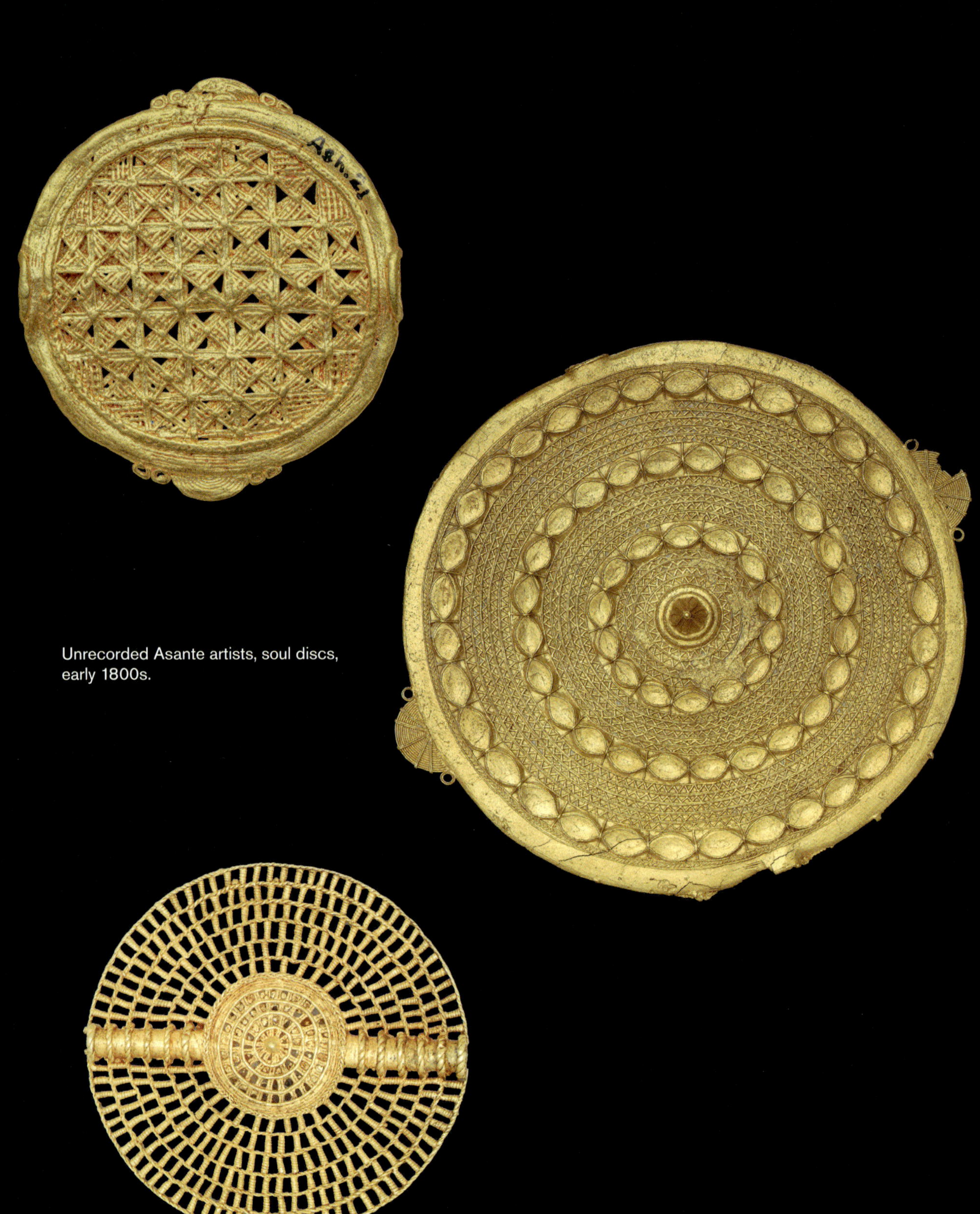

Unrecorded Asante artists, soul discs,
early 1800s.

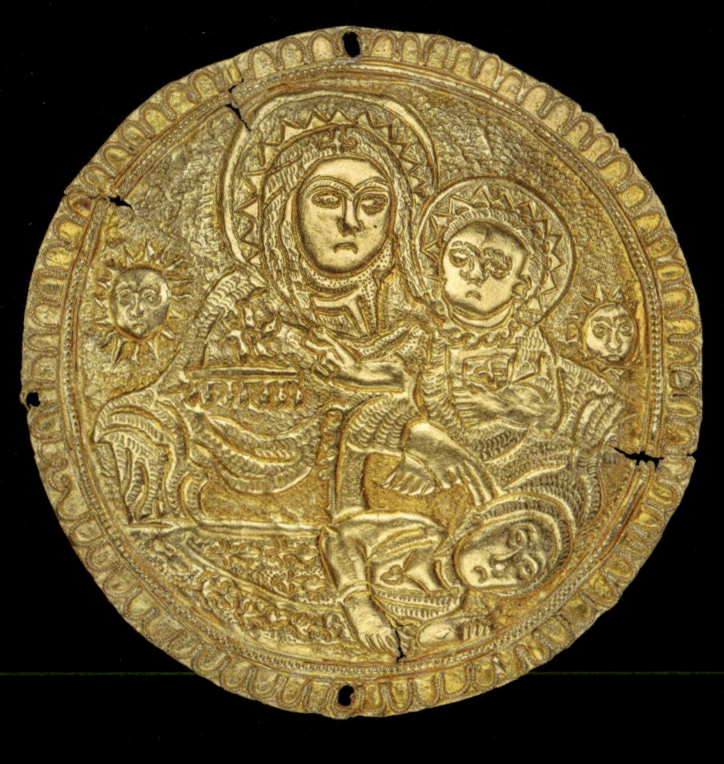
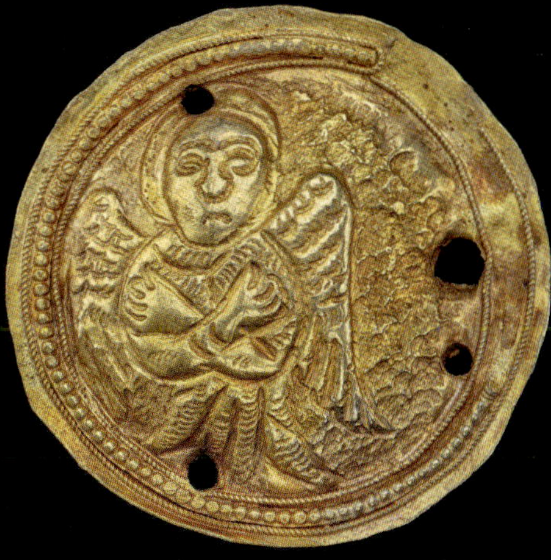

Unrecorded Ethiopian artists, gold discs,
1800–68.

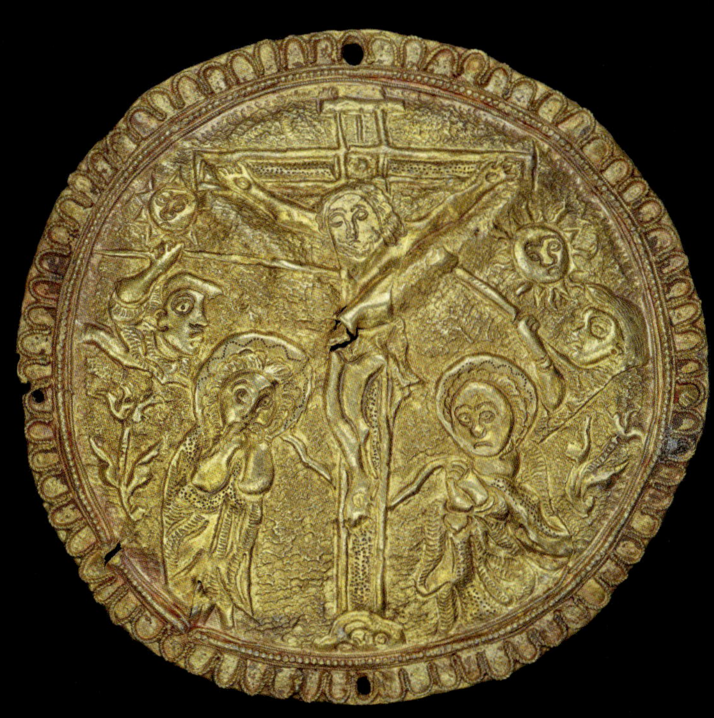

Ash. 18

West Africa.

Circular gold badge, with projecting centre, ornamented with five lobes, two tubular proper openings on the margin, and two hemispherical projections at the sides; from the centre proceed four leaves, and the rest of the surface is divided by ~~into band~~ into four pointed ovals containing trefoils.

Wt. 331 gr.

3 4/10 × 3 1/2 in

From Ashanti, part of the King's indemnity

Purchased from the Crown Agents for the Colonies.

December 1876.

Ash. 13

West Africa.

Circular gold badge, with projecting centre ornamented with six lobes; two tubular openings on the margin and two hemispherical openings at the sides; surface ornamented with three bands of raised ovals and within them bands of zigzags.

Wt. 6 oz. 53 gr.

From Ashantee, part of the King's indemnity.

4 7/10" × 4 9/10"

Purchased from the Crown Agents for the Colonies.

December 1876.

Ash 19

West Africa.

Circular gold badge, slightly projecting centre, surrounded with eight lobes, two tubular openings on the margin and two hemispherical openings at the sides; the surface ornamented with open-work forming an irregular cruciform pattern.

Wt. 232 gr.

From Ashantee part of the King's indemnity

full size

Purchased from the Crown Agents for the Colonies.

December 1876

Acquisition slips for soul discs, 1876.

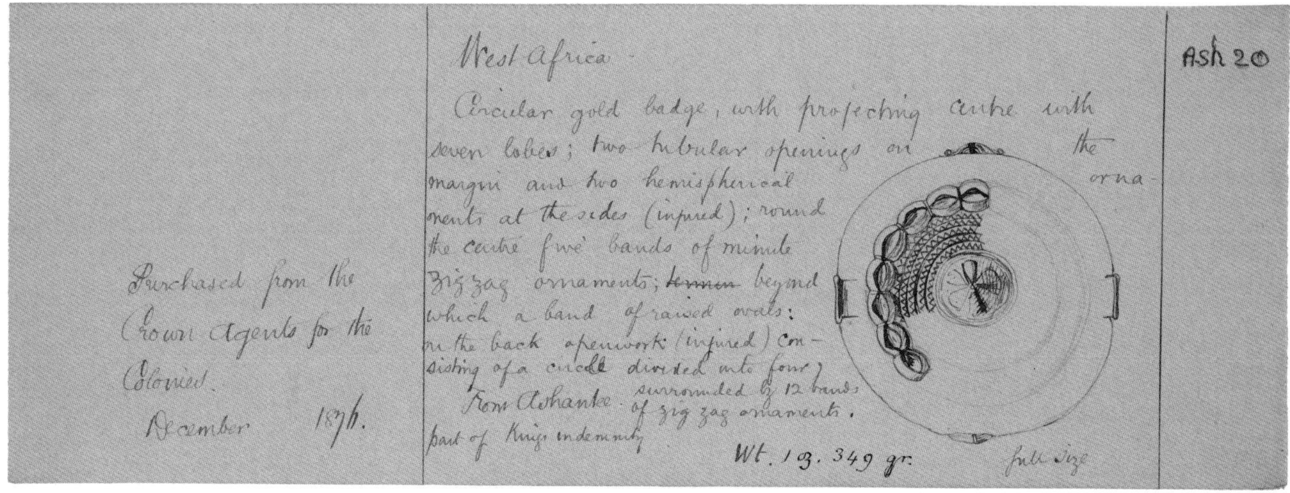

West Africa -

Circular gold badge, with projecting centre with seven lobes; two tubular openings on the margin and two hemispherical ornaments at the sides (injured); round the centre five bands of minute zigzag ornaments; terminating beyond which a band of raised ovals: on the back openwork (injured) consisting of a circle divided into four, surrounded by 12 bands of zigzag ornaments.

Ash 20

Purchased from the Crown Agents for the Colonies.
December 1876.

From Ashantee. part of Kings indemnity

Wt. 1 oz. 349 gr.   full size

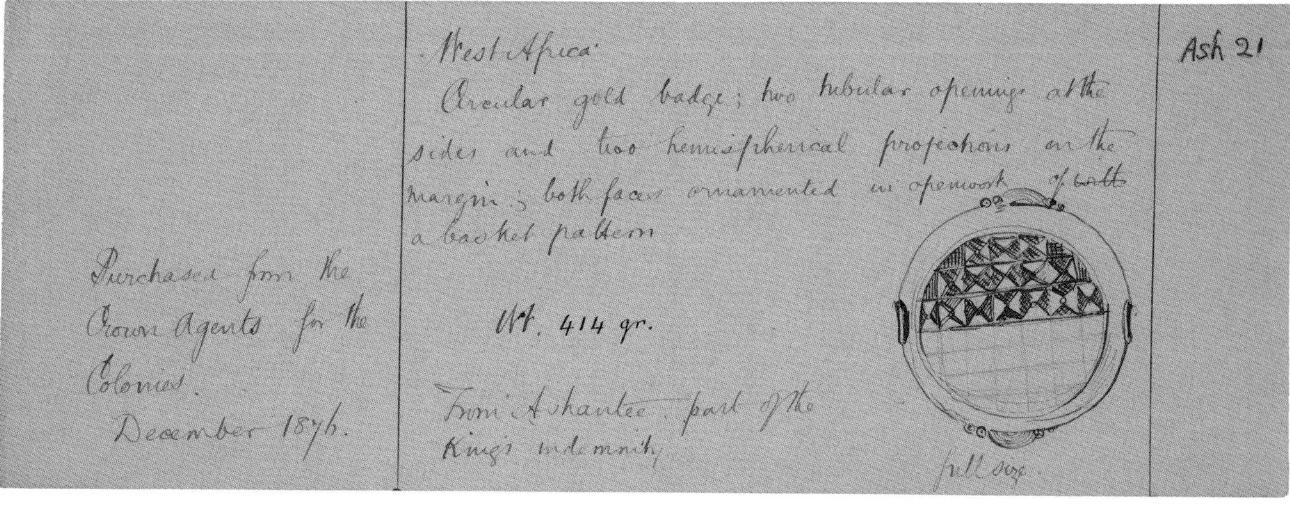

West Africa.

Circular gold badge; two tubular openings at the sides and two hemispherical projections on the margin; both faces ornamented in openwork of with a basket pattern

Ash 21

Purchased from the Crown Agents for the Colonies.
December 1876.

Wt. 414 gr.

From Ashantee, part of the Kings indemnity

full size.

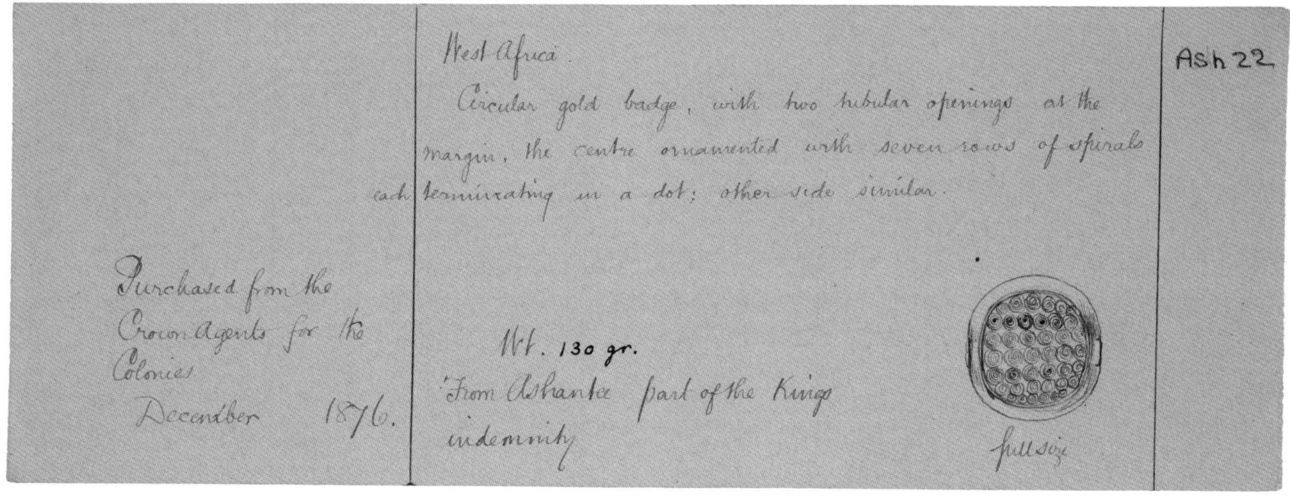

West Africa.

Circular gold badge, with two tubular openings at the margin, the centre ornamented with seven rows of spirals each terminating in a dot: other side similar.

Ash 22

Purchased from the Crown Agents for the Colonies
December 1876.

Wt. 130 gr.

From Ashantee part of the Kings indemnity

full size

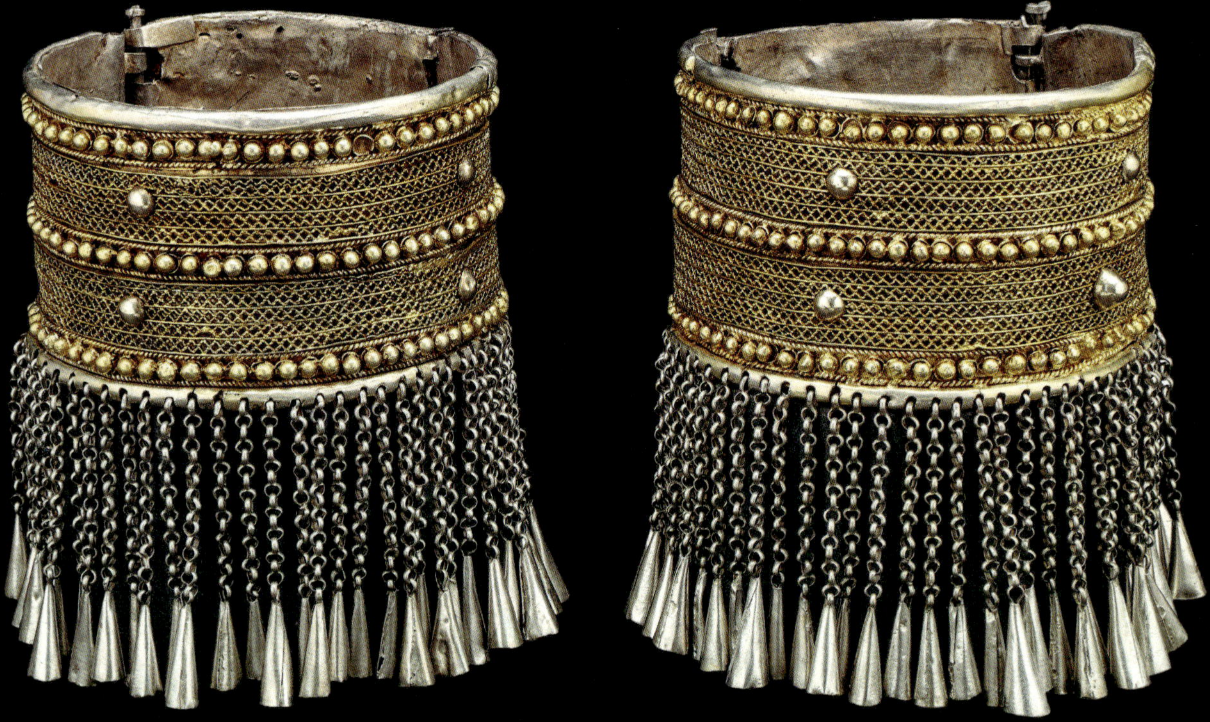

Unrecorded Ethiopian artist,
anklets, 1800s.

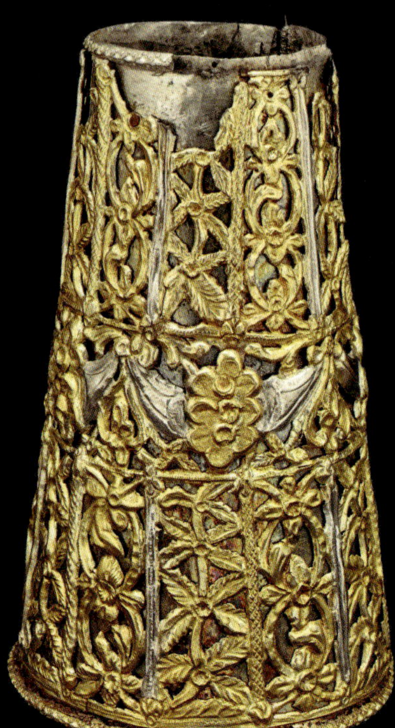

Unrecorded Ethiopian artist,
armlet, mid-1800s.

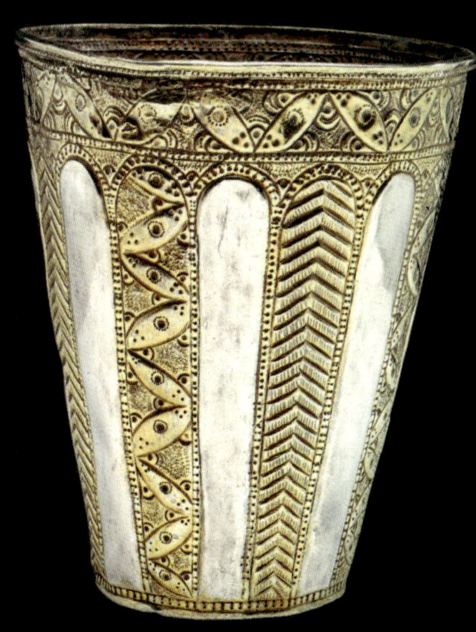

Unrecorded Ethiopian artist,
cup, 1800–68.

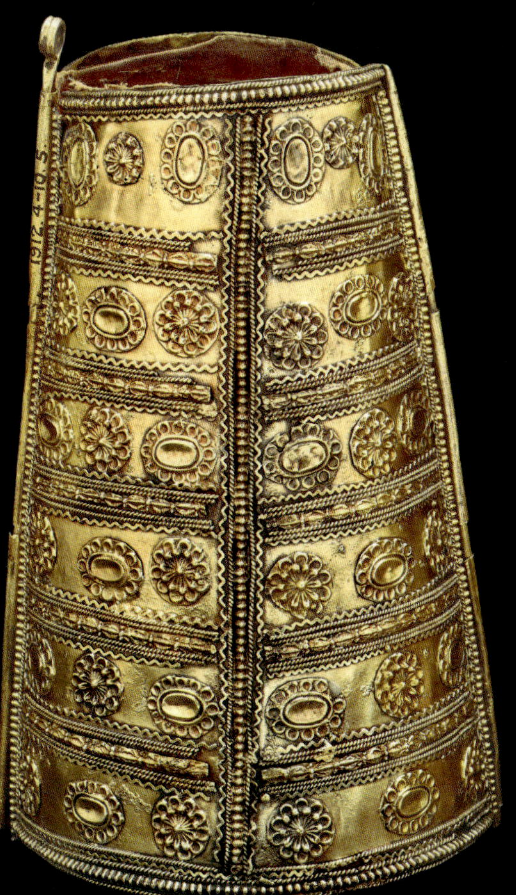

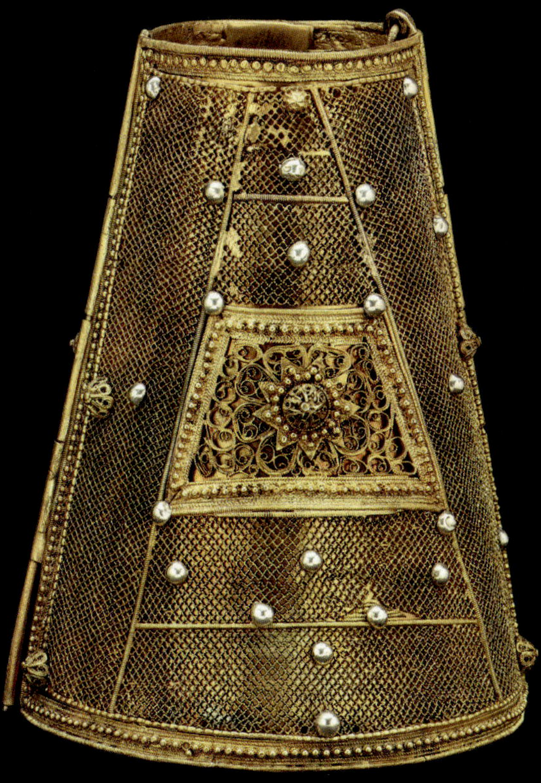

Unrecorded Ethiopian artists, armlets,
early to mid-1800s.

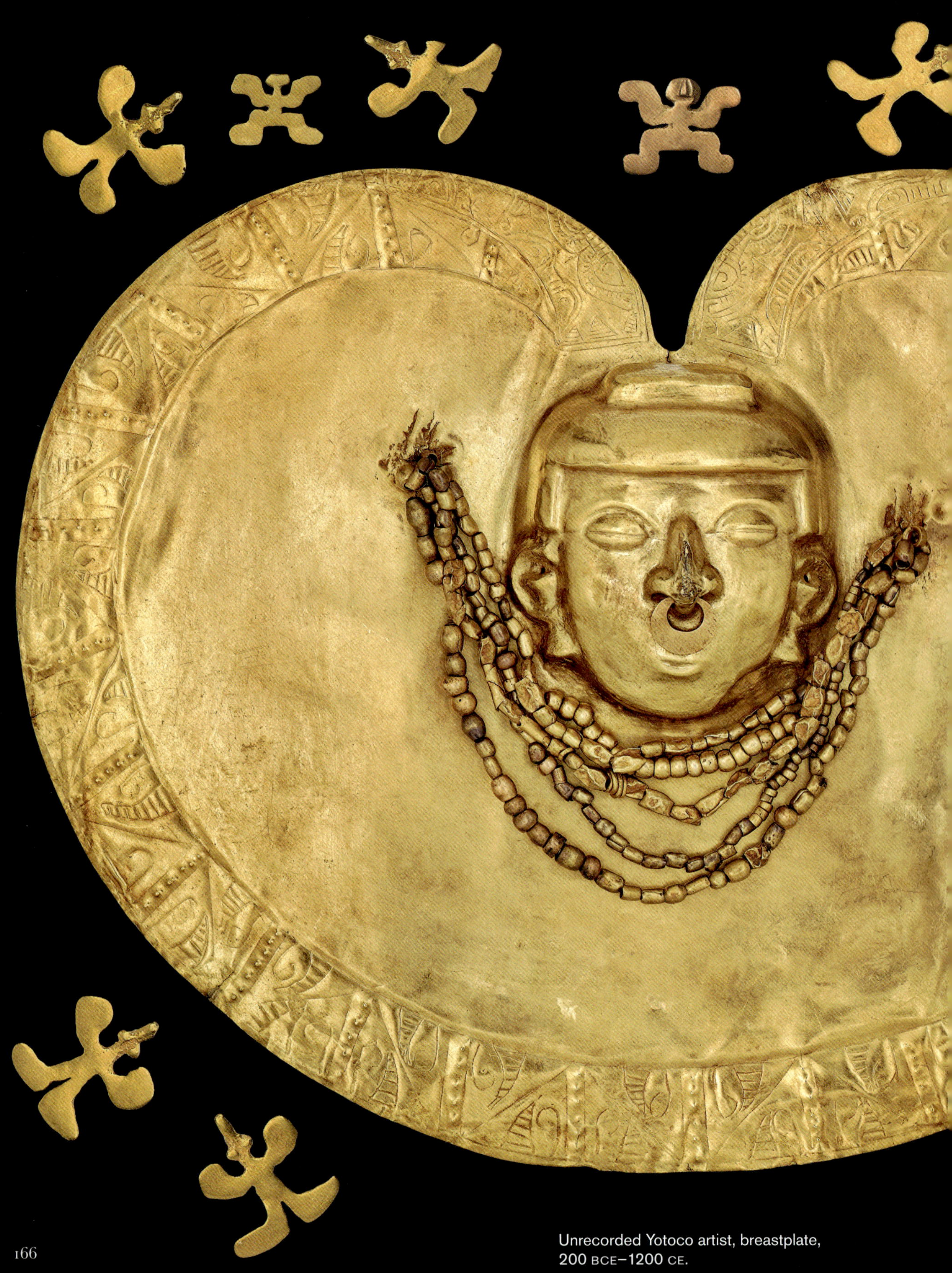

Unrecorded Yotoco artist, breastplate,
200 BCE–1200 CE.

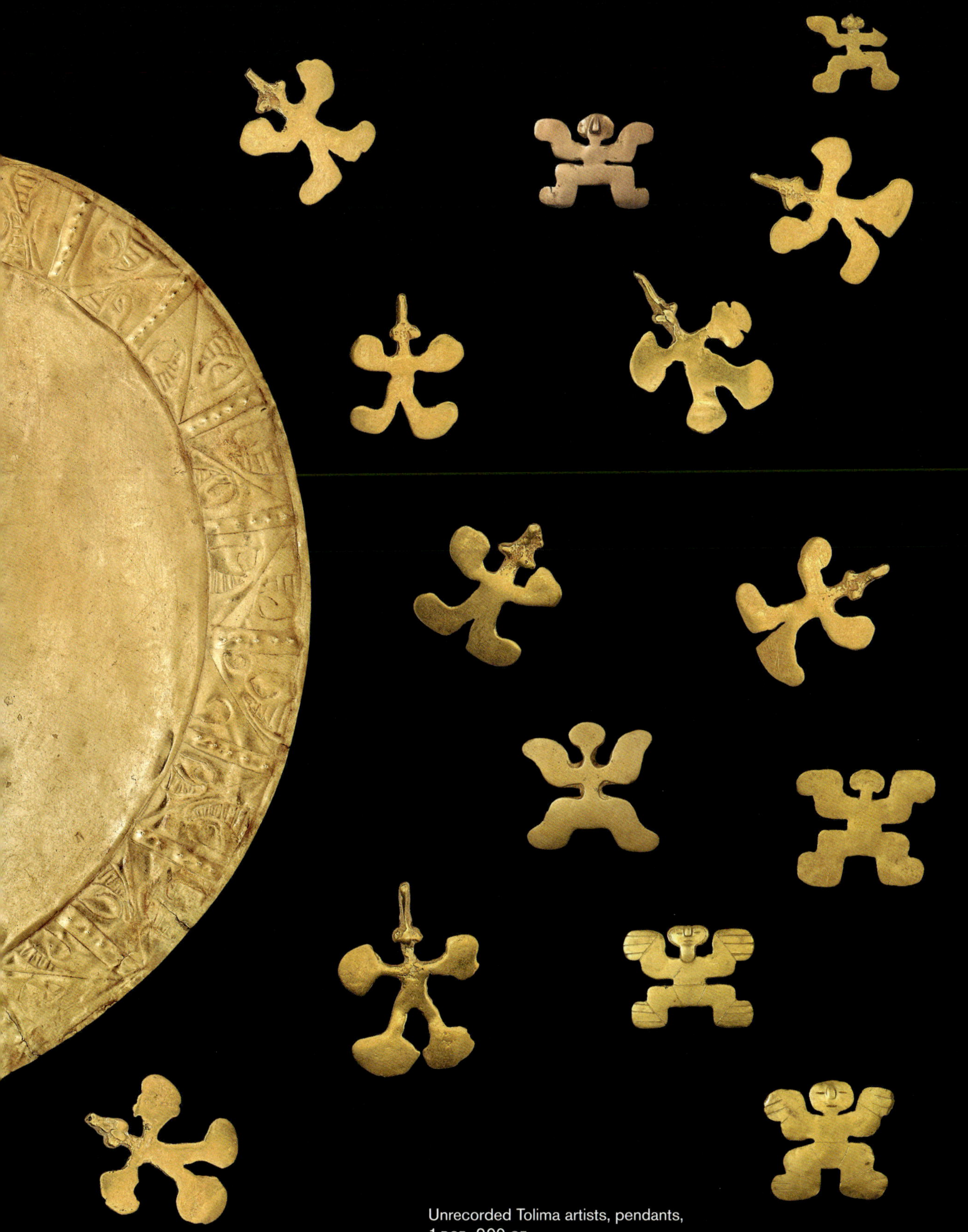

Unrecorded Tolima artists, pendants,
1 BCE–900 CE.

Dialogue

Indra Khanna and Hew Locke

Conversations between Hew Locke, Indra Khanna and the British Museum about the possibility of co-curating an exhibition began in May 2022. The following discussion took place during exhibition preparation in April 2024.

IK Let's talk about the process of selecting objects for this exhibition. For me, one of the great things about this project has been being able to go behind the scenes at the British Museum and see some things in storage – such as drawers upon drawers of seals, each contained in its own beautiful wooden box, and on each box is the name of a territory or country.

> **HL** I spent a lot of time looking at the Museum's Collection Online – it has millions of objects. I wanted to search randomly as well as specifically. That's how I found the Merian drawings, through looking at objects relating to Suriname. It was about giving myself a wide-ranging search term. Sometimes, if your terms are too narrow, you won't find what you're looking for.

IK And some of them were suggested by me or by Museum curators.

> **HL** Yes, forgot that one! Totally. The curators had been given a brief about where I was coming from and they pulled out stuff I would never have thought about – the 'good conduct' medal for example (p. 83). That was extraordinary.

IK Also, the engraved horns (p. 135) and the Asante Jug (p. 66).

> **HL** Yes. Sometimes my selections were prompted by you and the other curators. It's a genuine collaboration, otherwise it wouldn't work.

IK We talked a lot about what the point is of museums asking artists to curate things? So many museum exhibitions are chronological. There's a story: a beginning, middle and end. This exhibition feels more like an expression of how you behave when you visit museums, Hew. You wander from place to place randomly, making connections, and then you revisit them another day. You don't follow an order, no artist does. They go to what they like.

> **HL** Exactly. For me, it's random but it's not random – there's method in the madness. But it is very much about wandering from one thing to another and going 'oh that's interesting,' or 'that connects with what I was looking at a few minutes ago.'

IK Yes, we want people to make connections with objects that aren't displayed literally next to one another.

> **HL** Sometimes small brown objects are easy to walk right past in a museum, but they can actually be very beautiful and tell the most interesting stories.

The object is small, but the symbolism behind it is huge. And that's what this exhibition is – a colossal book of stories. Some are grand and beautiful, and some are more everyday.

IK *Ways of Seeing* [by John Berger, 1972] was a point of reference here. Berger alternated text chapters with image chapters that contrasted or spoke to one another.

    HL I work in a collaged, layering way. It's the way my mind works – I think of one object and then my mind jumps from that to something completely different and then back again. It hops from place to place.

IK We want visitors to see an object out of the corner of their eye and to make connections. People are usually asked to follow a suggested 'route', but we've purposefully not done that to echo the way that you [Hew] create your own artworks. You gather objects together and make visual and formal connections.

    HL Years ago, on holiday, we got told off for walking around an exhibition the 'wrong' way.

IK We had to follow a set route even though we were the only people there.

    HL I think that stayed with us for years and years as the benchmark for what not to do.

IK Definitely. As artist-curators we're trying to get people to think differently. And you often make visual echoes. Lots of the objects we picked are circular – the medals, coins, soul discs – which, as well as being a visual motif, encourages people to look from one to the other.

    HL And sometimes the links between them are the fact that the objects arrived at the Museum under similar circumstances. Speaking of discs, I've been thinking a lot about the Benin discs (p. 145). They are physical evidence from history – on the topic of the history of warfare and loot, the discs are scorched by a fire. It's the first time I saw something with actual clear evidence of the violence of its acquisition, shall we say. There was a time when I would look at Benin Bronzes, because we have two fibreglass replicas in our kitchen at home in Brixton, and every time I look at them I would think, 'Why is that broken off like that?' Some of them, it's just to do with age. But some of them you think 'Ah! That's been ripped off the wall!' That's the reason why that hole is there.

IK And what about the materials of the exhibition design? One of the great things about doing this exhibition has been the access we've had to parts of the British Museum that the public doesn't normally have. The back rooms, storerooms, safes, cabinets. We wanted to echo these materials and structures in the exhibition design. The structure looks a bit like the inside of your head, and it also reflects the process of selection – if we could have had open crates, we would have done.

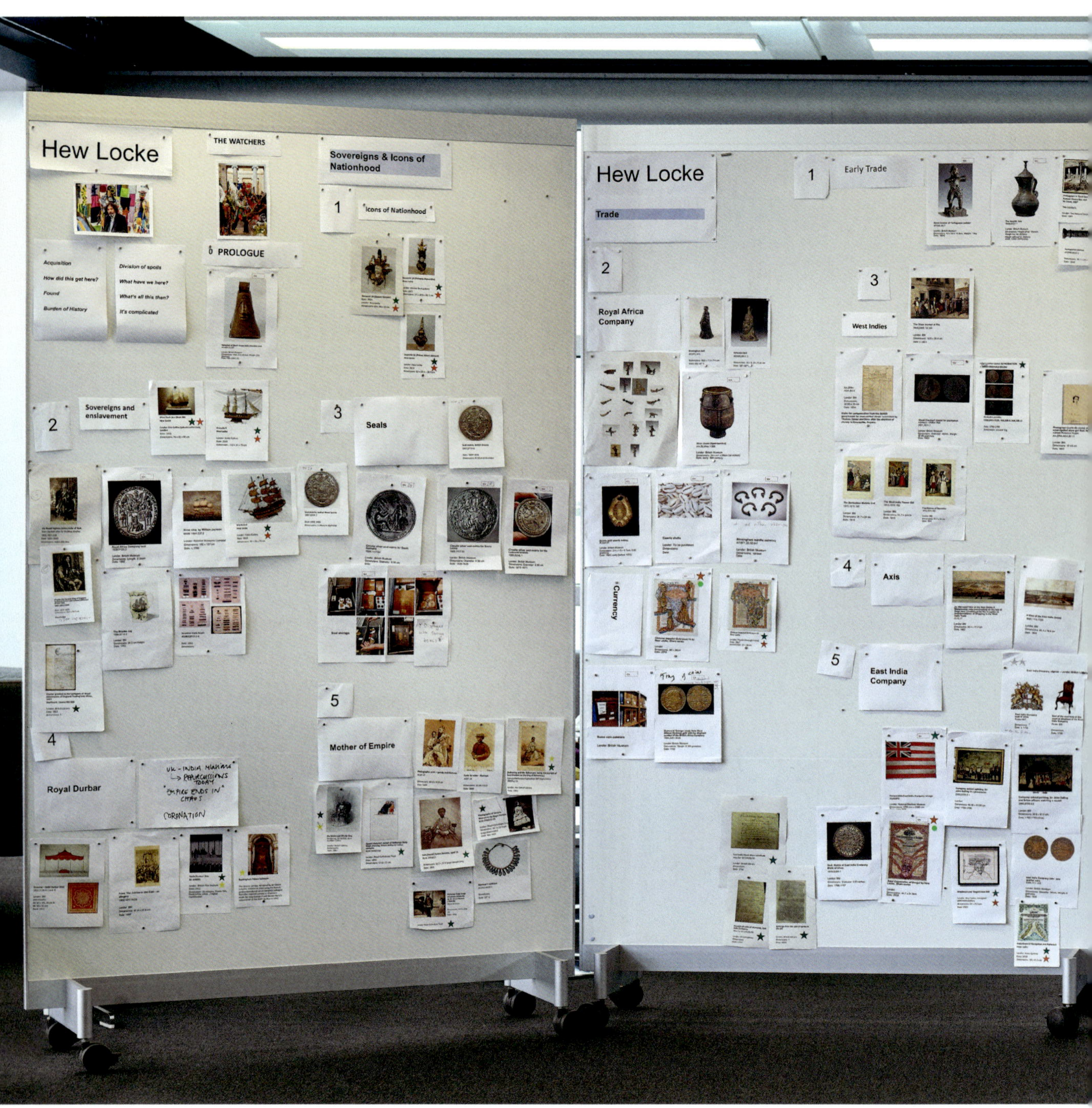

Exhibition planning boards, 2024.

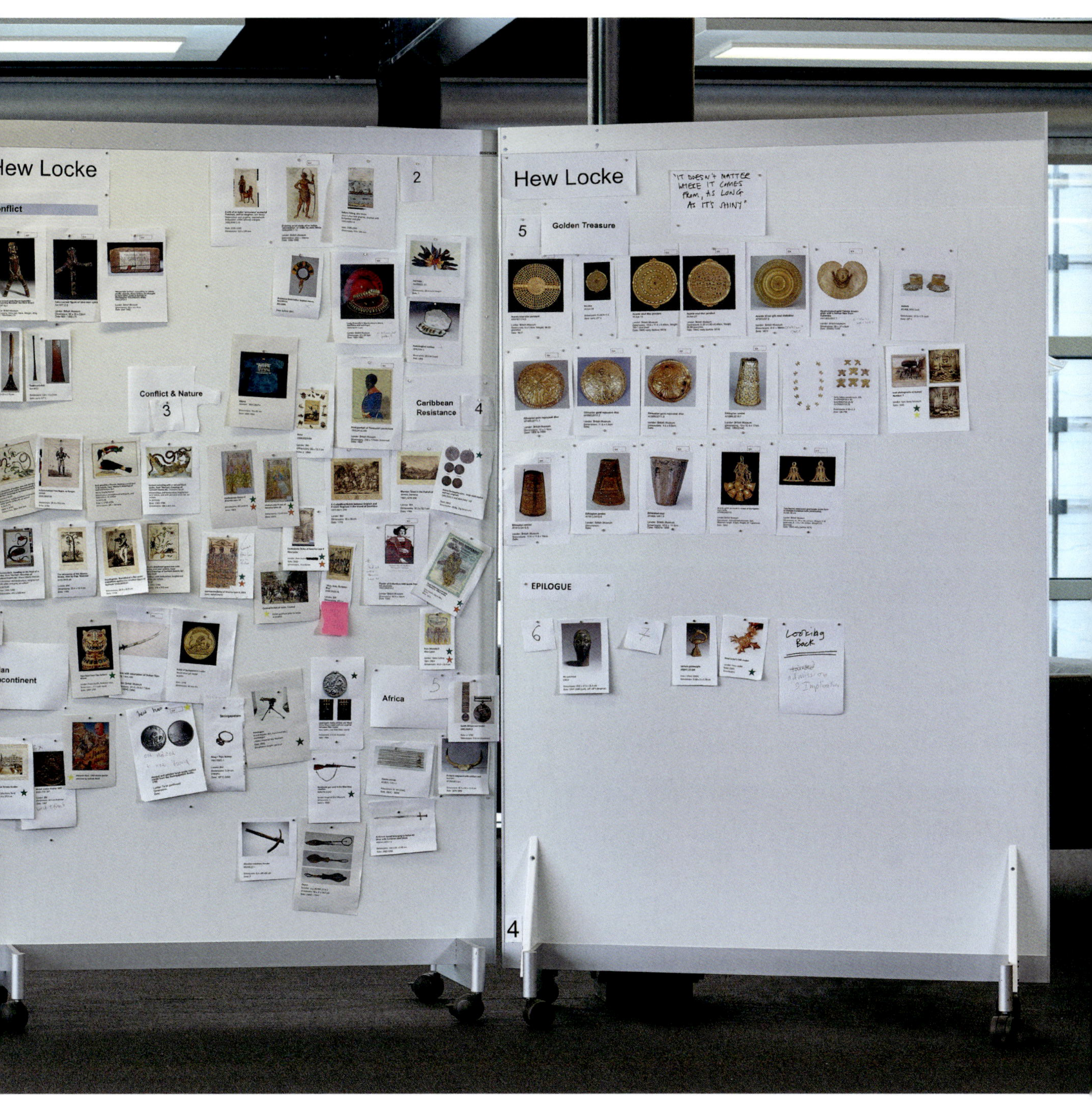

HL Well, I haven't had a lobotomy! But yes, it's very much like that. That's literally what my brain is like. You'll say, 'I'll follow you Hew, but you've gone down a rabbit hole!' And this show is one giant rabbit hole.

IK It's a warren!

HL It's a warren, exactly. And that's what I like about it. It's a product of genuine enthusiasm and excitement. When we discuss these things at home, we direct each other towards news articles or new information – this whole project keeps opening new avenues. You open one door, and there's another waiting behind it.

IK The original list had twice as many objects, but you can't fit everything in, or get everything you want – some objects couldn't be loaned, or there's too much demand for certain items. We have an exhibition in our heads that's even bigger than this one.

HL Yes, this is Part One! [Laughs.] The whole point is to pose a question to the viewers: what would you include? What would your show be? I'm sure some people will think 'how on earth could you exclude that?' And my answer would be 'the room is not infinite.' We are working to constraints. And in the case of this show, we have twice as many showcases as a 'typical' British Museum exhibition in this space. But it will still only be able to show a fraction of the collection.

IK We should talk about *The Watchers* (pp. 1–4, 6–7).

HL *The Watchers* were part of the original proposal. For me the show wouldn't work without an intervention. Interventions are what I do. My initial idea was figures with costumes and masks on the walls, looking over the walls, observing you, observing the exhibition and passing judgement or comment on the show. Pointing at something that they think is important. I want them to be something you see out of the corner of your eye, in the same way that you make connections out of the corner of your brain. It's a similar kind of thing – 'oh what's that up there?' – you know. Sometimes the figures might be having a conversation or a discussion. Are they judging the viewer? Or judging me, the person who's put this selection together?

IK Or the Museum. I originally wondered if they were judging the treasure or thinking about the objects' provenance.

HL It's one way of looking. The figures are from my own conscience but they're also observers. They're the 'Greek chorus', for want of a better word, commenting on the side about what they have seen, and commenting on you.

IK They're also a mirror of the viewers. Normally the audience is used to being the one looking, to be in the position of power.

HL Yes, this flips the script. To return to Benin, I think 'typical' images of treasure might be the Benin Bronzes, but other artefacts can reveal a lot about that moment and that society in just one object – like the crossbow from Benin (p. 134). We want people to think about these things more.

IK Yes, people think of gold, or art, but so many weapons were looted. That's why they feature so prominently in museum collections, and in this exhibition. The objects from southern Nigeria that form the 'Prologue' to this exhibition and book, the series of bells, are really important too. The starting point is a display but also a symbolic warning.

HL They seem to be sounding an alarm. The bells haven't been on display much [at the Museum] and aren't as well known as the bronzes or plaques. They make you think about what they would sound like, but also what they meant in the past and the present. The original significance of summoning the ancestors. They are a call to action too. Do we have a problem here? Well, obviously there is a problem.

IK The Epilogue (pp. 174–5) is a series of questions. It presents an Ife head, a gold-weight and two medals that you own – the one you received when you became a member of the Royal Academy of Arts and your OBE [Officer of the Order of the British Empire], which you received from the king.

HL The Epilogue draws everything together, but it's a strange one. These four objects – my medals, the Sankofa bird and the Ife head – are intrinsically linked. And my medals are symbolic of my personal entanglement with British history, which I am constantly reflecting on.

IK So the Ife head is a cast made by the Museum in the 1940s when they borrowed 12 Ife heads and other sculptures from Nigeria. The British Museum helped with conservation work and made plaster casts. The original head is in the National Museum Lagos, Nigeria.

HL It alludes to a long history of copies over the years. Plaster cast replicas were a common thing. The V&A's cast court is a well-known, iconic place, and this is a variation on that. This cast is scientifically valuable too, and it is its own thing, it's beautifully done. The question is – is this a suggestion for the future? Of how we can move forwards? Even at the V&A's Donatello show [in 2023], casts and replicas of original objects were on display and they were still appreciated by the scholars and visitors. We can understand what was intended. The Ife head cast is a work of art in itself, a loving replication.

IK The Sankofa bird is an Akan gold-weight that shows a bird with its head turned to look over its back, made in Ghana. It relates to a proverb that translates to 'go back and get it' or 'pick up what you left behind' – it means that we should look to the past and previous mistakes to become wiser.

HL Yes, and the exhibition itself is circular – its end links to its beginning.

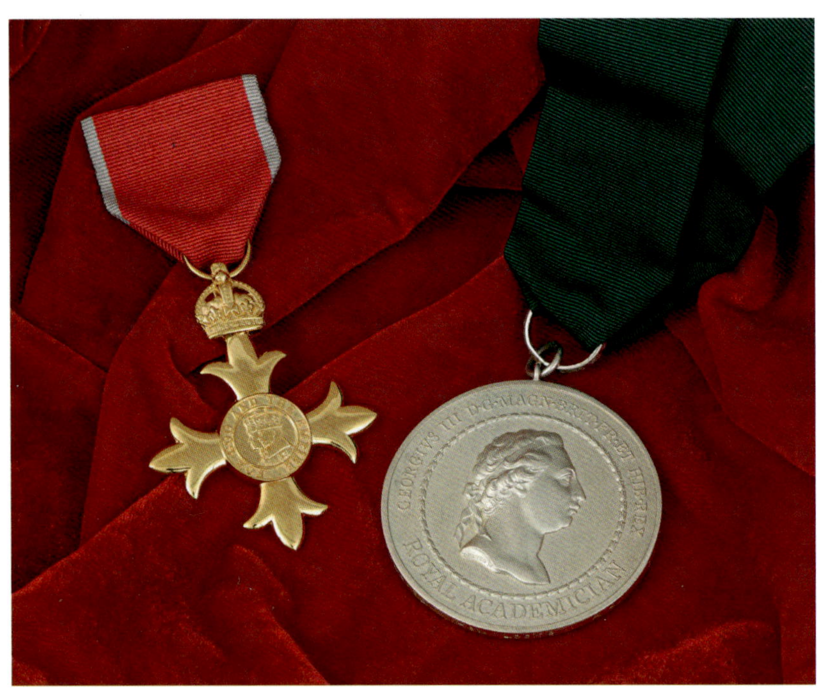

Hew Locke's OBE medal, 2023, and RA medal, 2022.

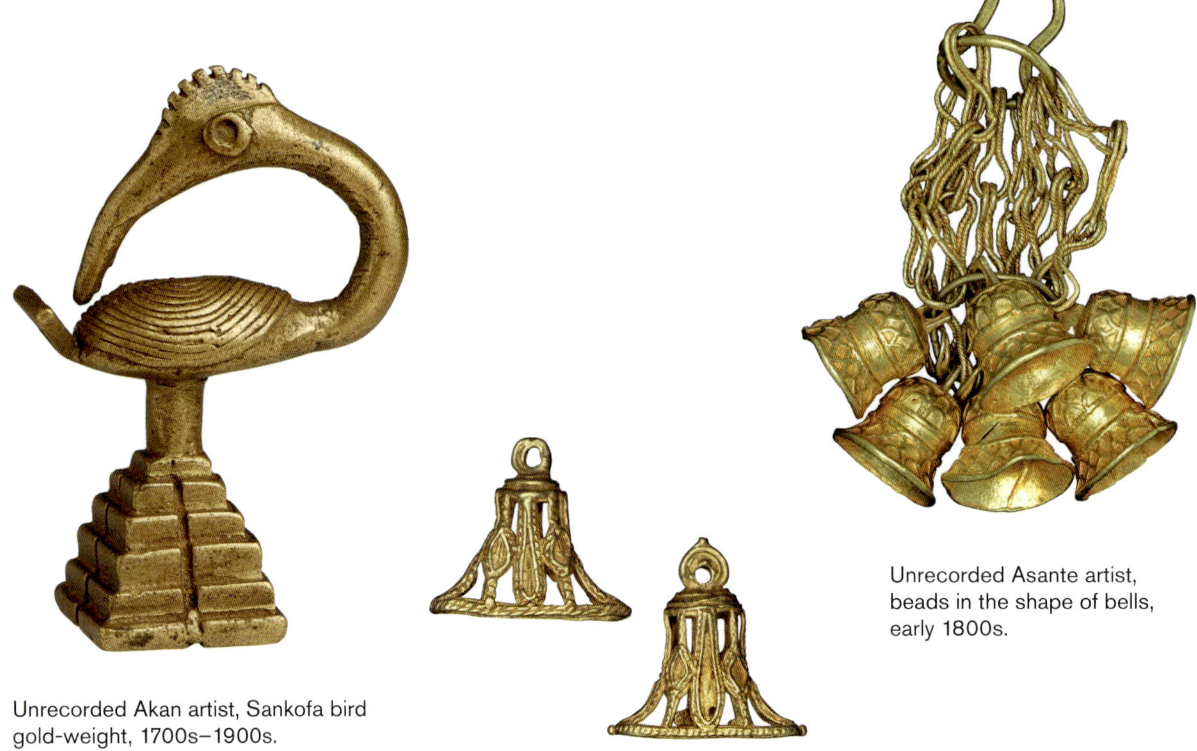

Unrecorded Akan artist, Sankofa bird gold-weight, 1700s–1900s.

Unrecorded Asante artist, bells, possibly for attaching to a bracelet, 1800s.

Unrecorded Asante artist, beads in the shape of bells, early 1800s.

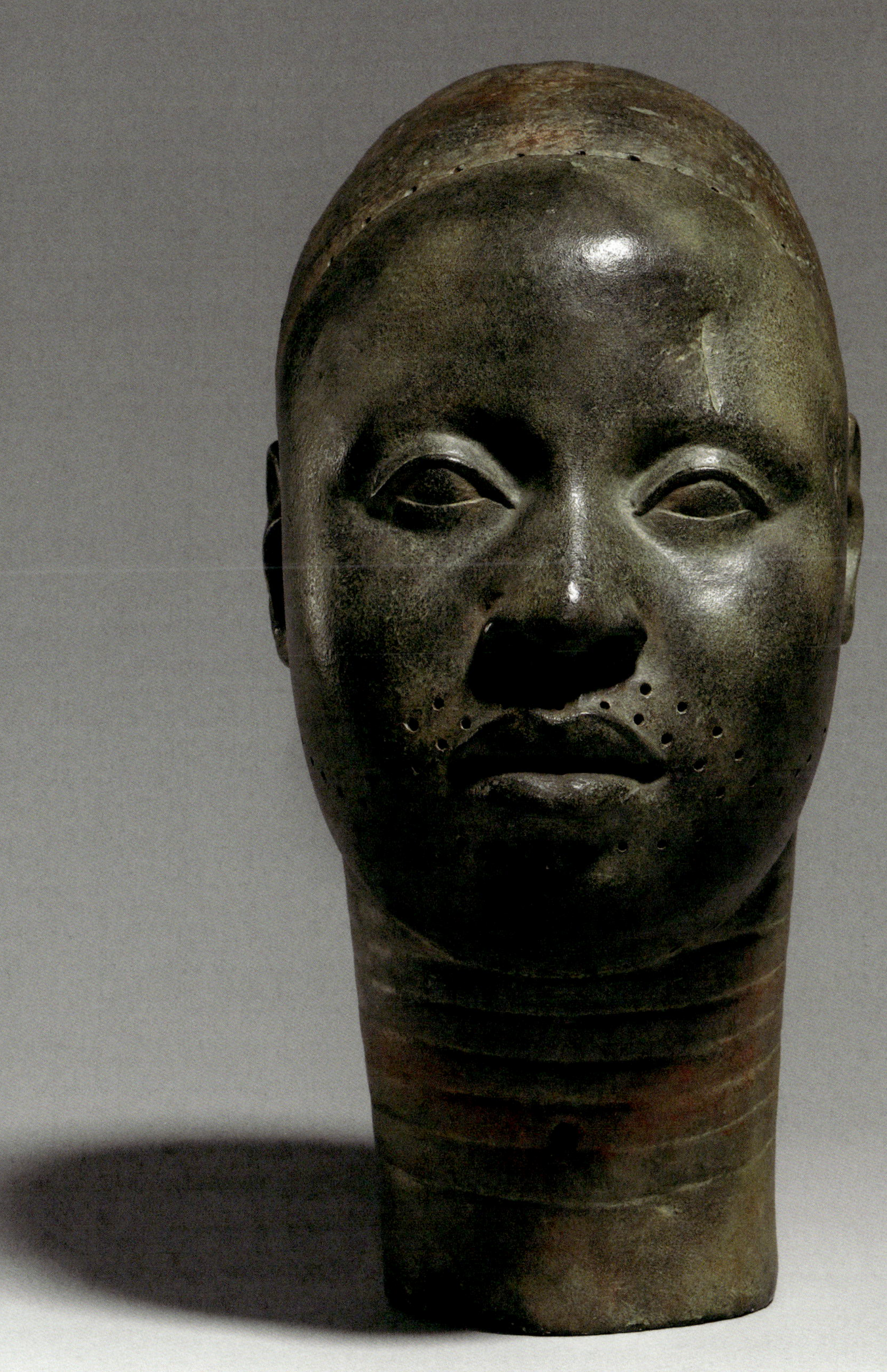

Unrecorded artist, cast of a sculpture of an Ife head, cast 1947–8,
original 1300s–early 1400s.

IK There are so many medals of war in the exhibition, so it's kind of beautiful to have yours, which you received as a result of your art – fighting battles with creativity not a gun. But there is a sense of absurdity in you being awarded a medal in the name of 'God and Empire' for critiquing empire.

HL When you're made an Academician, you sign your name into a vellum book. There are many great recent names in it. There's also a framed page with the signatures of Joshua Reynolds and J.M.W. Turner, and you become a part of that deeply troubled history – entangled pasts, as the RA called it [in their April 2024 exhibition]. This show is pulling at the threads of these histories and trying to bring them to light.

IK You also felt conflicted about accepting your OBE [in 2023].

HL When I got the letter of invitation, my instant reaction was that I wanted to accept it. A moment of wonder and joy turned into a stressful week where I had to process my reaction and decide what to do. Some of my friends were not happy. I was thinking about the late great poet Benjamin Zephaniah, who refused it. The poet Lemn Sissay commented that Zephaniah never judged him for accepting it. Historian David Olusoga accepted his too. He felt it would be worse if no Black Britons were honoured by the awards system. There is a campaign to change its name to 'Order of British Excellence', which I am part of. Maybe I've blown my knighthood, but there we go.

IK You and many other artists, writers and historians have been highlighting these issues of provenance and museological narratives for decades. It's only recently that it's been in the news and become a current topic of debate.

HL Yes, this exhibition is a beautiful can of worms.

IK People can also just come to the show and admire the beauty of the objects, and that's fine.

HL But then if they want to go deeper, they can. Every European power has a hand in this. It is a very human response with difficult decisions to kick the can down the road. Because what is the reality? Does everything go back? Is this exhibition the 'last chance' to see some objects before they are returned to their place of origin? But for the viewer, it's also an opportunity to see things that haven't been on display for a long time.

IK What do you want people to take away from this exhibition?

HL I want them to ask their own questions and make up their own minds. The Museum is one of the most visited in the world. People come to see certain things. What would happen if those things were no longer here? How would you deal with that? There is a lot of stuff in storage that doesn't get seen. And who funds that?

IK Museums are constantly changing. When I visit the Museum now, I am

much more aware about the Egyptian galleries being full of dead bodies,
and modern Museum curators are now reconsidering how to display human
remains.

> **HL** Yes. It's how we evolve the Museum and evolve with it. I've been coming
> here for decades. I saw the Benin Bronzes in the Museum of Mankind years ago
> and remember my mother explaining their significance to me as a child. She
> was English, by the way.

IK It's not that we're directing people towards a specific answer. We want to
open up the discussion, to encourage people to think more widely. It's not an
easy topic.

> **HL** It's a highly political one though, and it will become more urgent over the
> next decade. Every day there is a massive queue to get inside the building –
> there's such a desire to visit museums. The audience is just coming with more
> complicated perspectives now. We often joke about that James Acaster stand-up
> set [*Repetoire: Reset*]. 'Come and look at this stuff we're looking after for you, and
> we'll explain to you how important it is to you and your culture!'

IK What impact do you hope this exhibition will have on the audience's
perception of the British Museum, as well as its collections and their histories?
Personally I hope it will encourage people to think about the lesser known, non-
headline objects.

> **HL** Yes. On average people spend a few seconds looking at an object. I want to
> encourage close looking, to get people to think about the stories behind them.
> This is a treasure trove of complicated stories, messy stories, horrible stories
> sometimes.

IK All we can do is hope to intrigue people enough that they might stop to look
for more information, might follow up on something that caught their eye.

> **HL** Do they belong here or in their place of origin? What even is their point of
> origin? Sometimes it wasn't one country or owner.

IK And even when it is one country or nation, different competing groups
within a nation might have a claim to an object. But why do you think the
British Museum asked you to do this show?

> **HL** The other day I described myself as a 'sin eater'. Somebody who comes
> to your funeral after you've died, and there are cakes set on the coffin, and the
> person eats these cakes and takes the sins away from the deceased person.

IK Is the British Museum that cynical? They weren't asking you to do it just to
be a 'sin eater', were they?

> **HL** No, I know. I think they asked us to get involved because I take a complex
> view of things.

IK And why have they asked a contemporary artist in the first place?

HL Because the time is now. If not now, when? The cat is out of the bag. We don't know what the future will hold, but this is the time to dissect it.

IK The whole experience has been great. It's been good for us to learn and have a mutual dialogue with the Museum curators – it's been valuable for us but also for them.

HL I'm hoping that other museums internationally will pick up the approach of artist-curated exhibitions. This is a very important show to me personally, but I would hope it's an important show for the British Museum too. One that can't be ignored. Put it this way – in the words of the sitcom *Yes Minister*, it's a 'very brave' move!

IK It's also brave for us to do it because we know the criticism we might face. We know artists and friends who won't be happy. There's always something to criticise, because we're not giving a cut-and-dried opinion.

HL I am often deliberately vague and open-ended. I like to point out problems.

IK At the same time, the British Museum has also been more open to our process compared to other institutions. Why did you want to work with them?

HL You can't just say no or sit on the sidelines and throw stones. Once I realised the Museum was willing to try to be open, I saw it as a challenge, an opportunity. If they had the guts to do this, then what's the excuse for other museums? Things change and evolve. If you told me five years ago I'd be curating a British Museum exhibition, I would never have dreamt it.

IK And why is it so important to invite artists into museums?

HL I've seen exhibitions put together by academics that are wonderful shows, but I have a very different approach. Some artists are more archival than others, but for me, things are both political and aesthetic.

IK Many of the objects in the Museum have been made by an artist. It makes sense that you'd want an artist to respond to it. The Grayson Perry exhibition *The Tomb of the Unknown Craftsman* (2011) did this.

HL I come to this museum to think and to be inspired. There are often times, say on Sunday at 2.30 in the afternoon when I'm kicking my heels at home, and I think 'You know what, sod it, I'm going to go to the British Museum.' And I'm never disappointed. And that's why the museum should work with contemporary artists. This is where we're getting our inspiration from. We're the people making the stuff inspired by the stuff that you're showing. And an artist's approach is always different to a historian's. It's a very different way of looking at things.

IK The artist can make an image that endures, that lingers in the mind. More so than if you'd read an entire book. One for me was Fred Wilson's intervention *Mining the Museum* (1992) at the Maryland Historical Society. I didn't visit it in person, but images of this have stayed with me. They had a cabinet called 'Metalwork 1793–1880', in which Wilson placed lovely silver teapots and spoons alongside shackles for enslaved people that had been manufactured at the same time. It's very simple, but that image has stayed with me for 30 years.

    HL Yes, there's a long history of artists creating interventions in museum spaces, and I hope this exhibition continues that, and continues to raise questions and draw attention to contemporary issues. And I also hope that it will bring in a new audience. If you had an exhibition called 'Provenance', people might imagine it would be a bit dry.

IK Well, we would come! But lots of people might assume they wouldn't be interested. But if you can tempt extra people in with your own work, they might find out that there's lots to be interested in.

    HL Exactly, it's about not beating people over the head. If people want to come and see beautiful things, come and see some interesting artwork, that's enough.

Further reading

Hew Locke

Work made by Hew Locke: www.hewlocke.net.

Deborah Robinson and Emily Marsden (eds), Hew Locke, Kris Kuramitsu and Sarat Maharaj, *Hew Locke*, Walsall: The New Art Gallery, 2005.

Stephanie James, Peter Bonnell, Jens Hoffman and Kobena Mercer, *Hew Locke: Stranger in Paradise*, London: Black Dog Publishing, 2011.

Hew Locke, Richard Harry Drayton, Diana Tuite and Jonathan Watkins, *Hew Locke: Here's the Thing*, Birmingham: Ikon Gallery, 2019.

Hew Locke (guest ed.), *Entangled Pasts*, *Royal Academy of Arts Magazine*, no. 161, Winter 2023.

What have we here?

Contested objects in the British Museum's Collection: www.britishmuseum.org/about-us/british-museum-story/contested-objects-collection.

Digital Benin project (a digital inventory of Benin collections globally): digitalbenin.org.

Victoria Avery and Jake Subryan Richards (eds), *Black Atlantic: Power, People, Resistance*, London: Philip Wilson Publishers, 2023.

Nigel Barley, *The Art of Benin*, London: The British Museum Press, 2010.

C.A. Bayly (ed.), *The Raj: India and the British, 1600–1947*, London: National Portrait Gallery Publications, 1990.

Annie E. Coombes, *Reinventing Africa: Museums, Material Culture and Popular Imagination in Late Victorian and Edwardian England*, New Haven, CT: Yale University Press, 1997.

William Dalrymple, *The Anarchy: The Relentless Rise of the East India Company*, London: Bloomsbury, 2019.

William Dalrymple and Anita Anand, *Koh-i-Noor: The History of the World's Most Infamous Diamond*, London: Bloomsbury, 2017.

James Delbourgo, *Collecting the World: The Life and Curiosity of Hans Sloane*, London: Penguin, 2017.

Anthony Farrington, *Trading Places: The East India Company and Asia, 1600–1834*, London: The British Library, 2002.

Jeanette Greenfield, *The Return of Cultural Treasures*, Cambridge: Cambridge University Press, 2020.

Saidiya Hartman, *Scenes of Subjection: Terror, Slavery, and Self-Making in Nineteenth-Century America*, New York: Oxford University Press, 1997.

Saidiya Hartman, 'Venus in Two Acts', *Small Axe*, vol. 12, no. 2 (June 2008), pp. 1–14.

Sudhir Hazareesingh, *Black Spartacus: The Epic Life of Toussaint Louverture*, London: Allen Lane, 2020.

Andrew Heavens, *The Prince and the Plunder: How Britain Took One Small Boy and Hundreds of Treasures from Ethiopia*, Cheltenham: The History Press, 2023.

Nancy Neaher Maas and Philip M. Peek (eds), *Summoning the Ancestors: Southern Nigerian Bronzes*, Los Angeles, CA: Fowler Museum at UCLA, 2021.

Philip Marsden, *The Barefoot Emperor: An Ethiopian Tragedy*, London: Harper Press, 2007.

Olivette Otele, *African Europeans: An Untold History*, London: C. Hurst & Co., 2020.

Eduardo Paolozzi, *Lost Magic Kingdoms and Six Paper Moons from Nahuatl: An Exhibition at the Museum of Mankind*, London: The British Museum Press, 1985.

Grayson Perry, *The Tomb of the Unknown Craftsman*, London: The British Museum Press, 2011.

William A. Pettigrew, *Freedom's Debt: The Royal African Company and the Politics of the Atlantic Slave Trade, 1672–1752*, Chapel Hill, NC: University of North Carolina, 2013.

Barnaby Phillips, *Loot: Britain and the Benin Bronzes*, London: Oneworld Publications, 2021.

Dorothy C. Price, Esther Chadwick, Cora Gilroy-Ware, Sarah Lea, Alayo Akinkugbe and Rose Thompson, *Entangled Pasts, 1768–Now: Art, Colonialism and Change*, London: Royal Academy of Arts, 2024.

Sathnam Sanghera, *Empireworld: How British Imperialism Has Shaped the Globe*, London: Penguin, 2024.

Kim Sloan, *A New World: England's First View of America*, London: The British Museum Press, 2007.

Alison Smith, David Blayney Brown and Carol Jacobi (eds), *Artists and Empire: Facing Britain's Imperial Past*, London: Tate Publishing, 2015.

Objects

Objects marked with an asterisk did not feature in the exhibition.

pp. 1–4, 6–7: Hew Locke, *The Watchers*, 2024. Mixed media.
H. 130 cm, W. 60 cm, D. 55 cm (max, child *Watchers*), H. 242 cm, W.
110 cm, D. 90 cm (max, adult *Watchers*).

pp. 10–11. Unrecorded artists, bells and bell forms, *c.* 900s–1900s. 15
are illustrated but 12 more featured in the exhibition. Made in southern
Nigeria. Brass, bronze. H. 7.6 cm, W. 3.2 cm, D. 2.9 cm (smallest),
H. 21.6 cm, W. 12.8 cm, D. 11.5 cm (largest). British Museum,
London, Af1909,0811.2 & .4; Af1949,07.3–8; Af1954,23.235, .699,
.700, .710 & .714; Af1969,27.1; Af1979,01.4451. Af1909,0811.2
& .4 collected by Sir Claude MacDonald in 1890–5 while he was
Commissioner and Consul-General of the Oil Rivers Protectorate
and later the Niger Coast Protectorate; donated by his widow Lady
Ethel MacDonald in 1909. Af1949,07.3–8 sold to the Museum by
Mr W. Francis on behalf of his mother. Af1954,23.235 purchased by
John Comins on behalf of the Wellcome Institute for the History of
Medicine at a Sotheby's sale on 26 July 1932 (lot 50); donated to the
Museum in 1954. Af1954,23.699, .700 & .714 collected in 1931–2 by
British colonial government anthropologist Mervyn David Waldegrave
Jeffreys in southern Nigeria; sold to the Wellcome Historical Medical
Museum in the 1930s and donated to the Museum by the Wellcome
Institute for the History of Medicine in 1954. Af1954,23.710
purchased by Mr Webb on behalf of the Wellcome Historical Medical
Museum at a Glendining sale on 3 Dec 1934 (lot 212); donated to
the Museum in 1954. Af1969,27.1 was likely cast in Ijebu-Ode and
probably belonged to local Yoruba Chief Lisa; sold to the Museum by
New York dealer Mr Merton D. Simpson in 1969. Af1979,01.4451 is
of unknown provenance.

pp. 36–7. Hew Locke, *Société de Transit de Grand-Lahou 1*, 2014.
Acrylic on antique share certificate. H. 32 cm, W. 34 cm. Hales
Gallery, London.*

p. 38. Hew Locke, *Souvenir 20 (Queen Victoria)*, 2024. Parian ware
and mixed media. H. 63 cm, W. 46 cm, D. 19 cm. Private Collection.

p. 40. Hew Locke, *Souvenir 14 (Princess Alexandra)*, 2023. Parian
ware and mixed media. H. 57 cm, W. 19.5 cm, D. 18.5 cm. Almine
Rech Gallery, London.

p. 41. Hew Locke, *Souvenir 13 (Prince Albert Edward)*, 2023. Parian
ware and mixed media. H. 67 cm, W. 23.5 cm, D. 20.5 cm. Private
Collection.

p. 43. Hew Locke, *Wine Dark Sea Boat BB*, 2019. Wood, plastic,
brass, fabric, mixed media. H. 74 cm, W. 92 cm, D. 26.3 cm. Private
Collection.

p. 44. Hew Locke, *Windward*, 2019. Mixed media. H. 91 cm,
W. 36 cm, D. 72 cm. Hales Gallery, London.

p. 45. Hew Locke, *Armada 6*, 2019. Mixed media. H. 110 cm,
W. 34 cm, D. 75 cm. Hales Gallery, London.

p. 47. Unrecorded artist, seal-die with arms and motto of the Royal
African Company, after 1663. England. Copper alloy. Diam. 3.4 cm.
British Museum, London, 1838,0125.2. Previously belonged to
someone named 'Till', possibly coin dealer William Till, transferred
from The British Library in 1838.
 Isaac Beckett, after Sir Godfrey Kneller, *James, Duke of York*,
c. 1681–5. England. Mezzotint on paper. H. 43 cm, W. 25.5 cm.
British Museum, London, 1902,1011.118. Bequeathed by William
Meriton Eaton, 2nd Baron Cheylesmore.*
 Unrecorded English artist, *King Charles II*, *c.* 1660–80. England.
Engraving printed from two plates on vellum. H. 26.3 cm, W. 22.5 cm.
British Museum, London, 1961,0211.38. Purchased from Mrs K.M.
Hocking in 1961.*

p. 48. Charter for the Company of Royal Adventurers of England
Trading into Africa, 1663. London, UK. Paper. H. 44 cm, W. 29.5 cm,
D. 1.2 cm (closed volume). The British Library, London, Sloane
MS 205. Bequeathed by Sir Hans Sloane.

p. 49. Nicholas Hilliard, design for the obverse of Queen Elizabeth's
Great Seal of Ireland, *c.* 1584–90. UK. Pen and ink, with wash, over
graphite, on vellum. H. 12.4 cm, W. 12.4 cm. British Museum, London,
1912,0717.1. Donated by Mrs Peter Gellatly.*
 Brooks jug, 1793 or later. Liverpool, UK. Creamware. H. 24.2 cm.
British Museum, London, 1994,0718.2. Donated by William Geoffrey
Skillicorn.
 William Jackson, *A Liverpool Slaving Ship*, *c.* 1780. Britain. Oil
on canvas. H. 102 cm, W. 127 cm. National Museums Liverpool,
MMM 1964.227.2.

pp. 50–1. Trade beads, *c.* 1863. Venice (Murano) and Bohemia. Glass.
H. 29.5 cm, W. 30 cm, D. 1.8 cm (largest). British Museum, London,
Af1863,0717.3 & .4. Donated by London bead merchant Moses Lewin
Levin in 1863.

p. 53. Joseph Shepherd Wyon, seal-die for South Australia, *c.* 1858–
73. London, UK. Silver. Diam. 6.5 cm. British Museum, London,
1906,1117.54. Donated by Robert Crewe-Milnes, 1st Marquess of
Crewe, Lord President of the Council, in 1906.
 The Royal Mint, seal-die for Jamaica, 1901–10. Britain. Steel.
Diam. 7 cm. British Museum, London, 1914,0611.8. Donated by Lord
President of the Council in 1914.
 Joseph Shepherd Wyon and Alfred Benjamin Wyon, seal-die for the
Leeward Islands, 1872–3. London, UK. Silver. Diam. 8.9 cm. British
Museum, London, 1926,0316.1. Donated by Arthur Balfour, 1st Earl of
Balfour, Lord President of the Council, in 1926.
 Benjamin Wyon, seal-die for British Guiana, 1839–40. Britain.
Silver. Diam. 6.3 cm. British Museum, London, 1897,0719.6. Donated
by Spencer Cavendish, 8th Duke of Devonshire, Lord President of the
Council, in 1897.
 Benjamin Wyon, seal-die for Sierra Leone, 1838–9. Britain. Silver.
Diam. 3.6 cm. British Museum, London, 1906,1117.53. Donated by
Robert Crewe-Milnes, 1st Marquess of Crewe, Lord President of the
Council, in 1906.
 Benjamin Wyon, seal-die for Nova Scotia, 1838–9. Britain. Silver.
Diam. 6.2 cm. British Museum, London, 1897,0719.7. Donated by
Spencer Cavendish, 8th Duke of Devonshire, Lord President of the
Council, in 1897.

p. 55. After Godefroy Durand, *The Jubilee in the East*, supplement to
'The Graphic', 1887. London, UK. Wood engraving on paper. H. 48 cm,
W. 33 cm. British Museum, London, 1902,1011.9336. Bequeathed by
William Meriton Eaton, 2nd Baron Cheylesmore in 1902.

p. 56. Mayo School of Arts and Sir Edwin Landseer Lutyens, throne
canopy, 1911–16. Buckingham Palace, London, UK. Velvet, silk,
gilt wood. The Royal Collection, London / HM King Charles III,
RCIN 589.*
 Mayo School of Arts, drawing of the Royal Shamiana, 1911. Made
in Lahore, Pakistan. Pen and black ink with red watercolour and gold
pigment on paper. H. 66.3 cm, W. 55 cm. British Museum, London,
1915,1126,0.8. From the India Office in 1915.

p. 57. Mayo School of Arts, drawing of the Chandoa, hanging interior
of the canopy roof, 1911. Made in Lahore, Pakistan. Pen and black
ink with red watercolour and gold pigment on paper. H. 68.5 cm,
W. 101.2 cm. British Museum, London, 1915,1126,0.1. From the India
Office in 1915.

p. 59. M. & N. Hanhart after Frederick E. Forbes, 'Sarah Bonetta
Forbes: The African Captive', from *Dahomey and the Dahomans*,
1851. London, UK. Lithograph. H. 14.4 cm, W. 8.9 cm (image).
The British Library, London, 10097.d.21.*

William Bambridge, *Sally [Sarah] Bonetta Forbes*, 1856. Britain. Albumen print photograph. H. 28.2 cm, W. 22.9 cm. The Royal Collection, London / HM King Charles III, RCIN 2906613.

p. 60. Roger Fenton, *Princess Victoria Gouramma of Coorg*, 1854. Britain. Albumen print photograph. H. 19 cm, W. 14.7 cm. The Royal Collection, London / HM King Charles III, RCIN 2906573.

p. 61. Queen Victoria, *Maharaja Duleep Singh dressing Prince Arthur in Indian costume*, c. 1854. Britain. Watercolour on paper. H. 17.6 cm, W. 11 cm. The Royal Collection, London / HM King Charles III, RCIN 980023.br.
Ernst Becker, *Maharaja Duleep Singh of Lahore*, 23 Aug 1854. Isle of Wight, UK. Carbon print mounted on card. H. 17.3 cm, W. 25.2 cm. The Royal Collection, London / HM King Charles III, RCIN 2915314.

p. 62. Cornelius Jabez Hughes, carte de visite of Prince Alemayehu, 1868. Isle of Wight, UK. Photographic print mounted on card. H. 10.3 cm, W. 6 cm. British Museum, London, Af,B7.19. Donated by Ida Perrin, goddaughter of Captain Speedy.
Unrecorded Ethiopian artist, necklace, 1800s. See p. 63 for Prince Alemayehu wearing the necklace. Made in Ethiopia. Silver pendants, glass beads, silk cord. H. 24 cm, W. 20 cm, D. 2 cm (mounted). British Museum, London, Af1912,0410.7. Belonged to Prince Alemayehu. At some point after Alemayehu was brought to England in 1868, Captain Speedy took possession of the necklace. Donated to the Museum by his widow, Cornelia Mary Speedy, in 1912.

p. 63. Cornelius Jabez Hughes, carte de visite of Prince Alemayehu and Captain Speedy, 1868. See p. 62 for the necklace worn by Alemayehu. Isle of Wight, UK. Photographic print mounted on card. H. 10.3 cm, W. 6.2 cm. British Museum, London, Af,B7.22. Donated by Ida Perrin, goddaughter of Captain Speedy.

p. 66. Unrecorded English artist, the Asante Jug, 1390s. England. Bronze. H. 62.5 cm, W. 30 cm, D. 36 cm. British Museum, London, 1896,0727.1. Looted by British officers during the 1895–6 Anglo-Asante War; purchased from Major Charles St Leger Barter in 1896.
Frederick Grant, the Asante Jug in a courtyard associated with royal buildings in Kumasi, Ghana, 1884, from *Gold Coast, Views in Kumasi: Kwaka Dua and His Court*, 1887. Photograph. H. 21 cm, W. 14 cm. The National Archives, UK.*

pp. 66–7. Francisco Alvares, cannon, 1540. Lisbon, Portugal. Bronze. H. 36.1 cm, W. 23 cm, D. 162.8 cm. British Museum, London, Af1899,0610.1. Looted by British officers during the Benin Expedition in 1897; presented to the Museum in 1899 by Sir Ralph Moor, Consul General of the Niger Coast Protectorate, on behalf of the Crown Agents for the Colonies.

p. 67. Unrecorded Edo artist, figure of a Portuguese soldier, late 1600s–early 1700s. Benin City, Nigeria. Lost-wax cast in brass. H. 43 cm, W. 20 cm, D. 18.5 cm. British Museum, London, Af1944,04.7. Looted during the British Expedition to Benin City, 1897. Acquired by Herbert Child, captain of the SS *Ivy* (Benin Expedition). This figure was previously in the collection of the Cranmore Ethnographical Museum, established by Harry Geoffrey and Irene Marguerite Beasley in 1928. It was purchased by Beasley on 1 May 1934 from the Trustees of the Herbert Child Estate. This formed part of the donation made by Irene Beasley to the Museum in 1944.
Unrecorded Edo artist, figure of a Portuguese soldier, late 1500s to early 1600s. Benin City, Nigeria. Lost-wax cast in brass. H. 37.5 cm. British Museum, London, Af1928,0112.1. Looted by British officer Ralph Frederick Locke during the Benin Expedition in 1897. Sold to Sir Sydney Bernard Burney in or soon before 1928, then sold to the Museum in 1928.*

p. 69. Unrecorded Akan artist, drum, early 1700s. Made in Ghana. Wood (camwood, African cordia), fibre, deer or possibly antelope skin. H. 41 cm, W. 28 cm, D. 24 cm. British Museum, London, Am,SLMisc.1368. Collected in Virginia by Mr Clerk, given to Sir Hans Sloane, possibly in 1729, and bequeathed by him as part of the Museum's founding collection.

p. 70. Hew Locke, *Chinese Imperial Gold Loan 11*, 2017. Acrylic on antique share certificate. H. 50 cm, W. 38 cm. Private Collection of Jonathan Olsoff and Sophie de Bellissen.

p. 71. Hew Locke, *Chinese Imperial Gold Loan 14*, 2019. Acrylic on antique share certificate. H. 50 cm, W. 38 cm. Private Collection of the Hitchin family.

pp. 72–3. Unrecorded Akan artists, gold-weights, c. 1600s–1900s. Made in Ghana. Brass. W. 1.4 cm, D. 2.4 cm (smallest), L. 11.7 cm, W. 3.6 cm (largest). British Museum, London, Af,+.8218; Af1900,0513.41–2; Af1900,0513.69; Af1939,20.8; Af1946,20.8; Af1947,13.110, .171 & .231; Af1947,18.24; Af1948,21.58; Af1949,46.68; Af1954,23.2280 & .2284; Af1955,05.11; Af1956,27.81; Af1961,16.17.a-b; Af1978,12.7; Af1979,01.3609 & .3707; Af1992,12.9; Af1993,02.214. Af,+.8218 given to the Museum on 25 Jan 1882 by A.W. Franks, who had acquired them from Miss Josephine Campbell. Af1900,0513.41, .42 & .69 purchased from the dealers Janson & Sons in 1900. Af1939,20.8 donated by Miss D.A. Stock in 1939. Af1946,20.8 purchased from Captain John Robins in 1946. Af1947,13.110, .171 & .231 bequeathed by Robert Powley Wild in 1947 following his death; he worked as Inspector of Mines in the Gold Coast (modern-day Ghana) and in the Asante region 1920–38. Af1947,18.24 purchased from Philip Creasey Smith's executors in 1947; Smith was an artist who formed a collection of objects from Africa through the London art market. Af1948,21.58 donated by Mrs C. Chater in 1948; by inheritance from her father, Captain Bowyer-Bowes, who served in the 1895–6 and 1900–1 Anglo-Asante Wars; he was based in the Gold Coast 1895–1907. Af1949,46.68 purchased with a contribution from Art Fund (as NACF) from Dorothy K. Oldman in 1949 when she sold her deceased husband William Ockelford Oldman's collection; Oldman was an important ethnographic dealer in the UK from 1902. Af1955,05.11 collected by Frank N. Best, Managing Director of a gold mine in Northern Nigeria who visited the Gold Coast (modern-day Ghana) in 1898–1900; his daughter Miss M. Best donated them to the Museum in 1955. Af1956,27.81 donated by Margaret Plass, ethnographic collector and patron of the British Museum, in 1956; Mrs Plass was married to Webster Plass and together the couple formed a significant collection of African art, largely acquired through auctions in Europe, mainly between 1945 and Mr Plass's death in 1952. Af1961,16.17.a-b purchased from Lt-Col S.C. Askwith in 1961 who had collected gold-weights while on military duty in the Gold Coast (modern-day Ghana) in 1925. Af1978,12.7 donated by Mrs M. Holmes-Gore in 1978. Af1979,01.3609 & .3707 are of unknown provenance. Af1954,23.2280 & .2284 possibly purchased by Mr Stow on behalf of the Wellcome Historical Medical Museum at a Glendining sale on 29 July 1932. Af1992,12.9 collected by Miss McCarthy between 1919 and 1931 when she was matron of the hospital at Kumasi in the Gold Coast (modern-day Ghana); her descendants Paul and Mary Massey donated her collection in 1992. Af1993,02.214 bequeathed in 1993 by William Fagg, Curator and then Keeper of the Department of Ethnography between 1938 and 1974.

p. 74. Unrecorded Akan artist, bead in the shape of a cowrie shell, early 1800s. Made in Ghana. Gold. H. 2.4 cm, W. 1.9 cm, D. 0.7 cm. British Museum, London, Af,Ash.51. Formed part of the indemnity payment extracted by the Crown Agents for the Colonies through the Treaty of Fomena in 1874 from Asantehene Kofi Karikari. Part of the regalia of the Asantehene or his court. Purchased from the Crown Agents for the Colonies in 1876.
Cowrie shells (*Monetaria annulus*). H. 1.2 cm, W. 2 cm, D. 1.2 cm (each shell, approx.).

p. 75. Guinea, 1685. Minted in the British Isles. Gold. Diam. 2.5 cm, weight 8.4 g. British Museum, London, E.1652.
Guinea, 1703. Minted in London, UK. Gold. Diam. 3.8 cm, weight 41.7 g. British Museum, London, 1935,0401.8203. Bequeathed by Thomas Bryan Clarke-Thornhill.
Guinea, 1798. Minted by Matthew Boulton at Soho Mint, Birmingham, UK. Gold. Diam. 2.4 cm, weight 8.6 g. British Museum, London, SSB,20.34.1. Donated by Dorothea, Lady Banks.
Guinea, 1722. Minted in London, UK. Gold. Diam. 2.5 cm,

weight 8.4 g. British Museum, London, 1935,0401.8239. Bequeathed by Thomas Bryan Clarke-Thornhill.

Guinea, 1746. Minted in London, UK. Gold. Diam. 3.8 cm, weight 41.9 g. British Museum, London, E.1928.

Guinea, 1729. Minted in London, UK. Gold. Diam. 2.4 cm, weight 8.3 g. British Museum, London, 1935,0401.8275. Bequeathed by Thomas Bryan Clarke-Thornhill.

Manillas, possibly 1800s. Made in Europe and southern Nigeria. Brass, bronze. H. 2.5 cm, Diam. 7 cm (max). British Museum, London, Af1909,0511.1-5; Af1950,45.453.a-b, h-j, l, n-o & u; Af1950,45.454.a-b; Af1954,23.662; Af1954,23.976; Af1954,23.1578; Af2001,07.9-22; 2009,4092.1. Af1909,0511.1-5 collected in southern Nigeria and given to the Museum by the Crown Agents for the Colonies in 1909. Af1950,45.453.a-b, h-j, l, n-o, u & Af1950,45.454.a-b collected by Colonial District Officer Percy Amaury Talbot in Southern Nigeria from 1907 and donated to the Museum in 1916. Af1954,23.662 purchased by the Wellcome Historical Medical Museum at a Glendining sale on 24–25 Sept 1934 (lot 172); donated by the Wellcome Institute for the History of Medicine in 1954. Af1954,23.976 purchased at the Stevens' Auction Rooms on 1 July 1919 (lot 382) by the Wellcome Historical Medical Museum, then donated in 1954. Af1954,23.1578 collected by anthropologist and colonial administrator Mervyn David Waldegrave Jeffreys in the Bonny River area in Southern Nigeria; it was sold by Jeffreys to the Wellcome Historical Medical Museum in 1930 and donated by the Wellcome Institute for the History of Medicine in 1954. Af2001,07.9-22 bequeathed by Mrs A Fowler in 2001. 2009,4092.1 found in the wreck of the *Douro* off the Isles of Scilly and donated by Andrew Rancliffe in 2009.

p. 76. Unrecorded artist, Lower Niger Bronze Industries bell, 900–1500. Found in the Forcados River, southern Nigeria. Copper alloy. H. 16 cm, W. 8.1 cm, D. 8.1 cm. British Museum, London, Af1909,0811.3. Collected by Sir Claude MacDonald between 1890 and 1895 while he was Commissioner and Consul-General of the Oil Rivers Protectorate and later the Niger Coast Protectorate. Later donated to the Museum by his widow, Lady Ethel MacDonald.

p. 77. Unrecorded Birmingham artist, bell, 1892. Birmingham, UK. Bronze. H. 16.5 cm, W. 7.8 cm, D. 7.6 cm. British Museum, London, Af1973,14.1. May have been in use in Nigeria. Purchased by American collectors Ernst and Ruth Anspach, who donated it to the Museum in 1973.

p. 79. Agostino Brunias, A West Indian flower girl and two free West Indian women, published 1810. London, UK. Hand-coloured etching and stipple on paper. H. 31.7 cm, W. 24 cm. British Museum, London, 1913,1015.102. Purchased from Miss Frances Bowley.

p. 80. Agostino Brunias, Three West Indian women on Barbados, published 1810. London, UK. Hand-coloured etching and stipple on paper. H. 31.7 cm, W. 24 cm. British Museum, London, 1913,1015.103. Purchased from Miss Frances Bowley.

p. 81. Agostino Brunias, Free West Indian Dominicans, published 1810. London, UK. Hand-coloured etching and stipple on paper. H. 31.7 cm, W. 24 cm. British Museum, London, 1913,1015.104. Purchased from Miss Frances Bowley.

p. 82. Richard Newton, *Cruelty and Oppression Abroad*, 1792. London, UK. Hand-coloured etching on paper. H. 38.8 cm, W. 51.2 cm. British Museum, London, 2007,7058.2. Purchased from Andrew Edmunds with contribution from British Museum Friends and Ingrid Alexander CBE.*

John Gregory Hancock Sr, Barbados Penny, 1792. Issued in Barbados. Copper alloy. Diam. 3.2 cm, weight 15.9 g. British Museum, London, 1935,0401.9125. Bequeathed by Thomas Bryan Clarke-Thornhill.

John Milton, Barbados Penny, 1788. Issued in Barbados. Copper alloy. Diam. 3.2 cm, weight 13.7 g. British Museum, London, SSB,208.6. Collected by Sarah Sophia Banks, bequeathed to her sister-in-law, Dorothea, Lady Banks, who donated it to the Museum in 1818.

p. 83. William Wyon, medal for good conduct, 1842. British Isles. Bronze. Diam. 4.5 cm, weight 50.6 g. British Museum, London, 2021,4011.1. Acquired with funds from the Archibald Bequest, 2021.

Augustus Earle, *Slave Market at Rio Janeiro*, c. 1823. Brazil. Pen, grey ink and watercolour on paper. H. 18.3 cm, W. 26.4 cm. British Museum, London, 1845,0405.14.144. Donated by Sir Augustus Wall Callcott.

p. 84. Claim for compensation, 1834. Essequibo, Guyana. Paper. H. 32.5 cm, W. 20 cm. British Museum, London, Am,EPH-AOA,B2.5. Likely purchased by Jonathan C.H. King from dealer Judith Grant in 1999 and donated to the Museum.

p. 85. J.E. McClees, carte de visite of Rebecca Huger, 1863. Sold in New York, USA. Paper. H. 10 cm, W. 6 cm. British Museum, London, Am,EPH-AOA,B2.11. Purchased by Jonathan C.H. King on eBay in 2005 and donated to the Museum.

Letter describing the punishment of a runaway enslaved woman, 1832. Shrewsbury, Jamaica. Paper. H. 25 cm, W. 20 cm. British Museum, London, Am,EPH-AOA,B2.3. Donated by Jonathan C.H. King.*

p. 87. William Daniell, *An Elevated View of the New Docks & Warehouses now constructing on the Isle of Dogs near Limehouse for the reception & accommodation of Shipping in the West India Trade*, 1802. London, UK. Soft-ground etching and aquatint, hand coloured on paper. H. 46.4 cm, W. 77.6 cm. British Museum, London, G,13.17. Bequeathed by John Charles Crowle (from the Crowle Pennant).

William Daniell, *A View of the East India Docks*, 1808. London, UK. Soft-ground etching and aquatint, hand coloured on paper. H. 45.4 cm, W. 78.4 cm. British Museum, London, 1880,1113.1729. Purchased from John Gregory Crace.

p. 89. Unrecorded Indian artist, *Portrait of Jonathan Duncan*, c. 1800. Possibly Mumbai, India. Gouache on paper. H. 17 cm, W. 21 cm. British Museum, London, 2019,3010.1. Funded by the Brooke Sewell Permanent Fund.*

Quarter anna coin, 1835. Issued in India. Bronze. Diam. 2.6 cm, weight 6 g. British Museum, London, 2005,1111.263. Donated by Joan Towle, Donald Barbour and Fiona Barbour.

East India Company share certificate, 1766. London, UK. Paper. H. 21 cm, W. 16.3 cm. The British Library, London, Mss Eur G37/81/6/18.

p. 90. Possibly Thomas Mun, An estimate of yearly trade in spices, textiles and indigo carried out by the East India Company, 1620–1. London, UK. Paper. H. 33 cm, W. 21.5 cm. The British Library, London, IOR/H/39/ fol. 56v.

p. 91. East India Company coin, 1786, with later engraving. Minted in Calcutta, India. Copper alloy. Diam. 28.4 cm, weight 11.7 g. British Museum, London, 1952,0904.73.*

15-rupee coin, 1770. Minted in India. Gold. Diam. 2.3 cm, weight 11 g. British Museum, London, 1844,0425.49.*

Account for diamonds imported by Lord Clive, 1767. London, UK. Paper. H. 37.3 cm, W. 22.5 cm. The British Library, London, Mss Eur G37/82/5/26.

p. 92. Hew Locke, *Steel Corporation of Bengal 1*, 2009. Acrylic ink on antique certificate. H. 44.7 cm, W. 31.5 cm. Private Collection.

p. 93. Hew Locke, *Bank of Bengal*, 2012–24. Acrylic on antique share certificate. H. 20.7 cm, W. 34.8 cm. Private Collection.

p. 94. Unrecorded Company School artist, Sir John Dalling and fellow officers at a nautch and in procession, c. 1785–6. Made in Chennai, India. Black ink, body colour, gold paint and varnish on paper mounted on canvas. H. 61.5 cm, W. 90.8 cm (each painting). British Museum, London, 2005,0705,0.1–2. Funded by the Brooke Sewell Permanent Fund.

p. 95. Hew Locke, *Middleton & Tonge Cotton Mill*, 2023. Acrylic on antique share certificate. H. 24 cm, W. 26.5 cm. Hales Gallery, London.

p. 96. Unrecorded artist, coat of arms of the East India Company, *c.* 1730. England. Painted and gilded wood. H. 130 cm, W. 152 cm. The British Library, London, Foster 887.*
Honourable East India Company ensign, *c.* 1911. Britain. Wool, linen, rope, wood. H. 179 cm, W. 239 cm. Royal Museums Greenwich, London, Daniel Bolt Collection, AAA0970. Modern copy from a design supplied by Sir William Foster who was registrar and superintendent of the India Office Records.

p. 97. Seal-die of the East India Company, 1766–7. India. Silver. Diam. 6.7 cm. British Museum, London, 1970,0309.1. Donated by Mrs Estelle W. Fuller.
Unrecorded artist, seat of the chairman of the court of East India Company directors, *c.* 1730. England. Walnut with velvet upholstery, coloured silks and silver gilt thread. H. 155 cm, W. 75 cm. The British Library, London, Foster 905.*

p. 100. Hew Locke, *Confederate States of America Loan 4*, 2018. Acrylic ink and pen on antique share certificate. Private Collection of Jonathan Olsoff and Sophie de Bellissen.*

p. 102. Daniel Veneciano (Center for the Study of Political Graphics), *500 Years Since Columbus: the Legacy Continues*, 1992. Los Angeles, USA. Offset lithograph on paper. H. 62.8 cm, W. 35 cm. British Museum, London, 1993,0629,0.2. Donated by Carol Wells.

p. 103. T-shirt, *c.* 2000–10. Made in Mexico, sold in the USA by Inti Arts. Cotton. H. 76 cm, W. 85 cm. British Museum, London, 2012,2017.4. Donated by Jonathan C.H. King.
Brick, made after 1492, labelled in 1853. Possibly made in Hispaniola. Earthenware, paper. H. 5 cm, L. 30 cm, D. 14 cm. British Museum, London, 1853,0101.1. Possibly collected from church ruins after an earthquake in 1564 by Dr Jose de la Pería. Collected by Sir Robert Hermann Schomburgk, first Consul to the Dominican Republic, who sent it to the Secretary of State for Foreign Affairs in 1853, who donated it to the Museum.

p. 104. Unrecorded Taíno artist, birdman spirit figure, 1029–1156. Found in Carpenter's Mountains, Jamaica. Guayacan wood with inlaid shell. H. 87 cm, W. 70 cm, D. 22 cm. British Museum, London, Am1977,Q.2. Collected in a cave in Carpenter's Mountains, Jamaica, 1792. Probably acquired by David Rebello between 1792 and 1796, then passed on to his son Isaac Alves Rebello, who bequeathed it to the Museum between 1799 and 1802.

p. 105. Unrecorded Taíno artist, Boinayel the Rain Giver figure, 1256–1300. Found in Carpenter's Mountains, Jamaica. Guayacan wood. H. 104 cm, W. 52 cm, D. 15 cm. British Museum, London, Am1977,Q.3. Collected in a cave in Carpenter's Mountains, Jamaica, 1792. Probably acquired by David Rebello between 1792 and 1796, then passed on to his son Isaac Alves Rebello, who bequeathed it to the Museum between 1799 and 1802.

p. 106. Hew Locke, *Confederate States of America Loan 14*, 2023. Acrylic on antique share certificate. H. 68.5 cm, W. 43 cm. Private Collection.

p. 107. Hew Locke, *Confederate States of America Loan 16*, 2024. Acrylic on antique share certificate. H. 71 cm, W. 43.5 cm. Private Collection.

p. 109. John White, *North Carolina Algonquian people fishing*, *c.* 1585–90. Watercolour and graphite, touched with body colour, white (altered) and gold on paper. H. 35.2 cm, W. 23.5 cm. British Museum, London, 1906,0509.1.6. Purchased from Henry Stevens & Son.

p. 110. John White, *A North Carolina Algonquian woman (wife of a werowance or leader) and her daughter*, *c.* 1585–90. Watercolour and graphite, touched with body colour, white (altered) and gold on paper. H. 26.3 cm, W. 14.9 cm. British Museum, London, 1906,0509.1.13. Purchased from Henry Stevens & Son.

p. 111. John White, *A North Carolina Algonquian* werowance *(leader)*, *c.* 1585–90. Watercolour and graphite, touched with body colour, white (altered) and gold on paper. H. 26.3 cm, W. 15 cm. British Museum, London, 1906,0509.1.12. Purchased from Henry Stevens & Son.

p. 112. Phillips Brothers, beetle tiara, necklace and earrings, 1884–5. London, UK. Gold, weevil tissue (*lamprocyphus augustus*), silk, leather, wood. H. 20 cm, W. 31 cm, D. 30 cm (parure in case). British Museum, London, 2016,8037.1.a-e. The Granville family sold the parure to Wartski, London, in 2011. It was sold in 2013 to the Hawkins family, antique dealers of London and Tasmania, who lent it to the Museum of Applied Arts & Sciences, Sydney, Australia (MAAS) in Sept 2013. The MAAS then donated it to the British Museum in 2016.

p. 113. Harry Emanuel, hummingbird necklace, 1865. London, UK. Gold, ruby-topaz hummingbird (*Chrysolampis mosquitus*), short-tailed emerald hummingbird (*Chlorostilbon poortmani*), leather, silk. H. 3.2 cm (central bird's head, excluding setting), L. 23.3 cm (case). British Museum, London, 1993,0205.1. Purchased from Roger Garlick, funded by Robert C. Kwok.

p. 114. Unrecorded Akawaio artist, headdress, before 1865. Guyana. Feather, reed, cotton. H. 32 cm (without cord), W. 37 cm. British Museum, London, Am.2496. Found by the Demerara River, Guyana. Acquired by the Christy Collection and donated to the Museum 1860–9.
Unrecorded Wai Wai artist, hair-tube, before 1865. Found in Essequibo, Guyana. Bamboo, bird skin, beads. H. 25.4 cm. British Museum, London, Am1950,01.12. Collected by Philip Storer Peberdy, sold to the Museum in 1947.

p. 116. Maria Sibylla Merian, *Toucan eating a small bird*, *c.* 1701–5. Watercolour, strengthened with gum, and body colour on vellum. H. 28.5 cm, W. 38.3 cm. British Museum, London, SL,5275.80. Bequeathed by Sir Hans Sloane.
William Blake, after John Gabriel Stedman, An armed Coromantyn Free Ranger, 1793. First published in London, UK. Etching and engraving on paper. H. 25.4 cm, W. 19.5 cm. British Museum, London, 2006,0830.45. Purchased from Prof. David Bindman.
Maria Sibylla Merian, *Muscovy duck wrestling with a snake*, *c.* 1701–5. Watercolour and body colour, heightened with white and gold on vellum. H. 43.1 cm, W. 32.8 cm. British Museum, London, SL,5275.78. Bequeathed by Sir Hans Sloane.

p. 117. William Blake, after John Gabriel Stedman, *The skinning of the Aboma Snake, shot by Captain Stedman*, 1793. First published in London, UK. Etching and engraving on paper. H. 25.4 cm, W. 19.5 cm. British Museum, London, 2006,0830.48. Purchased from Prof. David Bindman.
Francesco Bartolozzi, after John Gabriel Stedman, *Frontispiece for Stedman's Narrative*, 1794. First published in London, UK. Stipple on paper. H. 23.5 cm, W. 15.9 cm. British Museum, London, 2006,0830.44. Purchased from Prof. David Bindman.
Attributed to Dorothea Graff, *Caiman wrestling with a snake*, *c.* 1701–5. Watercolour and body colour, heightened with white, and with pen and black ink on vellum. H. 30.6 cm, W. 45.4 cm. British Museum, London, SL,5275.61. Bequeathed by Sir Hans Sloane.

p. 119. Unrecorded Guyanese artist, club, *c.* 1600–50. Guyana. Wood. H. 114.2 cm, W. 11 cm, D. 2 cm. British Museum, London, Am.4913. Possibly collected by John Tradescant the Elder and donated to the Ashmolean Museum, University of Oxford. Given to the Museum as part of an exchange in 1868.
Unrecorded Guyanese artist, club, before 1836. Guyana. Wood. H. 72.5 cm, W. 19 cm, D. 2.8 cm. British Museum, London, Am1836,0901.66. Collected by Sir Robert Hermann Schomburgk and donated to the Museum in 1836.

p. 120. Thomas Wyon Sr, coin of Henri Christophe, president and king of Haiti, 1820. Issued in Haiti. Silver. Diam. 3.7 cm, weight 28.9 g. British Museum, London, 1866,0323.3. Purchased from George Eastwood.

Williamson & Parsons, *Toussaint L'Ouverture, Governor of St. Domingo*, 1802. First published in London, UK. Hand-coloured etching on paper. H. 23.6 cm, W. 17.5 cm. British Museum, London, 1926,0412.250. Purchased from David Alexander Edward Lindsay, 27th Earl of Crawford and 10th Earl of Balcarres.

p. 121. Unrecorded British artist, print showing a mother threatening to jump overboard with her child, *c.* 1850. Published in the British Isles. Varnished hand-coloured lithograph with letterpress on paper, with collaged animals. H. 20 cm, W. 13.1 cm. British Museum, London, 2006,0929.66. Donated by Jonathan C.H. King.

p. 122. Hew Locke, *West India Improvement Company 1*, 2021. Acrylic on antique share certificate. H. 34.2 cm, W. 16.8 cm. Private Collection.

p. 123. Hew Locke, *Para (Marajo) 3*, 2013. Acrylic on antique share certificate. H. 46.5 cm, W. 36.5 cm. Hales Gallery, London.

p. 124. James Heath, *Maroon Town in the Parish of St James Jamaica*, 1796. First published in London, UK. Etching and aquatint on paper. H. 35.3 cm, W. 53.1 cm. British Museum, London, 1881,1210.256. Purchased from Frederick Pontifex.

Agostino Brunias, A Cudgeling Match between English and French West Indians on the Island of Dominica, published 1779. London, UK. Etching and stipple on paper. H. 30 cm, W. 38 cm. British Museum, London, 1877,0811.209. Purchased from Thomas Toon.

p. 125. William Heysham Overend, after a sketch by Melton Prior, *Carnival in Port of Spain, Trinidad*, 1888.*

Isaac Mendes Belisario, *Koo, Koo, Or Actor-Boy*, 1837–8. Published in Kingston, Jamaica. Hand-coloured lithograph on paper. H. 29.5 cm, W. 20.7 cm. British Museum, London, 2006,0929.48. Donated by Jonathan C.H. King.

p. 127. Conrad Heinrich Küchler, Seringapatam medal, 1799. British Isles. Silver-gilt. Diam. 4.8 cm, weight 40 g. British Museum, London, M.4391.

John Wesley Livingston, *Windsor Castle: Proposal for the East Terrace Gardens*, 1883. Britain. Albumen print on paper. H. 21.4 cm, W. 27.2 cm. The Royal Collection, London / HM King Charles III, RCIN 2100723.

p. 128. Sword from the palace of Tipu Sultan, 1700s. Srirangapatna, Mysore. Iron, gold. L. 97.5 cm, W. 9.5 cm, D. 7.6 cm. British Museum, London, 1878,1101.450. Seized as a trophy after the death of Tipu Sultan in 1799, later donated to the Museum by Lt-Gen Augustus W.H. Meyrick in 1878.

Unrecorded artist, ring said to belong to Tipu Sultan, late 1700s. Srirangapatna, Mysore. Bronze. H. 3.2 cm. British Museum, London, 1997,0502.1. Donated by Nancy Henderson Cole, Dowager Countess of Enniskillen, in memory of David Lowry Cole, 6th Earl of Enniskillen.

Unrecorded artist, tiger's head from Tipu Sultan's throne, 1787–97. Srirangapatna, Mysore. Engraved gold set with rubies, emeralds and diamonds. H. 46 cm, W. 57 cm, D. 48 cm. National Trust, Powis Castle, NT 1180713. Seized as a trophy after the death of Tipu Sultan in 1799 and given to Henrietta Clive by Lord Richard Colley Wellesley, later the 2nd Earl of Mornington. Accepted in lieu of tax by HM Government and transferred to the National Trust in 1963.

p. 129. Anna Tonelli, *Tipu Sultan enthroned*, 1800. India. Watercolour on paper. H. 38.5 cm, W. 53.2 cm. National Trust, Powis Castle, NT 1180776.*

Samuel William Reynolds I, after Sir Robert Ker Porter, *The finding of the body of Tipu Sultan*, 1800. First published in London, UK. Mezzotint and etching on paper. H. 57.8 cm, W. 75. 2 cm. British Museum, London, 1870,1008.2812. Purchased from Colnaghi in 1872.

p. 130. Unrecorded artist, front cover of a souvenir booklet for the film *Jhansi Ki Rani* (Queen of Jhansi), directed and produced by Sohrab Modi, 1953. Booklet made in 1952. India. Paper, 34 pages. Private Collection of Mehelli Modi.*

p. 132. South African War medal with 24 clasps, 1910. London, UK. Silver. Diam. 3.6 cm, weight 110.4 g. British Museum, London, 1902,0105.2. Donated by Sir Horace Alfred Damer, Deputy Master of the Royal Mint, in 1902.

Anglo-Asante War medal, 1874. London, UK. Silver. Diam. 3.5 cm, weight 45.9 g. British Museum, London, 1935,0401.13478. Bequeathed by Thomas Bryan Clarke-Thornhill.

p. 133. Maxim machine gun, 1892. Enfield, UK. Brass, steel. L. 114 cm, W. 21 cm, D. 23 cm. Imperial War Museum, London, FIR 9397.

p. 134. Mau Mau gun, *c.* 1950. Kenya. Wood, metal, sisal plant. L. 82.5 cm, W. 11 cm, D. 5.8 cm. Imperial War Museum, London, FIR 11302. Captured by the Royal East Kent Regiment from a Mau Mau fighter in 1953–4, it was first kept by the regiment's museum before being given to the Imperial War Museum in 1955.

Unrecorded Edo artist, ceremonial *eben* sword, *c.* 1700s–1800s. Benin City, Nigeria. Iron. H. 114.5 cm, W. 34.5 cm, D. 21 cm. British Museum, London, Af1949,46.167. Purchased with a contribution from Art Fund (as NACF) from Dorothy K. Oldman in 1949 when she sold her deceased husband William Ockelford Oldman's collection. Oldman was an important ethnographic dealer in the UK from 1902.

Edo or Yoruba crossbow, 1900s. Nigeria. Wood. H. 8.4 cm, W. 66 cm, D. 82 cm. British Museum, London, Af1940,22.2. Collected by Lieutenant Colonel Percy Maclear, who commanded the Nigerian Regiment of West Africa Frontier Force. Believed to have been brought to the UK in 1906. His widow Mrs Ethel Maclear donated his collection to the Museum with the help of their daughter Mrs Eileen M. Bickford in 1940.

Kaskara sword engraved with the name of its owner, Ali Dinar, the last Sultan of Darfur, *c.* 1900–6. Blade made in Europe, engraved in Sudan. Steel, silver, gold. H. 109 cm, W. 18 cm, D. 5.9 cm. British Museum, London, Af1932,1014.1.a. Ali Dinar was killed in 1916 by troops from the Anglo-Egyptian Condominium of Sudan. Until his death, Darfur was an independent Sultanate but in 1916 it was incorporated into Anglo-Egyptian Sudan. The sword was likely taken at or soon after Ali Dinar's death. It was donated by a Mrs Hutton, whose identity is unknown. She might have been Stella Eleanora Hutton, the wife of J.H. Hutton, an anthropologist who gave Indian objects to the British Museum, or a relation of Captain Ronald Winder Hutton, who participated in the 1916 operations against Ali Dinar. It is uncertain how the sword came into Mrs Hutton's possession.

p. 135. Unrecorded Zulu artist, engraved cattle horns, *c.* 1879–99. KwaZulu-Natal, South Africa. Animal bone, horn. H. 37.5 cm, W. 68 cm, D. 25.5 cm. British Museum, London, Af1960,08.1.a-c. Transferred from the Natural History Museum collection.

p. 138. Unrecorded British artist, pendant mask cast, cast *c.* 1940–58, original 1500s. Cast at the British Museum, London, UK, original made in Benin City, Nigeria. Plaster, resin. H. 24.1 cm, W. 13.5 cm, D. 6.3 cm. British Museum, London, CRS.48.

Unrecorded British artist, pendant mask cast, cast mid-1900s, original 1500s. Cast at the British Museum, London, UK, original made in Benin City, Nigeria. Plaster, resin. H. 24.1 cm, W. 13.2 cm, D. 6.3 cm. British Museum, London, CRS.49.

Derrick C. Giles, pendant mask cast, cast 1977, original 1500s. Cast at the British Museum, London, UK, original made in Benin City, Nigeria. Resin, iron, metal. H. 23.5 cm, W. 12.2 cm, D. 5.1 cm. British Museum, London, CRS.50.

p. 139. Erhabor Emokpae, FESTAC '77 poster, 1977. Nigeria. Screenprint on paper.

pp. 141–2. Jonathan Adagogo Green, Oba Ovonramwen Nogbaisi on-board the British yacht SS *Ivy* with soldiers, 1897. Nigeria.

Photographic prints. H. 20.8 cm, W. 14 cm (largest). British Museum, London, Af,A47.70, Af,A46.25. Album of photographs owned by Arthur Prest, an English trader who lived and worked in the Niger Delta between 1896 and 1917.

p. 143. Jonathan Adagogo Green, Oba Ovonramwen Nogbaisi on-board the British yacht SS *Ivy*, 1897. Southern Nigeria. Photographic print mounted on card. H. 20 cm, W. 14 cm. Weltmuseum Vienna, 6185.*

p. 144. Unrecorded Edo artist, ceremonial crown (E̩rhu E̩de), corslet (Ukpo̩n) and flywhisk (Ugbudien Ugie), *c.* 1700s–1800s. Benin City, Nigeria. Coral, agate beads. H. 71 cm, W. 65 cm (corslet). British Museum, London, Af1898,0630.5, Af1944,04.63, Af1898,0630.3. The crown and fly-whisk were looted during the 1897 Benin Expedition by Captain Ernest Percy Stuart Roupell, who sold them to the Museum in June 1898. The corslet was purchased in 1934 by Harry Geoffrey Beasley, a wealthy brewer and collector, from the Trustees of the Herbert Child Estate. Child was Captain of the SS *Ivy* (Benin Expedition). After Beasley's death, his wife Irene donated the first portion of their collection to the Museum, giving over 2,000 items, including up to 80 bells, weapons, commemorative heads and regalia from Benin.

p. 145. Unrecorded Edo artists, ornamental discs (Emwiegbe), 1500s–1897. Benin City, Nigeria. Brass. H. 26 cm, W. 23 cm, D. 1.5 cm (largest). British Museum, London, Af1897,-.505, .504, .506. Looted from Benin City and sold to the Museum in 1897 by Major William Alexander Crawford Cockburn.

p. 146. Reginald Kerr Granville, British soldiers posing with Benin artefacts in the Oba's compound, 1897. Benin City, Nigeria. Photographic print. H. 12 cm, W. 16.5 cm. Pitt Rivers Museum, Oxford, 1998.208.15.11.*

p. 147. Unrecorded photographer, *Sample of old Benin Bronze work looted at Capture of Benin City*, 1897–1905. Nigeria. Photographic print. H. 10.7 cm, W. 14.5 cm. British Museum, London, Af,A46.24. Album of photographs owned by Arthur Prest, an English trader who lived and worked in the Niger Delta between 1896 and 1917.*
Jonathan Adagogo Green, Christmas card featuring architectural photographs, 1902–3. Bonny, Nigeria. Photographic print. H. 10.7 cm, W. 13.7 cm. British Museum, London, Af,A48.32. Owned by Sir Manuel Raymond Menendez, donated by Lady Menendez.

p. 149. Hew Locke, *Company of the Imperial Railway of Ethiopia 5*, 2024. Acrylic on antique share certificate. H. 42.8 cm, W. 64.8 cm. Private Collection.

p. 150. Ethiopian shield, mid-1800s. Ethiopia. Lion skin, silver, leather, cotton. H. 80 cm, W. 51 cm, D. 21 cm. British Museum, London, Af1912,0410.28. Emperor Tewodros II may have given the shield to Captain Speedy. Described as an 'Abyssinian curio', it was donated to the Museum in 1912 by Cornelia Mary Speedy.

p. 151. Lawrence Lowe, portrait of Captain Speedy, late 1800s. Photographic print. H. 11.1 cm, W. 15.7 cm. British Museum, London, Af,B2.23.*
Ethiopian sword and sheath, mid-1800s. Ethiopia. Iron, horn, silver, gold, brass, leather, velvet. H. 115.5 cm, W. 43.8 cm, D. 7 cm. British Museum, London, Af1912,0410.24.a. Collected by Captain Speedy. Described as 'Abyssinian curios', they were donated to the Museum in 1912 by Cornelia Mary Speedy.
Ethiopian spear, mid-1800s. Ethiopia. Iron, brass. H. 95.5 cm, W. 4.8 cm, D. 2.3 cm. British Museum, London, Af1912,0410.31.a. Collected by Captain Speedy, donated in 1912 by Cornelia Mary Speedy.

p. 152. Hintsa Selassie, processional cross, 1730–55. Made in Gondar, Ethiopia. Copper alloy, gold. H. 63.5 cm, W. 43.2 cm, D. 5.8 cm. British Museum, London, Af1868,1230.7. Looted during the 1868 invasion of Ethiopia and purchased by Lord Robert Napier, Commander of the British and Indian troops. Donated by him to

the Museum via the India Office in Dec 1868 as part of a donation described as 'cases of Abyssinian trophies'.*

p. 153. Sir Richard Rivington Holmes, drawing of the Maqdala expedition force, 1868. Ethiopia. Brush and brown wash, heightened with white, over graphite, on buff paper. H. 25.5 cm, W. 35.8 cm. British Museum, London, 1972,U.577. Donated by Sir Richard Rivington Holmes.

p. 155. Unrecorded artist, Ts'a-t's'a amulet, 1800s. Tibet. Bronze, paper. H. 10.5 cm, W. 9.5 cm, D. 3.5 cm. British Museum, London, 1905,0519.115. Sold to the Museum in 1905 by Major Herbert Augustus Iggulden, Chief Staff Officer of the Younghusband Expedition.

p. 156. Unrecorded artist, lama figure, 1400s. Tibet. Copper, gold. H. 45.2 cm, W. 37.3 cm, D. 32.4 cm. British Museum, London, 1905,0519.1. Looted from Tsechen Monastery, Gyantse. Sold to the Museum in 1905 by Major Herbert Augustus Iggulden, Chief Staff Officer of the Younghusband Expedition.

p. 157. Unrecorded artist, chalice, *c.* 1700s–1800s. Kangma, Tibet. Brass. H. 19.8 cm. British Museum, London, 1905,0519.49. Looted from Kangma. Sold to the Museum in 1905 by Major Herbert Augustus Iggulden, Chief Staff Officer of the Younghusband Expedition.
Wicker shield, *c.* 1700s–1800s. Tibet. Wood, leather, metal. Diam. 63.5 cm. British Museum, London, 1905,0519.169. Sold to the Museum in 1905 by Major Herbert Augustus Iggulden, Chief Staff Officer of the Younghusband Expedition.

p. 159. Unrecorded Asante artist and Garrard & Co., pendant, 1850–70, dish, 1874. Pendant made in the Asante Region, Ghana, dish made in London, UK. Gold, silver. Diam. 61.5 cm. British Museum, London, Af1973,07.1-2. The gold pendant was part of an indemnity payment from Asantehene Kofi Karikari to the British government after his defeat at the end of the Third Anglo-Asante War. The dish, with the pendant at its centre, was commissioned by William Alleyne Cecil, a former Treasurer of the Royal Household. It was passed to the family of Major-General Lord Cheylesmore, and was purchased by the Museum in 1973 from his step-daughter Mrs J. Coram Wright.

p. 160. Unrecorded Asante artists, soul discs, early 1800s. Made in the Asante Region, Ghana. Gold. Diam. 5.3 cm, D. 0.4 cm (smallest), Diam. 13.5 cm, D. 0.4 cm (largest). British Museum, London, Af,Ash.21, .13, Af1818,1114.5. Af,Ash.21 & .13 were part of an indemnity payment from Asantehene Kofi Karikari to the British government after his defeat at the end of the Third Anglo-Asante War; purchased from the Crown Agents for the Colonies by the Christy Collection Trustees in 1876, then transferred to the Museum. Af1818,1114.5 was an earlier diplomatic gift from Asantehene Osei Bonsu to Thomas Edward Bowdich in 1817 while visiting Kumasi on behalf of the African Company of Merchants, the successor of the Royal African Company; donated by Bowdich in 1818.

p. 161. Unrecorded Ethiopian artists, gold discs, 1800–68. Made in Ethiopia. Gold. Diam. 4.5 cm, D. 0.5 cm (smallest), Diam. 12 cm, D. 1.5 cm (largest). British Museum, London, Af1900,0711.1–3. Looted during the British military assault on Maqdala, 13 Apr 1868, possibly by Colonel W.J. Holt, who served in the Abyssinian campaign, or perhaps purchased at the auction of loot following the assault. Sold to the Museum in 1900.

pp. 162–3. Acquisition slips for soul discs, 1876 (see p. 160 for discs Af,Ash.21 & .13). London, UK. Paper. H. 10.2 cm, W. 26.7 cm (each slip). British Museum, London, Af,Ash.18, .13, .19–22.

p. 164. Unrecorded Ethiopian artist, anklets, 1800s. Made in Ethiopia. Silver-gilt. H. 10.5 cm, W. 8 cm (max), D. 7.5 cm. British Museum, London, Af1868,1001.3.a-b. Looted by Richard Rivington Holmes during the British military assault on Maqdala, 13 Apr 1868, but not included in the list of items purchased by Holmes on behalf of the

Museum at the auction of loot, suggesting that they may have been among those he took personally. Donated or sold to the Museum in 1868.

Unrecorded Ethiopian artist, armlet, mid-1800s. Ethiopia. Silver, gold, copper. H. 10 cm, W. 10.5 cm, D. 17 cm. British Museum, London, Af1866,0219.1. Collected in Ethiopia between 1841 and 1843 by Sir William Cornwallis Harris, then given by his daughter to music publisher Charles Henry Purday, who sold it to the Museum in 1866.

p. 165. Unrecorded Ethiopian artist, cup, 1800–68. Made in Ethiopia. Silver, gold. Diam. 10.5 cm, H. 12.5 cm. British Museum, London, Af1868,1001.9. Looted by Richard Rivington Holmes during the British military assault on Maqdala, 13 Apr 1868, but not included in the list of items purchased by Holmes on behalf of the Museum at the auction of loot, suggesting that it may have been among those he took personally. Donated or sold to the Museum in 1868.

Unrecorded Ethiopian artists, armlets, early to mid-1800s. Ethiopia. Silver, gold (?), velvet, white metal. H. 16 cm, W. 12 cm (largest). British Museum, London, Af1912,0410.5–6. Collected by Captain Speedy, donated by his widow Cornelia Mary Speedy in 1912.

pp. 166–7. Unrecorded Yotoco artist, breastplate, 200 BCE–1200 CE. Colombia. Gold. H. 28 cm, W. 37 cm, D. 6 cm. British Museum, London, Am1900,0517.1. Purchased from French dealers Rollin & Feuardent in 1900.

Unrecorded Tolima artists, pendants, 1 BCE–900 CE. Colombia. Gold plate. H. 2.5 cm, W. 3 cm (max). British Museum, London, Am1904,0718.6–7 & .9, Am1904,0718.12–34. Purchased from Enrique Cortes & Co. in 1904.

p. 170. Exhibition planning boards, 2024. H. 190 cm, W. 120 cm (each board).*

p. 174. Hew Locke's OBE medal, 2023. Worcestershire, UK. Silver. H. 6.5 cm, W. 5 cm. Hew Locke's RA medal, 2022. UK. Bronze. Diam. 5.7 cm.

Unrecorded Akan artist, Sankofa bird gold-weight, 1700s–1900s. Ghana. Brass. H. 5.6 cm, W. 2 cm, D. 3.7 cm. British Museum, London, Af1947,13.138. Bequeathed by Robert Powley Wild.

Unrecorded Asante artist, bells, possibly for attaching to a bracelet, 1800s. Made in the Asante Region, Ghana. Gold. Diam. 2 cm, H. 9.3 cm (each bell). British Museum, London, Af1900,0427.43. Looted from the palace of Asantehene Prempeh I in Kumasi during the Fourth Anglo-Asante War (1895–6). Purchased in 1900 from the Gold Coast government through the Crown Agents for the Colonies.

Unrecorded Asante artist, beads in the shape of bells, early 1800s. Made in the Asante Region, Ghana. Gold. H. 1.9 cm, W. 1.9 cm, D. 0.5 cm (max). British Museum, London, Af,Ash.58.a-b. Part of an indemnity payment from Asantehene Kofi Karikari to the British government after his defeat at the end of the Third Anglo-Asante War (1873–4); purchased from the Crown Agents for the Colonies by the Christy Collection Trustees in 1876, then transferred to the Museum.

p. 175. Unrecorded artist, cast of a sculpture of an Ife head, cast 1947–8, original 1300s–early 1400s. Cast in London, UK, original found in Wunmonije Compound, Nigeria. Plaster. H. 35.5 cm, W. 17.5 cm, D. 25.5 cm. British Museum, London, CRS.9.

Acknowledgements

I would like to thank Isabel Seligman, Billie Duch Giménez, Stephanie Jong and all the staff and curators at the British Museum who worked so hard on the exhibition. Also Tori Hitchens, Charlie Hubbard, Adam Vass, Brigid Vidler and friends and colleagues too numerous to mention whose discussions and advice over the years have helped shape my practice and get me to this point.

Thanks to Hales Gallery, P·P·O·W Gallery, Almine Rech Gallery and 291 Agency for their support, and to the British Museum fundraisers and Cockayne – Grants for the Arts: a donor advised fund held at The London Community Foundation, without whom nothing would have happened. And most importantly I'd like to thank my truly amazing wife Indra Khanna, for whom I don't have enough words.

Hew Locke

We are enormously grateful to Cockayne – Grants for the Arts: a donor advised fund held at The London Community Foundation and to the Stanley Thomas Johnson Foundation for supporting the exhibition.

I would like to thank Hew Locke and Indra Khanna for their genuine and generous collaboration with colleagues across the Museum, and for the creation of a compelling new body of work, including *The Watchers*, as well as additions to the *Share* and *Souvenir* series.

I am grateful to colleagues from many institutions across the UK for sharing their research, support and advice, including Alice Clanachan, Emily Hannam, Margaret Makepeace, Emma Martin, Lisa Newby, William Pettigrew, Sandra Sattler, Amara Thornton, Rebecca Spooner, Karen George, Martin Clayton, Lauren Porter, Alessandro Nasini, Sally Goodsir, Caroline de Guitaut, Alex Patterson, Bethan Stevens, Esther Chadwick, Damiët Schneeweisz and Malini Roy. I am also grateful to Mehelli Modi and Erhabor and Isaac Emokpae for their generosity in sharing their families' artistic endeavours.

At the British Museum, I would like to thank Hartwig Fischer, Mark Jones and Nicholas Cullinan for their support of the project, and Ruth Cribb, Jill Maggs and Rosalind Winton for their help developing the exhibition. I am indebted to Hugo Chapman, Keeper of Prints and Drawings, for his invaluable support and advice, and to former Keeper of Prints and Drawings, Antony Griffiths, for the same.

I have drawn deeply on the support and expertise of keepers of a number of different Departments, and my sincere thanks go to Lissant Bolton, Jane Portal, Jill Cook, Tom Hockenhull and Paul Collins. A vast number of curatorial colleagues have shared their expertise and I would like to thank Helen Anderson, Diego Atehortúa, Alice Christophe, Zoe Cormack, Julie Hudson, Sam Nixon and Danny Zborover from the Department of Africa, Oceania and the Americas; Richard Blurton, Luk Yu-ping and Imma Ramos from the Department of Asia; Rachel King and Naomi Speakman from the Department of Britain, Europe and Prehistory; Barry Cook, Vesta Curtis, Janet Larkin and Sabrina Ben Aouicha from the Department of Money and Medals; Stephen Coppel, Catherine Daunt, Olenka Horbatsch, Francesca Kaes, Grant Lewis, Jennifer Ramkalawon, Sarah Vowles and Charlotte Wytema from the Department of Prints and Drawings; and Tunde Babalola from Scientific Research. Special thanks are due to Zoe Cormack, Alicia Hughes, and Lloyd de Beer, for sharing their research on the British Expedition to Abyssinia, Sir Hans Sloane and his collections, and the Asante Jug respectively, as well as for their support throughout.

I would like to thank Christina Angelo and the Department of Conservation who worked to prepare objects for the exhibition. Thanks also to Joanna Fernandes and her team – David Agar, Marco Borsato, Stephen Dodd, Isabel Marshall and Bradley Timms – for their work on the photography, particularly the brilliant images of *The Watchers*.

Thank you to the exhibition's core team: Emily Castles, Shani Crawford, Lydia Fellgett, Rachel Finch, Nori Hung, Matthew Hutt, Ioli Karyka, Deklan Kilfeather, Peter Macdermid, Lauren Papworth, Rebecca Penrose, Jaime Prada, Lucy Romeril, Beth Rivers, Alexander Spreadbury, Victoria Stopar, Sam Waizeneker, Morgan Whatford and Keeley Wilson. And to other colleagues across the Museum, including Lizzie Barratt, Anna Chamberlain, Sarah Choy, Lynne Darwood, Stuart Frost, Hebe Halstead, Bea Hannay-Young, Maria Howell, Jadene Imbusch, Hannah James, Lizzie Loudon, Emma Lyttle, Sean McParland, Gideon Pain, Jane Parsons, Clara Potter, Angela Pountney, Miguel Roque, Jon Stephens, Valeria di Tommaso, Heloise Verity, Viktorija Vrublevska, Gregor Wittrick, Vicci Ward and to external designer Helen Eger.

I would especially like to thank Claire Edwards, Interpretation Manager, for her thoughtful and thorough work on the exhibition text, and Stephanie Jong, Project Manager, for calmly steering the project to fruition.

Above all, I would like to thank Billie Duch Giménez, Project Curator, for their exceptional work, creativity and critical insight, which have been essential to every aspect of this project, and in particular for their work on the case study texts in this book.

Thank you to Yvonne Thouroude for her brilliant work in realising this publication, and to Lydia Cooper for the same. I would like to thank Toni Allum and Claudia Bloch, and Beata Kibil for her work on the production with Nathaniel Balch, as well as Jules Bettinson, Harry King and Rob King at Altaimage. Fraser Muggeridge and Manon Veyssière created a beautiful design and I am grateful to copyeditor Danai Denga, proofreader Phoebe Colley and indexer Amanda Speake.

Finally, I would like to thank my family and friends, especially my partner Paul Evangelou, for everything.

Isabel Seligman

Contributors

Hew Locke OBE RA is a Guyanese-British artist who lives and works in London. He is Curator of the exhibition *Hew Locke: what have we here?* at the British Museum.

Indra Khanna MA is an independent curator and arts administrator. She is Assistant Curator of the exhibition *Hew Locke: what have we here?* at the British Museum.

Isabel Seligman is Curator of Modern and Contemporary Drawings at the British Museum and Curator of the exhibition *Hew Locke: what have we here?* at the British Museum.

Billie Duch Giménez is Project Curator of the exhibition *Hew Locke: what have we here?* at the British Museum.

Credits

Index

Figures are shown by a page reference in *italic*.

A

abolition 26, 27, 46, 118, *121*
Abyssinia *see* Ethiopia
Africa
   'scramble for Africa' 28–9, 131
   FESTAC '77 33–4, 137
   trade with Europe 19, 65, 68
   weapons 28, *134*
Akan people *see* Ghana (Gold Coast)
Alam II, Mughal emperor 88
Albert, British prince consort 54, 98
Alemayehu, prince of Ethiopia 18, 58, 59, *62, 63*, 148
Alexandra, queen consort of Great Britain 15–16, 18, *40*, 54, 108
Americas *see also* Caribbean
   Columbus's journey to 24–5, 101
   enslavement 24–5, 78–85, *100, 106, 107*
   Indigenous peoples 24–5, 101, *104–5*, 108, *109–11*
   New World companies 118, *122–3*
   Tolima pendants 158, *167*
   Yotoco breastplate 158, *167*
Anne, queen of Great Britain 13
Asante Kingdom *see* Ghana (Gold Coast)
Australia 52, *53*

B

Barbados 13, 22–3, 78, *80, 82*
Barlowe, Arthur (explorer and author) 25
Bartolozzi, Francesco (artist) *117*
Baule people 9, 14, 32
Beche, Henry De la (plantation owner) 78
Belisario, Isaac Mendes (artist) 118, *125*
Benin Bronzes 21 *see also* Queen Mother Idia Mask
   in Locke's work *19*, 32, *20*, 169, 177
   photos of looted Bronzes *146*
   Portuguese mercenary figures *20*, 65, *67*
   replicas 9, 32, 169
Benin (Kingdom of)
   artefacts in the British Museum collection 14, 32
   British looting of artefacts 20, 140, *146*
   British 'punitive' expedition to Benin City 16, 31–2, 33, 65, 131, 137, 140–6
   court of the Oba (king) 20, 21, 31, 65
   Edo ceremonial sword 131, *134*
   Edo ornamental discs 140, *145*, 169
   Edo or Yoruba crossbow 131, *134*, 173
   Oba Ovonramwen Nogbaisi 140, *141–3*
   the Oba's regalia 140, *144*
   Portuguese cannon 65, *66–7*
   sculptures 9, 32
Berger, John (art critic) 169
Black Lives Matter movement 12
Blake, William (artist) 25–6, 115, *116, 117*
boats
   Armada series, Hew Locke 17, 20, 33, *45*
   Brooks ship 46, *49*
   Egyptian boats 9
   A Liverpool Slave Ship 49
   in Locke's work 9, 17, 42
   memento mori 17, 22, 39
   Windward, Hew Locke 42, *44*
   Wine Dark Sea, Hew Locke 17, 20, 42, *43*
brass manillas 21, 68, *75*

British Empire
   benevolent image 19
   imagery of in seals 17
   Imperial Durbars 18, 54, *55*
   mementos 16, *16*
   mythologisation in film 131
   'punitive' expeditions 140
   seals 52, *53*
   Souvenir series, Hew Locke 15–16, 33, *33, 38, 39, 40–1*
   West and East India Docks 86, *87*
British Guiana *see* Guyana (British Guiana)
British Museum *see also Hew Locke: what have we here?*; Museum of Mankind
   ethnography galleries *27*, 28
   imperial activities and object acquisitions 13–14
   Sloane's collections 13, 21
Brunias, Agostino (artist) 22, 78, *79–81, 124*
Burke, Edmund (politician) 23

C

Caribbean *see also* Barbados; Haiti; Jamaica
   Barbados penny 23, 78, *82*
   Barbados Slave and Servant Acts 13, 21–2
   Carnival 26, 27–8, 118, *125*
   indentured Indian labourers 23
   Maroons 25, 26, 118, *124*
   racial hierarchies 21–2, 78, *79–81*
   resistance of enslaved people 21, 26–7, 118, *120, 124, 125*
   rise of chattel slavery 13, 21–2
   sanitised depictions of enslavement 22, 78, *79–81*
   Taíno figures 24, 101, *104–5*
   trade in enslaved people to 16
   the 'triangular trade' 17, 21, 68
Carnival 26, 27–8, 118, *125*
cartes de visite (calling cards) 23, *62, 63*, 78, *85*
Charles II, king of England, Scotland and Ireland 16, 17–18, 23, 46, *47*
Charles III, king of the United Kingdom 16
Christophe, Henri (Haitian ruler) 27, 118, *120*
clubs 25, 118, *119*
coats of arms 17, *17*, 47, 53, 65, *96*
Colombia 158
Colston, Edward (merchant and enslaver) 12, *12*, 21, 46
Columbus, Christopher (explorer and colonial governor)
   500 Years Since Columbus 102
   in the Americas 24–5, 101
   brick for ballast 24, 101, *103*
Company of Royal Adventurers of England Trading into Africa 16, 19, 46, *48 see also* Royal African Company (RAC)
conflict
   colonial 'punitive' expeditions 14, 16, 18, 30–2, 140–59
   within imperial structures 24–9, 30, 131
   'scramble for Africa' 28–9, 131
currency
   Asante gold dust 68
   Barbados penny 22, *82*
   the Bombay Mint 88, *89, 91*

   brass manillas as 21, 68, *75*
   in the colonies 22–3
   cowrie shells 21, 68, *74*
   exchanged for enslaved people 21, 46, 68
   glass beads 21, 46, *50–1*
   guineas 68, *75*
   Haitian 27, 118, *120*

D

Dalling, Sir John (soldier and colonial administrator) 88, *94*
Daniell, William (artist) 87
Dessalines, Jean-Jacques (Haitian revolutionary) 27
Dolpopa Sherab Gyeltsen (Tibetan Buddhist monk) 154, *156*
Duncan, Jonathan (East India Company official) 88, *89*
Dutch Guiana *see* Suriname (Dutch Guiana)

E

Earle, Augustus (artist) 78, *83*
East India Company
   Bengal famine 24
   the Bombay Mint 88, *89, 91*
   bureaucracy 88, *89*
   coat of arms *96*
   defeat of the Mughal Empire 23–4, 88
   defeat of the Sikh Empire 18, 59
   defeat of Tipu Sultan 29, 126, *129*
   in Locke's *Share* series 24
   Honourable East India Company ensign *96*
   Indian Uprising 29, 88
   seal-die *97*
   share certificates 88, *89*
   as a sovereign state 23–4, 88, *94, 97*
   trade 19, 23, 86, 88, *90–1*
Edo people *see* Benin
Edward VII, king of the United Kingdom (Prince Albert Edward) 15–16, 18, *41*, 54
Egypt 9, 108
emancipation *see also* abolition movement
   carte de visite (calling card) 78
   compensation payments to enslavers 23, 78, *84*
   transition to apprenticeships 23
Emokpae, Erhabor (artist) 33, 137, *139*
enslavement
   in the Americas 13, 24–5, 101
   anti-abolitionist prints 78, *79, 82*
   branding practices 16, 46
   British royal family's links with 16, 46
   compensation payments to enslavers 23, 78, *84*
   currency exchanged for enslaved people 21, 46, 68
   in English colonies 13, 24–6, 101
   global trade 46
   punishment of enslaved people 26, 78, *84*, 115
   resistance of enslaved people 21, 26–7, 118
   by the Royal African Company 12, 16–17
   sanitised portrayals of 22, 78, *79–81*
   ships 46, *49*
   Slave Market at Rio Janeiro 78, *83*

and the Sloane collection 13
in Suriname 25, 26, 115
transition to apprenticeships 23
the 'triangular trade' routes 17, 21, 68
Esigie, Oba of Benin 32, 137
Ethiopia
anklets 158, *164*
armlets *165–6*
British looting of artefacts 14, 30, 148,
158
British 'punitive' expedition to 14, 18,
30–1, 148, *153*
*Company of the Imperial Railway of
Ethiopia*, Hew Locke 31, *31*, *136*, *149*
cup 158, *165*
gold discs *161*
necklace *62*
processional cross 148, *152*
shield *150*
spear and sword *151*
under Tewodros II 14, 18, 30, 59, 148

F
FESTAC '77 33–4, 137
Forbes Bonetta, Sarah *see* Omoba Aina
French Revolution 27

G
George I, king of Great Britain and Ireland 13
George II, king of Great Britain and Ireland
13
George III, king of Great Britain and Ireland
27, 118
George V, king of the United Kingdom 18, 54
Geronimo, Apache leader 101, *103*
Ghana (Gold Coast)
Akan drum 21, 34, 68, *69*
Akan gold-weights 68, *72–3*, 173
Akan Sankofa bird 34, 173, *174*
Anglo-Asante Wars 20, 34, 68, 131, *132*,
158
Asante bells *174*
Asante court 19
Asante Jug 19, 65, *66*, 168
Asante soul discs 160, *162–3*
awisiado (soul priest's ornament) 34, 158,
158, *159*
British looting of artefacts 19–20, 34, *66*,
68, *74*, 158, *159*
indemnity payments to the British 34, 68,
158
Gibbes, Sir Philip (plantation owner) 23, 78
Gladstone, William (British prime minister)
31, 148
gold
Asante bells *174*
in the Asante Kingdom 34, 68
Asante soul discs 160, *162–3*
awisiado (soul priest's ornament) 158,
158, *159*
Chinese Imperial Gold Loan series, Hew
Locke *64*, 68, *70–1*
cowrie shell 68, *74*
Ethiopian discs *161*
guineas 68, *75*
Gold Coast *see* Ghana (Gold Coast)
Gouramma, Victoria, princess of Coorg 18,
59, *60*
Graff, Dorothea (artist) 25, 26, 115, *117*
Grant, Frederick (photographer) 66
Green, Jonathan Adagogo (photographer)
Oba Ovonramwen Nogbaisi 140, *141–3*
stamp *147*

Guyana (British Guiana)
borders 118
clubs 24, 118, *119*
compensation payments to enslavers 78,
84
as a Dutch colony 19
featherwork 108, *114*
independence from Britain 15, 39
Indigenous peoples 108
Locke's childhood in 14, 15, 19, 33–4
seals 52, *53*

H
Haiti 26–7, 118 *see also* Caribbean
Hew Locke: what have we here?
as an artist-curated exhibition 14–15,
168–9, 177–9
audience interactions with 35, 77, 179
exhibition design 169–71
object selection 168–72, *170–1*
The Watchers, Hew Locke *1–4*, *6–7*, 35,
15, *172*
Heysham Overend, William (artist) *125*
Hilliard, Nicholas (artist) *49*
Huger, Rebecca 23, 78, *85*
hummingbirds 108, *113*

I
Idia, Iyoba of Benin 32, 137 *see also* Queen
Mother Idia mask
Igbinovia, Joseph Alufa (artist) 33, 137
Iggulden, Major Herbert Augustus (British
army officer) 154
imperialism
collection of objects for museums 13–14
the Colston statue and 12
display of objects from former colonies 14
and the foundations of the British
Museum's collections 13
intersections with British sovereignty
15–19
intersections with trade 19–24
romanticised portrayals of 25, 108,
109–11
India *see also* East India Company
Bengal famine 24
colonial troops 148
English imperial expansion in 23–4
fall of Seringapatam 29, 126, *127*
Imperial Durbars 18, 54, *55*
indentured labourers in the Caribbean 23
Middleton & Tonge Cotton Mill, Hew
Locke 24, 29, 88, *95*
resistance to British rule 24, 29, 88, *95*,
126–30
Royal Shamiana 54, *56–7*
Steel Corporation of Bengal 88, *92*
Indigenous peoples
of the Americas 24–5, 108
of the Caribbean 24
in European iconography 17–18
of Guyana (British Guiana) 108
romanticised portrayals of 108, *109–11*
on seals 17, 52

J
Jackson, William (artist) 46
Jahan I, Mughal emperor 98, *99*
Jamaica
enslavement and the British Museum's
foundations 13
*Maroon Town in the Parish of St James
Jamaica 124*

medal for good conduct 78, *83*, 168
seals 17–18, *53*
James II, king of England 16, 46, *47*
jewellery *see also* Koh-i-Noor
beetle parure *112*
Ethiopian necklace *62*
exoticism in 108, *112–13*
hummingbird necklace *113*
ring said to belong to Tipu Sultan *128*
Jonkonnu (or John Canoe) figure 27, 118,
125

K
Kenya 131, *134*
Kofi Karikari, Asantehene (king) 34, 68, 158
Koh-i-Noor 18
Koh-i-Noor, Hew Locke 28
ownership history of 98, *99*
re-cutting 34, 98, 158
surrender of 58

L
Landon, Perceval (British Museum
representative) 32, 154
Locke, Hew
as an artist-curator 14–15, 168–9, 177–9
biography 14–15
childhood in Guyana 14, 15, 19, 33–4
collage and assemblage techniques 15,
169
explorations of British history, empire and
museum culture 12–13, 14, 35, 168–79
'mindful vandalism' 12
OBE 34, 173–5, *174*
relationships between museums and
history 12–13, 14, 16
Royal Academy 34, 173–5, *174*
Share series *19*, *31*, *36–7*, *64*, *70*, *71*, *92*,
93, *95*, *100*, *106*, *107*, *136*, *149*
Souvenir series 15–16, 33, *33*, *38*, *39*,
40–1
visits to the British Museum / Museum of
Mankind 9, 14, 20, 65, 158, 175, 178
The Watchers 1–4, *6–7*, 35, *15*, *172*
Louverture, Toussaint (Haitian general) 27,
118, *120*
Lower Niger bells 68, *76*, 77
Luba people 9, 14, 32

M
Maroons 25–6, *124*
Mary, queen of the United Kingdom 18, 54
masquerade 27–8
Mau Mau 131
medals
from African conflicts 28–9, 131, *132*
in Locke's work 16, 22, *33*, *40–1*
medal for good conduct (Jamaica) 78,
83, 168
Seringapatam medal 126, *127*
Menelik II, emperor of Ethiopia 31
mercenary figures
in Locke's work 14, *20*, 24, *42*, *43*
Portuguese mercenary figures *19*, 20, *20*,
65, *67*
Merian, Maria Sibylla (artist) 25, 26, 115,
116, 168
Museum of Mankind 9, 14–15, 20, 65, 158,
177
museums
Eurocentric cultural classification 13
exhibition curation 168–9
tradition of copies and casts 173

N

Nader Shah, Persian ruler 98, *99*
Napier, Sir Robert (field marshal) 30, 148
nationhood
    heroes and identity-building 12, 14, 15, 16, 39
    iconography of 18
    national self-image 15, 16, 17, 29, 39
    symbols of 15, 39
Nelson, Horatio (vice-admiral) 16
    bullet that killed him 16, *16*
Newton, Richard (artist) 78, *79*, *82*
Nigeria *see also* Benin (Kingdom of)
    bells *10–11*
    FESTAC '77 33–4, 137
    Ife head 137, 173, *175*

O

Olusoga, David (historian) 176
Omoba Aina, Yoruba princess (Sarah Forbes Bonetta) *58*, 59
Ovonramwen Nogbaisi, Oba of Benin 140, *141–3*

P

Paolozzi, Eduardo (artist) 14–15
Para (Marajo) 3, Hew Locke *122*
Perry, Grayson (artist) 15, 178
photography *see also* Green, Jonathan Adagogo
    Colston, Hew Locke 12
    east terrace Windsor Castle 29, *29*
    How do you want me?, Hew Locke *28*
Porter, Sir Robert Ker (artist) 126
The Procession, Hew Locke 20, *20*, 28, 29

Q

Queen Mother Idia mask
    in the British Museum collection 32, 33, 34, 137
    ceremonial function 32
    cultural symbolism 9, 33, 137
    FESTAC '77 33, 137
    in Locke's work 9, 14, 32–3, *32*, *33*, 34, 42, *45*
    pendant mask casts *138*
    replicas of 33, 137, *138–9*

R

Rani of Jhansi, Lakshmibai Newalkar 29, 126, *130*
Ranjit Singh, Sikh maharaja 98
Restoration, Hew Locke 12
Richard II, king of England 19, 65
Rivington Holmes, Richard (British Museum employee) 14, 30, 148, *153*, 158
Royal African Company (RAC) *see also* Company of Royal Adventurers of England Trading into Africa
    Edward Colston and 12
    gold trade 20
    guineas 68, *75*
    monopoly charter 16, 46
    trade in enslaved people 12, 20, 68

S

Schomburgk, Robert (explorer and surveyor) 118
sculptures
    Ambassador 1, Hew Locke *26*
    Ambassador 2, Hew Locke 22, *22*
    Benin Portuguese mercenary *19*, 20, *20*, 65, *67*

Foreign Exchange, Hew Locke *29*
Locke's drawings of 9, 14, 32
Taíno wooden figures 24, 101, *104–5*
The Watchers, Hew Locke *1–4*, *6–7*, 15, 35, 172
seals
    of colonial territories 17–18, 52, *53*
    of the East India Company 97
    as expressions of sovereignty 17–18
    imperial uses of 52
    Indigenous peoples on 17–18, 52
    The Procession, Hew Locke 17, *17*
    of the Royal African Company 46, *47*
share certificates *see also* Share series
    East India Company 89
Share series, Hew Locke 19, *36–7*, 92, 123
    Bank of Bengal 93
    Benin Portuguese mercenary on *19*, 20
    Chinese Imperial Gold Loan series 64, 68, *70*, *71*
    Company of the Imperial Railway of Ethiopia series 31, 136, 149
    Confederate States of America Loan series *100*, 101, *106*, *107*
    image of a Taíno figure *20*, *122*
    Middleton & Tonge Cotton Mill 88, 92–3, 95
Singh, Duleep, Sikh maharaja *18*, 18–19, 58, 59, *61*, 98, *99*
Siraj-ud-Daulah, Nawab of Bengal 24
slavery *see* enslavement
Slavery Abolition Act 23, 78
Sloane, Sir Hans (physician and collector) 13, 21
Société de Transit de Grand-Lahou 1, Hew Locke *36–7*
South Africa 131, *132*
Souvenir series, Hew Locke 15–16, 33, *33*, 38, 39, *40–1*
sovereignty *see also* coats of arms; seals
    Black sovereignty in Haiti 26–7
    of the East India Company 23–4, 88, *94*, 97
    Evil to Him who Thinks Evil, Hew Locke 17, *17*
    iconography of 17
    Imperial Durbars 18, 54, *55*
    intersection with imperial power 15–19
    in the *Souvenir* series, Hew Locke 15–16
Speedy, Tristram (captain and explorer) 58, *63*, 148, *151*
Stanley and African Exhibition 27, 28
Stedman, John Gabriel (Dutch army officer) 115, *116*, *117*
Suriname (Dutch Guiana)
    drawings of botanical and animal life 25, 26, 115, *116*, *117*, 168
    enslavement in 25, 26, 115
    Maroons 25–6

T

Taíno people 24, 101, *104–5*
Tewodros II, emperor of Ethiopia 14, 18, 30, 59, 148
Tibet
    British looting of artefacts 32, 154, *155–7*
    books and manuscripts in the British Museum collection 32
    Younghusband Expedition 13–14, 32, 154
Tipu Sultan, ruler of Mysore
    defeat by the East India Company 29, *129*
    fall of Seringapatam 29, 126, *127*
    possessions *128*, *129*

tiger symbolism 29, 126, *128*
Tiruwork Wube, empress of Ethiopia 18, 59
trade *see also* enslavement
    and commerce in London 86, *87*
    currency systems 21, 46
    imperial expansion through 19–24
    pre-colonial Euro-African trade 19–20
Tradescant, John (collector and naturalist) 24

U

United States of America (USA)
    Confederate bonds 25, 101
    Confederate States of America Loan (Song of the South), Hew Locke 25, *100*, *106–7*
    enslavement in 13, 101
    Indigenous peoples 101, *103*

V

Veneciano, Daniel (artist) 102
Victoria, queen of the United Kingdom
    as Empress of India 18, 54, *55*
    godchildren 18–19, *18*, 58–9, *59–61*
    the Koh-i-Noor 98
    as 'Mother of Empire' 14, 19, 39, 59
    promise of Indian rights 29
    Souvenir series, Hew Locke 15–16, 33, 38

W

Waddell, Lawrence Augustine (British Museum representative) 13–14, 32, 154
Walcott, Derek (poet) 42
The Watchers, Hew Locke *1–4*, *6–7*, 15, 35, 172
weapons
    Edo ceremonial sword 131, *134*
    Edo or Yoruba crossbow 131, *134*, 173
    Ethiopian spear and sword *151*
    in ethnographic museum displays 27, 28
    European firearms in the Asante Kingdom 68, *72–3*
    handmade Mau Mau firearms 131, *134*
    in Locke's work 28–9, *28*
    Maxim gun 29, 32, 131, *133*, *136*, 148
    as military trophies 28, *28*, 131, 173
    Sudanese Kaskara sword 131, *134*
    sword from Tipu Sultan's palace *128*
    Wai Wai clubs 24
West India Improvement Company 24, *122*
West India Improvement Company 1, Hew Locke *122*
West India Planters' and Merchants' Association 23
White, John (artist) 24, 108, *109–11*
Wilberforce, William (abolitionist) 46, *79*
Williams, Aubrey (artist) 34, 137
Winterhalter, Francis Xaver (artist) *18*, 19
Wolseley, General Garnet (British army officer) 158
Wunderkammers (rooms of wonder) 13, 158
Wyon, Joseph Shepherd (artist) 53
Wyon Sr, Thomas (engraver) 27, *120*

Y

Younghusband, Francis (British army officer) 13–14, 32, 154

Z

Zephaniah, Benjamin (poet) 176
Zulu people
    British invasion of Zululand 131, 135
    engraved horns 131, *135*, 168